CARE IN PRACTICE

for Higher

Second Edition

Edited by
Janet Miller *and* Susan Gibb

Written with
George Baker *and* Ellen Lancaster

n
A MEMBER OF THE HODDER HEADLINE GROUP

The Publishers would like to thank the following for permission to reproduce copyright material:

Photo credits Pages 114, 140,147,194, 206, 229 and 270 © Gerry McCann/Scran

Acknowledgements
The BBC: www.bbc.co.uk; The Care Commission: www.carecommission.com/index.php?option=com_content&task=view&id=47&Itemid=76; 'The developmental psychology of Erik Erikson', Richland College: www.rlc.dcccd.edu/MATHSCI/anth/P101/DVLMENTL/ERIKSON.HTM; Housing Report: www.drc.org.uk/docs/10_454_Housing%20Report.doc; Moyhing case: www.eoc.org.uk/Default.aspx?page=18838&theme=print; Schools League Table, Scotsman 21 May 2007: http://news.scotsman.com/topics.cfm?tid=1361&id=2241002005; Scottish Household Survey: www.gov.uk/Topics/Statistics/16002/shs-search; Scottish Women's Aid (Domestic abuse: facts and figures): www.scottishwomensaid.co.uk/facts.html; Statistics on civil partnerships in Scotland: www.gro-scotland.gov.uk/press/2006-news/first-statistics-on-civil-partnerships-in-scotland.html; C5P20; Statistics on mental health/suicide: www.scottishexecutive.gov.uk/Topics/Statistics/Browse/Health/TrendMentalHealth; www.scotland.gov.uk/stats/bulletins/00284-00

Every effort has been made to trace all copyright holders, but if any have been inadvertently overlooked the Publishers will be pleased to make the necessary arrangements at the first opportunity.

Although every effort has been made to ensure that website addresses are correct at time of going to press, Hodder Gibson cannot be held responsible for the content of any website mentioned in this book. It is sometimes possible to find a relocated web page by typing in the address of the home page for a website in the URL window of your browser.

Hodder Headline's policy is to use papers that are natural, renewable and recyclable products and made from wood grown in sustainable forests. The logging and manufacturing processes are expected to conform to the environmental regulations of the country of origin.

To

Anna, Lewis,
Margaret, Marion and Roseanne

Orders: please contact Bookpoint Ltd, 130 Milton Park, Abingdon, Oxon OX14 4SB. Telephone: (44) 01235 827720. Fax: (44) 01235 400454. Lines are open 9.00–5.00, Monday to Saturday, with a 24-hour message answering service. Visit our website at www.hoddereducation.co.uk. Hodder Gibson can be contacted direct on: Tel: 0141 848 1609; Fax: 0141 889 6315; email: hoddergibson@hodder.co.uk

© George Baker, Susan Gibb, Ellen Lancaster and Janet Miller
First published in 2007 by
Hodder Gibson, an imprint of Hodder Education,
An Hachette Livre UK Company
2a Christie Street
Paisley PA1 1NB

Impression number 5 4 3 2 1
Year 2010 2009 2008 2007

Cover photo © Photofusion Picture Library/Alamy (L), © Bubbles Photolibrary/Alamy (R)
Illustrations by DC Graphic Design Limited, Cartoons © Andrew Parry and Robin Maclean
Typeset in ITC Century Light 10.5pt by DC Graphic Design Limited, Swanley Village, Kent
Printed in Italy

A catalogue record for this title is available from the British Library
ISBN-13: 978 0 340 92962 9

Contents

Contents *continued*

Contents *continued*

Figures and Tables

Foreword

Social Service Workers work with some of the most disadvantaged and vulnerable people in society. It is work that is demanding, complex and requires skilled and trained staff. Workers must be able to access good quality training and learning opportunities and be able to continue to learn throughout their working lives if they are going to do their jobs well and feel competent and confident about what they are doing. This book is a very helpful contribution to meeting the training and development needs of the social service workforce. It is full of sound, helpful and practical advice, and it steers the learner in the direction of good practice. The use of case material brings to life the learning, and grounds the text in day-to-day work.

The context in which care services are delivered has changed over the past 50 years, and it will continue to change. Workers need to be equipped to practise in this ever changing and complex environment. We know that people are living longer and demands for services will increase. At the same time there will be fewer children born and fewer people to enter the workforce. Technology is playing an increasing part both in the workplace and in the delivery of services, and inequalities in society continue. Employers will be looking for workers who are resilient, adaptable and flexible and have the confidence to work with colleagues from other services such as health, housing and education. Users of services and their Carers have rising expectations. They increasingly expect services to be personalised, to focus on meeting their needs. They want workers to listen to them, respect them and to recognise their expertise. Users and Carers will increasingly plan and buy their own services and this will present particular challenges to providers and their staff. Care practice has always been grounded in a strong value base, one that respects the individual, guards privacy and confidentiality, and promotes independence. We know from surveys and from talking to service users that they value the care and the services they receive and that good quality services delivered by caring staff can make a real difference to people's lives. Workers in turn get considerable job satisfaction by helping users to make a contribution to society and live more independently.

Caring is very much a practical activity, and no amount of reading or attending courses will replace doing and learning on the job. However, what learning, reading and undertaking qualifications will do is help you do the job better and make you feel confident in what you are doing. This in turn will make the people you are helping feel confident because they know you are committed to learning and improving your skills, and all of this will contribute to better quality services.

Carole Wilkinson

Chief Executive, Scottish Social Services Council (SSSC)

Acknowledgements

Second edition

In addition to all of the people who helped with the first edition, we would like to thank the following people for their contributions. Laura Weir of the Voluntary Sector Social Services Workforce Unit (Scotland) provided invaluable administrative assistance, charts and diagrams. Our employing agencies (VSSSWU, CCPS and Cardonald College), our colleagues, families and friends were all supportive of our endeavours. Kibble Education and Care Centre (Paisley) and the Retail Trust (Glasgow) provided examples of good practice. Marion Miller provided further writings. Carole Wilkinson, Chief Executive of the Scottish Social Services Council (SSSC), has kindly provided a foreword to this edition. We are grateful to Doris Graham for permission to adapt her material from the first edition of this book. John Mitchell and Katherine Bennett of Hodder Gibson in Scotland and our editor Mairi Sutherland gave generous help and encouragement throughout the editing process. Andrew Parry and Robin Maclean have once again contributed their talent to the cartoons.

First edition

Many people helped us to put this book together. The following list hardly does justice to all of the people who gave us assistance. If we didn't mention you by name we apologise and say thank you anyway. Thanks to service users and staff of Sense Scotland, Crookfur Cottage Homes and East Dunbartonshire Social work Department; to Lorna Trainer, Section Leader, and our colleagues at Cardonald College, who had to keep the team going whilst we were busy writing; to Rachel Ball and Laura Smith at Outlook, Kirkintilloch, and to SHS, Edinburgh for information on person-centred planning; to Rev. Alastair Ramage of the Heatherbank Museum of Social Work, Glasgow Caledonian University; to the Social Care Association in Scotland and in Surbiton; to Mary Cartledge and Sharon McBean of the Graphics Department, Michael Gaughan, art student, library staff and HNC Social Care students at Cardonald College; to Margaret and Roseanne Miller for diagrams and Marion Miller for her writings; to Mike, Siobhan and Martin Hollis; to Alexis Horsfield and John Hamilton of Greater Glasgow Health Board and to Steven Ryecroft of Eastbank Health Promotion Centre; to Dr. Andy Furlong of the Department of Sociology, University of Glasgow; to Elisabeth Tribe at Hodder and Stoughton; to Tom Stannage of the Higher Still Development Unit; to Robin Maclean and Andrew Parry for cartoons; The Scottish Office Department of Health; Blackwell's Publishers; Health Education Library, Scotland; SHEPS; Care Sector Consortium; HarperCollins; Waheeda Parveen; Bob Holman; and to our families, friends and colleagues.

Introduction

> *The person is at the heart of everything. This means that your service should start from where you are. It means services must see 'service users' as people, and not just see their labels.*
>
> Scottish Executive, *Changing Lives: Report of the 21st Century Social Work Review*, User and Carer Panel 2006

Care in Practice aims to open doors for you, so that you can open others for the people with whom you work now or in the future. It emphasises that you can make a positive difference to people's lives if you gain a value base, knowledge and skills which relate to care practice. Although the book won't make you an expert it does offer signposts, suggestions and opportunities to begin the process of becoming as good as you can be in the helping process. The chapters have been written for those who are setting out on a career or course in 'care' or who wish to further their knowledge in this and related areas. The subjects and format of the book do, however, specifically cover the syllabuses of the Scottish Higher in Care at Intermediate 2 and Higher levels.

The work is a group effort written by people with varied and extensive practice experience and academic expertise. As such, there may be some areas of repetition, even occasional contradictions which represent some of the different viewpoints current in this field. We are all aware of the rewards and difficulties of care practice and wish to emphasise that for the people you work with it is often the small things that really matter: how you address people, your manner, the little things you do to make a difference to someone's life. It helps if you also have practical skills and brilliant, original, creative ideas but, if you do, it is still the ways in which these are put into practice that make a difference to the quality of life of those with whom you work.

We have attempted to reach some agreements about terminology, emphasising that the language used by care workers is extremely important in avoiding confusion, discrimination and patronisation. In general we have used the term 'service user' to refer to people who use care services. This is the term adopted by the Social Care Association and is the term which is most in evidence in much of the current care and social work literature. It is a term which avoids stigma, implications of possession, dependence or patronising overtones. It places a firm emphasis on the people being worked with as users of a service, and this comes with the expectation that this service will meet needs in ways that respect the worth and dignity of individuals. The term 'client' is also in current usage and possesses similar advantages to those of 'service user'. As long as the implication of possession, as in 'my client', is avoided, this term is perfectly acceptable. 'Client' is currently used in counselling and some social work literature, and on some occasions in this book. The term 'care worker' is used to refer to anyone working in the care field. It is an all-embracing term, though it is recognised that in practice such workers have many different titles.

Care practice is essentially a practical subject and no amount of reading and study can replace the value of actually doing the job. It is the combination of learning and practice, the application of knowledge and skills to practice situations, which determine the quality of the service provided. Although a practice placement is not a requirement of the Higher Care course, it is recommended that participants should try to gain as much experience as possible through voluntary work, a voluntary placement, visits to care agencies or employment in order to complement the rather more academic content of the syllabus.

The aims of this book, and those of the national specifications for the Intermediate and Higher courses, coincide to emphasise the provision of the following opportunities:

- to acquire useful knowledge and understanding
- to consider the needs of self and others
- to develop the ability to analyse and evaluate
- to apply theories and concepts to a range of care contexts.

The book is divided into seven chapters. This division is somewhat arbitrary since the chapters are all related to one another and in the end come back to providing the value base, knowledge and skills which are needed to work with service users. The relationships among disciplines are frequently emphasised and it is hoped that the reader will be able to appreciate these relationships to gain an integrated and 'holistic' approach to care practice. This approach stresses not only that disciplines are related to one another but that the whole person in a social situation should be seen as possessing inter-related needs which are social, physical, emotional, cognitive, cultural and spiritual. This theme of interconnectedness and integration is returned to in the final chapter, which attempts to pull together the various threads of the book into a coherent whole. A summary of each of the chapters follows. A table of the relationship between the chapters of the book and the Intermediate and Higher syllabuses is provided at the end of the introduction.

Chapter 1, The Care Context, is essentially an introductory chapter which sets the scene for caring, examining the concept of care and the contexts in which it takes place. It looks at formal and informal care, the nature of care work and reasons for the growth in demand for formal care in British, and especially Scottish, society. Some sociological concepts are introduced, whilst leaving a more detailed consideration of these to future chapters. There is an examination of legislation and the providers of formal care, placing this provision within the context of the development, and partial demise, of the Welfare State. The concepts of institutionalisation and community care are also introduced. Examples from practice are provided where relevant, as they are elsewhere in the book. This chapter provides an introduction to all units of both the Intermediate 2 and the Higher in Care.

Chapter 2, Values and Principles in Care, begins with an examination of the values and principles that underpin all care practice, including the principles of the National Care Standards (Scotland). Discrimination and anti-discriminatory practice are looked at in some detail. The chapter proceeds to discuss effective communication and relationships, with the oomph factor seen as 'that bit extra', adding enthusiasm and enjoyment to the mix of skills that a care worker needs. The work of Carl Rogers and Gerard Egan is considered in relation to using communication skills to work with service users. The personal qualities and roles of the care worker are discussed and the whole chapter is illustrated with helpful examples from care situations. This chapter underpins all care syllabuses.

Chapter 3, An Introduction to Human Development and Behaviour, examines the concepts of development and behaviour, the strands of development (social, physical, emotional, cognitive, cultural and spiritual), and the influences on development and behaviour. This includes a consideration of the Nature/Nurture debate and socialisation. Human development is then examined from birth to old age. This section is full of generalisations, although it is emphasised that the changes outlined differ from person to person and culture to culture. A multi-cultural approach is promoted. This chapter underpins the Intermediate and Higher syllabuses and is important in setting the scene for understanding Chapters 4 and 5.

Chapter 4, Psychology for Care, considers what is meant by psychology and goes on to look at how this can help to explain human development and behaviour. Among the topics considered in this chapter are attachment and separation; loss and transition; three psychological approaches – psychodynamic, cognitive/behavioural and humanistic. This chapter covers the syllabus for the Intermediate 2 and Care Higher Units 'Psychology for Care'.

Chapter 5, Sociology for Care, includes a consideration of what is meant by sociology and how this can help to explain human development and behaviour. The chapter proceeds to look at four different sociological theories: functionalist, conflict, interactionist and feminist. It then goes on to look at two aspects of society (the family and deviance) from these four theoretical perspectives. Social inequality is considered in relation to people with disabilities. Illustration is provided through case study material, and activities relate to a case study presented in the final chapter of the book. This chapter covers the syllabus for the Intermediate 2 and Care Higher Units 'Sociology for Care'.

Chapter 6, Care in Practice, aims to present a model of care practice based on assessment, care planning, implementation and evaluation. Two models of care planning are presented: the exchange model and person-centred planning. There is a detailed examination of the concept of need. Implementation of care plans is examined in terms of a positive care environment approach, looking at therapeutic, organisational, physical and community environments.

Chapter 7, Integration and Conclusions, aims to make connections among the different sections of the book, especially through the use of frequently asked questions (FAQs), and case study materials. Connections are made, for example, between psychology, sociology and care practice, together with an account of the meaning of ethnocentrism and its avoidance. The account of the MacDonald and Ahmed families is updated from the first edition. The concluding section attempts to pull together the various threads of the book, pointing the way forward for further study and re-emphasising the importance of a person-centred and holistic approach to care practice.

	Intermediate 1	Intermediate 2	Higher
Psychology for Care		**Outcome 1 all PCs** Strands, stages, nature/nurture *Chapter 3.* **Outcomes 2 all PCs** Psychological approaches and theorists *Chapter 4.* **Outcomes 3 all PCs** Attachment *Chapter 4.*	**Outcome 1 all PCs** Nature/nurture *Chapter 3.* **Outcome 2 all PCs** Psychological approaches and theorists *Chapter 4.* **Outcome 3 all PCs** Life changes *Chapter 4.*
Sociology for Care		**Outcome 1 all PCs** Concepts *Chapter 5.* **Outcome 2 all PCs** Discrimination *Chapters 2 and 5.* **Outcome 1 all PCs** Promoting equality *Chapters 2 and 5.*	**Outcome 1 all PCs** Sociological thinking *Chapter 5.* **Outcome 2 all PCs** Aspects of society *Chapter 5.* **Outcome 3 all PCs** Social inequality *Chapter 5.*
Values and Principles in Care	**Outcome 1 all PCs** Needs *Chapter 3.* **Outcome 2 all PCs** Discrimination *Chapter 2.* **Outcome 3 all PCs** National Care Standards *Chapter 2* **Outcome 3** Qualities *Chapter 1*	**PC1a:** Needs *Chapter 3* **PC 1b:** Types of provision *Chapter 1* **Outcome 2 all PCs** National Care Standards *Chapter 2.* **Outcome 3 all PCs** Care Plan Process *Chapter 6.*	**Outcome 1 all PCs** Caring relationship *Chapter 2.* **Outcome 2 all PCs** Legislation *Chapter 1.* **Outcome 3 all PCs** Care Plan Process *Chapter 6.*
Sociology and Psychology for Care	**PC 1a,c:** *Chapter 5.* **PC 1b,c:** *Chapter 4* **Outcome 2 and 3** *Chapter 3.*		

Figure 0.1 Links between the syllabus and the chapter topics

CHAPTER 1
The Care Context

George Baker

> *There are political, social and demographic drivers which are forcing changes across the public sector and in particular social work and social care.*
>
> (Lishman, 2005)

This chapter introduces you to a number of the themes and issues that will be developed in the following chapters. Although a lot of the content is not related to any particular unit it provides an overview of care in Scotland today, where it has come from and where it is going.

This chapter covers material for Values and Principles in Care, Intermediate 1 Outcome 3, Intermediate 2 Outcome 1b, Higher Outcome 2. It also underpins all other units of the Care syllabuses at Intermediate 1, 2 and Higher.

By the end of this chapter you should be able to:
* ★ describe what is meant by care and care practice
* ★ explain what makes a good care worker
* ★ describe legislation related to care
* ★ give reasons for the growth in demand for care
* ★ describe future developments and trends in care
* ★ explain care work in the past and today
* ★ explain the meaning of institutionalisation
* ★ describe the main providers of care.

Care and care practice

Care practice covers a wide variety of activities which are carried out with a range of different individuals and groups in a wide spectrum of settings and locations. Care practice today often involves working across traditional boundaries such as those between health, social care, housing and education.

This chapter is written at a time when care services in Scotland are going through a period of substantial change and there are many new challenges for those working in the field. The changes have mostly arisen as a result of new legislation and substantial reviews of how services are delivered. They have often been driven by the most important people of all – those who use services.

Changes include:

- a move away from care in institutions towards community care
- increasing provision of hospital treatment on a short visit rather than in-patient basis
- more rigorous registration and training requirements across all professions
- much more focus on inter-agency and partnership working
- increasing demands on care workers to develop a broader range of knowledge and skills.

The development of good-quality care services depends ultimately on developing and maintaining a workforce which is well motivated, well trained and, most importantly, able to reflect critically on practice. The best care practitioners are those who never lose the capacity to ask questions of themselves and the work they do. This is a theme that will be revisited throughout the book.

In 2007 the Care Commission regulated over 15,000 care services used by almost 320,000 people (www.carecommission.com). It was estimated that there were 130,000 social service workers employed in these services (SSSC, 2005). The total number of people employed in this area is predicted to rise over the early part of the 21st century and possibly beyond, as a number of factors combine to mean that the demand for care will continue to rise. These factors will be examined in greater detail later in the chapter.

Many people come to this line of work after working in different types of employment or having raised families. Such people often bring wide experiences of life with them and are an invaluable asset to employers. It is assumed that you are reading this chapter because you are embarking on a course designed to build or enhance your career opportunities in the field of care practice. You have chosen an interesting and meaningful career that is sure to stretch and challenge you in many ways. You will be doing important work, helping to address social injustices and making significant contributions to the lives of other people. It is not an easy job, and there may be times when you might wonder why you ever took the decision to work in this area, but there will also be times when you see how your input has helped to make life a whole lot better for someone – and that can be very rewarding.

Work in the field of care encompasses a wide range of activities. It covers particular areas such as social care, health care, child care, social work, nursing and a wide range of other professional roles in health and social services, each of which involves specialised skills and knowledge. The word 'care' itself has a number of different connotations, but essentially means 'to look after or provide for'. A degree of caution has to be exercised, however, because an unfortunate connotation of the term is that it can imply a degree of dependency or powerlessness on the part of the user of a service. This can serve to exaggerate further the predicament in which people might find themselves. One way to reduce this effect is always to consider the relationship between the person using a care service and the person who is providing that service as a partnership where each of the people involved brings particular expertise. You may bring a good knowledge of your particular area of care practice to this partnership, but remember that generally the real experts in individuals' lives are the individuals themselves.

Tom

Consider the case of Tom who lives at home and has a number of health problems. He experiences periodic bouts of extreme depression which have led to him trying to take his own life in the past. At one stage in his life, Tom's needs were assessed and he was using input and support from nine different agencies, few of whom talked directly to each other and many of whom operated from different care philosophies and perspectives. His district nurse attended to his dressings and general health care needs and couldn't understand why his support workers insisted on making sure he went out every day, as he needed to rest. His community psychiatric nurse visited every three weeks to give him his medication by injection and check on his mental state and always experienced frustration as he never kept his appointments. His social worker, who had only met him once after an initial referral, had recently been appointed as his care manager and was fighting desperately to maintain his current level of services after having her budget cut. Staff at his day centre encouraged him to become as independent as possible and consider a move out of the housing support project where he lived. Housing support staff encouraged him to stay where he was as they felt he was making good progress with them. His advocacy worker was trying to involve him in person-centered planning and his social work assistant was undertaking an assessment of his needs as part of his Community Care Assessment. A common feature of all of their reports was that Tom appeared confused at times!

The move towards joint working is an attempt to bring more focus and clarity to the delivery of services. Many of the services that Tom was using were being duplicated by different agencies and the only time they ever got together to discuss aspects of his care with Tom was once a year at his review.

Activity   What does care mean to you?

Recent emphasis is upon the service user being an active partner in the care process, a chooser and user of services rather than a passive receiver of other people's decisions. What pictures of care spring to mind when you read the following terms?

- Care professional
- Terminal care
- Acute care
- Care services review coordinator
- Community care
- Personalised care

(Level Int 1) ## What makes a good care worker?

There are a number of factors that contribute to making a good care worker. The attributes of a good care worker are outlined in the following chart, and these apply whatever field of care you may be practising in. It may of course take some time before you feel competent or confident in all these areas. Remember that in this area of work you never really stop learning. If you should reach a point in the future where you begin to feel you know it all, then it may be time for a change, because you may have become infected with a degree of cynicism or arrogance, which are not very desirable qualities in any care worker.

Knowledge
Understanding of needs of service users
Awareness of psychological theory
Understanding of social issues
Awareness of sociological theory
Awareness of how organisations work
Specialised knowledge related to role
Knowledge of legislation

Skills
Good communication (verbal and written)
Ability to be analytical
Ability to use counselling skills
Good at building relationships
Ability to work as part of a team
Ability to work with initiative

Values
Commitment to social justice
Appreciation of worth of all individuals
Appreciation of boundaries of confidentiality
Promotion of anti-discriminatory practice
Support for rights and choices
Acknowledgment of differences
Support and understanding of inclusion

Personal qualities
Sensitivity
Warmth
Patience
Enthusiasm and sense of humour
Imagination and adaptability
Dependability and reliability
Ability to be reflective
Confidence in your competence

Figure 1.1 Attributes of a good care worker

Activity   *Attributes*

Consider your own attributes in relation to Figure 1.1. Award yourself a mark for each one on a scale of 1 to 5. Add up the total. The maximum possible score is 140. If you are anywhere near this then you are either reading the wrong book, too arrogant for your own good or you cheated! Keep a note of your score and check yourself out again as you progress in your studies and experience.

In care work today great attention is paid to work practices which serve to empower people and help them lead independent lives, as far as possible. There is also great emphasis on developing services which enable people to live normal and ordinary lives. This is one of the great challenges in care work and calls for skilled and knowledgeable workers who understand and can respond sensitively to the needs of people.

We are also beginning to build a much better knowledge and understanding of how people are affected by various illnesses, disabilities and experiences. Although knowledge is crucial, nothing surpasses interacting with the individual to understand their particular situation. The example of John below illustrates this.

John and Ben

John had worked for many months with young Ben and was beginning to feel that he was getting nowhere. Ben lived in a world of his own. He had autism and there just didn't seem any way that John was able to break down the wall that Ben had built around himself. It seemed almost that Ben had made a deliberate choice not to communicate with anyone else. He sat at the desk on the other side of the room playing with a toy truck, but not playing with it in the way that other kids would. Ben had placed it upside down on the desk and had been spinning one wheel for about an hour now, all the while making noises which John could only describe as gentle screams. Now and then he had stopped, placed his hands over his ears, and let out a series of extremely loud and high-pitched yells.

He had some other strange quirks as well. He only ate things which were round. Small pizzas, potato fritters, hamburgers and Smarties were fine but chips, sausages and chocolate bars were thrown across the room. His mother cut his toast with a round pastry cutter.

Autism was a condition which John, who was an experienced practitioner in his field, was only beginning to learn about. He had started to work with Ben and other children like him in order to gain more experience in this specialised field. For months now he had tried every way he could think of to establish some type of communication or connection with Ben but always to no avail. Ben didn't even show any signs of recognising him or acknowledging his presence (despite all the Smarties!), turning away and covering his face when John came too close.

Ben had stopped playing with the truck at last and had now picked up the phone on the desk and was holding it to his ear. Without thinking too much, John picked up the phone on his own desk, flicked the connection, and spoke into it.

'Hi Ben, when you going to speak to me?' he said.

'Hi John', replied Ben.

After he had picked himself up from the floor, John built on this indirect method of communication with Ben and they went on to work very closely together. They learned from each other how they could communicate in other indirect ways.

Developing professional skills and knowledge

One of the major developments in care over the last decade has been the development of a broad range of training and learning opportunities. In most areas of care work there are now regulatory bodies which have established qualifications criteria for registration, which means that you will be required to become competent for the specific requirements for your role. This in turn will contribute to you becoming as good a care worker as you can be.

Table 1.1 Agencies responsible for regulating health and social care professionals in Scotland

Care workers, qualified social workers and social work students on approved degree courses	Scottish Social Services Council (SSSC)	**www.sssc.uk.com**
Dentists, dental nurses, dental hygienists and technicians	General Dental Council	**www.gdc-uk.org**
Doctors	General Medical Council	**www.gmc-uk.org**
Opticians	General Optical Council	**www.optical.org**
Art therapists, podiatrists, dieticians, occupational therapists, paramedics, physiotherapists, radiographers	Health Professions Council, or for some roles, Scottish Social Services Council (SSSC) if working in a care setting	**www.hpc-uk.org**
Nurses, midwives	Nursing and Midwifery Council, or SSSC if working in a care setting	**www.nmc-uk.org**
Pharmacists, pharmacy technicians	Royal Pharmaceutical Society of Great Britain	**www.rpsgb.org**

There are many routes you may be able to follow in order to achieve the necessary qualifications. Training providers have been charged with the task of making access to training as flexible as possible in order to maximise opportunities for people from different backgrounds, and with various prior experiences of learning, to move into a career in care.

The notion of portfolio building has also been gradually introduced into the care sector in Scotland. This is an approach to learning which means that as you progress through your career you can add to your training and experience portfolio in a range of different ways. A further development in this area has been the Scottish Credit and Qualification Framework (SCQF), which places all qualifications in Scotland in a coherent framework to make it easier to determine the equivalence of qualifications and easier to transfer learning. There are now lifelong learning opportunities offering training to people at all stages in their careers. Many care practitioners also have a requirement for continuing professional development (CPD) for re-registration. Another trend is that the emphasis in learning care practice is shifting to a system where 'learning is brought to the learner', which is designed to further ease access to learning opportunities for all by addressing the difficulties people in the care sector have often had in balancing work, domestic and learning needs.

CARE IN PRACTICE

Sally

Sally's story may help to illustrate the types of options that are now available to individuals working in the care field. Sally left school early without any formal qualifications. She did various part time and temporary jobs in retail and barwork, and then spent time bringing up three children. She became interested in voluntary work with young people with family difficulties and found that the skills and understanding she had learned as a mother were very useful in appreciating the challenges posed by some of the young people she worked with. With the encouragement of friends and staff at the family unit where she had been volunteering, she took the plunge, went to college and completed her Higher Care followed by an HNC in Social Care. College was a very liberating and empowering experience for her as she discovered she actually enjoyed the challenges of learning. After college she took up a full-time position with a national organisation specialising in family support and then completed her SVQ Level 3 in Health and Social Care with them. After this she went back to college one evening a week to do a specialist counselling course which she felt would help her to develop skills in her work with young people. She is currently considering doing a Professional Development Award in Care Management with a view to applying for a Team Leader's post. Her story is fairly typical of the routes being followed by care workers in Scotland, and the range of available opportunities for training is continuing to increase.

(Level Higher) ## Summary of major legislation

Below are details of some of the major pieces of **legislation** affecting care services in Scotland. It is essential that you make yourself aware of legislation as some of it places a duty on you as an individual to carry out your care practice in particular ways. This is intended as a general introduction to the various types of legislation relating to care in Scotland and is by no means a comprehensive guide. It is important for you to keep up to date with changes in legislation relevant to your practice.

A guide to current legislation in Scotland can be found at **www.scotland.gov.uk/ Topics/Justice**. All Scottish legislation can be viewed and copies of acts and guidance notes can also be downloaded at **www.opsi.gov.uk/legislation/scotland/s-acts.htm**. It can be heavy going to look at the official version of a piece of legislation. Often it is better to go to the website of the agency which monitors the legislation, as this will give you a summary of the key features and current examples of how it is put into practice. Another good source of information about legislation are the main organisations whose services are affected by the legislation – local government, health boards and other care providers. They will have brief summaries and explain how they are implementing it.

Adult Support and Protection (Scotland) Act 2007

This Bill was introduced to the Scottish Parliament on 30 March 2006. The main provisions of the Bill are: a new power of right of entry to settings where abuse is thought to be taking place; the creation of banning orders so that perpetrators of abuse are removed from those settings; establishing Statutory Adult Protection Committees, operating on a multi-agency basis, to further develop strategic inter-agency working and collaboration.

www.scvo.org.uk/PolicyAndParliament Scottish Council for Voluntary Organisation.

Equality Act (2006)

This Act establishes the Commission for Equality and Human Rights (CEHR) that will come into being in October 2007. The Commission will tackle discrimination in relation to gender, gender reassignment, disability, sexual orientation, religion or belief, age, race and promote human rights.

www.cehr.org.uk Commission for Equality and Human Rights

Employment Equality (Age) Regulations 2006

Part of the European Union's 'Equal Treatment in Employment and Occupation' Framework, these regulations outlaw direct age discrimination: less favourable treatment on grounds of age in employment and vocational training, including education courses provided by further and higher education institutions. They prohibit unjustified direct and indirect age discrimination, and all harassment and victimisation on grounds of age.

www.agepositive.gov.uk Information on the age discrimination directive

Disability Discrimination Act 2005

The Disability Discrimination Act (DDA) 2005 amends and extends the existing provisions of the DDA1995, including: extending protection to cover people who have HIV, cancer or multiple sclerosis, from the moment they are diagnosed; making it unlawful for operators of transport vehicles to discriminate against disabled people; making it easier for tenants to make disability-related adaptations; and requiring public bodies to promote equality of opportunity for disabled people.

www.drc-gb.org Disability Rights Commission
www.update.org.uk Scotland's National Disability Information Service

Protection of Children and Prevention of Sexual Offences (Scotland) Act 2005

This Act introduces a range of measures to strengthen the protection of children from sexual harm and abuse. It creates a new offence related to the 'grooming' of children for the purposes of committing sexual offences. It also contains a number of other significant measures such as making it an offence to purchase any services at all from someone aged under eighteen which could be construed as sexual and introduced Risk of Sexual Harm orders.

www.nch.org.uk National Children's Homes
www.barnardos.org.uk Barnardo's

Smoking, Health and Social Care (Scotland) Act 2005

This Act aims to protect the general public from the harmful effects of passive smoking by making it an offence to smoke in public places. A few exemptions to the law are made, mainly on humanitarian grounds, so that people who have no choice about their main residence are still able to smoke, if they desire. Exemptions include residential accommodation, designated rooms in adult care homes, adult hospices, designated rooms in psychiatric hospitals and units and designated rooms in offender accommodation premises.
www.clearingtheairscotland.com Scottish Executive site
www.ashscotland.org.uk Anti-smoking organisation

Mental Health (Care and Treatment) (Scotland) Act 2003

This Act is primarily concerned with the provision of care for people with mental health difficulties and came into force in October 2005. It provides for the continuation of the Mental Welfare Commission and the duties of local authorities to provide care and support services (although they do not have to do this directly). It creates a number of new roles for professionals who have to carry out certain duties, such as Mental Health Officers in Social Work and Approved Medical Practitioners. It also makes stipulations regarding hospital detention and compulsory treatment orders. All people working in mental health services have to abide by ten principles of good practice, such as participation and the least restrictive alternative.
www.nes.scot.nhs.uk/mha/ Scottish NHS website on the Act
www.wellscotland.info/mentalhealth/index.html National Programme for Improving Mental Health and Well being
www.mentalhealth.org.uk Mental Health Foundation

Employment Equality (Sexual Orientation) Regulations 2003.

These regulations make discrimination on the grounds of sexual orientation in the field of employment unlawful. It is unlawful to deny people jobs because of prejudice about their sexual orientation. The regulations also cover perceived sexual orientation and association, i.e. being discriminated against on grounds of the sexual orientation of those with whom you associate (for example, friends and/or family).
www.stonewallscotland.org.uk Equal rights for lesbians, gay men and bisexuals
www.equality-network.org Campaign for equality for lesbian, gay, bisexual and transsexual people

Employment Equality (Religion or Belief) Regulations 2003

These regulations prohibit discrimination on grounds of religion, religious belief or similar philosophical belief. They cover discrimination, harassment and victimisation in work and vocational training, on grounds of perceived as well as actual religion or belief (i.e. assuming – correctly or incorrectly – that someone has a particular religion or belief). The regulations also cover association, i.e. being discriminated against on grounds of the religion or belief of those with whom you associate (for example, friends and/or family).
www.cre.gov.uk Commission for Racial Equality

Community Care and Health (Scotland) Act 2002

This Act makes personal and nursing care available without charge for everyone in Scotland aged 65 and over who needs it, whether at home, in hospital or in a care home. Free nursing care is available for people of any age. People who require social care will still be means tested. **www.scotland.gov.uk/Topics/Health/care/17655**

Regulation of Care (Scotland) Act 2001

This Act establishes the two main regulatory bodies for social services in Scotland: the Scottish Social Services Council and the Scottish Commission for the Regulation of Care. These bodies carry out the functions detailed below.

The Scottish Social Services Council (SSSC) is the organisation that is responsible for registering individuals who work in social services and also regulating their education and training. This registration is intended to increase the protection of people who use services by ensuring that workers are trained, have the right qualifications for the job and are regulated properly. It is also involved in development of training and workforce development and acts as the Sector Skills Council for the sector. Staff and services are expected to meet agreed standards of conduct and practice which are laid down in the Code of Practice for Social Service Workers and the Code of Practice for Employers of Social Service Workers. **www.sssc.uk.com** (see Appendix 2, page 296)

The Scottish Commission for the Regulation of Care (the Care Commission) is the independent regulator of care services in Scotland. It is responsible for regulating services used by adults, and children and young people, throughout the country in a wide range of locations including care homes, housing support services, early education and childcare services, home care and nurse agencies. In total it regulates the services used by about 320,000 people in Scotland each year. **www.carecommission.com**

Adults with Incapacity (Scotland) Act 2000

This Act allows Sheriff Courts to appoint guardians to make decisions on behalf of those who are not able to do so. Guardians may have to account to the Public Guardian, Mental Welfare Commission or supervising Social Work Departments. The act stipulates that anything that is done on behalf of an adult with incapacity will be required to benefit him or her, take account of the person's wishes and those of the nearest relative, carer, guardian or attorney, and achieve the desired purpose without unduly limiting the person's freedom.
www.publicguardian-scotland.gov.uk The office of the Public Guardian
www.mwcscot.org.uk Mental Welfare Commission in Scotland

The Race Relations Amendment Act 2000

This act requires that public authorities (including the Police) need to eliminate unlawful discrimination and 'be expected to consider the implications for racial equality of all their activities . . .'
www.cre.gov.uk Commission for Racial Equality
www.onescotland.com Scottish Executive anti-racist campaign

Mental Health (Public Safety and Appeals) (Scotland) Act 1999

This was the first piece of legislation passed by the devolved Scottish Parliament. It was felt to be necessary to close a loophole after an individual who had been sent to the State National Hospital for shooting a policeman, and was subsequently diagnosed with a personality disorder, had to be released after making a legal claim that as he couldn't be treated he therefore should not be in hospital. Previous legislation only provided for the detention of people who could be treated.
www.mwcscot.org.uk Mental Welfare Commission in Scotland

Data Protection Act 1998

This Act protects the rights of individuals in relation to data obtained, stored, processed or supplied about them. The Act requires that appropriate security measures will be taken against unauthorised access to, or alteration, disclosure or destruction of personal data and against accidental loss or destruction of personal data. The Act applies to both computerised and paper records. Breaches are investigated by the Information Commissioner.

www.ico.gov.uk The Information Commissioner's site

Human Rights Act 1998

This Act incorporates most of the articles of the European Convention on Human Rights into UK law. Many of these have to be tested in UK courts, and some have significant implications for care work, such as the right to respect for private and family life, and the right to freedom of expression.

www.direct.gov.uk/en/RightsAndResponsibilities/DG_4002951

The Police Act 1997

Part V of this Act was implemented in April 2002. This allows the Scottish Criminal Record Office (SCRO) to issue criminal record information certificates to individuals and organisations. This is the legislation under which all forms of disclosure are carried out. The scheme is now administered by Disclosure Scotland, which is a partnership between DT and the SCRO.

www.scro.police.uk Scottish Criminal Records Office

Community Care (Direct Payments) Act 1996

This Act enables the direct payment of money to someone who has been assessed as in need of services to allow them to purchase their own services. This Act was initially discretionary, but many local authorities did not implement such schemes. It was subsequently made mandatory for them to do so.

www.direct.gov.uk/en/DisabledPeople/FinancialSupport/DG_10016128

Children (Scotland) Act 1995

This is the main piece of legislation relating to the welfare and protection of children in Scotland. It is broadly seen as a well-balanced Act which promotes the rights of children while attempting to ensure their protection where necessary. The Act puts children first. Each child must be treated as an individual who is encouraged to form and express views on matters affecting them and has the right to be protected from all forms of abuse, neglect and exploitation.

www.children1st.org.uk formerly the RSPCC
www.childline.org.uk has a good section on 'influencing policy'

Carers (Recognition and Services) Act 1995

Section 2 of this Act enables local authorities to assess the needs of carers, as well as individuals thought to be in need of community care services. It does not, however, entitle them to any services that such an assessment might indicate a need for, although this may have been improved by the Community Care and Health (Scotland) Act 2002.

www.carerscotland.org Carers' support organisation
www.scottishcarersalliance.org.uk Carers' support organisation

Disability Discrimination Act 1995

This Act made it illegal to discriminate against disabled people in employment, access to goods, services, transport and education. Unlike the SDA and the RRA (see below), positive discrimination is allowed for people with disabilities.
www.drc-gb.org Disability Rights Commission

National Health Service and Community Care Act 1990

This Act introduced massive changes in the way social care services were delivered in the UK. It introduced into social care the whole notion of care in the community, needs-led rather than service-led provision, a mixed economy of care and market forces. It gives special duties to local authorities as the 'lead partner' in collaboration among agencies, one of their roles being to publish a three-yearly plan of needs and proposed services in their area. Copies of these reports can be obtained from your local council, e.g. **www.aberdeencity.gov.uk; www.dumgal.gov.uk; www.cne-siar.gov.uk**

Race Relations Act 1976

This Act makes it unlawful to discriminate against anyone on the grounds of race, colour, nationality (including citizenship), or ethnic or national origin. All racial groups are protected from discrimination. The Act applies to the fields of employment, planning, housing, the provision of goods, facilities and services, and education. Exemptions to the Act are allowed where race is a 'Genuine Occupational Qualification' (GOQ) for the job. In care settings, this includes providing personal services to people from a particular racial group, defined by colour or nationality, in connection with their welfare.
www.cre.gov.uk Commission for Racial Equality

Sex Discrimination Act 1975

This Act makes it unlawful to discriminate against someone on the basis of gender or marital status in employment, education, and the provision of goods, facilities and services. It also prohibits harassment in employment, vocational training and further education, and victimisation because someone has tried to exercise their rights under the SDA or Equal Pay Act. Sex discrimination is lawful if one of the defined 'Genuine Occupational Requirements' (GORs) applies. This can be the case in some care settings where a job needs to be held by a person of the same gender as the service user in order to preserve their privacy and decency. There are special provisions prohibiting discrimination on the grounds of gender reassignment in the employment field, with certain exceptions.
www.eoc.org.uk Equal Opportunities Commission
www.womenandequalityunit.gov.uk Government site for the Women's Unit

Health and Safety at Work Act 1974

This Act outlines the responsibilities that employers and employees have in relation to developing safe working practices and creating a safe environment. For example, employers have to provide suitable training, and employees have to operate machinery properly: in a care setting this might involve using hoists and other lifting aids.
www.hse.gov.uk Health and Safety Executive

Rehabilitation of Offenders Act 1974

This Act allows some criminal convictions to become spent and ignored after a fixed period of time. The main relevance to care work is that an 'exceptions order' to this Act means that no offences are ever regarded as spent in regard to obtaining employment in this field.

www.sacro.org.uk Aims to safeguard communities and reduce offending

Social Work (Scotland) Act 1968

This Act was the main platform for the creation of Social Work Departments providing social work services in Scotland. It required each local authority to provide advice, guidance and assistance to people in need of care and attention arising out of infirmity or age, or those suffering from illness or mental disorder. Some aspects of it still apply today. It also created the Children's Hearing System.

www.chscotland.gov.uk Children's Hearings website

One of the key ways in which society responds to social problems is through the creation of laws (legislation) which seek to redress some of the inequalities in society. Conflict theorists (see Chapter 5) would maintain that legislation reflects the values of the ruling political party. From an interactionist perspective (see Chapter 5), however, all parties are now generally more responsive to public opinion than they have been in the past. The Scottish Parliament, in particular, consults widely with a number of representative groups before deciding on any new legislation. You can see what issues they are currently consulting on at **http://www.scottish.parliament.uk/vli/consultations/index.htm**

Most pieces of legislation go through quite a long process before they finally become an Act of Parliament. Special groups may have met and prepared reports which outlined the need for change and detailed proposals for parliament to consider. For example, the Millan Committee (2001) set out the points that were developed into the Mental Health (Care and Treatment) (Scotland) Act 2003; the Griffiths Report (1983) led via two White Papers to the NHS and Community Care Act 1990.

The growth in demand for care – a historical perspective

In order to understand why the demand for care has increased in our society a number of different factors will be examined which are believed to have contributed to this process.

1 Demographic changes

2 Changes in the nature of family and community life

3 Changes in political and personal ideologies and values

1 Demographic changes

The major demographic change in relation to the increasing need for care is the growing number of people who are living longer. This is linked with other changes occurring in society, which means that an increasing number of people are no longer able to meet their care needs within their family.

Demography is the study of populations, in particular the way in which individual characteristics may be distributed throughout the population. It comes from the combination of two Greek words – *demos* meaning the people and *graphein* meaning to write – thus literally 'writing about the people'. Information is gathered and analysed to examine changes in patterns between the past and the present to try to identify and predict present and future trends. In this way changes in a range of matters such as family size, life expectancy, divorce rates and ethnic distribution can be examined. For instance it is forecast that, by 2030, 25% of the Scottish population will be over 60 and that the number of people aged over 75 will rise by a massive 60% by 2028 (Scottish Executive, 2006a).

> **Activity**   *Trends in population change*
>
> Identify the trends in population change which will have an impact on care services, using information from the graph below.

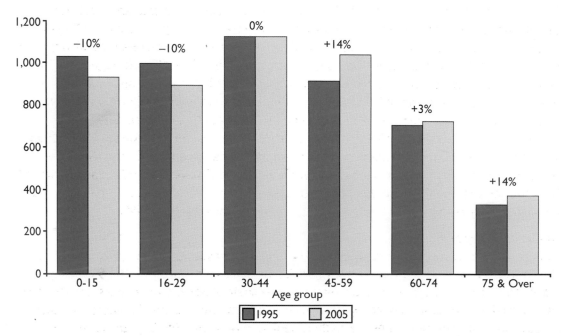

Figure 1.2 The changing age structure of Scotland's population, 1995–2005 (Source: General Register Office for Scotland)

Why are people living longer?

There are a number of reasons why people are now living longer. Over the last hundred years or so the rise in life expectancy has been quite dramatic. Men born in the 1890s could expect to live only into their forties, whereas now men can expect to live to their mid seventies in Scotland, and late seventies in some other parts of Europe. Listed below are some of the factors which are thought to have contributed to this increase in longevity.

Improved health care

The general availability of free, or at least relatively inexpensive, health care for everyone has made a significant contribution towards people living longer. The most important event in this regard was the National Health Service (Scotland) Act 1947, which promised free health care to everyone at the point of delivery. This meant that people no longer had to pay for the services of a doctor or for hospital treatment or medicines. Although it has come under threat a number of times in its history, and costs and charges are now made for different services such as prescriptions, the National Health Service remains one of the institutions in Britain of which we can be justly proud.

Improved public health

Just as vital as the provision of medical and health services is the supply of basic necessities such as clean safe water and sewage disposal facilities. These have helped to eradicate a number of diseases such as cholera, which used to wipe out significant numbers of the population in epidemics that regularly swept the country. Public health services also monitor and help maintain the quality of the food we eat through environmental health agencies.

Technological advances

Certain technological advances have also contributed significantly towards increasing our lifespan. Most homes now have a fridge freezer which keeps food safe and fresh for longer. Modern methods of storing and transporting foodstuffs by freezing, chilling or canning also mean the general availability of safe food. Other inventions have also played their part. Scotsman Alexander Fleming invented penicillin in 1927, although it did not come into general use until some twenty years later. Antibiotics have played a huge role in combating diseases and infections. They been used so much that there are now great fears that new 'superbugs' are evolving which are resistant to a large number of antibiotics. One such bug which is being increasingly encountered is MRSA (Methicillin Resistant Staphylococcus Aureus), which although probably not much of a threat to healthy care workers can prove fatal to people whose ability to resist infection is lowered by other factors. In 2003–4 all hospital-acquired infections contributed to the deaths of about 5,000 patients in the UK (Comptroller and Auditor General, 2004).

Reduction of poverty

This is an area where a certain amount of controversy exists. Some people take the view that poverty has been eliminated from Britain. While few people in Scotland actually starve to death for want of food, for many people their lifestyle and chances are affected by not having a lot of money at their disposal. Using the most generally accepted half average income measure, some 1.2 million people in Scotland live in poor households (The Scottish Parliament, 1999). The nature of the society in which we live determines that those with money will tend to get richer and those without will get poorer. Evidence for this can be found in 'Social Justice – The Report of the Commission on Social Justice' (1903), which states '. . . the poor have become poorer. Between 1979 and 1992 the poorest 10% saw their real incomes fall by 17% while the richest 10% saw their real income rise by just over 60%'. More recent figures confirm that this trend continues. Between 1997/8 and 2000/1 the proportion of people in Scotland living in households with less than 60% of median income after deducting housing costs – the most commonly used poverty threshold – rose slightly from 21.5% to 23.5% (Joseph Rowntree Foundation, 2002).

Protective legislation

In the last century there has been a steady increase in the amount of legislation designed to protect people in their work and living situations. Laws exist to safeguard people from exposure to hazardous substances such as asbestos or toxic chemicals in their work environments. Clean-air laws have reduced the hazardous emissions from factory and domestic chimneys, which used to cause life-threatening smogs in the big cities. Legislation to reduce emissions from motor vehicles by removing lead additives from petrol should also be of benefit. Health and Safety at Work legislation has forced employers and employees alike to take steps to reduce industrial risks and hazards. A major area still to be worked on is the reduction of road accidents, which, with our continuing obsession for faster and more powerful vehicles, continue to kill and maim a large number of people each year. In 2005 286 people were killed and 2,594 were seriously injured on Scotland's roads (Scottish Executive, 2006b). These accidents also provide care services with a large number of service users with serious head injuries.

Healthier lifestyles

Some people may consider that we are living much healthier lifestyles today than our grandparents did, which is contributing to us living longer. Certainly there has been a huge growth in the health and fitness industry. Many people go to health clubs to work out and keep themselves in shape, and others have healthy outdoor hobbies such as cycling or hill walking. Many people also pay a lot of attention to the food they eat and avoid foods known to contribute to things that cause poor health. On the other hand many people have sedentary lifestyles and take no exercise at all. An estimated 21% of adults in Scotland are now obese (Earle, 2003). Smoking remains a killer and major contributor to reducing your lifespan, although Scotland can be proud of its recent introduction of legislation to ban smoking in public places. Overuse of, and dependency on, alcohol and other drugs remains high for some individuals and this often can have a particularly nasty series of consequences, not only for these people themselves but for those they live with.

2 Changes in the nature of family and community life

Until fairly recently in historical terms, people tended to assume that when they became old and reached a stage where they might need help to look after themselves this role would be carried out by their children. Indeed, in some cultures this role was ascribed and it was the assumed duty of the eldest daughter to forsake marriage and instead look after her parents until they died. Parents might therefore have had an interest in having as many children as possible in order to ease the future burdens of old age.

The nature of the changes which have occurred in families is examined in Chapter 5, but a few points are considered here. Some argue that the traditional extended family, where the family lived in close proximity and looked after each other, with Granny watching the kids and the kids watching Granny, has become replaced in many instances by smaller nuclear families who have moved away from the area where they were brought up. While this may reflect the situation to an extent, it is perhaps more accurate to think of these families as part of a dispersed extended family because they will tend to maintain regular contact using means of communication not available to their ancestors. The nature of support which families are able to offer, while continuing to be substantial, is different from that of previous generations. This places additional demands on service provision to supplement what family members can no longer provide.

3 Changes in political and personal ideologies and values

Societies throughout history can be seen as originally evolving according to collectivist principles as people saw the benefits of working together and looking after each other's interests. People formed tribal units, clans and eventually nations because of strength in numbers and the ability of large groups to protect themselves. To some extent individuals subordinated their own selfish interests for the good of the larger society. Only recently, it can be argued, has the trend emerged for members of particular societies to put their own self-centred interests first, a tendency which is sometimes referred to as individualism. Historically, this tendency can be seen to have started with the onset of the Reformation and later the industrial and other revolutions, but we need to look back only at the last few decades in Britain to see how individualism took off, especially in the sense of how it might be tied up with the other factors mentioned above.

Although it is difficult to generalise about any particular era, the 1960s presented a time of great change in Britain. It was an age of emancipation and liberation, civil rights movements, the growth of feminism. Everything from music and cinema to fashion and contraception spoke of difference from previous eras, of protest, of people no longer willing to be pushed around and bullied by people in power. Individuals wanted to be heard, to make a difference in the world, wanted to exercise rights and choices in fundamental areas of their lives, and they wanted to enjoy themselves. The times they certainly were 'a-changin'. This extended into the 1970s, reinforced by the perceived successes of the protest generation.

The British population underwent several changes of government during these times, and important anti-discrimination legislation was introduced attempting to iron out some of the injustices built into the fabric of society.

Things proceeded with no great fundamental alterations until May 1979, when a new Conservative government under the leadership of Margaret Thatcher was elected to power. The following decade and a half saw a time of radical change to many of the country's institutions and the lifestyles of its citizens. This new government had a set of political ideas mainly driven by the ideologies of the 'New Right', which were pursued with zeal. The government openly promoted the idea of self-responsibility and individualism. It tried to create opportunities for people to 'get ahead', to make a success of their lives. Individual effort was what counted and what would be rewarded.

The cult of individualism seemed to say it all. Look after number one first. Make money. Get rich. Buy a house. Have a career. Get ahead in life. Be successful and show it. This was the message of the 1980s: the 'me first' generation. As the 21st century becomes established there are other trends affecting political ideology indicating a move away from a totally 'me first' philosophy. There are differing, and sometimes conflicting, personal and political ideologies that are changing the political and social landscape. With globalisation, large multi-national companies hold huge power in terms of driving the global economy; environmentalism is placing a new emphasis on saving the environment and taking personal and political measures to reduce 'greenhouse' gases; fundamentalism has in some cases led to terrorism, and the threat of terrorism has affected many countries; the expansion of the European Union has given rise to a new wave of immigration from Europe; people escaping unjust treatment in their own countries have come to Britain to seek asylum.

Much recent legislation has promoted ideas of social inclusion, responsibility and rights for people who have experienced long years of discrimination. The Scottish Parliament established in 1999 aims to be accessible to everyone and is encouraging citizenship and participation in the development of national policy. This has particular relevance to the care sector where there is wide consultation about new policy and legislation, and service users are encouraged to participate in areas that affect them. In *Changing Lives: Report of the 21st Century Social Work Review* (Scottish Executive, 2006a), for example, there was a service user forum, and service users reported on the kind of service they would like to have.

Figure 1.3 illustrates the main political parties operating in Scotland today and Figure 1.4 shows historical trends.

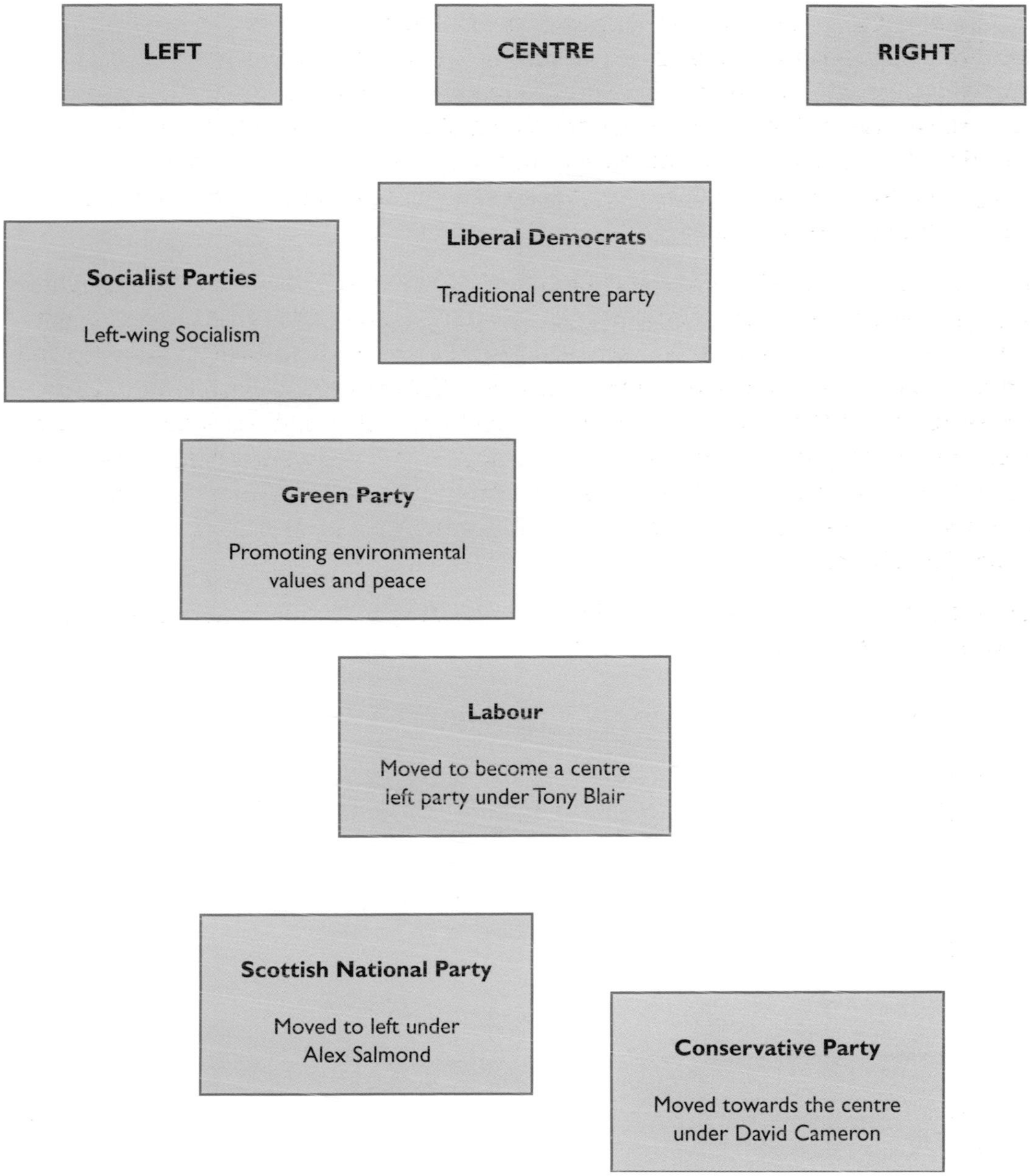

LEFT	CENTRE	RIGHT

Socialist Parties

Left-wing Socialism

Liberal Democrats

Traditional centre party

Green Party

Promoting environmental
values and peace

Labour

Moved to become a centre
left party under Tony Blair

Scottish National Party

Moved to left under
Alex Salmond

Conservative Party

Moved towards the centre
under David Cameron

Figure 1.3 The political spectrum in Scotland

Figure 1.4 Timeline: 1939–2007

	World	UK/Scotland	Social legislation	Spirit of the age
2007	Will Iran develop its nuclear capacity?	Alex Salmond first SNP leader of Scottish Parliament	Adult Support and Protection Act Equality Act	**21st century**
06	N. Korea nuclear bomb test			Environmentalism
05	Earthquake on Pakistan/India border	Make Poverty History G8 Summit at Gleneagles	Smoking Health and Social Care Act	War on Terror Powerful multi-national companies
04	Bush re-elected in USA Tsunami in Indonesia	McConnell elected Blair re-elected		Disaffection with Blair Government
03	War on Iraq begins		Mental Health (Care and Treatment) Act Community Care and Health Act	SNP First Minister for Scotland
02	Moscow theatre siege by Chechen rebels	Soham murders		
01	9 / 11 Attacks		Regulation of Care Act	
2000			Adults with Incapacity Act	
99		Scottish Assembly		**The nineties**
98	Peace in Ireland			Age of computer
97	Princess Diana dies	Tony Blair new PM		Collapse of Communism
96		Dunblane massacre	Scottish Local Govt Reform	Globalisation
95	OJ Simpson Trial		Disability Discrimination Act	
94	Rwandan Civil War			
93	Bill Clinton new US President	James Bulger murder	Poll Tax abolished	
92				
91	Gulf War		NHS Patients Charter	
1990	Nelson Mandela released	John Major new PM	NHS and Community Care Act	
89	Berlin Wall comes down		Children Act	**The eighties**
88	George Bush new US President	Lockerbie disaster		'Me First' generation
87		Zeebrugge disaster	Poll Tax introduced	Individualism
86	Chernobyl nuclear accident		Disabled Persons Act	Privatisation The New Right
85	Live Aid Concert			Market forces
84	Aids virus identified	Miners' strike	Mental Health (Scotland) Act	
83				
82	Falklands War	Greenham Common anti-nuclear protest		
81	Ronald Reagan new US President	Inner-city riots	Education Act	
1980	John Lennon shot			
79		Margaret Thatcher new PM		**The seventies**
78			Homeless Persons Act	Increasing individualism
77	Jimmy Carter new US President			Energy crisis Terrorism
76		James Callaghan new PM	Race Relations Act	Recession
75	Vietnam War ends	Regional Authorities formed	Sex Discrimination Act	
74	World oil price soars	Harold Wilson new PM	Rehabilitation Offenders Act	
73		3-day working week electricity consumption		
72	Bloody Sunday			
71			Decimalisation	Divorce Reform Act

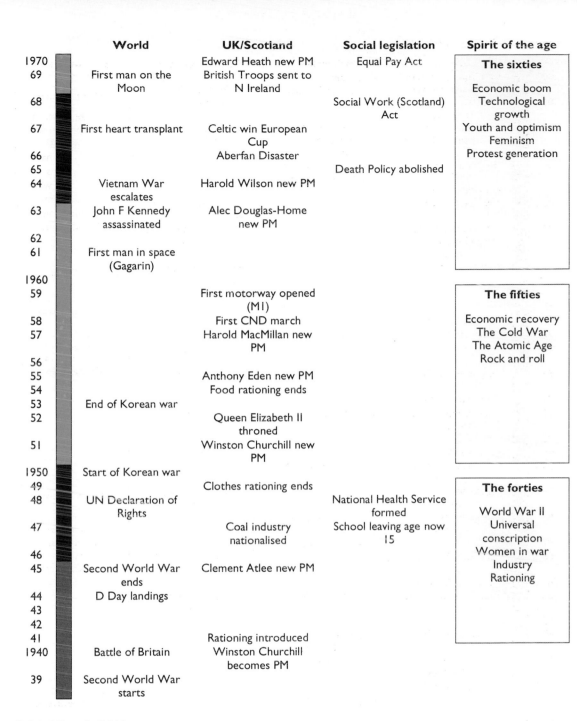

	World	UK/Scotland	Social legislation	Spirit of the age
1970		Edward Heath new PM	Equal Pay Act	**The sixties**
69	First man on the Moon	British Troops sent to N Ireland		Economic boom
68			Social Work (Scotland) Act	Technological growth
67	First heart transplant	Celtic win European Cup		Youth and optimism Feminism
66		Aberfan Disaster		Protest generation
65			Death Policy abolished	
64	Vietnam War escalates	Harold Wilson new PM		
63	John F Kennedy assassinated	Alec Douglas-Home new PM		
62				
61	First man in space (Gagarin)			
1960				
59		First motorway opened (M1)		**The fifties**
58		First CND march		Economic recovery
57		Harold MacMillan new PM		The Cold War The Atomic Age
56				Rock and roll
55		Anthony Eden new PM		
54		Food rationing ends		
53	End of Korean war			
52		Queen Elizabeth II throned		
51		Winston Churchill new PM		
1950	Start of Korean war			
49		Clothes rationing ends		**The forties**
48	UN Declaration of Rights		National Health Service formed	World War II
47		Coal industry nationalised	School leaving age now 15	Universal conscription
46				Women in war
45	Second World War ends	Clement Atlee new PM		Industry Rationing
44	D Day landings			
43				
42				
41		Rationing introduced		
1940	Battle of Britain	Winston Churchill becomes PM		
39	Second World War starts			

Political Party in British government:

Conservative

Labour

Coalition / National

(Level Int 2) Care work today

In the past, care work tended to be carried out in a wide range of settings, often institutional in nature, which operated very much in isolation from each other, separated by practice, agency and professional boundaries. A significant change which is occurring in the field of care work at the present time is a realisation that the work carried out in different fields actually shares many common factors. This is leading to a recognition that boundaries have to be much more flexible and that much can be achieved by closer working practices. This realisation of common factors may be illustrated by the formation of UNISON, which is the biggest public sector workers' trade union, and was formed by an amalgamation of a number of local government and health service unions. This reflects a dismantling of traditional barriers which previously existed between such professions as nursing and social work. There is now a greater understanding of the commonality of the caring task, and less demarcation between the various professions involved.

This has very positive implications for people entering the field of care work because it means that the opportunities for moving around and gaining skills and experience in a number of fields have greatly increased. It also has significant implications for the people on the receiving end of care services, potentially improving inter-disciplinary and collaborative work between agencies with positive effects in terms of the quality of services. Scotland has done a lot of work on the Joint Future Agenda (Scottish Executive, 2001) which has been the vehicle used to introduce new methods of working such as single shared assessments discussed in Chapter 6.

The focus of work has also moved away from institutional settings to smaller units within the community. This has changed the nature of care work so that today it is much more complex, often community-based and sometimes quite challenging.

A definition of the care task today would need to include the following:

- **direct work with individuals which provides support to them in overcoming the effects of temporary or permanent difficulties**
- **empowerment and a person-centred approach**
- **promotion of social inclusion.**

This involves the worker in a range of processes and supportive interventions working in partnerships with individuals in a structured way. It accords with the Social Care Association's definition of care, which emphasises that care is essentially about improving the quality of people's lives. This goes some way towards answering the question of what care workers do, and the following examples may give an idea of the range of work they are involved in.

Harry, Janet and Gina

Harry is 25 and works for a 'not for profit' organisation which provides social care services for people with learning disabilities who have recently moved out of a large institution. He works directly with John, who lives in his own house now and is gradually being helped to build a meaningful life for himself, despite the fact that he has been labelled as having challenging behaviour and limited communication skills.

Janet is 32 and employed as a home support services organiser for a local authority social work department. Part of her job is to assess the needs of vulnerable older people living in the locality and ensure they receive the support they need to continue living in their own homes. Such people, she reflects sometimes, would previously have been automatically admitted to a residential care home for older people, whether or not it met their needs.

Gina is 22 and works for a voluntary organisation providing support for children with autistic spectrum disorders who attend the local mainstream school. This enables the two children she works with to continue to receive schooling and the same sort of normal experiences as other kids. Five years ago they would have been sent to a special school and effectively excluded from normal educational opportunities. Nothing impresses her more in her job than the support offered by other children.

Institutionalisation

One aspect of care which care work today sets out to avoid is the effect that some institutions (especially large ones') have had, and sometimes continue to have, on people. Such institutions may be places such as hospitals for people with learning disabilities or mental health problems, or homes or entire villages for children or older adults.

In the past such institutions were often located in remote places away from centres of population and in country locations where people would enjoy the benefits of plenty of fresh air. Many institutions were characterised by having large numbers of people living in them, who were cared for by small numbers of poorly trained and poorly paid staff.

Institutions developed for a number of different reasons and were very much the product of dominant thinking of the day about what to do with people who were different. Many institutions for people with learning disabilities, for example, were built in order to provide safe refuge as well as an alternative, less challenging and safe lifestyle for people. There was another agenda, however, which was concerned with removing such people from society and placing them in locations where they would not be allowed to have any children of their own because it was felt, quite wrongly, that the moral fabric of society was threatened by a growth in the population of people with such disabilities.

It wasn't until the 1960s that anyone really started to check out the effects of institutions on people, and some of the first to do so were sociologists who began to recognise and research the phenomenon which became known as **institutionalisation**. Erving Goffman's (1968) book *Asylums* has been particularly influential in promoting analysis of this process.

Institutionalisation describes a process by which the needs of the people whom the institution exists to serve become secondary to the needs of the institution. Individuals start to lose their identity and everything becomes secondary to the smooth and efficient running of the institution. Order and routine become the dominant factors. Both staff and the people for whom the institution is providing a service become depersonalised.

The following characteristics are also usually present:

- large numbers of people being cared for by small numbers of staff
- little contact with the outside world
- few meaningful activities, lots of empty time and enforced idleness
- large social distance between staff and service users, with staff in uniforms to emphasise differences
- staff behaving in an authoritarian manner
- working to a medical model with emphasis on treatment and attention to physical needs
- little chance of leaving the establishment either temporarily or permanently
- lack of respect for dignity of individuals, demonstrated through pejorative language or lack of regard for privacy
- an almost total preoccupation among staff with the practical, task-oriented aspects of the job (mealtimes, bathtimes, etc.) with little thought or effort applied to imaginative ways of improving quality of life for service users
- staff pre-occupied with their own affairs and communicating with one another as if service users weren't there.

People who spend a significant amount of time in such institutions will usually become institutionalised, displaying the following features.

- They become indifferent to their surroundings, other people, the world, the future, anything in fact.
- They lose any motivation to do new things or sometimes anything at all.
- They lose the ability to make choices, decisions or plans of any sort. They expect others to do this for them.
- They become obedient to what people tell them to do.
- Standards of personal habits and cleanliness may go down, as they have little sense of pride in themselves.
- Expectations are that little will change and that today, tomorrow and the next day will all be the same.

- Every now and then there is an outburst of temper or aggression which is quickly dealt with.
- There can be a complete lack of enthusiasm.

The end result of this process is that the individual comes to depend on the institution for everything and finds it difficult to cope independently away from it. Many people with learning disabilities who have moved out of institutions after many years find it difficult to adapt to life in the community. This is often a direct result of the effects of institutionalisation. They have not had interactions with a wide range of people or situations, so they lack confidence when faced with new activities of daily living such as handling money, using public transport or making decisions about what food to buy.

An important factor to recognise is that many of the establishments which offer care to service users continue to have elements of institutions about them. One of the major tasks of care workers is to recognise the effects of institutionalisation and take measures to reduce or minimise these effects on individuals.

Counteracting institutionalisation

It is not the size of the institution that is most critical. People do not necessarily become institutionalised just because they live in or attend an institution which provides care. It all depends upon how the service is delivered. Some ways of counteracting institutionalisation are:

- providing choices
- not sticking to strict routines but being flexible according to need
- staff wearing casual clothes, not uniforms
- plenty of stimulating activities on offer for those who wish to participate
- showing respect for the worth and needs of all individuals
- the privacy of single rooms
- privacy when bathing, dressing, etc.
- staff trained in the values and skills of care work
- making the building as 'homely' as possible
- wherever possible, using/adapting services which are available to everyone rather than offering specialised services
- wherever possible, supporting people in their own homes rather than in institutional settings.

Some people believe that the closure of the large old institutions meant the end of institutionalisation, but unfortunately this is not necessarily the case. There is a current trend once again to build large homes for older adults, and great care needs to be taken not to replicate the mistakes, depersonalisation and disempowerment of the past. Even in small units or domiciliary settings, institutionalisation can occur if workers do not practise a positive value base which promotes the worth, dignity and inclusion of everyone.

Who are the users of care services?

> *Service users . . . are normally defined as those people who currently use services or those who have used services in the past.*
>
> (Levin, 2004)

The above definition covers a huge variety of people. For example, in the report *Making Service User Involvement Work* (Branfield and Beresford, 2006) the following people were identified: older people, people with physical and sensory impairments, people living with HIV/AIDS, mental health service users/survivors, people with learning difficulties, young people with experience of growing up in care, people with drug and alcohol problems, and users of palliative care services. As you can see, the range of people who use care services is extensive. It is also important to realise that, while all the above people may use care services, the type and degree of service they require will also vary enormously. Compare the different range of needs of someone who has a drug dependency which is ruining their lives with those of someone who has sustained a severe spinal injury in a road traffic accident, who no longer has the ability to manage even their basic physical movements. It is because the range of need is so wide that there is an increasing requirement for care workers to develop a wide range of skills.

The power of the care worker

As a care worker, it is important to realise the extent of the potential power and influence that you have over the individuals and groups of people with whom you work. This may be very obvious in some cases where you may, for example, be speaking on behalf of individual service users who have limited communication abilities. You will be, literally, speaking for them. In other cases, by simply carrying out your assigned duties, you may be perpetuating an element of disempowerment. This may happen, for example, every time you help to 'manage' someone's 'challenging behaviour'. 'Challenging behaviour' is itself a controversial concept since there can be many reasons for behaviour that care workers often find difficult. This includes the behaviour and actions of care workers themselves (they may appear to be intimidating or dismissive) or the environment in which the situation occurs (it may be too noisy or too hot).

Good intentions and well-meaning actions are often not enough to ensure that your practice is really acting in the best interests of the people you are paid to serve. The black civil rights leader Martin Luther King once said:

> *Shallow understanding from people of good will is more frustrating than absolute misunderstanding from people of ill-will.*
>
> (quoted in Oates, 1982)

This was said in relation to racism, but also expresses a sentiment which may be felt by many people using care services. You need a degree of vigilance at all times to ensure that your actions do not serve simply to continue any forms of institutional discrimination or oppression.

This caution is added not without reason for, at various times in the history of care, a number of agencies charged with the care of different service user groups have acted more as a force for social control than anything else. Examples here are children's services which colluded in the forced resettlement of 'orphans' to Australia; home helps who locked confused older people in their homes for their own safety; nurses who assisted in giving massive doses of sedatives and tranquillisers to difficult patients or helped remove the teeth of 'biters' – the list is long and does not make comfortable reading.

These are extreme examples but should act as a reminder of the responsibilities of care workers not to collude, unconsciously or otherwise, in systems which treat people badly or disrespectfully while purporting to care for them. If you are ever faced with such a dilemma you should not hesitate to seek advice which is available from a variety of sources e.g. Public Concern At Work or the Care Commission (www.pcaw.co.uk; www.carecommission.com). If you base your practice on the value base outlined in Chapter 2, you should not go too far wrong.

An important point is that you will develop the ability to act as an agent of change. You will develop skills and confidence in promoting good practice. You will be able to challenge practices which you feel are not in the best interests of service users and thereby help to ensure that practice continues to be improved. Building upon your learning, experience and reflection are essential. Sometimes reading a book can be helpful in expanding your thinking in new directions as in the example below.

The noise of the world
In an excellent book which re examines the history of the world by looking at the different sorts of relationships which have existed between people in times gone by, Theodore Zeldin (1995) makes what at first sight seems to be an enigmatic and contradictory statement when he says 'The noise of the world is made of silences.' This starts to make sense, however, when you think of all the times when, instead of shouting out about unfair treatment or injustice, people remain silent or turn their heads away. They fail to get involved or make an effort. Sometimes this happens in professional contexts in situations such as case conferences where people may fail to speak out to defend the real best interests of those whom they are supposed to be serving. The consequences of not speaking up, of saying nothing, are often dire for the individuals involved, and their subsequent protests might contribute significantly to the noise of the world.

Formal and informal care

There is an important distinction between what is known as 'formal care', which is care provided by people on a paid basis, and 'informal care', which is usually provided by relatives for no material reward whatsoever. In 11.5% of households in Scotland there is someone who needs regular care (Scottish Household Survey). In Scotland today there are a significant number of people who act as carers for someone. They may be parents who care for a child with a disability, a man caring for his partner with Alzheimer's disease or a woman who has given up her own career to look after her frail, elderly parent. Although many people willingly take on roles such as these, the lot of such carers is not always a happy one. They may be left to get on with things, with little or no support from professional services, necessitating sacrifices socially and economically. For example, they may be unable to work, have little social contact with others or be forced to rely on benefits in order to live, which generally means existing close to poverty. It can be a 24 hours a day, seven days a week job for some carers. It is estimated that there are about 5.7 million carers in the UK (Department of Health 2000). Carers' rights to be assessed in their own right have been reiterated in a number of pieces of legislation, e.g. the Carers (Recognition and Services) Act 1995 and the Community Care and Health (Scotland) Act 2002. However, as with users of service, there are not always adequate services to meet their needs.

Many people who undertake the role of informal carer have not had much choice in the matter, but have been forced by circumstances. There is also a great gender imbalance here as this role tends to be undertaken by women rather than men.

Formal care, on the other hand, refers to care which is received by people in a wide variety of settings, usually with support given by people who are paid to work with them. Formal care may be defined as caring for people in society, other than self or family, in an agency whose codes of practice are dictated to and guided by legislation, policy and professional ethics. The different types of provider of formal care and the areas in which they operate are examined below.

There are a large number of organisations who provide formal care in a wide variety of settings and for a wide variety of client groups. These organisations can be classified as belonging to the statutory, voluntary or private sector, although sometimes those belonging to the last two categories are known as 'independent' sector providers. Changes in the proportion of services provided by each sector between 1994 and 2004 can be seen in Figure 1.5.

The statutory sector

The statutory sector contains organisations which provide health services, social work services and increasingly joint or combined services with housing, education and justice. They are known as statutory services because they perform some of their functions, or have been set up, under Acts of Parliament. Every Scottish local authority must by law provide a range of certain social work services. It used to be the case that Scottish local authorities were the direct providers of most of the services themselves – they had big Social Work Departments which ran a whole range of care provision such as home helps,

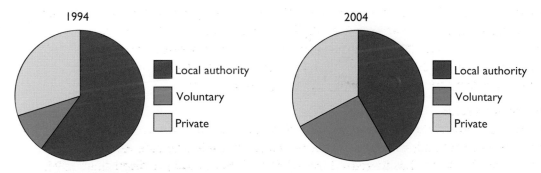

Figure 1.5 Social service split by sector

day centres for people with learning disabilities, intermediate treatment services for offenders, adoption services and fieldwork services. Since the National Health Service and Community Care Act (1990), such departments have adopted a mixed economy approach to the provision of care, and many services are now provided by and/or commissioned from the independent sector. The proportion of services actually provided by the statutory sector has fallen from 60% in 1994 to 42% in 2004 (Scottish Executive, 2006c).

The voluntary sector

The voluntary sector is one half of the independent sector. It has traditionally been seen as the area where new services tend to be developed in order to fill the gaps that statutory services don't cover or to provide creative approaches in the provision of service. Some of the first services for people with learning disabilities, for example, were provided on a local level by groups of volunteers such as parents who, in the absence of any provision, grouped together and ran their own services. At the same time such groups lobbied to get the statutory services to take notice of the plight of the people they were caring for and create pressure for proper services to be provided. Some of these groups grew up to become service providers themselves. One example is Enable, formerly known as the 'Scottish Society for the Mentally Handicapped', which was an amalgamation of local groups of parents all of whom worked very hard for the benefit of their sons and daughters. They opened and ran their own day centres and respite care units, some of which were eventually taken over and managed by local authority services. Enable continues as a campaigning group for this service user group and also functions as a direct provider of quality services through a number of affiliated service provision agencies.

The voluntary sector is the fastest growing sector in Scotland providing over a quarter of all services (Scottish Executive, 2006c). Sometimes, but not always, voluntary organisations will also be registered charities and depend on voluntary giving for part of their income. This has proved a problem in the past because, in order to gain the sympathy of the public and encourage them to make donations, these organisations often portrayed the people they cared for in a very negative way, with images of dependency and helplessness. One woman I met, who was a wheelchair user, recounts the story of waiting outside a major department store drinking from a can of cola, when suddenly a man approached her and absent mindedly tried to put some coins in her can. Many service users were extremely angry at being portrayed as objects of sympathy and having to rely on people's charity.

Associated with and sometimes confused with the voluntary sector are social enterprise companies. Many of these are run essentially on models borrowed from commercial undertakings, and can often outperform traditional voluntary organisations, especially in terms of flexibility and responsiveness to peoples' needs. Together with voluntary organisations they comprise the newly emerging 'third sector'.

The private sector

The private sector is the other half of the independent sector and continues to grow at a steady pace in Scotland, especially in the provision of residential care for older adults. Provision by this sector has increased from 30% to 33% of total provision since 1994. Private sector services are run as businesses which make a profit so only operate in areas of the care sector where profits can be made such as care homes, hospitals and child care facilities.

Is there a mixed economy of care?

A 1998 survey into the 590 providers of domiciliary care in Scotland discovered that, despite the abundance of private and voluntary providers, the market share of the independent sector was found to be relatively small (see Figure 1.6). The statutory sector was still by far the major provider of domiciliary care in Scotland. Of the total hours of domiciliary care provided per week in Scotland, 76% were provided by social work providers. The private and voluntary sectors combined represented 15% of the total hours of care provided, and the health sector accounted for the remaining 9%.

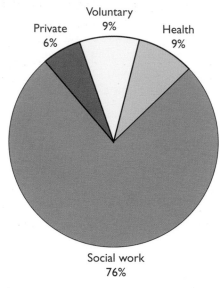

Figure 1.6 Proportion of domiciliary care hours provided by each sector (Scottish Office, 1998b)

Activity

The mixed economy of care

Figure 1.6 relates to domiciliary care (care in a person's own home) only. If the graph referred to residential care for older adults, the share of provision among the sectors would be very different. Can you find information on the Scottish Executive website to support this statement?

Care work: the shape of things to come

A number of factors which will have a significant influence on the shape of work across all fields of care are identified in the Scottish Executive (2006a) publication *Changing Lives: Report of the 21st Century Social Work Review*, and some of these are explored below. Many of these issues are discussed in more detail in Chapter 5.

Ageing population

This trend has been identified for some time and was referred to earlier in the chapter. *Changing Lives* recognises the tremendous challenge this poses to health and social care but also points out the large pool of talent within this group which could potentially be better used for the benefit of communities.

Children in need

The fall in the birth rate has led to a decrease in the number of children in Scotland. In 2006 the pre-school population was half what it was in 1968 (277,000 compared with 478,000) but in the same period the number of children looked after by local authorities rose by 4%. So while there may be fewer children in the future, more of them may need to be looked after, and this is a massive challenge for those organisations charged with a care and protecton role. This is an area where results to date have not been good. Of children who have been looked after in care, 60% leave school with no qualifications and a similar percentage never enter employment or training.

Changing needs

In a paradoxical way, medical advances have led to an increase in the number of people with significant disabilities because babies born prematurely, or with what would once have been life-threatening conditions, will now survive into adulthood. There is also a rise in the incidence of chronic mental health conditions related to stress, anxiety and depression.

Fractured relationships

The nature of society is changing in that the strong social relationships that may have existed in the past are rapidly changing to more fluid, complex and fractured associations. Many more people are making life choices to live alone, many children are growing up with changing sets of parents and family members, and support that might have previously been available from extended families might not be available and indeed may have to be purchased instead, which puts increasing financial pressure on families.

Social polarisation

While there is continuing slow growth in overall wealth in society, the gap between the richest and the poorest also continues to grow. In 2010 it is predicted that the difference in life expectancy between the most and least affluent areas will have grown to about 9.2 years.

Activity

Changing lives

Read the section on the changing context of care in the *Changing Lives* report (Scottish Executive, 2006a). It adds a number of other factors to those identified above.

You can download the report from the Scottish Executive at **www.scotland.gov.uk/Resource/Doc/91931/0021949.pdf**.

Working on your own, or preferably in a small group, identify three of the changes you think are most relevant for one of the following: young people, older adults, people with mental health difficulties.

SUMMARY

This chapter has provided an examination of the context of care, so that you can see where and how care practice fits into a historical and social context. The nature and meaning of care and care practice were examined, with an emphasis on improving the quality of people's lives. Recent important legislation was introduced, and developments and possible future trends in care examined. Reasons for the growth in demand for care were put forward. Care work in different fields and the factors common to all of these were looked at. Examples both of care workers and service users were provided. Consideration was given to the power of the care worker and empowerment of the service user in order that practice is always in the best interests of service users. The concept of institutionalisation was introduced to enable you to understand how institutions can disempower people, and the measures that are needed to counteract it. The differences between formal and informal care were examined and accounts given of statutory, voluntary and private sector provision of services. The chapter also looked forward to care work in the future and the shape of things to come.

Care work is going on all over the country every hour of the day and night and it would be hard to overstate the value of this work, which is carried out usually in a quiet, undemonstrative manner and sometimes in difficult and demanding circumstances. It is hoped that the contents of this book will assist you in becoming a confident and competent practitioner.

Activity · *Comparing care services*

Read Julie's story below and the descriptions of the care sector units in Chapter 7: Queen's View, The Five Trees Nursery, 6-8 Newton Road, The Dorward and The McTavish Unit.

Choose one of the units and compare practice with that of Julie's story, identifying:

a five features of institutionalisation in Julie's story

b five features that may counteract the occurrence of institutionalisation in your chosen unit.

Julie's story

It was a summer day in the mid 1970s and Julie's first shift on the ward in the local hospital for 'mental defectives', where she had been offered a summer job as an assistant nurse during her break from university. The ward she had been assigned to was called a villa but she could see little resemblance between the dilapidated red-brick building she now stood in and her uncle's holiday home in Spain. Sixty people appeared to spend every minute of their lives confined to this ward where they were looked after by three or four nurses. The worst thing was the smell — a heady mixture of sweat, urine, stale food and disinfectant.

Julie felt ill at ease and self-conscious in her new nurse's uniform. She wasn't a nurse so why was she dressed like one? She also felt uncomfortable at being locked in this place, even though she had a bunch of keys securely attached to her belt. She was, if truth be told, even a little scared of the patients, some of whom looked quite frightening and were behaving in strange ways, pacing up and down like caged animals or sitting rocking on the floor.

So far today she had helped to bath 20 of the patients in the ward, ticking off their names in a big bath book as they were processed two at a time in the white walled bathroom with its two baths sitting in the middle of the floor. Each patient was bathed and received a change of underwear twice weekly. She had been amused to see the communal underwear at first, all marked with the hospital name and ward number until she thought what it must be like not even owning your own pants.

Now it was dinner time and she had been asked to help with the two dozen patients in wheelchairs who were unable to feed themselves. 'You can do the feeders', she had been told by the kindly old charge nurse. As she looked at the two rows of patients lined up against each side of the wall and away from the others sitting at tables, a big trolley with steaming hot steel cans of food was wheeled in by Bessie, the other assistant nurse on the shift.

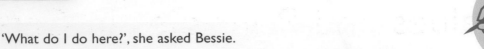

Activity   *Comparing care services* continued

'What do I do here?', she asked Bessie.

'Just fill the bowls and feed them', replied Bessie, 'and watch out for chokers.'

She watched as Bessie spooned food from the steel containers into the large plastic bowls. Three half-slices of buttered bread were dropped in each first, followed by a ladleful of soup, brown mince, mashed potato and then a couple of splashes of milky tea from a huge battered teapot. The resulting mixture was mixed to a runny consistency.

'That's how you do the soft diets, love' said Bessie. 'Sometimes if you're in a hurry you can put the custard in as well. All goes down the same way you know. Now you do that side and I'll do this.'

This story refers to practice which actually occurred in a Scottish hospital. The practice came to an end when a young student nurse who had been placed in the ward on temporary secondment was so appalled that she threatened to go straight to the press.

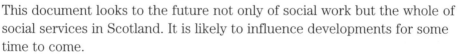

Suggested reading

Scottish Executive (2006) *Changing Lives: Report of the 21st Century Social Work Review.* Edinburgh: Scottish Executive.
This document looks to the future not only of social work but the whole of social services in Scotland. It is likely to influence developments for some time to come.

Zeldin, T (1995) *An Intimate History of Humanity.* London: Minerva.
Some very personal accounts about life and how it is lived and thought about.

CHAPTER 2
Values and Principles in Care

Ellen Lancaster

> *Implicit in care practice is the recognition of the dignity and value of every human being.*
>
> (Social Care Association, 2002)

This chapter covers material for Values and Principles in Care, Intermediate 1 Outcome 2, Intermediate 2 Outcomes 2 and 3, Higher Outcome 1; Sociology for Care, Intermediate 2 Outcomes 2 and 3.

By the end of this chapter you should be able to:

★ understand and apply the value base in care

★ explain the significance of values in care

★ explain the meaning of discrimination and anti-discriminatory practice

★ explain the role of communication in the caring relationship

★ analyse caring relationships in terms of care values and communication.

The value base

In all areas of care practice a commitment to the values and principles of care is essential. Values and principles provide the foundations for good practice. A **value** is defined as 'that which is worthy of esteem for its own sake, that which has intrinsic worth' (Oxford English Dictionary). **Principle** is defined as 'a rule of conduct, especially good conduct' (Oxford English Dictionary). The principles of care are derived from two core values: respect for the worth and dignity of every individual; according social justice and promoting the social welfare of every individual. Social justice means that everyone has the right to fair and correct treatment in society. Welfare should ensure that those who are in need of care should have the opportunity to improve their personal situation through the promotion of their right to services and benefits.

Value statements

In the light of these values, read and think about the quotes below:

'I find it pointless talking to old Mary. She's got dementia and never knows what you are saying to her.'

'That is the lassie McKay. She's deaf and dumb and has a carer who takes her out shopping. It's a waste of time if you ask me.'

'It's a danger to us all, these "nutters" who are living among us. They should be kept in hospitals.'

'That man of hers is out of prison now and living in a resettlement unit. They will never change him. He has always been an addict.'

'These Asian folk will just need to be like us and do what we do. It is costing enough catering for our own without them.'

How often have you heard such statements or similar statements made? What have you thought of them or have you just accepted them?

On reflection you may conclude that the people making these statements think that those people talked about have no value, do not deserve a chance in life, a choice in life or acceptance as fellow human beings worthy of dignity or respect.

Unfortunately in many walks of life these attitudes are apparent and reflect a lack of the understanding and acceptance to which every human being should be entitled. In care work there should be no such attitudes. In today's society, which is multi-cultural and multi-racial, those who need the help of care services are entitled to good care practice enriched with values and principles. If care practice is anything less, then people are being let down by the workers who are there to support them. The differences between good and poor practice can be seen below.

Table 2.1 Characteristics of a person using care services

Good care practice	Poor care practice
Happy	Unhappy
Optimistic	No hope
High self-esteem	Very low self-esteem
Choice	No choice (given orders)
Privacy	Exposure of their lives
Important	Lonely
Comfortable with oneself and others	Awkward and no confidence
Accepted and relaxed	Intimidated and bullied
Safe	Scared, in danger

Never look down on anyone unless you are helping them up.

(Jesse Jackson, American activist)

It is obvious from Table 2.1 that a person receiving good care will have a far better quality of life than a person receiving poor care. Good care rests upon a solid value base and it is for this very reason that it is imperative that care values and principles are adhered to and practised devotedly at all times.

The necessity for a value base with a set of guiding principles has been outlined many times since the 1980s. The Wagner Report (Wagner, 1988), the Social Care Association's Code of Practice (1994), the National Health Service and Community Care Act (1990), Scotland's National Care Standards (Scottish Executive, 2001) and the Code of Practice for Social Service Workers (SSSC, 2002) all emphasise the importance of values and principles. As far back as 1946 the Universal Declaration of Human Rights, published after the Second World War, gave prominence to 'fundamental human rights, the dignity and worth of the "human person" and equal rights for men and women'.

The principles of care

The main principles considered in this chapter are those set out in the National Care Standards. These are:

- Dignity
- Privacy
- Choice
- Safety
- Realising potential
- Equality and diversity

Activity *National Care Standards*

Acquire a copy of the National Care Standards relevant to your workplace (this can be obtained free from **www.carecommission.gov.uk**). Examine your practice and ensure that it reflects these standards.

Dignity

Everyone has a right to:

- be treated with dignity and respect at all times
- enjoy a full range of social relationships.

The application of this principle involves individualisation and respect for this particular person, whoever he or she may be. It also involves empathy, acceptance and encouragement from the care worker to heighten the self-esteem of the person. Individualisation is the recognition and understanding of each person's own qualities, distinctive character and personality. It is based on the right to be treated not just as a human being but as *this* human being with his or her personal differences.

Elaine and Beth

This example should enable you to reconsider the value statement quoted earlier: 'I find it pointless talking to old Mary. She's got dementia and never knows what you are saying to her.' Elaine is a support worker in a care home and describes working with Beth who has dementia:

'It can be difficult to communicate with someone who has dementia and very discouraging if the service user shows no interest in communicating. However, I feel empathy for those who appear to be trapped in their own world and I always feel positive that I will succeed in communicating with them. My training in communications and my patience, tolerance and knowledge give me confidence and enthusiasm. For example, when I first met Beth in her home I felt that previous support workers, families and the outside agencies had carried on doing things for Beth without waiting for her response. This I felt was making Beth a passive recipient of her care and encouraging 'learned helplessness'.

'I would spend time with Beth sitting straight in front of her, at the same level, slightly leaning toward her to try to get her to make eye contact with me. I would speak slowly to her and use simple words, have a friendly expression on my face, open body language and a friendly tone of voice. Gradually Beth showed signs of wanting to communicate with me by touching my face and hand. I would ask her if I could take a photograph off her sideboard and ask her who the people in the photograph were by suggesting 'is this your grand-daughter?' or 'is this you?' She would nod or even say 'yes'. I used the same method to find out what Beth would like to eat by showing her different types of actual food or pictures of food. At one point I asked her if I could turn on her radio to which she nodded and I watched her face as I tuned in the stations and observed her smiling when Scottish music was playing. I had a wonderful feeling when I actually saw Beth smiling and felt very good for her. I was succeeding by treating Beth as an individual with her own likes and dislikes, by using my imagination to find out what she liked and also by treating her with respect and promoting her dignity.'

Privacy

Everyone has a right to:

- have their privacy and property respected
- be free from unnecessary intrusion.

Everyone has the right to privacy, to have his or her own 'space'. It is not difficult to imagine how it would feel if someone accompanied you to the bathroom and insisted on staying, or barged in without permission when you were in your own bedroom, or listened in to your telephone conversations, or discussed your financial affairs with you in front of others. If you consider the humiliation and embarrassment this would cause *you*, then you will appreciate the need for care workers to give service users the privacy that is their human right. Sometimes, when a carer knows a service user very well, the carer may assume it is acceptable to look through a bag, look in drawers or open a letter without permission. However, such behaviour is disrespectful and ignores common courtesy.

Chris

Chris, a student on placement in a care home, had to assist a care worker one morning in waking up residents and then helping them to wash and dress. Chris was horrified when the care worker boldly walked into each resident's bedroom without knocking, switched on the lights and proceeded to help them out of bed. Chris did not follow suit. He knocked on the doors first and then, when told to enter, went up to the resident and kindly spoke to her before switching on the light, allowing time for the resident to decide when she wanted to get out of bed. Chris was given a 'ticking off' for his actions by the care worker and told that they did not have time for this. Realising that this was common practice in the home, Chris discussed his concerns with his supervisor. The supervisor, without hesitation, discussed this practice with all staff and it was agreed that in future this type of practice was not acceptable. It is only by not accepting poor practice and by good example that long-standing 'well, that is the way that we do it' poor practice will change.

Confidentiality

Confidentiality is maintaining the right to privacy of information and is an extension of the privacy principle. It is not only an ethical obligation of the care worker but is also necessary in order that the service user will trust and confide in the worker. The principle of confidentiality appears deceptively simple. You may think that it can be equated with secrecy but this is not the case. It is about the appropriateness of sharing, transmitting or storing information about a service user where a number of competing factors may influence decisions about the information usage.

It may appear to present a dilemma for the care worker when a service user offers to tell him or her something of a confidential nature. In this instance the worker should explain to the service user that what is told to them may have to be shared with their line manager. Confidence needs to be instilled in the service user that this would solely be in his or her interest.

Suggested methods of maintaining confidentiality are by keeping all records in a secure place when not in use, by gaining permission from the service user if information has to be shared with other professionals, by restricting access to records, by keeping confidences unless there are limitations imposed by law and agency policy, by not talking about service users or their carers behind their backs or to others who are not members of the care team.

It is wise not to talk about any area of work in caring to anybody other than those involved, whether it is about service users, their carers, their family or any incident.

Prevention is better than cure. Even to discuss an issue using different names is not recommended, as some people will probably be able to recognise who or what is being talked about. There could be times when you are in a place or talking to people whom you would never associate with your workplace or service user when in fact they do have connections. How many times have you started to talk about someone when you have been away somewhere only to find out that they know someone you know or are even related? Remember the familiar saying 'it is a small world'.

Choice

Everyone has a right to:

- make informed choices, while recognising the rights of other people to do the same
- know about the range of choices
- get help to fully understand all the options and choose the one that is right for them.

Applying the principle of choice encourages **independence**. Independence may be defined as 'opportunities to think and act without reference to another person, including willingness to incur a degree of calculated risk'.

Many service users were previously accustomed to, and capable of, making decisions and choices for themselves. Others, for example people who were severely institutionalised as a result of spending many years in hospital, may never have had the opportunity of being independent. Irrespective of the service user's circumstances it is the care worker's duty to ensure that those in his or her care are enabled and empowered to maximise choice and independence.

Choice can in many situations result in an element of risk. This is embodied in the following quote from the principles of practice of one home for older adults:

> *Responsible risk taking is regarded as normal. Excessive paternalism and concern with safety may lead to infringements of personal rights. Those who are competent to judge the risk to themselves are free to make their own decisions so long as they do not threaten the safety of others.*

(The Retail Trust, Glasgow)

Choice **empowers** people who might be seen as powerless and vulnerable in some aspects of their lives. Giving service users choices, a form of control over their own lives, does empower them. It also involves making sure service users are given sufficient information to enable them to make informed choices, that is choices which are based on a sound understanding of their situation and any options which may be available.

Choice also promotes independence, encouraging people to take control of their own lives, to make decisions and choices, no matter how small or how big. It follows then that the service user has to be given a full range of choices and not just those which are compatible with the care worker or the agency that is providing care. Too often the service user is not given the power of choice because of inconvenience, apathy or over-protection. This type of practice is in complete contrast to the key factors stated in government reports and legislation such as the National Health Service and Community Care Act (1990), the Wagner Report (1988), the Citizens Charter (1991) and *The Same As You?* (Scottish Executive, 2000) which all state that service users have the right of choice and should be given encouragement enabling them to be independent.

Examples of this principle in practice are:

- a resident in a care home choosing to go to bed when it suits her rather than when it is convenient for the night shift workers
- a young person who is being looked after in a children's home choosing to travel to school on public transport rather than in the local authority named bus
- a person with learning difficulties choosing to cook his own meal
- a person who is blind choosing to travelling independently to and from wherever they wish to go.

Finally, the following quotation makes points about choice and the way in which this is empowering:

> *Sevice users want two other issues to be prioritised in 2007. First is that choice becomes a reality, with people able to live their lives how, where and with whom they want and the right to the support they want, instead of relying on what scraps of services are thrown their way. They want choice and control taken out of the hands of managers and clinicians who think they know what's best . . .*

(Beresford, 2007)

Safety

Everyone has a right to:

- feel safe and secure in all aspects of life, including health and well-being
- enjoy safety but not be over-protected
- be free from exploitation and abuse.

It is the duty and moral obligation of the care worker to enable service users to feel safe and secure and to protect them from any form of abuse. Abuse includes behaviour which is intended to exploit, dominate and/or damage another person. There are several forms of abuse. Physical abuse occurs where one person may hit, punch, push, pull or cause pain to another. Emotional abuse, including verbal abuse, occurs when a person is humiliated, intimidated, shouted at, belittled and/or bullied. Financial abuse occurs when one person is exploited by another or others for financial gain. Sexual abuse is exploiting another for sexual pleasure against their wishes. Lastly there is neglect, sometimes called passive abuse. Neglect can be intentional or unintentional and occurs when a child or other vulnerable person is deprived of the appropriate or continuous care needed, thus resulting in the deterioration of their physical or emotional well-being.

In many situations the service user's reasons for being in need of care have occurred because of one or more of these forms of abuse. Rightfully, then, they should not be exposed to the same painful treatment by those who are supposed, and legally bound, to ensure in them a feeling of safety and security. Care workers who are guilty of abusing those in their care misuse the power of 'being in charge'.

Unfortunately abuse in many forms still rears its ugly head, as is apparent in examples taken from issues of community care magazines (1998 to 2007), such as: 'social worker sexually abuses adolescent in care', or 'private nursing home closed down because of a catalogue of neglect' or 'a resident of a home suffered horrendous bedsores and subsequently died' or 'residents found to be in a state of coma due to being drugged' or 'home care worker embezzles thousands of pounds from elderly lady in her care' or 'staff at care home did not treat human beings as adults'.

These acts of abuse should never happen and it is imperative that care workers should never practise in this way. They should also be aware of, prevent and report any care worker whose behaviour is considered to be abusive.

Realising potential

Everyone has a right to have the opportunity to:

- achieve all they can
- make full use of the resources that are available
- make the most of their lives.

Care workers should be committed to providing more than just basic care and should enable service users to lead rich, fulfilling lives in which they are encouraged to achieve their ambitions and goals and realise their maximum potential.

The following guidelines aim to assist care workers in this task. Care workers should:

- make themselves knowledgeable of the service user's previous lifestyle by consulting with them or someone, such as a relative, who knows them well – in this way the worker becomes aware of the service user's expectations and wishes in relation to independence
- help and encourage the service user to think and act as independently as possible
- encourage, enable and participate, if required, with the permission of the service user
- provide a suitable physical environment which is safe for the service user to do as much as possible for him/herself
- continually monitor the service user's achievements and ensure a practical and safe progression
- praise achievements or kindly explain the justified limitations
- offer and make the service user aware of services outside their own residence or local environment
- offer information on training, educational provision such as further education colleges, choice of outings, holidays, choice of creative and leisure activities.

Peter

The following case study is written by a support worker who works in a resettlement unit for people who have been released from prison. It should enable you to reconsider the value statement quoted earlier: 'That man of hers is out of prison now and in a resettlement unit. They will never help him. He has always been an addict.'

Peter grew up on a large council estate. He lived with his mother and father and four brothers and sisters. His father was continually unemployed and his mother had a part-time job. Life was not easy for Peter when he was growing up as he was the eldest and expected by his father to provide for the family. He first started to drink when he was fourteen and became addicted to alcohol by the time he was eighteen. Peter, who generally had a pleasant and amicable personality, would 'lash out' when he was drunk. Eventually he lost his job and after being arrested many times for fighting, breach of the peace and assault he was given a six-month sentence in prison and then was released into a resettlement unit.

When Peter arrived at the unit he was very embarrassed and angry with himself that he had become an alcoholic. He was also fearful that he might end up like some of the older residents in the unit whom he felt had no future. Fortunately the unit he was living in had very dedicated staff who accepted others for who they were and gave wonderful encouragement and support. Peter's support worker built up a good relationship with him. Over time, Peter, who was the youngest in the unit, found himself helping other residents in the unit. After a year, Peter moved into his own flat, which was not too far from the unit. He was actively seeking employment and rather than having nothing to do he offered to work voluntarily in the unit.

It was soon realised that Peter had many good qualities and skills in caring, and he was offered part-time paid work in the unit. The manager arranged training for Peter and not long after that he was accepted onto the HNC in Social Care. Peter now says: 'My aim is to support people the way I was supported and encouraged to realise my potential. I know how they feel and how when others believe in you it gives confidence, optimism and happiness to your life.'

From this case study it is clear that the support workers gave Peter the opportunity to achieve his own goals. They accepted Peter, were non-judgemental and genuinely interested in Peter, which helped him to believe in himself.

George

George had lived in a 'long-term' hospital for the largest part of his life and had been discharged from hospital to live in the community. He has now lived in his own house with the support of paid support workers for almost a year. George enjoys travelling into the city to shop. However, because of the expense of bus travel, he is limited to how often he can do this. When a student support worker realised George's plight, he made inquiries about why George did not have a concessionary travel card. Unfortunately, George's right to this benefit had been overlooked by his support workers. Their negligence had caused George to be deprived of his leisure pursuits and he had been limited in his number of trips into the city. His right to receive a concessionary travel pass should have been made known to him when he originally moved into his own home. The support workers involved failed to ensure that George's support needs were fully met, and he was deprived of living his life to the full. Care workers should ensure they know and find out about all benefits, resources and facilities available.

Equality and diversity

Everyone has a right to:

- live an independent life, rich in purpose, meaning and personal fulfilment
- be valued for their ethnic background, language, culture and faith
- be treated equally and be cared for in an environment which aims to be free from bullying, harassment and discrimination
- be able to complain effectively without fear of victimisation.

So far in this chapter the great necessity for, and the essentials of, values and principles in care work have been discussed. All of these values and principles underpin the promotion of equality and diversity, anti-discriminatory and anti-oppressive practice.

Every carer has a duty and responsibility to:

- demonstrate an awareness of both individual and institutional discrimination
- be sensitive to all people's needs, regardless of differences
- challenge discrimination in words and deeds.

Activity   *Value base*

Copy the list below and tick the things that you value.

Living in your own home

Being free to come and go as you please

Living in a rented flat with other people

Having to ask permission to leave your own home

Living in a hospital ward

Having worthwhile employment

Having to repeatedly apply for state benefit

Choosing your own clothes

Going on holiday abroad

Sharing underwear and clothes with someone else with someone else

Going to a seaside boarding house for a week once a year

Spending the day doing 'arts and crafts'

Doing work for which you do not get paid

Going to college

Having a speech impediment and not being able to communicate clearly

Going to the hairdresser

Being neat and well dressed

Winning an athletic event

Passing your driving test

Having your teacher, hairdresser and doctor come to see you only at your place of work

Having the right to marry if you wish

Not being able to drink without help

Having your needs discussed by other people at a meeting

Being told the truth about a medical condition you have

Going out for a drink with your friends

Consider the statements you have not ticked and think why you do not value them. It may be because they do not give you choice, because they do not give you privacy and/or because they take away your dignity or your right to equality.

When the above values and principles are practised competently the foundations have been established for a 'meaningful relationship' with the service user. This will not only give a good feeling of friendship, acceptance and safety but more importantly it will enable him or her to progress in all areas of development.

The following section aims to enable you to understand the ways in which practising equality and diversity are underpinned by an understanding of discrimination and anti-discriminatory practice.

Discrimination and anti-discriminatory practice

> *Anti-discriminatory practice challenges people's values and their taken-for-granted assumptions in constructing their own sense of reality. Such a challenge can prove to be very threatening and destabilising. If not handled sensitively, exposure to anti-discriminatory ideas and values can be so alien and threatening as to arouse considerable resistance and barriers to change . . . The focus needs to be on educating and convincing, not bullying*
>
> (Thompson, 2006)

Introduction

As a worker in a care setting, it is essential to develop a clear understanding of **discrimination**, **prejudice** and **stereotyping** and to develop a variety of strategies to combat them. Few people would deny that discrimination exists, but there is still disagreement and confusion about exactly what it is, why it exists and what can be done to change things. Discrimination is a complex subject, and one that is prone to a hostile response because people feel threatened when their views are challenged.

What is discrimination?

- Discrimination is treating someone differently: it can be positive or negative.
- Negative discrimination is the unequal and unfair treatment of an individual or group.
- Discrimination is based on prejudice towards people who are seen as being different.
- Prejudice is learned from picking up negative attitudes from our families and society.
- Discrimination is built in to the way we run our social, political and economic institutions.

What is prejudice?

A prejudice is an attitude about an individual or a group, based on judgements which are often founded on ignorance, fear or speculation, rather than fact. Prejudice – the pre-judging of someone – can be either positive or negative. You can be prejudiced in favour of, or prejudiced against, a person. Everyone has prejudices: once we become aware of what they are for us, we can begin to do something about them.

The way prejudice works in relation to discrimination is that a negative, biased and intolerant attitude against someone is maintained, even in the face of contradictory evidence. These prejudices are often based on negative stereotypes of a group.

Figure 2.1 When one group is disadvantaged, another is advantaged (© Andrew Parry and Robin Maclean)

A stereotype is a label which is applied to all members of a group. A quality or characteristic is taken as applying to all members of the group, for example: people with Down's syndrome like music; girls don't like playing football; all gay men are promiscuous; all Aberdonians are mean. People within that group are not seen as individuals with unique needs and interests. They are treated as if they are the same as everyone else in that group.

Apart from being based on a lack of correct information, prejudices and stereotypes such as these disadvantage people because negative assumptions are made about them, based on one aspect of their identity. People are not seen as a 'whole person', but are categorised according to one feature – being black, disabled, homeless – and related to only on that basis. That one aspect of their identity defines them in the eyes of the prejudiced person. Assumptions are made about their abilities and interests based on these stereotypes and prejudices. This limits their opportunity to construct their own feeling of positive self-esteem, because they so often meet with negative or misinformed reactions, and this limits their opportunities to participate equally in society.

On a piece of paper, write 'Who am I?' at the top. Answer this question 20 times with as wide a range of responses as you wish: I am female, I am small, I have brown hair, I'm a joker, I am a grandfather, I have a hearing impairment, I help out at the youth club, I am chinese, I am fat. The list might contain descriptions of what you look like, what you do or an aspect of your personality.

Place a large piece of paper sideways and draw a line with your date of birth at the left-hand side and today's date at the right-hand side. For each of the 20 responses to the question 'Who am I?', write or draw on the paper when you first became aware of that part of your identity. Things like 'I am a grandfather' will be easy to date, but you might need to think about exactly when you first became aware of your colour or your gender. The purpose of this exercise is to reflect on exactly *when* you developed your sense of what makes up your individual identity. Discovering and creating an identity is an active process for everyone.

Prejudice and stereotypes don't occur randomly. They reflect the divisions within any society, whereby those who have power are able to define what is good or bad, and what is acceptable or not. Power is the ability to control or to influence other people. Prejudice reflects the power that the dominant group has over other groups. When one group is disadvantaged, another group is advantaged. Conflict theory is examined in Chapter 5, and the point about the power of dominant groups is returned to later in this chapter.

How do we develop our prejudices? The process of **socialisation** (the way in which we develop our values, attitudes and ideas) will be dealt with in more detail in Chapters 3 and 5, but it is touched on here because it is central to the process of developing prejudice. The messages you pick up, firstly from your family (agent of **primary socialisation**) and later from friends, school and the media (agents of **secondary socialisation**), influence the way you see the world.

Where did these attitudes and values come from? Historically, the Christian Churches exerted a strong influence on British society and helped define what was seen as being right and wrong. The limited position of women and perceived sinfulness of homosexuality stemmed directly from interpretations of the Bible. The Church was part of the 'establishment', along with aristocratic men who served in Parliament, and it was their views that were enshrined in laws. Married women couldn't own property in their own right until 1882. Women couldn't vote until 1918 and it was not until 1946 that the civil service dropped its rule against employing married women in certain jobs. Britain's colonial past and role in maintaining the slave trade provides the basis for many of the negative stereotypes of black people still current today.

The Commission for Racial Equality produced an exhibition called 'Roots of the Future' which looked at the history of migration to Britain. They ran workshops for schoolchildren, who made the following comments: 'I didn't know that curry didn't come from here', 'I didn't think there could be 20,000 black people in London in 1787', 'I've always related Jews to the Holocaust, never back to the Norman Conquest'. Lack of knowledge about the variety of groups in society enables discrimination to continue, because our false and negative impressions of what needs people have, and what rights they should expect, limit their opportunities. Our culture – schooling, entertainment, religion and so on – helps to create and perpetuate this lack of understanding.

Prejudice exists because we are brought up with negative pictures of certain groups, which are often based on views developed many generations ago. The negative message still exists today because it is ingrained in legal, political, educational and other structures in society. However, not everyone brought up with these negative images agrees with them or acts on them. Once people are able to make up their own minds about issues, they can reject the attitudes and behaviour they have been socialised to accept. However, some people, even if they can see that the values they have learned are wrong, still continue to hold them. This may be because of pressure from friends or family to 'fit in with the crowd'. People who have low self-esteem, and a need for acceptance by others, are more likely to conform with values they don't hold, in order to remain part of the crowd. People who have higher self-esteem are able to disagree and not fear the consequences of disapproval, because they have a stronger sense of their own identity.

Prejudice is learned during the process of developing identity, and we tend to accept unconsciously that this is 'just the way things are': it is part of our culture. However, as care workers it is important that we don't assume that it is only gay people who have to think about their sexuality, or black people who develop a sense of belonging to an ethnic group. We have all had to make choices about our sexuality, and construct our own sense of what being a member of a certain racial group means to us. Some people who belong to the 'mainstream' may not have had to give much conscious or active thought to how their identity has been created; it just seemed 'normal'. Anyone who is outside the 'mainstream' will have had to give more active thought to aspects of their identity because it has been stigmatised or is devalued in our society.

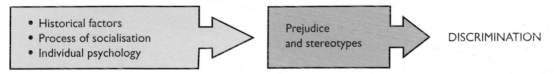

Figure 2.2 Causes of discrimination

Types of discrimination

Discrimination can occur in a number of different ways. It is important not to get too get caught up in defining what type of discrimination any particular situation is. If it's negative, it's wrong, and it should be challenged, whatever type it is. In a care setting, the main reason for trying to categorise the type of discrimination is so that you can work out the best way of challenging it. If it is a one-off situation, where it just needs to be pointed out to the person that they are being rude or dismissive, and they accept this, then no further action is needed. If it turns out that the person doesn't think it is wrong and in fact has picked it up as being acceptable from someone else in the organisation, it then needs to be tackled at an organisational level.

Conscious discrimination

Conscious discrimination occurs when a person knows they are acting negatively and wants to disadvantage someone. In a care setting, this would be against the equal opportunities policy and breaks the law. The person should be reported and, depending on the situation, may receive supervision, training or be disciplined. They may lose membership of their professional organisation, and have their professional registration taken away.

Unconscious discrimination

Unconscious discrimination occurs when a person discriminates against someone without realising that they are discriminating. It can be seen in the everyday behaviour and language that people have routinely used, without being aware that they may be infringing someone's rights or disrespecting them. Many actions disadvantage people because they perpetuate stereotypes of people being weak and helpless. This is the 'Does he take sugar?' syndrome, where people talk to the person who is pushing the wheelchair rather than the person using the wheelchair. The unconscious prejudice is shown through thinking that the person who has a physically disability is also unable to think or talk on their own behalf.

As a care worker, it is possible to fall into another version of this patronising behaviour. Under the guise of 'helping' someone, you may do things for them that they could do independently. This creates a dependency on the worker and keeps a power imbalance in their favour.

> One significant aspect of ageist ideology is the process of infantilisation – treating older people as if they were children . . . In recognising this, we must also recognise that the more protective we become the more we challenge older people's rights to make their own decisions and be responsible for themselves.

(Thomson and Manuel, 1997, p. 104)

The language we use is one of the most obvious ways of unconsciously showing our prejudice. Many of the words, phrases and expressions we use are insulting to, or undermining of, others without us being aware of it. For instance, shortening the 'difficult-to-pronounce' Asian name to a Western nickname can be seen as an attempt to make the person part of the group, but underlying this assumption is the fact that people can't be bothered to find out and use the proper pronunciation. Examining and changing the words you use is more than just window dressing. Although it is apparently a small step, it is something you as an individual can start thinking about, and acting on, immediately. It is a symbolic step, because you notice it and so do others around you.

Language is an important representation of our thoughts and feelings, therefore it is important to consider what message is given by the words we use. Changing the term 'disabled toilets' to 'accessible toilets' gives a different message to everyone. It emphasises the attributes of a building, not of a person. A number of organisations for disabled people have changed their name because they wanted to portray a more positive and modern picture of their work. The Spastics Society renamed itself Capability Scotland and the Scottish Society for Mental Handicap changed its name to Enable.

Our use of language changes all the time, and terms that were once commonplace are now rarely used. Most people would agree that it is unacceptable to call someone who is mentally ill a 'moron', or someone with learning disabilities an 'imbecile', but these terms were once the normal medical terms. This is not about political correctness, but about being aware of the effect of your words on those around you. Two of the qualities required to be a good care worker are respect and sensitivity. Appropriate use of language is one of the ways in which you can display these qualities.

Levels of discrimination

There are many levels on which discrimination can occur. Discrimination can take place at personal, organisational and structural levels. In reality, these levels are not separate: our personal views are influenced by the culture in which we live, and the organisations we encounter, but it is useful initially to look at the way in which each level operates independently. It is important to analyse at what level we believe discrimination occurs, because then we will know at which level to challenge it. It is of little use treating a broken leg with a sticking plaster, and it is equally pointless trying to tackle large-scale inequalities only with small-scale solutions.

Personal discrimination

When someone attacks a black person because of his colour, or bullies a child with learning disabilities, or sexually harasses an employee, he or she is individually discriminating against that person. Although this individual behaviour exists because that person has been brought up in a culture that devalues certain groups, it is still *individual* discrimination because it is that person acting alone. It doesn't need to be literally only one person. If a small group of people harass or intimidate someone, this can still be described as an example of personal discrimination, because the essence is that they are operating independently and not as part of a wider structure. There is no official backing for their behaviour.

Individual responsibility for discrimination also occurs when we see an act of discrimination and don't seek to stop it or change it. We say 'I don't want to get involved', or 'It's not my problem, someone else will do something about it.' However, discrimination continues to exist because people don't challenge it. It is not just the perpetrators who keep groups oppressed by acting against them, it is also the people who do nothing to stop it or change it. The system of discrimination is perpetuated by individual people doing nothing to challenge it. In care settings this might mean not reporting an incident of bad practice, or failing to support someone who is experiencing harassment.

Organisational discrimination

Discrimination is organisational when it operates within the rules, regulations and practices of an organisation. When an instance of personal discrimination is backed up by an organisation, or when it happens so often that it is part of everyday practice, it can be seen as being organisational discrimination. It is part of the way an organisation is structured.

Rules and regulations

Discrimination occurs because it is built into the rules and regulations of an organisation. For example, a white woman was told on starting her job as a receptionist with a van hire company that it was not the company's policy to hire vehicles to 'coloureds or Asians'. She resigned and took her case to an employment tribunal, claiming she had been asked to carry out discriminatory instructions.

Everyday practices within an organisation

Most organisations have rules and regulations which forbid discrimination, but nonetheless discrimination still occurs. That is because the *culture* of the organisation allows certain bad practice to occur, and people don't do anything to challenge it. There has often been no formal discussion among the people involved about what is happening – it is just 'the way things are done around here' and there is a strong pressure to fit in or leave.

Sexual harassment

In 1986 Jean Porcelli won a landmark case which established sexual harassment in the workplace as a form of sex discrimination under the Sex Discrimination Act (SDA). Yet today sexual harassment remains all too common, according to the Equal Opportunities Commission (EOC). Jean Porcelli worked as a school science technician for Strathclyde Regional Council; she brought her case after experiencing a sustained campaign of harassment from two male colleagues, some of which was sexual in nature. Initial harassment included stealing her keys, disturbing her experiments and emptying out her desk drawers. It soon escalated to rubbing up against her, blocking her path in stairways and corridors, and threatening her with physical violence.

Speaking on the 20th anniversary of the case, Jean Porcelli said: 'it disheartens me that sexual harassment still happens – sadly my own daughter has experienced it. And I can certainly understand why so many women are reluctant to come forward – I know I paid a great price, both personally and professionally. Despite changing jobs, I was labelled a "troublemaker" until the resulting stress and ill health eventually prompted me to take early retirement. In my day, there was no shortage of managers – and even my union officials – who told me to sit down, keep quiet and get on with my job, a response some women still experience today. I hope employers – prompted by the new EOC guidelines – will take a strong leadership role, and in another twenty years time we'll be telling a very different story.'

(Based on: Equal Opportunities Commission, 2006)

This would have been an example of personal discrimination if the council had followed their own procedures and backed the person's complaint. However, the fact that the council and unions chose not to support Mrs Porcelli meant it became organisational discrimination, because it was now the organisation as a whole that supported the discrimination, not just a few individuals within it.

Structural discrimination

The way society operates can disadvantage certain groups. Sometimes this is enshrined in law, but often it is due to the way society has developed historically. Similar instances of discrimination can occur in so many different places that it can be said to be part of the 'normal' functioning of that part of society. It is not just a few people, and it is not just the occasional organisation: it is structured into the way that society operates. This topic is considered in more depth in Chapter 5 when deprivation and inequality are examined. It is therefore only briefly considered here, in the following two examples.

Disabled people continually come up against negative messages that they are not suitable romantic partners. Segregated education, for example, limits their interaction with non-disabled children and reinforces negative stereotypes about disabled people being asexual. Opportunities to interact socially with others, let alone chances to be sexually intimate, are all too scarce for many disabled people. It is challenging enough for some members of society to accept that disabled people have sex, and even more difficult for some to contemplate that they might engage in same-sex relationships. Special education and other segregated systems create informal networks which often have values that do not accommodate difference (**www.drc.org.uk/library**).

There is an under-representation of a number of groups, such as ethnic minorities, in key positions in society. Some individuals in these groups have managed to break through the invisible barrier – the 'glass ceiling' – having managed to escape from the 'sticky floor', which keeps so many people from oppressed groups in unpromoted posts.

How do the different levels of discrimination interact?

Developing an awareness of the structural and organisational aspects of discrimination helps to change the focus of discussion away from the personal limitations of individuals towards the barriers they face in society. At these levels, it can be seen that disadvantage is not just a random, individual problem, but is systematic and embedded in the day-to-day rules and practices of the organisations that make up society.

The structural, organisational and personal levels interact in a different way for every individual. We share some similarities in the wider cultural influences we experience but, even at the structural level, we develop a unique interaction with the society in which we live. This individual relationship with our surroundings continues throughout our lifetime in the experience we have within the organisations we come into contact with and the family and friends we have. Figure 2.3 shows how individuals share certain experiences at the structural level, but these begin to differ at the organisational level and become unique at the personal. Structurally, we all live with the same laws, we all have access to the media in one form or another and we all receive some kind of education. However, our experiences of school might have been quite different: we might have attended a Roman Catholic school, a special school, a private school or a Rudolph Steiner school. We might feel our needs were met within school or perhaps, as a girl, a Sikh, or a person with visual impairment, that our needs were not clearly recognised, or not fully met, and that had an effect on the jobs we were able to apply for. In this way, our experience of discrimination and the positive or negative messages we receive as an individual – depending on our gender, racial origin, disability, etc. – will be different for each person within the wider structural and organisational framework.

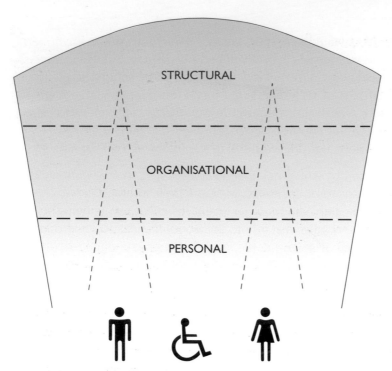

Figure 2.3 Levels of discrimination: how they interact and influence individuals in different ways

Level Int 2 The effects of discrimination

The net result of the various levels and types of discrimination is that someone is disadvantaged, denied an opportunity or refused access to something. Whether it happens once or repeatedly, it can have an effect on that person's identity. Their sense of self-worth is diminished because of the negative treatment, and their potential to achieve what they are capable of is reduced. A person with learning disabilities is frightened to walk down a street because they are being taunted and bullied, so they may miss the bus to college; a woman harassed at work takes long-term sick leave due to stress-related illness; a gay person, who has disclosed their sexuality to a colleague who now avoids him, is concerned that he will be isolated within his team and not gain the promoted post he has just applied for.

The result of not being accepted, not having your concerns taken seriously or not being listened to can be a feeling of alienation. Alienation is a sense that you don't belong to society and that you are often excluded from participation in mainstream activities and events. People who are discriminated against don't have the same rights as other people, or are constrained from asserting their rights.

Another way of looking at this is the invisibility of some groups in sections of society: their needs are just not recognised or addressed. Their experience is marginalised; they feel as if they have no voice, no platform, and no one to listen when they try to express themselves. This can lead to groups feeling as if the services that are supposedly for their benefit are seen as another way in which their experience is undervalued.

Activity — *Assumptions of normality*

If 1 in 10 people are gay, then in a class or workplace of 30 people, statistically there are 3 gay people. Similar statistics can be applied to other aspects of identity which are not immediately visible: the percentage of people with mental health problems, the 50% of women who experience some form of sexual abuse (from flashing to rape) before their 18th birthday, and nearly 40,000 people in Scotland who have epilepsy.

It is probable that some of the people you live and work with will fall into these categories, but because of the general 'assumption of normality' – that everyone is the same – people who are different may not feel free to talk about their experience openly. They may fear that people will misunderstand their situation because of negative stereotypes and prejudice, or that they become stigmatised and people start avoiding them or making jokes at their expense.

The next time you are talking about any of these issues, bear in mind that if someone in the room was gay, had been raped, or experienced mental health problems, would you talk about things in the same way? Would you make the same 'innocent' jokes and comments? Is the way you make assumptions about the normality of people you work with one of the factors that perpetuates their silence, and therefore their continued invisibility?

All the examples of discrimination in this chapter are of real-life situations and show not only the variety of negative effects of oppression but also the desire to fight back (see Figure 3.3 on page 104). A lot of people in the examples have stood up against discrimination and taken a variety of approaches to seek redress for the negative treatment they have experienced. They have spoken out, found support and used the law and other tools in an effort to change their personal situation, and this often has the effect that the discrimination is less likely to occur for other people in other situations. They have taken individual action or joined together in groups to campaign against the discrimination they faced.

Level Int 2 Discrimination in a care setting

In a care setting both service users and workers can be affected by discrimination. Some of the factors which affect each group are examined below.

1 Discrimination against service users

Care services are in an uneasy position when it comes to discrimination. They are part of the social service, benefits, housing and health systems in which people may have experienced institutionalised oppression, but part of their function is to help these same people challenge this discrimination and assert their rights.

The NHS and Community Care Act (1990) emphasised the need to promote choice and develop needs-led services, yet the experience of a lot of service users is that their choices are limited and their needs are not being recognised. One of the aims of the Act was to reduce the number of people in large institutions which clearly could not meet their individual needs. However, discrimination still exists in community-based services, because many people with disabilities or mental health problems still do not have access to resources which would enable them to live an autonomous life. There is not enough money to provide the required services, and there is no consistency in the rights and services available to people in different parts of the country. Care can be seen as a service which has increasing demands on it because of problems in society such as poverty, addiction and homelessness, while it has diminishing resources to deal with these problems because of changes in the funding and organisation of the Welfare State.

The role of care worker implies a certain amount of power and, in any situation of power, abuse may occur. It is possible to behave in a way that devalues, suppresses or dismisses the beliefs or needs of the service user. Not all examples of bad practice in care settings are necessarily also examples of discrimination, but when the misuse of power by workers is based on a denial of the rights of certain people, then it can be seen as discrimination.

2 Discrimination against staff

Staff in care services can experience discrimination from colleagues, their organisation or service users. As a potential employee, a care worker can face discrimination during the recruitment and selection process and, once they have a job, they can face discrimination when applying for promotion. Workers can experience harassment and bullying from colleagues and service users. Violence against staff by service users in care settings is an increasing problem. Some women workers have been sexually assaulted by service users, and some black workers have been racially abused by service users. As a worker, you still have the right to be respected as an individual and expect to have your rights recognised by colleagues and service users.

CASE STUDY

Discrimination against male nurses

Andrew Moyhing, a 29-year-old former student nurse, left the profession over concerns about how male nurses were treated. He was told that a female member of staff would have to chaperone him while using an ECG machine with a female patient, but female staff were allowed to provide intimate care to male patients with no chaperone present. This was based on the stereotype that all men are sexual predators and that therefore female patients automatically need extra protection when being treated by male nurses. The Equal Opportunities Commission helped Andrew take his case to an employment tribunal as they wanted to highlight the problems that men experience from outdated stereotypes when they seek employment in areas previously considered as 'women's work' (www.eoc.org.uk).

Level Int 2 Promoting equal opportunities

Anti-discriminatory practice is not about treating everyone the same: it is about recognising the differences, negotiating with service users how best to meet their needs, assert their rights and challenge the inequalities they face. The different levels of discrimination have been examined. Now consideration will be given to the ways in which discrimination can be challenged at these three levels: personal, organisational and structural.

1 Personal strategies

There are a number of things any individual can do to combat discrimination. Strategies include increasing your self-awareness to ensure that you are less likely to discriminate unconsciously and more likely to challenge discrimination when you see it.

Increase your self-awareness

The most immediate action you can take is to examine your own attitudes and behaviour. The first step to being a good care worker is the development of self-awareness, because you can only change those aspects of your attitudes and behaviour that you have recognised. Workers need to become alert to the ways in which they present themselves to, and respond to, service users. Increased self-awareness reduces the likelihood of unconscious discrimination. Becoming more aware of your value and belief systems is essential for competent care practice and is addressed elsewhere in this chapter.

Challenge prejudice and discrimination when it occurs

This requires you to be clear in your own mind about what discrimination is, and to develop interpersonal skills so that you can tackle situations assertively. Challenging is not the same as confrontation. If you are prepared and informed there are non-aggressive ways of discussing your views with people. A lot of training courses use role play to help people plan and prepare how they would tackle difficult situations. This gives you a chance to 'try things out' in a supportive atmosphere, so that you are more able to deal with the problem in real life.

The secret of success when challenging discrimination is to choose the best time and place to raise the issue. It is impossible to counter every statement or action you see that is directly, indirectly, consciously or unconsciously discriminatory. It is also too easy to think that the time is never right, because there is always the potential for hassle when you raise it as an issue. However, if you choose not to tackle a phrase or an action, you are colluding with the discrimination: you are part of it; you are part of the culture of acceptance. Things will never change if you just leave it up to other people, or to Parliament, to make a difference. If people did not allow phrases and actions to pass by unchallenged, a culture of non-acceptance would develop. There would be zero tolerance of discrimination. In this way anti-discriminatory practice would become institutionalised – it would be the accepted way of doing things in an organisation: the routine, regular way of dealing with things. This has already been established in some organisations and workplaces because individuals in them had the strength of their convictions to start challenging bad practice.

When talking about prejudice and stereotypes, people often start sentences with 'I'm not prejudiced, but what about . . .' and go on to speak negatively about a group, based on prejudices they have picked up from newspapers, TV, etc. An example would be 'I'm not prejudiced, but what about young women who get pregnant just to get a house – they shouldn't go to the top of the council house list', or 'I'm not prejudiced, but I know a Pakistani grocer who sells cigarettes to under-age kids and the police are too scared to get him into any trouble in case he says it's racism.'

It is important to note that, when discussing prejudice with other people, the point is not to score points or be more politically correct than someone else, but to become aware of the kind of assumptions that are being made and on what evidence they are based. Since prejudice is based on lack of knowledge you could ask 'what evidence do you have for what you have just said?' or, if it is accepted that, in a society where discrimination is structured into all levels, we will all have a number of unconscious prejudices, you could say 'everyone has some prejudices, why do you think you don't have any?'

What other comments might you use to counter the prejudices shown in the above statements?

2 Organisational strategies

Employers are responsible in law for acts of discrimination conducted by employees, whether or not they are done with the employer's knowledge or approval. Employees can be personally responsible for discriminatory acts if the employer mounts a defence to show that they took all reasonable and practical steps to prevent the discrimination. Employers are responsible if they instruct employees to act in ways which discriminate. Within an organisation, there are many actions which can be taken to prevent discrimination and promote equal opportunities for staff and service users, such as positive action, a clear equal opportunities policy, diversity training and promoting anti-discriminatory practice.

Positive action

Positive discrimination is not allowed by law, except in the case of people with disabilities, and some other very specific situations. This means that an employer cannot give a job or promote someone only on the basis of their gender or race. However, positive action is allowed under sections 47 and 48 of the Sex Discrimination Act and sections 37 and 38 of the Race Relations Act. Certain groups are more likely to be unemployed or in lower-grade jobs because of the discrimination they have faced, not only in a specific job but owing to, for example, poor access to education in the past, or lack of response to their needs. The main aim of positive action is to make equality of opportunity more of a realistic possibility. Even if racial discrimination, for instance, could end immediately, many people from ethnic groups would continue to experience the effects of discrimination and disadvantage from the past. They would still not be 'on a level playing field' and able to compete equally with those who have not been systematically disadvantaged over a period of time.

In a work setting, positive action can take the form of encouraging people from certain groups to apply for vacant posts. Employers might put 'applications especially welcome from members of ethnic minorities' or 'people with disabilities are currently under-represented in our workforce' in an advertisement. The job can still only be awarded on the basis of merit of the applicants, but the message is intended to encourage under-represented groups to apply. The Equal Opportunities Commission had the following statement on a job advertisement: 'the EOC is committed to the promotion of equality in all fields. Men are currently under-represented in the EOC Scotland office. We therefore particularly welcome applications from men as well as women.'

An employer might advertise in newspapers and magazines aimed at gay people or members of an ethnic group, or talk to community groups to convey the positive desire to increase the diversity and representation of a variety of groups in their workforce. They might organise training specifically aimed at groups under-represented at certain levels, for example 'Women in Management' courses. The purpose of such training is to equip people with skills and abilities that they have not had the opportunity to develop in the past, so that they are qualified on merit to be appointed or promoted. Workplace awards such as 'Investors in People' emphasise this need for training and utilisation of existing staff as being good for morale and commitment to the organisation.

Equal opportunities policy

Positive action measures are just one piece of the equality jigsaw in the workplace. If the measures aren't embedded into a clear equal opportunities policy, which is applied and monitored effectively, they will be little more than window dressing. A lot of organisations have a written equal opportunities or diversity policy, which states behaviour that is not acceptable, outlines avenues of complaint and provides strategies for monitoring and evaluation of the policy.

It is crucial for any care organisation to have a written policy in order to safeguard the rights of workers and service users. Most established organisations should have a policy and all new organisations have to develop one as a prerequisite for obtaining funding and registration. It is important, however, that these policies are not meaningless pieces of paper, full of fine principles that cannot be implemented or measured, which have been decided only by management.

It is good practice to have a process of consultation when developing or changing an equal opportunities policy in order to give all workers and service users a sense of ownership over the policy (i.e. they helped draft it and so have a sense of responsibility for implementing and monitoring it too). They will have thought about the reasons why certain things are included and how they might need to change to conform to the requirements. Management will have had to listen to all points of view and make some attempt to integrate them into a policy which is acceptable to everyone who has a stake in the process. There is a parallel here with good care planning, because it involves consultation with all relevant stakeholders and is not determined solely by orders from above.

How will anyone know if the equal opportunities policy has made a difference? Organisations are now bound by legislation to promote equality, so there has to be some form of measurement from year to year to see if there has been any progress. An organisation might include statistics on such questions as: have under-represented groups had more success in gaining promotion? Does the mix of service users reflect that of the target population? What training have employees had? It might also include some more subjective data on the quality of service and levels of satisfaction that staff or service users feel they receive. This could be obtained by questionnaires, interviews, group discussions, personal development meetings with staff and re-assessment of care plans with clients.

Diversity training

Organisations now have a duty to promote equality in the workplace, and one way they can demonstrate this is to provide suitable training on diversity. Best practice is to make it compulsory for all staff, including senior management and part-time workers, so that every employee is knowledgeable and informed about the range of diversity issues in general, and specifically in relation to their role in the organisation. Organisations such as Stonewall, Leonard Cheshire and local Racial Equality Councils work with employers to provide relevant training and support.

Anti-discriminatory practice

The commitment to equal opportunities in an organisation extends much further than developing and implementing a policy. A commitment to anti-discriminatory practice can be shown in many ways. It can be demonstrated with service users in everyday practice by promoting independence, maintaining dignity, supporting choices, respecting beliefs and valuing opinions. Many care agencies have a published 'Charter of Rights' which specifies the rights and choices a service user can expect (see Chapter 6). These rights include the right to confidentiality, the right to take risks and the right to make relationships.

Other policies and practices that care organisations implement to encourage active participation of service users in decision making – therefore giving them a voice and some power in the decision-making process – include: service user committees and involving service users in the recruitment and selection of new workers. Regular training and supervision sessions will give staff the opportunity to update their skills and knowledge, and provide an opportunity to discuss any problems they are experiencing.

Anti-discriminatory practice is also about visibility. It is about promoting positive images of people in publications and leaflets about your organisation, and it is about having a representative workforce and range of service users. Anti-discriminatory practice has an impact on the way services are delivered. It has to address the wider issue of re-distribution, not just of scarce resources such as funding or accommodation, but of the power imbalance which exists between workers and users, staff and management, funders and providers of services.

Barriers to achieving equality in an organisation

There are a number of barriers which a care organisation may encounter when trying to achieve equality, for example:

- insufficient funds to implement changes or provide staff training
- resistance or hostility from some staff or service users to changes
- lack of information for new staff and service users about policies and how they work
- ineffective policies with no monitoring mechanism
- fear of 'political correctness' impinging on people's behaviour.

An organisation should be aware of these potential problems and try to address them when developing their anti-discriminatory policies, procedures and ways of working.

3 Structural strategies

There are many things that have to happen at a structural level in society before any real change will be experienced by oppressed groups. Discriminatory norms and rules have to be tackled at societal level for structural change to occur. Some ways that discrimination and inequality can be challenged at this level is through legislation, and by the work of pressure groups.

Legislation

Personal and organisational strategies are crucial to raising awareness of discrimination and developing ways to counteract the effects of discrimination, but if they are to have any major effect they need to have strong and clear backing at the structural level, and that means legislation. If there is no legislative framework to provide people with rights and the freedom to make choices, then personal and organisational strategies are merely isolated acts which are less likely to make a significant impact at anything other than the local level.

Adult Support and Protection Act (Scotland) 2007

All legislation goes through a process of consultation, but sometimes conflicts cannot be resolved, as can be seen from the following article.

Passing of Bill belies problems

Ann Ferguson

The passing of the Adult Support & Protection (Scotland) Bill with the unanimous backing of the Scottish Parliament last week belies the problematic passage of legislation designed to help vulnerable adults who experience harm or mistreatment. Described by some MSPs as a 'difficult' bill, the amendment was reported as being the longest yet in the life of the parliament. The Convenor of the Health Committee remarked on the sharp division of opinion between older people's groups and those for people with disabilities.

Since the late 1990s, Age Concern Scotland has campaigned for improved legislation and protection for older people who are abused or at risk of abuse. All too often the charity was made aware of cases of abuse which were not investigated and where victims were left unsupported, and although there were powers available to key agencies it was not a requirement to respond and the sorely pressed statutory agencies prioritised the 'must do' cases. Frail older people

being abused by those paid to care for them or totally at the mercy of uncaring, abusive relatives often didn't make the cut.

The key obstacle to changing legislation and introducing new statutory requirements and powers has been around the difficult balance between individual human rights and the state's responsibility to intervene.

Some disability groups believed such legislation stigmatises people who have a disability and makes them more vulnerable to unwanted state intervention, which would not apply to a person who was not disabled.

The counter argument is evidence of the disempowering affects of abuse often rendering victims unable to protect themselves and sometimes enduring terrible mistreatment because they are unable to seek help. Adults who have to rely on others for help with daily living are known to be most at risk of the mistreatment cited in the bill.

(Ferguson, 2007)

A description of legislation relevant for care can be found in Chapter 1. The Scottish Parliament cannot develop its own equal opportunities legislation: that is one of the powers reserved for Westminster. However, the issues that are the responsibility of the Scottish Parliament – education, social work, transport, health and housing – still provide an opportunity to make an impact on the inequality and disadvantages that people face. The role of legislation in tackling inequality is further discussed in Chapter 5.

Pressure and campaigning groups

Thompson (2006, p. xii) notes that anti-discriminatory practice is 'a broad undertaking that needs to incorporate sociological, political and economic concerns above and beyond narrow legal requirements'. Many pressure and campaigning groups provide a focus for both one-off and long-term challenges to discrimination. Sometimes they are campaigning for a change to legislation, but often they are trying to raise awareness of an issue and encourage people to become more informed. Many groups are working to challenge stigma and prejudice, such as seemescotland, One Scotland and Women's Aid.

People might mobilise a group overnight to highlight a particular incident of racial violence, while many organisations run campaigns for many years to highlight inadequacies in the law, and campaign to change the way they are treated. Many of these groups are well funded and very powerful. They provide statistics and information for MPs to use when issues are being discussed in Parliament. Many groups also provide services such as informing people of their rights in relation to existing law. The role of these groups is discussed further in Chapter 5.

Level Higher — Effective communication

Another factor essential to establishing a positive helping relationship is effective communication.

'Communication' is defined as 'the imparting, conveying or exchange of ideas, knowledge etc. (whether by speech, writing or signs); interchange of speech' (Oxford English Dictionary) and 'effective' is defined as 'producing a desired result; impressive; operative'. From these two definitions it is apparent that communication is more complex than just speaking to a person. The ways in which care workers communicate convey to the service user how they value that person.

Think of someone in your life whom you admire and find it easy to speak to, perhaps a friend or a relative. It is likely that the reasons why you find them easy to speak to are that you know that person well, and they know you well, they accept you, they are warm and understanding, they listen to you and they do not criticise or judge you.

Effective communication involves many features, including:

- a caring, valuable relationship
- listening skills
- non-verbal communication
- using appropriate language
- using the right pace and tone.

Vocation

Enthusiasm

Enjoyment

Dedication

Humour

Genuine
interest

Positive
self-disposition

Figure 2.4 The oomph factor: 'I love what I do!'

A caring, valuable relationship

To form and sustain a caring, valuable relationship is the main essence of effective communication between a service user and a care worker. Without a good relationship there will be no mutual respect. This is likely to result in failure to meet the needs of the service user. The ingredients necessary to form relationships are the practice of all the values and principles, a knowledge of human behaviour, a knowledge of the person and also that bit extra – *the oomph factor* (see Figure 2.4).

The oomph factor

The ingredients which bind together the oomph factor are as follows:

- **Enthusiasm** is ardent interest, eagerness and includes encouraging and having a great faith in others. Care workers need to be energetic and possess inspiration in what they are practising. If there is a day when the carer does not feel 100% then it is best to apologise and explain this to the service user without going into too many details. The service user will then realise that any reserve is not because of them.

- **Dedication** is consistent support and commitment to the well-being of the service user. As far as possible try to be reliable and let your service user know where you will be. When you do have to be away, always explain that you will not be there and state when you will be back.

- **Vocation** emphasises the professionalism of care work and that it is 'not just a job'. Your heart really has to be in caring for other people. If you work 'by the clock' then you should not be in care.

- **Genuine interest** includes being interested in all people, knowing people's likes and dislikes, frustrations, expectations and also being truthful.

- **Enjoyment** and **humour** involve the worker in showing and feeling genuine pleasure in what they are doing and sharing successes or even failures, however great or small. What a difference a smile makes, and that pleasantness needs to be evident from the minute you start work until you finish. A real challenge!

- **Positive self-disposition** emphasises that the care worker should be confident and happy with him or herself in what he or she is doing, and striving to share this confidence and happiness with the service user. If the care worker does not feel this way then the service user will sense it. There may be a time when the care worker does not feel happy. He should then reflect on and evaluate his own life to decide whether there are changes that need to be made.

In addition to these attributes, other factors are essential in establishing helpful relationships. Carl Rogers (1902–1987) emphasises three core conditions to promoting good relationships (Rogers, 1991): empathy, congruence and unconditional positive regard. These help the service user to have self-esteem, to make choices and to solve problems.

Empathy

Rogers saw the idea of **empathy** as 'the ability to experience another person's world as if it was your own world'. Service users may have completely different experiences from the care worker so it is important to try genuinely to understand a service user's thoughts and feelings. Through the carer's expression of empathy and the opportunity of talking freely, many service users experience great relief at being able to tell their innermost feelings without getting a negative reaction from the care worker. This process is sometimes referred to as 'ventilation'. It can lower anxiety and can, if the care worker provides empathy, be sufficient in itself to let the service user find their own solution to their problem.

Also, when service users feel comfortable with the care worker they will be more likely to talk about themselves, which will enable the care worker to learn more about that person and understand their views. Understanding can grow from a conversation which conveys value for the service user. Understanding is also conveyed when the care worker is competent in showing knowledge of a particular physical, intellectual, emotional or social need of a service user.

Congruence

Congruence is genuineness: being totally sincere. Being sincere is paramount. It means that care workers have to be honest, open, be themselves and be giving to others. There is no room for acting or using language that confuses the service user. This only gives the impression that the care worker is superior to others. When a person talks to a friend or relative there may be no barriers if each is relaxed, natural and genuinely interested. When a care worker talks to a service user it should be just the same. It is essential that a care worker conveys a little of what kind of person they are and shares information which may help the service user feel relaxed and comfortable. In some situations this could encourage the service user to be more forthcoming with information about themselves.

Like any other skills, forming a supportive relationship with a service user improves with practice, and care workers should continually evaluate themselves. It is necessary for care workers to accept feedback from colleagues, supervisors and most importantly the service users. It is possible to tell if communication is effective by the response of service users. They will show trust, be honest with the care worker and show that they enjoy the care worker's company. Without these kind, humane ingredients the relationship will be doomed and very difficult to redeem.

Unconditional positive regard

Unconditional positive regard means accepting someone unquestioningly as having worth, whoever they are and whatever they may have done. It is conveyed through showing both acceptance and warmth. This will ensure that the service user feels valued as an individual. A service user may be feeling helpless, threatened, embarrassed or a nuisance. The care worker may reflect warmth by *non-verbal communication*, such as:

- a warm smile (facial expression)
- open, welcoming gestures
- a confident manner – this reassures the service user that they can be helped
- offering physical help – for example a guiding arm to an elderly or distraught person
- the general appearance of the care worker
- calm and gentle gestures and movements.

The care worker may also reflect warmth by verbal communication, such as:

- a friendly tone of voice and not in a patronising way
- using friendly words that show respect, e.g. instead of saying 'tell me', say 'would you like to tell me' or 'can you tell me'
- expressing a wish to help
- explaining clearly what the care worker is trying to do
- giving reassurance about confidentiality
- showing clear understanding of what has been achieved and what can be achieved.

In developing the skill of showing unconditional positive regard it is important to be oneself, to be natural and genuine. If the care worker pretends to be interested, warm or understanding then the service user will sense this and it will jeopardise the whole relationship.

Listening skills

Trying to get them to listen is . . . well let's just say it's a Herculean task and I aren't no Hercules.

(Branfield and Beresford, 2004)

Listening is as important as verbally communicating. It shouldn't be a Herculean task to get a care worker to listen to you. Listening should not be 'passive' but active, and this involves more than just hearing but also concentrating on what the person is saying, responding to what has been said and then acting on it. To be a good listener involves practising all the values, principles and attributes in caring, as well as being attentive, using prompts and using appropriate questions, as explained below.

Being attentive

Being attentive means actively listening and concentrating on what is being said, being aware of what is not being said by sensing that the service user is perhaps shy, feeling awkward, embarrassed or unable to express how they feel. They may show signs of these feelings by silence, eye movements, nervous movements like wringing their hands or turning a ring on their finger. Facial expressions, posture and other forms of body language all give clues to a person's feelings. The care worker should try to understand these signs and allow the service user time to relax and feel confident to talk.

Using prompts

Service users who may be shy, nervous or hesitant about talking for various reasons may need encouragement from the care worker. This can be done, for example, by nodding at appropriate times to show acceptance and understanding, by eye contact to show that attention is being given, and by using words and sounds such as 'oh', 'really', 'mmm' to show they understand what is being said and are happy to listen further.

Using appropriate questions

Questions may be asked to clarify what the service user has said and to establish more information. To encourage service users to talk, it is better to use 'open' questions which invite answers that are longer and more involved; these usually start with words like 'how', 'why', 'what', 'when', 'where'. For example, rather than asking a young person 'Do you like your new school?' which would probably be answered with a 'yes' or 'no', it would be better to ask 'What do you think of your new school?' The care worker is then more likely to learn more information about how the young person feels about the school.

Non-verbal communication

Non-verbal communication comprises appearance, gestures and movements. There are four main ways in which non-verbal communication is used: eye contact, posture, facial expressions and physical contact.

Eye contact

Eye contact is very useful to show that the care worker is paying attention to the service user when they are speaking; it also conveys sincerity and genuineness. However, it would not be appropriate to stare continually at someone: it is best to be natural.

Posture

When two people are talking they generally feel more comfortable if they are at the same level. If a care worker were to tower over a service user, the service user might feel intimidated, or that they cannot move away. The care worker should be sufficiently relaxed to be friendly and calm. Positioning of seating is important: it is better to be facing the service user and leaning forward slightly, showing willingness to listen. Such mannerisms as hands in pockets, playing with hands or running hands through hair should be avoided as these would be distracting to the service user.

Facial expressions

The expression on a person's face can often convey how that person is feeling and can be used effectively to communicate feelings. Therefore it is essential that the care worker shows warmth and friendliness. It is difficult to communicate with someone who shows no emotion in their face and it can be very unsettling. Of course, the expressions that the care worker shows should be appropriate; they should not, for example, show signs of laughing, sneering or superiority.

Physical contact

When a service user is distressed or frightened then a care worker might show understanding and empathy by giving a child a cuddle or an older person a reassuring arm around their shoulder. However, the care worker has to be careful that their familiarity is not misinterpreted. It can be difficult to know when physical contact is not appropriate. Generally, when a good relationship has been formed with a service user, the care worker will know whether physical contact is appropriate or not. This is a controversial subject and it helps to discuss appropriate physical contact at team meetings and to know your agency policy in relation to this subject.

Using appropriate language

Each service user is an individual with their own social background, culture, character and abilities. For these reasons it is necessary for care workers to adapt and tailor their language to suit each individual service user. The choice of words, the length of what is said and the content are all important. Too often care workers, without thought, use 'jargon' such as 'goal setting', 'empowerment' or 'interaction', which will only confuse the service user.

The age of a service user has to be considered. An older person, for example, should never be spoken to as if they are a child, by using childish words. This is patronising and shows no respect for the person. Would you like to be spoken to in this manner? Similarly, when speaking to a child, language should be kept simple so that the child can understand. It is useful to check, in an appropriate way, that what is being said has been understood.

When working with service users who have a hearing impairment it is best for the care workers to be familiar with sign language and know the different meanings that service users attach to signs; alternatively an interpreter could be present. Also, when working with those who have a visual impairment, it is advisable to describe objects and situations. It would be ineffective and insensitive for the care worker to show the service user something and ask 'Do you want this just now?'

Care workers may work with service users who speak a different language. This should not cause a barrier in communication nor should the service user be made to feel inferior because they do not speak English. In this situation an interpreter would be required. Ideally the care worker could make an effort to learn the service user's language, or at least a few words of it.

Service users who have a learning disability need the care worker to be patient and capable of using words that they will understand. The length of what is being said should take into account the service user's ability to understand. It is advisable to repeat what has been said so that the service user understands. Adults should not be spoken to as if they are children, and time should be given for service users to express themselves. To aid communication, facial expressions, gestures and appropriate touch is useful.

Eric and Jennifer

This case study should enable you to reconsider the value statement quoted earlier: 'That is the lassie McKay. She's deaf and dumb and has a carer who takes her out shopping. It's a waste of time if you ask me.' Eric is a support worker, working with adults who are deaf and blind. Here he talks about working with Jennifer.

'At present I support Jennifer, who is 21 years of age and has complex learning difficulties including deafness and partial blindness. Before commencing support of Jennifer I read her Personal Passport and her Care Plan, which stated that Jennifer communicates through gestures, i.e. pointing and facial expressions. I then requested some observation shifts so that I could observe how she communicated with other people and in her surrounding environment and I was told that she had no verbal communication at all but appeared to understand simple words. Jennifer seemed to spend most of her time crumpling pages of magazines and putting them in a plastic bag. Over time I built up a relationship with Jennifer by using communication skills, speaking to Jennifer in simple language, sitting opposite her at the right level and showing friendliness in my face. As Jennifer's trust and confidence began to build up with me I began using simple communication skills with her, by asking her to take off her own jacket and showing her, by example, taking off my own jacket. After several weeks Jennifer would happily take her jacket off when required.

Jennifer and I went out one day into a supermarket. While out, Jennifer preferred to hold my hand as she can only see short distances. When I got the trolley Jennifer let go my hand and pointed to it. I went to give her my hand again and she pushed it away, pointing to the trolley again. I went through the process of getting eye contact with her and asked her clearly at a pace and level she could understand what it was she wanted. Jennifer then put both her hands on the trolley and began to wheel it around the supermarket. She communicated to me that she was really enjoying this activity by laughing and clapping her hands. I passed this information on to her other key workers and family, and now she enjoys weekly shopping trips with her father and mother, which is helping to build up the communication in her home environment.'

Eric also realised that Jennifer loves music especially when it is played loudly. Jennifer is now able to choose and enjoy things that she likes to do, thanks to the support worker who used good values and communication skills, treated Jennifer as an individual and respected her wishes.

Usha

A student who recently took up part-time employment as a care worker in a local authority home for elderly people noticed that an Indian woman, Usha, who was in the home for a period of assessment and respite, seemed very unhappy and isolated. When she asked another care worker about Usha she was told that English was her second language. The staff had assumed that there was no point in speaking to her as she would not understand. They believed that she was in the home for a short time and they did not have the time to communicate with her. They had attended to her physical needs, washing her, dressing her, giving her meals, but they had not attempted to communicate with her. When they did have to speak to her they had used inappropriate language such as 'You sit up', 'Me feed you'.

The student approached Usha with a smile and introduced herself. She found that Usha understood what she was saying and continued to tell Usha her name and a little about herself. The student realised that the other staff had assumed that because English was Usha's second language she would not understand what they were saying. By not speaking quickly or shouting and by being patient and repeating some words, the student had been able to communicate with Usha. If there were words that Usha did not understood then the student had used facial expressions and hand gestures. Some of the other staff noticed the attempt made by the student and they too made more effort to speak to Usha. The student found that after a few days Usha seemed happier and had made friends with other service users.

Using the right pace and tone

The pace of the communication used by a care worker should, like the language used, take into account the age, the ability and culture of the service user. There would be no point in talking on and on very quickly when in fact the service user was still trying to understand what was first said. The tone of voice that is used by the care worker should also be appropriate to who is being spoken to. They should not 'talk down' to service users, and there is no place for abruptness. The tone should be friendly and warm, irrespective of who is on the receiving end. Civility costs nothing and goes a long way. For example 'What do you want?' with the emphasis on 'what', would be better replaced with 'What would you like?', said in a warm and friendly tone with an emphasis on 'like'. The first question and tone would make the service user feel that it was a bother for the care worker, whereas the second reflects that the care worker is genuinely interested in those they are talking to. There are times when the tone of voice has to be different, for instance when the service user has received disturbing news, and then the tone should be comforting. Care workers have to be sensitive about what they say and how they say it and this should stem from a good understanding and interest in the person they are working with.

Finally, to be successful as an effective communicator, care workers need to be aware of their own ability to communicate with others and use the necessary skills to form good relationships with service users. Where effective communication is practised the service user will feel accepted, understood and know that their needs have been recognised. Effective communication is an important way of helping to promote independence, ensuring equal opportunities and achieving self-empowerment.

Barriers which impede communication

Care workers need to be aware of personal and physical obstacles which impede communication and deter a service user from expressing their feelings. Failure to understand and detect these obstacles will affect communication and make it impossible for the care worker to understand and respond to the needs of a service user. Below is a list of possible barriers:

Personal barriers

- A person who is very nervous
- A person who is distressed
- A person who feels uncomfortable with any care worker
- A person who feels their problems are too personal to discuss with the care worker
- A person who feels embarrassed or ashamed
- A person who is angry
- A person who fears being ridiculed
- A person who fears being abused
- A person who fears being misunderstood
- A person who fears being neglected

- A person who has no self-esteem
- A person who is wary of confidentiality
- A person who has a different mother tongue
- A person who feels inferior and prejudiced
- A person who is unable to express their feelings
- A person who is uncomfortable with age difference

Sensory barriers

- A person who has a hearing impairment
- A person who has a speech impairment
- A person who has a visual impairment

Consider the *environment* where communication is taking place. For instance:

- Is the meeting place the choice of the service user?
- Is it safe and comfortable?
- Is it private and quiet?
- Is it free of any interruptions?
- Is it appropriate, with suitable lighting (for those with visual impairments)?
- Are the seating arrangements positioned in a friendly way?
- Is the care worker sitting in full view (for those with hearing impairment)?
- Is there refreshment available?

The care worker who is sensitive to these aspects will be competent in achieving effective communication with those with whom they are working.

Activity *Barriers to communication (1)*

Work with a partner for this activity.

Imagine you are unable to speak, write and walk following a stroke. You are able to understand what people say to you.

1 Tell your partner that you are hungry.

2 Tell your partner you need to go to the toilet.

3 Tell your partner you want to go out.

4 Explain to your partner that you are uncomfortable and want to be moved.

What were your feelings during this exercise?

What did your partner do that was most helpful?

What could she have done that she did not do?

How did your partner feel?

Can you suggest a method of communication that would be useful in this situation?

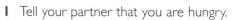

Activity — Barriers to communication (2)

Work with a partner for this activity.

Imagine you are unable to speak or write following a stroke. You are able to understand what people are saying to you. You cannot use your hands.

1 Tell your partner that you are thirsty.
2 Tell your partner you would like the TV on.
3 Tell your partner you want a friend to come and visit you.
4 Explain to your partner you are concerned about how hard they are working to look after you.
5 Tell your partner that you are worried about the future.

What were your feelings during this exercise?

What did your partner do that was most helpful?

What could she have done that she did not do?

How did your partner feel?

Activity — Barriers to communication (3)

Read the following case studies and write down what factors may impede communication in each case, and how you could maximise communication with each service user, for example, which methods could you use; which you should avoid and what else might help. Think about what or who might also be of assistance to you.

CASE STUDIES

1 Hayley Anderson (age 35)

Hayley has spent periods of time in hospital for depression. She now lives in her own flat and is supported by community support workers who are based in premises nearby. When Hayley is depressed she self-harms but knows she can call on her support workers.

2 Antonio Biagi (age 55)

Antonio has had Alzheimer's disease for two years and lives with his wife. A care worker visits him twice a week for three hours to give his wife time to herself.

3 Amir Patel (age 16)

Amir is deaf and blind. He lives at home with his mother and father. He attends a resource centre twice a week.

4 Frankie Hughes (age 23)

When Frankie was released from prison he was ordered by the court to reside at a resettlement unit, where he has his own flat within the unit. He had been on drugs since he was fifteen years of age. He has been off drugs since entering prison and he is hoping to find employment.

5 Natalia Kuger (age 17)

Natalia is an asylum seeker who arrived in Scotland two weeks ago after fleeing from her own country where she was physically abused. She speaks limited English. She is at present living in a hostel for young women.

6 Margaret McKinnon (age 72)

Margaret lives alone in her own home. She has recently suffered a stroke, which has left her with her right arm paralysed, unsteady on her feet and her speech affected. She needs a care worker daily to help her with household chores and shopping.

Strategies for improving communication

Case study 1 Hayley Anderson

- Be non-judgemental.
- Accept Hayley for who she is and show her she is valued.
- Support Hayley to express her feelings.
- Allow her time and space.
- Use good body language.
- Use gestures and touch.
- Do not treat her like a child.
- Work closely with the Community Psychiatric Nurse (CPN).

Case study 2 Antonio Biagi

- Sit facing Antonio and at the same level.
- Speak clearly without raising your voice.
- Use simple sentences.
- Try using photographs, pictures or objects.
- Learn from Antonio's wife what things he likes to do, e.g. listening to music, reading to him, gardening.
- Read up on new approaches in care of people with Alzheimer's disease.

Case study 3 Amir Patel

- Approach Amir gently and touch his hand to let him know that you are there.
- Sit close to him and if you have to move let him know.
- Use touch alphabet on his hand to communicate. Touch is important and reassuring.
- Give Amir assistance in eating and drinking by putting a cup or food in a comfortable position in his hand.
- Encourage Amir to speak to you and listen attentively to what he says.
- Talk to Amir's mother and father and find out how they communicate with Amir and how they know how he is feeling

Case study 4 Frankie Hughes

- Be non-judgemental, accepting Frankie and his ambitions.
- Be encouraging, enthusiastic, genuine, helpful.
- Help Frankie to find out about benefits and grants to pay for training.
- Support him to find out about training and employment.
- Ask him what support he needs.
- Give him praise when he accomplishes even a small thing like making an enquiry by himself.
- Be consistent.

Case study 5 Natalia Kuger

- Be welcoming and friendly with kind gestures.
- Speak slowly and use facial signs, movement signs and pictures to communicate.
- Make an effort to learn some phrases in Natalia's language, e.g. good morning, how are you, thank you.
- Offer to accompany her to English classes initially.
- Introduce Natalia to others in the hostel, especially those who may speak Natalia's language.
- Suggest to Natalia that you show her round the city.

Case study 6 Margaret McKinnon

- Introduce yourself and ask Margaret how you can support her.
- Remember that Margaret is mentally aware.
- Do not treat her like a child.
- Be patient and listen to her.
- Be cheery and let her know what is going on in the community.
- Offer to contact her friends.
- Suggest an outing.
- Find out about dial-a-bus or voluntary transport.
- Make arrangements for entering her home.
- Always make sure that you leave her home in a safe condition, for example that there are no objects, papers or furniture which obstruct Margaret moving about.
- Find out about utensils that are available for those with the use of only one hand. An occupational therapist (OT) is a good source of information.

Gerard Egan's three-stage model of helping

Gerard Egan (1986) presented a model of helping which is based on all of the above communication skills, and also provides a model for helping people to deal with their difficulties and problems. Egan's model rests on the assumption that, with a little help to identify and talk through things that concern them, most people can reach their own satisfactory solutions. He presented three stages in the helping process:

- Stage 1 – exploration; the service user is helped to ask herself 'what is going on?'
- Stage 2 – developing new understanding; the service user is helped to ask herself 'what do I want instead?'
- Stage 3 – action; the service user is helped to ask herself 'how might I get to what I want?'

These stages are illustrated through an examination of the work with Aisha Bibi (see 'Case study – A tale of two families' in Chapter 7) at the Westgate Clinic, to which she was referred by her doctor. Aisha was widowed four years ago. She has two sons: Tanveer, who is a student at Glasgow University, and Nabeil, who is taking art courses at the local further education college. Nabeil has severe physical disability and lives in supported accommodation.

Stage 1

At the Westgate Clinic Aisha was allocated a worker who used communication skills (Rogers' empathy, congruence and unconditional positive regard) to enable Aisha to explore her situation and to look at what was going on in her life. The worker listened to what Aisha said and helped her to understand that she was still grieving for her husband and that this was a completely 'normal' process; Aisha also realised that both of her sons leaving home during the past year had led to her feeling very lonely and unsure about how to face the future. The worker didn't offer any advice to Aisha but just asked open questions such as 'tell me about how you have been feeling this week' and 'what do you think may be making you feel like this?' In this way Aisha was helped to explore all of the factors that could have a bearing on her current feelings.

Stage 2

During the second stage Aisha was helped to look at her situation in different ways so that she could work towards some decisions about her future. It was at this stage that the worker suggested that it was going to be very difficult for Aisha to make much progress because she still needed to mourn for her husband. Aisha joined a bereavement group at the clinic for six weeks and this helped her to meet other people who were experiencing loss. She talked a lot about her husband and began to feel that she could now tackle discussion about her future. The group also helped her to see that her sons moving away from home was something she would need to build into her new way of life and that this presented opportunities for her as well as losses. She returned to her discussions with the worker with some new perspectives about her situation and having dealt with a lot of her feelings of loss. When Aisha stated that she thought she would like to make some decisions about what to do with her life in the future, the worker rephrased this for her and helped her towards stating what life might look like. Aisha was able to make the suggestion that she would like to go back to work and perhaps eventually gain further qualifications, as well as support her sons through whatever decisions they made for themselves.

Stage 3

At this stage Aisha was helped to be practical and to take action. Every week the worker and Aisha agreed at least one task that Aisha would pursue in her search for employment. In this way Aisha was able to identify that she would like to go back to work for a voluntary organisation since she had enjoyed work in this sector before. When she found a post for which she would like to apply she discussed this with the worker and was offered encouragement to complete the forms and go for the offered interview. Aisha also tackled areas of her personal life, joining a social group for outings and conversation. At all times it was Aisha who made the decisions and the worker who offered support.

Level Int 1 Personal qualities of the care worker

> There are no 'golden rules' to learn in order to become an effective carer – we each do the job differently according to our own personalities.
>
> (Tossell and Webb, 1994)

This quote is true to an extent. However, there are areas where a care worker may improve and develop. Throughout this chapter many of the required attributes and skills have been discussed, such as the ingredients of the 'oomph factor', applying the value base, showing understanding, warmth and empathy, using communication, including listening skills, and being anti-discriminatory. Embedded within these skills are essential personal qualities. No one care worker will possess all of the personal qualities, but each individual should be aware of the qualities they already possess and build on these to develop them and other qualities and skills. As a comparison, a person who knows he or she is a good singer may decide to sing as a career. But the decision is not enough. In order to succeed he or she has to pursue studies in music theory and spend hours practising to become skilful and even famous.

What qualities can potential care workers possess? There are many qualities, some overlap, and with 'fine tuning' some can develop into skills. Personal qualities include:

- patience and tolerance
- respect, acceptance and empathy
- sensitivity and discretion
- reliability, dependability and flexibility
- positive attitude, cheerfulness and willingness
- politeness and kindness

- honesty and humility
- autonomy and teamwork
- self-awareness
- readiness to learn
- readiness to do a share of unpleasant tasks.

Patience: a care worker should never lose their patience or show annoyance. This could upset a service user and make her feel a nuisance.

Tolerance is patience, understanding and accepting others.

Respect is considering, accepting the views of others even if they differ from your views.

Acceptance is taking people as they are without judging them: an absence of rejection.

Empathy is putting yourself in another person's shoes and seeing the situation from their point of view.

Sensitivity is being aware of others' feelings, embarrassment, fears, discomfort.

Discretion means not making a show or a fuss; it comes with respect and maintaining privacy and confidentiality.

Reliability is always doing what you said you will, on time and in a meaningful manner.

Dependability means being reliable and giving others confidence in your actions.

Flexibility means adaptability: open-mindedness and a willingness to learn from the skills of others.

Positive attitude is being able to see the best in a situation. This is aptly explained in the phrase 'the glass is half full' and not 'the glass is half empty' or a more common phrase like 'this is not a problem'.

Cheerfulness is being a 'happy' person who enjoys their work, which makes others feel happy.

Willingness is accepting readily what you have been told to do and also performing tasks without being told.

Politeness is being mannerly, respectful and giving others recognition.

Kindness means showing compassion, interest and natural friendship.

Honesty is being truthful, trustworthy, genuine and keeping your word.

Humility is being humble, admitting that you do not know how to do something or accepting constructive criticism. This is not failure; it is evaluating your practice and being able to enhance it accordingly.

Autonomy is being able to work on your own initiative.

Teamwork is being able to work with other care workers, being tolerant of their ideas and methods of working, accepting help, guidance and support.

Self-awareness is being aware of yourself, your strengths and areas which need development.

Readiness to learn is willingness to think about what you do, to ask questions and to be ready to learn throughout your career. It is now expected that all care workers must be able to show evidence that they have continuous professional development (CPD), i.e. they embark on learning in areas new to them and also update existing skills and knowledge.

Readiness to do a share of unpleasant tasks: not all tasks are lovely but use empathy and respect and be willing to play your part in the team.

CARE IN PRACTICE

Jenny

Jenny, a care worker in a home for elderly people, always arrives at work on time; she usually smiles at everyone and says a cheerful 'good morning'; she asks people how they are feeling and waits to hear their replies. She gets upset when a service user dies or becomes ill. She admits that there are parts of her job she does not like such as cleaning up vomit. This makes her feel sick but she says that it is not the person's fault that they are sick and she knows they must feel embarrassed that someone else has to clean it up

Autonomy, *teamwork* and *honesty* are explained in the following case study.

CARE IN PRACTICE

Helen

Helen, a day release student who is employed in a small residential unit for people with cerebral palsy, works mainly on night shift. More often than not she works on her own. There is a senior member of staff available if Helen needs assistance. There are occasions when service users are not well or cannot sleep. In these situations Helen has to work on her own initiative. She has become very attached to the service users. They depend solely on her during the night and early morning. Once a week, the unit has a team meeting and Helen has to attend this meeting. There are times when she finds it difficult to share information about service users, and accept new methods of working from other team members. She does appreciate, however, that she is not the 'sole' carer and that any change is in the interest of the service user. At these meetings Helen has had to be truthful and not conceal any information that may jeopardise the service user.

The care worker may have many of the qualities and attributes shown in Figure 2.5 but it is also important that personal qualities are well balanced. Care workers should be aware of what qualities they possess, build on these and recognise what they still have to learn. To be an effective care worker it is not enough 'just to like people', because effective care work involves energy, stamina, knowledge, skill and a strong desire actively to help others. To succeed as a competent care worker these qualities should be practised in your own life and not just reserved for work.

The many roles of the care worker

This section is about the interplay of practical, emotional and management roles and skills.

The role of the care worker varies with the setting in which care takes place, the needs of service users and the position occupied by the worker in the organisation. If you look back at Chapter 1 you will see that the aim of the care worker is to improve the quality of people's lives. The three short examples which follow outline the work of three different care workers and provide a good starting point for a discussion of role. These workers have already been introduced in Chapter 1. 'Role' is the part an individual plays in a group and the behaviour that is expected from a person in that position.

CARE IN PRACTICE

Harry and John

Harry's role is to work directly with John in helping him to build a meaningful life. This role involves communication, assisting with some physical tasks such as shaving and washing, and coping with John's challenging behaviour. Harry is also a part of a community care team in the 'not for profit' organisation for which he works. He attends team meetings and communicates with other professionals involved in John's care. He prepares a review report every six months and keeps brief records on John's progress and achievements. Harry is also John's keyworker, a role discussed in greater detail below, and is supervising a student on placement who is taking a course at the local further education college.

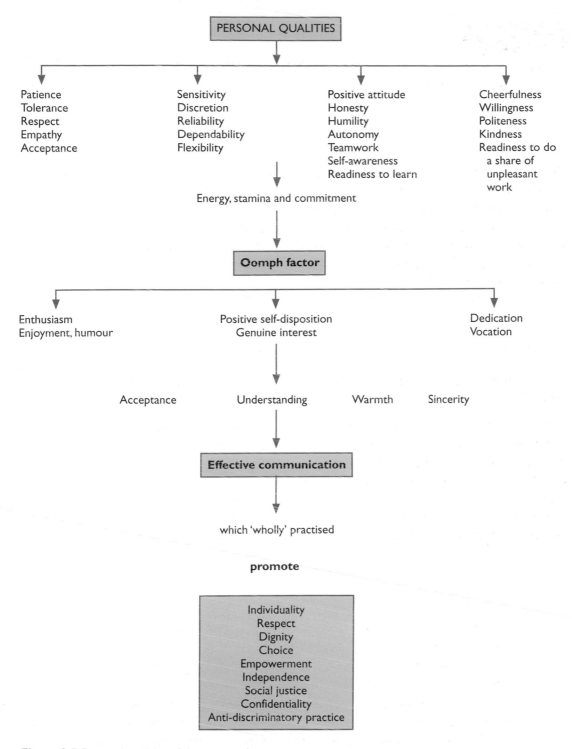

Figure 2.5 Personal qualities of the care worker

Janet

Janet's role as a home support services organiser is to assess service users' needs, ensuring that appropriate support is provided for them to be able to remain in their own homes for as long as they wish to. Her role involves assessment, organisational and communication skills. She also has a management role in leading a team of home support workers. She provides these workers with supportive supervision, she arranges induction training for them and runs the team meetings every two months. She also liaises with other professionals such as social workers, GPs, district nurses and occupational therapists.

Gina

Gina provides support for two children with autistic spectrum disorders who attend a mainstream school. This support involves helping them with educational tasks, supervising them at break times and helping with their lunch and physical needs. She also communicates with their teachers about the educational programme and with their parents about their school day, their progress and their needs. Her role includes direct care, education and liaison.

Below is a description, written by Laura, of her role as a facilitator in person-centred planning.

The role of the facilitator working with person-centred planning includes:

- talking and listening to the individual
- helping the individual communicate their expectations to others
- supporting the individual through a process of change
- helping to deal with and work through conflicts that can arise
- allowing everyone the opportunity to speak, so that no one person can dominate the meeting.

When an individual takes on the role of the facilitator he or she must bring with them the underpinning values and the personal knowledge of the tools of person-centred planning.

Before starting work on a person-centred process, each facilitator must first have gone through the process themselves. This allows the facilitator to experience the emotions that can arise. All of the work done with the individual should be shown with graphics as this is often the best way of communicating with the person and allowing him or her to be in control of the situation. A good facilitator will check everything with the individual first to ensure it is recorded accurately as part of this process.

Keyworking

The role of keyworker is included as part of the tasks of many care workers. Ian Mallinson wrote extensively about this role in *Keyworking in Social Care* (1995), and much of what follows is based on his excellent book.

Many workplaces have keyworkers or linkworkers. Their tasks vary from place to place, but they generally involve special responsibility for assisting one or more service users, forming a special relationship with them and coordinating work in relation to them. Essentially the role should be seen as a partnership which empowers service users to maximise potential and improve their quality of life. Keyworker tasks may include:

- developing a dependable relationship
- coordinating care and the care plan
- advocacy and empowerment
- being there as a reliable, approachable, dependable person, an ally in good and difficult times
- maintaining, exploring, encouraging and expanding the service user's network of links with family, friends and other agencies
- liaising with social workers and other professionals
- attending reviews and case conferences with the service user, ensuring that their views are heard and that decisions made are understood
- ensuring that records are up to date and accurate
- monitoring care to ensure that it is as good as it can be.

Keyworking is not always as straightforward as it seems. Sometimes the relationship between keyworker and service user is less than ideal: at times representing the needs of the service user conflicts with a worker's other roles, and sometimes the task is misinterpreted as favouritism. These occasional disadvantages do not detract from an otherwise valuable role. They alert the worker to the possible pitfalls and should encourage development of the role in the best interests of the service user.

Activity  (Level **Higher**) *Keyworkers*

If you are on placement or working in a care agency check whether there are keyworkers. What are the tasks of these keyworkers? What do you think are the good points about keyworking? What are its weaknesses? How could the system of keyworking be improved?

It is evident in the many roles of care workers that at the core of all care roles is:

the respect for the worth and dignity of all individuals and the promotion of social justice.

Rosemount View

Rosemount View is a day centre for older adults. The staff have to collect the service users in the morning and escort them home in the afternoon. Many service users live alone, and staff have to go into their houses to help them with coats, shoes, handbags, etc. All the service users have a keyworker who has a special interest in their care. One day Mrs King tells Billy (her keyworker) that she is low in mood because she does not get on with her husband and has never had a happy marriage. Billy tells Mrs King that he would like to share this with other team members, and she agrees but specifically asks that her family, and particularly her husband, should never find out. At the next meeting of keyworkers, Billy tells the other team members about Mrs King, and they agree on ways in which they can help her.

On the way home one of the keyworkers, Harry, meets a colleague from another day centre. They start to discuss their work and Harry recounts the story of Mrs King to his friend. Harry is on duty next day and receives a phone call from Mrs King's daughter. She says she is very worried about Mrs King as she seems depressed. Harry suggests that it might be something to do with Mrs King's marriage. The daughter is very shocked and visits her mother to find out if there is any truth in the story. At her next attendance at the day centre Mrs King is very withdrawn and angry. When asked about it she says she feels 'let down' and will never 'trust the staff again'.

Activity   (Level **Higher**)   *Rosemount View and Mrs King*

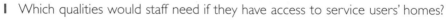

Answer these questions after reading the case study above.

1 Which qualities would staff need if they have access to service users' homes?

2 Which quality did Billy have which made Mrs King able to tell him about her troubles?

3 Was it appropriate that Billy told the other team members about Mrs King and why?

4 Which particular context did Billy choose to tell staff members about Mrs King?

5 What 'rule' did Harry break when he told his friend about Mrs King?

6 Did Harry break this rule when he told Mrs King's daughter about her mother?

7 Do you think there was a difference in what Billy did and what Harry did?

8 What was the result of Harry's actions?

CARE IN PRACTICE

Routenburn

Routenburn is a unit for service users who need a lot of support. The work is very hard and tiring but the staff are enthusiastic. There is also a keyworker system in place where each member of staff is allocated to a group of service users and is responsible for their care for the duration of the shift. This makes the work more interesting and rewarding but requires staff to be reliable in all aspects of their work.

Jan lives 15 miles away from the unit but is always on time for work and has never been off sick. Sandra is also very punctual but has had two weeks off because she had to go into hospital for a minor operation. Christine is a very good worker, has an excellent rapport with the service users, and comes forward with exciting ideas for improving service user's care. However, she also has frequent absences from work and is late at least once or twice a week. This sometimes causes friction between herself and other staff members, and also disrupts the planning of service user care as other members of the team do not know if she is going to be late or if she is off sick.

Another very good member of the team is Helen. She is extremely reliable, caring and intelligent. She is polite and professional at all times in her manner. However, Helen tends to be a bit sloppy about her personal appearance and often has an unpleasant body odour. Her colleagues feel too embarrassed to say anything and, although they like and respect her, they feel uncomfortable when they have to work alongside her. The service users also prefer it when she does not attend to them, even though she is kind and caring, and visitors have been overheard to say unkind things about her.

Activity　　(Level **Int 1**)　*Christine and Helen*

Answer the following questions based on the case study above.

1　Christine appears to have many good qualities. Which two aspects of her behaviour are letting her down?

2　Which two consequences result from this?

3　Which two aspects could Helen improve on?

4　Helen is neglecting these at the moment. What effect does this have on staff, service users and visitors?

Activity   *Feelings about yourself*

Copy and complete the following incomplete sentences. Do not spend a great deal of time thinking about the most appropriate way to finish them. Be as spontaneous as possible.

1   I get angry at myself when . . .

2   I like myself best when . . .

3   I feel ashamed when . . .

4   I trust myself when . . .

5   When I fail, I . . .

6   I feel encouraged when . . .

7   I puzzle myself when . . .

8   I'm pleased with myself when . . .

9   I get down on myself when . . .

10   I feel confident when . . .

11   When I violate my own principles, I . . .

12   When I succeed, I . . .

13   It troubles me when I . . .

14   I'm most at peace with myself when . . .

15   I feel good about myself when . . .

16   When I do not understand myself, I . . .

17   I get depressed when . . .

18   I am buoyed up when . . .

19   I get annoyed with myself when . . .

20   When I take a good look at myself, I . . .

21   When I think of what others have told me about myself, I . . .

Review the ways you have completed the sentences and see if you can identify characteristic ways you feel about yourself. How do you feel about the way you feel about yourself? How do your feelings about yourself facilitate or interfere with your involvement with others?

Activity

Level **Int 1 & 2**   *Your qualities*

Check what qualities you possess by writing down your answers as you read through these questions.

Questions: can I think of …

1   Anything I do regularly which helps others?

2   Any skills I have?

3   Any time I was generous?

4   Anything I achieved which took a good deal of effort?

5   Any feature of my personality?

6   Any special relationship?

7   Any spare time activity?

8   Any work I do in my spare time?

9   Any strengths/qualities I have?

10   Any award/recognition I have received?

11   Any membership of any group?

12   Any way in which I have changed?

13   Any way in which I have stayed the same?

14   Anything I have done for myself?

15   Anything I have won?

16   Anything I do to: help society; protect the environment; give support to the less fortunate?

17   Any fears I have overcome?

18   Any time I have been positive rather than negative?

19   Anything I do to maintain/improve my health?

20   Anything else not covered by this list?

SUMMARY

This chapter has introduced you to the value base for care, upon which practice is based, exploring the principles of the National Care Standards as well as anti-discriminatory practice. Essential components of interpersonal skills associated with communication, including relationship skills, 'oomph', listening skills and non-verbal communication have been explored. Barriers to effective communication have been examined. Personal qualities required by care workers were described, and opportunities have been provided to examine your own qualities. The roles of care workers, with some examples, have given you the opportunity to see how qualities, values and principles, knowledge and skills are practised in care settings.

Activity

Level Int 1 & 2 *Qualities and skills*

Refer to the MacDonald/Ahmed case study in Chapter 7. Linda MacDonald and Aisha Bibi both work as care workers.

1 What qualities do you think they need in their work?

2 Take four of these qualities and give an example of how each one can be put into practice.

3 Imagine that you are a worker in one of the following units described in Chapter 7:

- the McTavish Unit
- Queen's View
- Five Trees Nursery
- 6 and 8 Newton Road

Discuss in small groups or write down:

a the interpersonal skills that a care worker needs to develop in this setting;

b the barriers which there may be to communication with this group of service users;

c ways of overcoming at least two barriers.

Suggested reading

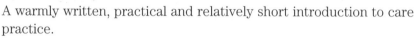

Rogers, J. (1990) *Caring for People: Help at the Frontline.* Milton Keynes: Open University
A warmly written, practical and relatively short introduction to care practice.

Social Care Association (2002) *SCA Handbook.* Surbiton: SCA
Useful guidance for organisations about many aspects of care practice.

Thompson, N. (2002) *People Skills*, 2nd edition. London: Palgrave Macmillan.
A clear and useful text to enhance your communication and interpersonal skills.

Thompson, N. (2006) *Anti-Discriminatory Practice,* 4th edition. Hampshire: Palgrave Macmillan
A discussion of the historical background and theoretical base of anti-discriminatory practice. A variety of areas of discrimination are discussed, with chapters specifically on gender, race, age and disability. It includes discussion of the debate about the differences and similarities between oppression and discrimination.

CHAPTER 3
An Introduction to Human Development and Behaviour

Janet Miller

> *Normal development includes a wide range of individual differences . . . Some influences on individual differences are inborn. Others come from experience. Family characteristics, the effects of gender, social class, race and ethnicity, and the presence or absence of physical, mental or emotional disability all affect the way a person develops.*
>
> (Papalia et al., 2001)

In this chapter you will look at human development and behaviour, and the strands which make up these processes. These are considered under the six main headings of social, physical, emotional, cognitive, cultural and spiritual (SPECCS). The influences upon development and behaviour are also considered, ranging from genetic to cultural and social. There is reference to the nature/nurture debate and to the importance of socialisation. Human development is examined from birth to older adulthood.

The material covered in this chapter is relevant to Values and Principles in Care, Intermediate 1 Outcome 1, Intermediate 2 Outcome 1; Sociology and Psychology for Care, Intermediate 1 Outcomes 2 and 3; Psychology for Care, Intermediate 2 Outcome 1; and underpins the content of Higher Psychology for Care. It provides essential background knowledge for an understanding of Chapters 4 and 5 on Psychology and Sociology.

By the end of this chapter you should be able to:
*   ★ define human development
*   ★ understand what stages we go through
*   ★ define human behaviour
*   ★ explain the needs we have
*   ★ explain the strands of human development and behaviour
*   ★ explain the influences on human development and behaviour
*   ★ understand the meaning of socialisation
*   ★ understand the nature/nurture debate

★ explain how people in general develop and behave at each stage of development

★ apply the understanding gained to care practice.

Introduction

This chapter is about all of us: you, me and everyone else. One major source of information is yourself and those with whom you live and work. These are not the only sources of information, however. In a multi-cultural world your analysis needs to be wide-ranging in order that you can take account of the influence of cultural, socioeconomic and other factors. You provide a good starting point, but remember that your development will be taking place in a particular set of social, economic and cultural circumstances that will exert an enormous influence on your development. Most of the generalisations made in this chapter refer to human development in Western Europe in the 21st century. Anthropologists, sociologists and psychologists have shown us that this is only one view of human development. Some of the examples in this chapter are drawn from other cultures to illustrate that we cannot make global assumptions about the nature of human development.

(Level **Int 1 & 2**)   ## Development and behaviour

Development can be seen as a gradual unfolding, as an increase in complexity involving change and movement. Where there is change there is also transition, passing from one stage or situation to another. There is also loss and gain connected with change, and transitions are associated with both of these in varying proportions. Development involving increasing complexity (e.g. speech going from babbling to talking clearly in whole sentences) can be distinguished from growth, which is an increase in size that can be measured (e.g. height, weight).

Behaviour refers to how people conduct themselves, the way they do things themselves and in their relationships with others. Development and behaviour are very much interconnected and, though they are not the same thing, they exert influences upon one another. Some behaviour patterns are typical of certain stages in development while other behaviours reflect personal traits which, although they may alter in many ways during the life cycle, are characteristic of a particular individual and are woven into the way that person does things throughout life.

> ### Activity   *Development*
>
> To make a start in the study of human development and behaviour, examine how you have changed since you were born. List the things you do well … and the things you do not do so well.
>
> Your answer may mention such things as:
>
> - I can run really fast
> - I've learned a lot
> - I have developed the ability to have conversations
> - I have made a lot of friends, different ones at different ages
> - I have developed an interest in music and like to sing
> - I've learnt to swim and play basketball
> - I've just got my first girlfriend/boyfriend
> - I can do things for myself – as a baby I needed to be fed and now I can cook
> - I'm good at languages
> - I'm terrible with figures
> - I take part in discussions about society at the community centre
> - I think a lot more before I make decisions than I used to
> - Sometimes I enjoy spending time by myself just day dreaming

The six strands of development (SPECCS)

The changes and skills noted above have formed part of your development and can be grouped into six main strands known as social, physical, emotional, cognitive, cultural and spiritual. These strands can conveniently be remembered as making the word SPECCS. They are not entirely separate from one another, and their separation here is only because that is a convenient way to discuss them. In fact development is holistic, with all of the strands interacting with one another and inseparable from the others.

- **Social development** is about how we interact with others, develop relationships and take on social roles. Socialisation underpins social development and is about enabling people to develop the knowledge, skills, attitudes and qualities not only for successful relationships but also to function effectively in our multi-racial and multi-cultural society.

- **Physical development** refers to how our bodies change, increase in skill and develop the ability to perform more complex activities. It includes sensory development, the development of the processes of vision, hearing, touch, smell, taste and proprioception, the sense that lets us know where the mobile parts of our body (e.g. arms and legs) are in relation to the rest of our body.

- **Emotional development** concerns the development of feelings, coping with feelings, developing self-esteem and gaining a sense of our own identity.

91

- **Cognitive development** refers to our thought processes and how we make sense of the world, especially through the development of language and learning. It concerns the development of the mind in terms of recognising, reasoning, knowing, understanding, decision-making and making sense of what is perceived through the senses.

- **Cultural development** concerns how we acquire thoughts, beliefs and behaviours particular to the groups and institutions in society to which we belong. It concerns developing an understanding of our own culture, and developing respect for the values and assumptions of other cultures. Culture is closely linked with all other aspects of development. Like emotional development it contributes to the sense of self. It requires the cognitive skills associated with language development in order to communicate, receive and modify shared cultural values. Rogoff (2003) sees an understanding of cultural development as absolutely fundamental to understanding other aspects of development. She focuses on people's participation in their communities.

- **Spiritual development** concerns developing a sense of what matters, what is of genuine value, what is believed in and gives meaning to life. It may involve reflection, thought and special activities such as praying or meditation. For some people religion plays a large part in spiritual development. Other people have very positive spiritual development without holding any religious beliefs. Like other aspects of development, it contributes to the development of a sense of self and self-esteem.

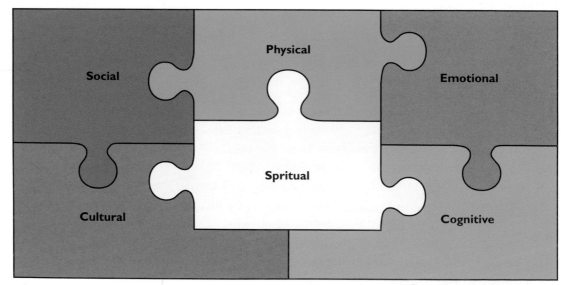

Figure 3.1   The six strands of development: SPECCS (social, physical, emotional, cognitive, cultural and spiritual)

These strands will form the basis of a discussion about development and behaviour throughout the life cycle. Another set of factors which must also be considered before tackling the life cycle stage by stage are the influences upon development and behaviour. Why are people different from one another? Why do some people develop different skills from others? Why do some people experience differences in physical and other strands of development? Why are you different from me? These differences can largely be explained by looking at influences. There are many influences upon development and behaviour which, though they may not on their own determine how an individual develops and behaves, in combination do make for many differences among individuals.

Activity **SPECCS**

Draw an image of yourself surrounded by six boxes. Label the six boxes social, physical, emotional, cognitive, cultural and spiritual, and place the changes and skills which you listed in the previous activity in the appropriate box(es). You will probably find that some things fit into several boxes as in the example in Figure 3.2.

Social
Able to have conversations
Made a lot of friends
Plays basketball
First boyfriend/girlfriend

Physical
Learnt to swim/play basketball
First boyfriend/girlfriend
Can do things for myself

Spiritual
Time by myself
Day dreaming
Interest in music
First boyfriend/girlfriend
Take part in discussions

Emotional
Made a lot of friends
Interest in music
First boyfriend/girlfriend

Cultural
Ability to have conversations
Take part in discussions
Interest in music
First boyfriend/girlfriend

Cognitive
Learned a lot
Able to have conversations
First boyfriend/girlfriend
Take part in discussions
Think to make decisions

Figure 3.2 Aspects of development

 Level Int 1 Influences on development

Activity *Influences*

Read the three short case studies that follow and write down what you think are some of the influences on the individuals concerned.

CASE STUDY

Tanni

Tanni Grey Thompson is Britain's most successful wheelchair athlete. She was born in Cardiff in 1969 with Spina Bifida, and is paralysed from the waist down. She grew up in a sporty family and had a go at many sports before discovering athletics. Her hero was Chris Hallam and she remembers saying to her Mum that one day she would do the London Marathon, just like him. She says:

'It was my dream to be there on the starting line with everyone else. And if you've got that kind of dream it gives you something to aim for. It's important to have something you can focus on or have a plan to work towards ... My biggest motivation is the fact that I desperately want to beat my husband, who is also an athlete ... I'm also a very selfish person, in that I want to be the best I can. I like pushing myself to the limit. I'm very strong-minded and if I decide I want to do something, then I'll go for it.'

(Based on BBC, 2005)

CASE STUDY

John

John is seven. He was born prematurely to his mother Jan, who was then a lone parent. He is quite small but is lively and about average for his age at school. Jan lost contact with John's father before John was born and says that she doesn't mind this since he was a drug user and very unreliable. Jan is very determined to be a 'good' mother. She is warm and loving and believes that children should be given time and attention. She gave up smoking when she was pregnant and now struggles to provide a decent environment for her son. She makes her local authority house on the outskirts of Dundee comfortable and always keeps it clean and tidy. She spends her spare money on toys and even though she works part-time she always makes time to spend with John. Jan's mother lives nearby and helps with childcare. John loves going to see his gran, who gives him a lot of love and encouragement. Two years ago, when John was five, Jan married Frank (not John's father) and shortly afterwards John's half-sister, Rita, was born. John at this time started to be really upset about going to school and started bed-wetting during the night. Frank had little patience with him at first but gradually John and Frank started to enjoy a few activities together, especially football. They still have some furious arguments but gradually during the past year John's behaviour has improved and he is almost back to being the happy and loving child he was two years ago. His bed-wetting is only very occasional now.

CASE STUDY

Nadia

Nadia is 24. She is a student at a Scottish university though she grew up in Birmingham. Both of her parents emigrated from Pakistan before Nadia was born, and lived with her father's brother and his wife and two children in a terraced house in an area of predominantly immigrant families not far from the centre of Birmingham. Nadia's father is a doctor at a large hospital and is increasingly frustrated that he has never been appointed as a senior consultant. Her mother helps in her brother-in-law's shop occasionally, as Nadia did throughout her childhood. The family are very close-knit and, although they have never been wealthy, they have given priority to education. They have also encouraged their children to feel proud of their Islamic culture, Muslim religion and their colour. Although Nadia went through a phase of identifying with white people and wanting to be white when she was about twelve, she is now very positive about her black identity. Sometimes she jokes and says she has five disabilities in Scotland: being a woman, being black, being English, being a Muslim and being a student. She is, however, really very cheerful and confident about her identity.

When you have read these accounts and written down what you think are some of the influences on development and behaviour, you can check these against the list below. Each of these influences will be dealt with in more detail. The main influences are:

- genetic/hereditary
- socioeconomic
- cultural (including the influence of socialisation)
- gender and sexuality
- racial identity
- disability
- unexpected/unplanned life changes.

Genetic/hereditary influences

Every individual, with the exception of identical twins, has an absolutely unique set of genes at birth. Genes are present in all human cells and are responsible for inherited characteristics. Sometimes one gene codes for one characteristic of an individual such as blue eyes, though it is much more usual for the products of several genes to combine and interact with one another and the environment to create particular individual characteristics. Genes play a part in appearance, in intelligence and in some illnesses such as cystic fibrosis and Huntington's disease. Table 3.1 shows that there is a genetic aspect to intelligence.

Table 3.1 The average correlations between IQs of relations: the higher the number, the greater the link between genes and intelligence (Thomson et al., 1995)

Between parents and their natural children	0.40
Between identical twins	0.86
Between fraternal twins	0.60
Between siblings reared together	0.47
Between siblings reared apart	0.24
Between parents and their adopted children	0.31

Although these figures do show a link between genes and intelligence they also indicate that other influences are at work here. If there were no other influences than the genetic, then the intelligence of siblings whether reared together or apart would be the same and there would be very little correlation between parents and their adopted children. This raises the whole issue of the nature/nurture debate in relation to human development – are people a product of their inherited, genetic characteristics or a product of their environments and the way they are brought up? This is a convenient place to examine this issue before proceeding to an examination of other influences.

Activity   *Inherited illness*

Research an inherited illness such as haemophilia, cystic fibrosis or Huntington's disease and examine how it affects the person's development and behaviour.

The nature/nurture debate

Although some theorists lean more in one direction than the other, i.e. some attribute more to nature (inherited characteristics) and some attribute more to nurture (the environment in which people develop and grow, and the way in which they are looked after and socialised), it is generally agreed that the ways in which people develop depend on a mixture of these factors, interacting with one another. The interaction of factors is a very important point to grasp. Think about baking a cake. There are certain given ingredients – flour, sugar, margarine, eggs – and often some additional items such as flavouring and colouring. These can be compared to inherited characteristics. Many things can affect the way the cake turns out: the vigour with which the ingredients are mixed together, the order in which they are mixed, the kind of oven used, the temperature of the oven, the care taken to line the cake tin, and so on. It is the nature of the ingredients, the nurturing of them into a cake and the interactions between these two sets of factors which determines the eventual nature of the cake. It is similar with people in the interaction of nature and nurture.

The section above, describing genetic/hereditary influences, has dealt with the 'nature' side of the nature/nurture debate. It is now appropriate to consider influences on the 'nurture' side. These include the influences of socioeconomic factors, culture (including socialisation), gender, disability and unexpected life changes.

Socioeconomic influences

Socioeconomic influences include social class (based upon occupation), income and wealth, housing situation and educational opportunity. In Chapter 1 it was shown that there is substantial evidence that the gap between rich and poor people in Britain is getting wider, not only in terms of income but all kinds of associated opportunity. This is discussed in more detail in Chapter 5. Approximately 80% of service users of social work departments have incomes at or below income support levels, as a result of being unemployed, experiencing long-term illness or disability or earning a low income from unskilled labour. Richard Wilkinson (2005) in a recent study shows that those at the bottom of unequal societies suffer psycho-social effects which make them depressed, apathetic and angry. The outcomes can include anti-social behaviour, violence, crime, ill-health and early death. This has enormous implications for the development of individuals in the areas of greatest socioeconomic deprivation.

Activity   *Low income*

From the above account and your own thinking, make a list of five possible effects on human development of living in a low-income household.

Cultural influences

Cultural differences exist in society that influence development and behaviour from conception to death. These differences may be related to nationality, religion, social class, geographical or community variations. For example, island populations may have different practices from mainland urban areas, and Protestants may have different cultural practices from Catholics.

Rogoff (2003) gives the example of West African mothers who had recently immigrated to Paris. They criticised the French use of toys to get infants to learn something as tiring out the babies and focusing too much on objects instead of people. Their culture prioritised social relationships above individual accomplishment.

In Britain, BBC2 aired a programme in December 2006 about the former inhabitants of the Island of Mingulay. This remote island was inhabited for over 2000 years until it was finally abandoned in 1912. The people were thought by the outside world to be uneducated but they had a rich culture which was closely bound up with island life, the Gaelic language and the work of fishing, keeping cattle, weaving and plucking bird feathers. They had a rich tradition of stories, songs and proverbs passed from generation to generation by word of mouth. The Mingulay Boatsong, which would have been sung in Gaelic, reflects their sea-faring traditions:

Wives are waiting on the bank, boys,
Looking seaward from the heather
Pull her round boys, and we'll anchor
'Ere the sun sets at Mingulay

Their culture was closely bound up with their spiritual beliefs. It is said that, being so isolated, 'they knew they were in God's hands every day of their lives'. Superstition and a belief in ghosts was just as strong as religion, and all were laced together through custom, song and story. After the inhabitants moved from Mingulay because of the difficulty of life there, they missed the island. It was such a close-knit community that they were unable to replicate it once they had moved away (**www.bbc.co.uk/coast/programmes2/07-outer-hebrides.shtml**).

Activity   (Level (Int 1 & 2)   *Mingulay*

Describe five differences between the cultural influences on you and those on the people of Mingulay above.

Socialisation is the process or way in which people learn the culture of their society. Its consideration forms a large and important section of this chapter and, although it is appropriate to look at it when examining culture, its importance is emphasised by devoting a special section to it.

Socialisation and its influence on development

Socialisation is relevant to a discussion of development from both a psychological and sociological perspective, from the viewpoint of the individual's development in society and the influence of society on the individual. It has, therefore, a place both in this chapter and in Chapter 5. Rather than discuss it twice, the main examination takes place here with only brief reference made to it in Chapter 5. Socialisation, defined above as the process or way in which people learn the culture of their society, begins at birth and continues throughout life. It can be seen as preparation for taking adult roles, for taking a responsible and acceptable part in society. Socialisation takes place at both a formal level (e.g. in school) and at an informal level (e.g. through play). What is learned through socialisation in early life is critical to what happens later on. For care workers an understanding of socialisation is essential. John Bowlby (1953) argued that children deprived of emotional stability failed in all sorts of ways. They were often unable to form lasting, meaningful relationships later in life. Although this failure was to a very great degree one of emotional deprivation, it was often compounded by a lack of positive socialisation. Socialisation is influenced by and influences the other topics discussed in this chapter, and is itself determined by what are known as the main **agents of socialisation**: the family, education, work, religion and the mass media, each of which is examined in turn below.

The first agent of socialisation is the family and it is here that most, but not all, children learn how to behave appropriately, how to relate to other people, how to eat, drink and so on in ways which are socially and culturally acceptable. This initial socialisation is called **primary socialisation**. Its impact becomes evident through contrast with situations in which no primary socialisation has taken place. The following account demonstrates what is likely to occur in the absence of socialisation:

> *Police who entered a house in The Hague found a scrawny girl in the attic unable to walk or talk. She had not been let outside by her mother since her birth nearly four years ago. A police spokeswoman said the girl, who was surrounded by rubbish, flies and mosquitoes, was now being treated for malnutrition.*

(Anon, 1998b)

Activity   Level Int 1 & 2   *Socialisation of a four year old*

When you have read the above account, write down the things you would expect a four year old to have acquired through the socialisation process.

Not all children in the same culture gain the same things about that culture during primary socialisation. Rayner (1986) makes this same point as follows:

> *Since each child is exposed to and has to adapt to a different environment from other children, he must structure his mental life differently from the child next door or in the next continent. He is being socialised in ways particular to him.*

Thus socialisation is both a general cultural concept and a particular individual concept. Your family will provide you with some aspects of culture which are common to others of your culture but it will be served up in a particular way, with some things emphasised more than others, so that your experience of socialisation is different from everyone else's. An example here is the way people are socialised into gender roles of male and female within the family.

In British society it is still common for some families to encourage girls to think of themselves as budding housewives and mothers. This kind of socialisation is called anticipatory socialisation because it anticipates adult roles. Other girls are encouraged to think of themselves as equal to boys in their career prospects, but even here there are likely to be cultural influences at work. Ann Oakley (1997), a feminist sociologist who has done research into the gender division of housework, says that even her father, the sociologist Richard Titmus, relied on her mother to do most of the housework and childcare while he wrote his books. Although she was socialised to think of herself as equal to boys, her parents presented role models of very differentiated roles, with the father's career taking precedence over that of his wife. This relates to the discussion in Chapter 5 of a feminist perspective and also the examination in that chapter of inequality.

As a child grows up he or she comes into contact with more aspects of society than the family, and these are responsible for **secondary socialisation**. Education provided through the school system is the second main socialising influence upon the developing child. Schools and other agents of secondary socialisation promote learning in relation to appropriate conduct in society and in behaviour towards people with different degrees of status and authority. The sociologist Emile Durkheim (1938) emphasised the importance of education in the development of the individual as a social being. The social being comprises the beliefs and behaviours which express a person's awareness of being a member of society. The culture transmitted by the education system is a subject of debate. Nowadays there is a whole curriculum devoted to children's spiritual, moral, social and cultural development (Eaude, 2006). The notion of citizenship is emphasised, and many parents prefer it if topics such as sexual health and drugs awareness are covered in the school curriculum. There is emphasis upon cultural awareness and a consideration of cultural diversity and tolerance. This indicates the potential of schools to change cultures and thinking through the secondary socialisation process.

Activity   Level Int 1 & 2   *School*

Think of your attendance at school. Suggest five attitudes or behaviours that your school promoted, and three ways in which you think that secondary socialisation in school took place.

Work is also an agent of secondary socialisation. People do exercise some choice about the kind of work they do but once they are in work roles they need to learn the appropriate behaviours and attitudes of these roles. In this way they are socialised into the world of work. In order to maintain their place within it they must conform, at least to some extent, to the beliefs, aims and regulations of the workplace. Many sociologists argue that work is gendered, that 'society' has views about what is women's work and what is men's work. There is evidence (see Chapter 5) to suggest that this continues to be the case.

Activity   Level Int 1 & 2   *Work*

Consider three occupations which you think are usually regarded as 'men's work' and three regarded as 'women's work'. What part has socialisation played in this view?

Religion has been a powerful source of socialisation throughout history. Different religions promote different cultures comprising teachings about morality, the place of men and women in society, marriage and the family. Religion can be regarded as a belief in some form of supernatural power, and every known society has some form of religion. What religions can you identify in the area in which you live? You may have identified Protestants, Catholics, other Christian denominations, Jews, Hindus, Sikhs, Muslims and perhaps others. All of these include a set of beliefs and practices into which followers are socialised. For Christians the Ten Commandments set out principles which include instructions to members to honour their parents, not to steal, not to kill, not to commit adultery. For Muslims the Qur'an sets out the rights and functions of men and women, expounding a philosophy of equal but different, with women playing a major role in family affairs and men in social affairs.

Activity   Level Int 1 & 2   *Religion*

Research a religion which is unfamiliar to you. Describe five behaviours or rituals that a person following that religion is expected to demonstrate.

The *mass media* are the final agent of socialisation to be considered here. They consist of television, radio, newspapers, books, advertisements, films, recorded music, the Internet – anything which reaches a very large audience. Most people are exposed to some of these agents. They fill in where the rest of experience stops. It is impossible to experience directly more than a small portion of culture, life and the world. It is the media which form the link, mediating between the real world and what we come to think of as the real world. The media are responsible to some degree for what people share in common. What happened on TV is often the first topic to be discussed at school or work. Influence, however, is a two-way process. People process information from the media alongside the other influences upon them.

The influence of gender and sexuality

The different experiences of males and females in society exert an influence on development. These differences result from a mixture of biology and culture transmitted through socialisation. They are certainly not all necessarily biological in origin. This is considered further in Chapter 5.

A person's sexuality is of great significance in development, and for some people can be the most significant factor. This may be particularly so for homosexual people since adjustment to sexuality is often accompanied by discrimination. Dalrymple and Burke (1995) provide an interesting account of homosexuals as second-class citizens. They explain that homosexuals are denied equality in law (though this is improving) and are subject to institutional discrimination in virtually every aspect of their lives. Seonaid, in the account later in the chapter (see emotional development in adulthood) describes her own experiences in relation to sexuality and several other factors that have influenced her development.

> ## Activity   `Level` `Int 1 & 2`   *Gender and sexuality*
>
> Consider yourself and how gender and sexuality may have affected your development. You could write a short essay about this, giving consideration to some of the issues mentioned below:
>
> - how was I socialised to think about men and women, heterosexual and homosexual people?
> - what social attitudes affected my development in relation to gender and sexuality?
> - did I experience any discrimination?
> - what part did biological factors play?
> - what part did emotional factors play?
> - what impact did gender and sexuality have on the choices I have made, e.g. about subjects at school, career, friends?

The influence of racial identity

Although a person's racial identity has been given some consideration in the sections on culture and religion, it also deserves some consideration in its own right. Race can be very closely allied with the development of identity and with issues of discrimination. Lena Robinson (2002) examined black identity. She developed a Nigrescence model looking at how positive racial identity could be fostered through helping black children to build positive self-images of themselves. However, racial identity is complex in a multi-cultural society, where there is a huge spectrum of people, many from mixed parentage.

The influence of disability

When you think about disability what image springs into your mind? You perhaps thought about someone in a wheelchair who has problems getting about. Yet the term 'disability' covers many conditions and degrees of disability. People can be born with disabilities or acquire them through accidents, or sudden or progressive illness. Some people have a physical disability, others a learning or behavioural or sensory disability, or a long-term illness. Some people have a combination of some or all of these. Since the early 1990s, there has been an increase in the number of long-term sick and/or disabled people in Great Britain from 1.8 million in 1991–2 to 4.1 million in 2004–5 (Sharp, 2006). This only concerns the population of people who are registered disabled. The actual figure is considerably more. According to the Family Resources Survey of 2003-4 (Office for National Statistics, 2004) it is over 10 million, taking a definition of disability to include a wide spectrum of disabilities ranging from arthritis, cancer, multiple sclerosis and heart disease to depression, Down's syndrome and diabetes. The influence of disability varies from person to person but has two strands: the effects of the disability itself and the effects of social factors including attitudes and access to such things as buildings, jobs, education and leisure facilities.

John

John was born with spina bifida, as a result of which he is unable to walk. This is certainly a limiting factor on his development because it is difficult for him to get from place to place. He has also spent quite a lot of time separated from his family in hospital and experiences times when he is so ill that he has to stay in bed for a few days at a time. John is now 21, he has a wheelchair which gives him a great deal of mobility and a specially adapted car, further enhancing his mobility. He is very intelligent, has completed a college course in computing and is trying to get a job. This is proving extremely difficult. Usually he doesn't even get an interview and when he does he finds that the job always goes to someone who is not disabled. What factors are at work here? John has to a very great degree overcome the physical disadvantages of his condition but other factors are involved. Many workplaces are still not well-adapted to wheelchairs despite legislation such as the Disability Discrimination Act 1995 and 2005, many employers have an image of people in wheelchairs as less able intellectually and socially than people who are not. Social factors are at work here. These include prejudice, language and lack of consideration for the needs of people with a disability who should have the same civil rights as anyone else.

Claire

Claire, a student at Aberdeen University, wrote the following about her experience of an epileptic seizure:

> My first memory on coming round afterwards is of saying . . . 'Oh no, I'm epileptic!' and bursting into tears. It was the stigma associated with epilepsy . . . that frightened me – the fear that people would think me different, or strange, or weak, or that my life would no longer be 'normal'.

(*Scotland on Sunday*, 1999)

The label and stigma attached to disability can be worse or as bad as the disability itself. This can lead either to a process of disempowerment or, more positively, to a desire to challenge the discrimination and to a feeling of empowerment. This is illustrated in Figure 3.3, which applies to all forms of discrimination.

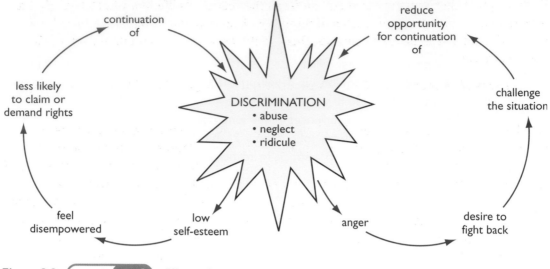

Figure 3.3 (Level (Int 2)   Effects of discrimination

The prospect for people with a disability may present difficulties but it is not all negative. These are exciting times for challenging long-held attitudes. Disabled people themselves are increasingly playing a political role and the Disability Discrimination Acts have begun to tackle some of the problems which people with disabilities have faced.

Activity   *Disability and development*

Look at the descriptions of Linda MacDonald and Nabeil Ahmed in the case study in Chapter 7. Give an account of the ways in which you think that their disability may influence their development.

(Level (Int 1)   ## The influence of unexpected/unplanned life changes

For most people there is a fairly steady progression through the life cycle. There will be good times and bad, sad times and happy times, gains and losses, but usually the impact of these will not profoundly affect the course of development. Some changes, however, are not expected or anticipated and can have profound effects. Edward Rainey's account (in Alexander, 1995) is an example:

> *I had an ordinary happy childhood with my younger brother and older sister at our home in Pollok . . . I just enjoyed life as it came. After leaving school I worked in a butcher's until one day I felt there was more to life than working inside all the time. So I joined the Royal Highland Fusiliers because I wanted adventure . . . Then, when I was twenty four I went to Spain for a holiday with my friend Eddie – we were known as 'the two Eddies' – and as soon as we arrived at our hotel in Marbella we decided to have a swim in the pool. I dived into the shallow end by mistake and struck my head on the bottom.*

Eddie's spinal chord was severed and he faces the rest of his life in a wheelchair. He has experienced some of the influences of disability discussed above, but there have been other adjustments to be made because this event was so sudden and unexpected. He goes on to say:

I was so depressed that I cried an ocean at the beginning. I kept asking 'Why me?'

Eddie's response was characteristic of what many people experience when something major and catastrophic happens to them: he experienced depression, then anger, and then gradual adjustment to completely changed circumstances. Eddie went through all of the stages of grief, explained in Chapter 4, before coming to terms with what had happened. The outcome for Eddie was influenced by many factors: a lot of support from family and friends, his strong religious convictions, his previously high level of physical fitness, his previous optimism and positive outlook, and chance. The chance was a calendar which an aunt gave to him from the Mouth and Foot Painting Artist's Association. Eddie, who had never painted in his life before, decided to give art a try and has been sponsored through art school by the Association. He now says:

At times I enjoy a wonderful sense of peace and I am happier than I was before the accident – it has made me a better person spiritually.

Of course the outcome could have been completely different, and is for many people who experience dramatic change. Eddie, if he had not been supported and encouraged, might have remained depressed. If he had not been sponsored he would have remained relatively poor. If he had not been strong before the accident he might have experienced more physical complications and would probably have died. The influence of unexpected events can be positive or negative or a mixture of the two, but they often do alter the course of development.

Activity *Unplanned pregnancy*

Unplanned pregnancy is an example of an unexpected change. How might this influence a young person's development if she is 15 years old? How different would this be if she was 35 years old and already had three children? List four possible negative influences and four possible positive ones in each case. What factors are likely to affect the outcome?

Level **Int 1 & 2**

Development at different ages and stages

It is interesting to look at the process of development as it occurs at different times in the lifespan. You will quickly realise if you look around you that people differ enormously in what they do at different ages and stages, and that any account here can only be about what can generally be expected. Joe at twelve months is already saying a few words and can walk. Ryan at twelve months is still crawling everywhere and makes a few incomprehensible sounds. By five Ryan might have overtaken Joe and be able to catch a ball and give a good account of his day to his Mum, whereas Joe may not yet have mastered these skills. Linda at 50 may be very tired, overweight, unfit and depressed. Pat is 50 too but she is active, optimistic and thinking about taking a college course and changing her job. We are all different and affected to different degrees by all of the influences considered in the previous section. Below is an account of what generally happens from infancy to older adulthood, considered in the separate sections infancy (0–2); early childhood (2–5); middle childhood; adolescence; adulthood; and older adulthood. Social, physical, emotional, cognitive, cultural and spiritual development will be examined at each stage.

Infancy: birth to two years

At birth a baby undertakes a phenomenal journey from being totally connected to the mother to being outside her body. Although the baby is still completely dependent upon others for the fulfilment of needs, this transition has enormous implications. One day 'ventilation, nutrition and excretion take place through the placenta and umbilical cord' (Rayner, 1986); the next day the baby breathes independently; feeding by sucking starts in the next couple of days, and so does excretion. Other people have to reorganise their lives around this new, dependent person.

Activity — *Observing babies*

Obtaining permission from their parents or carers first, try to watch babies and children in the first two years of their lives. Look at and make notes on their social, physical, emotional, cognitive, cultural and spiritual development, noting the age at which observations are made. You could record your results in a chart like the one below, adding other stages as you progress through your course. Remember that the divisions are in many ways artificial ones and that many observations may apply to several forms of development.

	Social	Physical	Emotional	Cognitive	Cultural	Spiritual
Birth to two years						

Social development

Most people who have been with small babies a lot will be convinced that they are sociable from a very early age. Whether or not they have any sense of a separate identity, a small baby's smiles and cries elicit responses from others to play, to comfort or just smile back. From these beginnings the child between two and eight months usually begins to bond with and show attachment to one or more adults who are close to the child. This early sociability is thus very much linked with the emotional development discussed below. A baby has little interest in other children in the first six months of life, though familiar children, such as brothers and sisters, are recognised and often elicit a response such as a smile of pleasure. From about eight months onwards the young child begins to spread his or her sociability to other people, though will often seek the reassurance and closeness of the most meaningful person if threatened, unsure, hungry, uncomfortable or tired.

Life becomes a series of going forth into new situations and retreating back for comfort. There is increasing interest in other children. Most children aged one will happily be with other children but actions are not yet an exchange between them. For example, at one year old a child who goes to playgroup may happily play alongside other children for up to an hour, but then may retreat to her mother for comfort. By two she may become much more independent and sociable but still her play will be what is known as parallel play. It does not yet rest upon ideas of sharing and exchange. That has to wait for the next stage of development.

Physical development

Here are some of the physical developments you may have noticed in a child from birth to two years. There is increasing control over the body, beginning with control of head and upper body. This progresses to the ability to sit independently, then to crawl, then to pull up onto two feet and stand, then to walk with help, perhaps in a walker or pushing a toy trolley. Hand movements become finer with the ability to grasp things and then to finely hold objects in a pincer grip at around nine months old. Then that remarkable day arrives, usually between ten and eighteen months, when the child takes those first independent steps.

CASE STUDY

Rachel

As an example of one child's physical development, let's look at Rachel. At seven months she has learned to turn over from front to back. She can sit momentarily without support but soon flops forwards or backwards; she can hold a cloth book but can't yet turn the pages. By fourteen months Rachel is walking and can sit in a small chair at a small table holding crayons or small objects and transferring them from one container to another. She can turn the pages of a book, usually several pages at a time. By eighteen months she is running, though not very confidently and with rather a lot of falls. She can walk upstairs one at a time holding someone's hand but comes down on hands and knees backwards. She pushes a small trolley full of toy bricks everywhere. By two years she runs confidently and has learned to turn door handles to open and close doors. Climbing is one of her new discoveries and she can 'escape' from her cot. She has a little tricycle and moves it by walking her feet along the ground. She now turns book pages one at a time. It has become evident that she is left-handed. She likes to build a tower with bricks, picking them up very carefully with her thumb and first finger; and she loves to knock the whole thing down again – with great hilarity.

Emotional development

A child's early experiences are crucial to emotional development. The presence of at least one consistent, caring and loving individual has been shown to be invaluable to the child's ability to thrive and to develop emotional stability, an integrated sense of self and relationships with others. Babies deprived of a close relationship may lose vitality, become apathetic and show many symptoms of depression. Sometimes they die. This is why there is so much emphasis on preventing the separation of young children from their families. When separation cannot be prevented, or is in the child's best interests, as in abusive situations, it is important to provide a situation which is as close as possible to a loving, warm parent–child relationship. Fortunately the days of routinely separating children with disabilities from their parents have passed. Whenever possible the emphasis is on support within, rather than outside, the family. Parents are now encouraged to stay with their children in hospital, nurture their babies as soon as possible after birth and to respond to a baby's need for warmth, love and physical closeness.

At first a baby is not able to distinguish between him/herself and other people, to distinguish the breast or bottle as something separate. At this stage begins what Rayner calls the synchrony between a close parent or parent substitute and a baby. They fit themselves around each other, are in tune, and a baby establishes communication with at least one close 'significant other' within the first few weeks of life. Both parents and babies vary in the nature of the synchrony that is established, but without it a baby is likely to be distressed. This synchrony is the basis for bonding and attachment between parent and child on which the baby's later ability to gain a separate sense of self depends. It is also the basis of love, trust and a feeling of security.

Slowly but surely the baby begins to gain a sense of him/herself as separate from other people and things, so that somewhere between six months and a year a separate identity begins to emerge. Crying changes in nature and becomes a call for someone else. Smiling, which has probably been present as a sign of pleasure from the first month of life, becomes increasingly a response to other people. Crying and smiling are the baby's main ways of communicating pain and pleasure and need a response in order that the child can begin to gain a knowledge of communication as an exchange. At this stage too the child begins to test the world, to throw things away which are then put back, to get anxious if the closest person to her goes out, and to be reassured when she or he returns. As long as the person does come back the child learns to trust other people, to see that they can be relied upon, and to form a close bond with at least one significant other. Initial synchrony helps in this bonding process, though bonding at this stage is entirely possible for children who have had early health difficulties and/or have been separated from their parents. Continued separation, however, increases the difficulties of bonding once a child reaches the stage of seeing him/herself as separate. This is looked at in more detail when attachment theory is discussed in Chapter 4.

Although children thrive and survive in all kinds of different parenting, and can and do recover from short periods of separation, children deprived of love and closeness and the opportunity to bond and form a consequent attachment to an adult are unlikely to trust others or to develop a satisfactory self-concept. This can lead to difficulties in their relationships with others. Such emotional deprivation has also been shown to be associated with slow intellectual development and poor physical health. Spitz (1965), for example, observed children in large institutions where they were well fed and clean but had little personal attention or stimulation. These children had extreme difficulties with learning and responding emotionally to others, and were prone to infections. Their illness and death rates were much higher than those for children in less clean but more warm and friendly places.

Cognitive development

Cognitive development includes the child's thinking, language development, some aspects of play and the whole process of learning and understanding about the world. The five senses of sight, smell, touch, taste and hearing are used to learn about and explore surroundings. Memory is used to store up information which can be adapted, initially to the same situations and subsequently to different ones. At first there is memory of the same face(s) meaning the same things: usually food and love. Recognition of one meaningful person, usually but not necessarily the child's mother, is among the first cognitive steps the child takes. For example, at a few weeks old a baby will stop crying at the sight of his or her mother's face, or the face of whoever happens to be the most significant person to that baby.

One way in which babies seem to learn is through imitation of those in their surrounding world. Even though adults and older children may not realise it, they are having an effect on a baby. What they do is very important from the earliest days of the child's life, not only in terms of the child's emotional security but also in terms of intellectual growth. There is evidence that babies imitate their mother's mouth movements from the age of about a month, even though they can't speak; similarly, body movements are imitated and learned. This topic is covered in more detail when Bandura's work is considered in Chapter 4.

Exploration develops to the stage where by eighteen months a child remembers where objects belong, explores new environments with great interest and can manipulate building blocks so that they become towers. The development of language is perhaps one of the most fascinating aspects of cognitive development. From crying and cooing at three months of age the child develops to babbling a whole mixture of sounds by six months. By nine or ten months the language of a child's culture can be recognised and by twelve months the first words are usually spoken. By two there is usually a vocabulary of a hundred words or so. Andrew was saying Da, Ma, do (dog), ca (cat) and something which resembled 'hello' by his first birthday, whereas his friend Sam called everything 'ducker'. As the second year progressed both boys grasped the meaning of 'me' and 'mine' and parts of the body: nose, face, feet. By two they could also recognise most colours. They pretended to 'phone' one another on their toy telephones and had 'conversations'.

Cultural development

You may think that 0–2 years is rather early to be talking about cultural development. However, an infant is surrounded by cultural influences that have a major impact on how she develops culturally: the institution of the family, rituals such as baptism, the use of language, the beliefs of the family and society; all of these begin to permeate the infant's development so that the development of a cultural identity is well under way by the time a child reaches the age of 2. At this stage infants are becoming habituated to their culture, usually and predominantly through their family, but they are not yet at a stage where they question it or try to change it. They accept that what is there is there; they have no ability or reason to question things . . . yet. Cultural development can best be illustrated by comparing differences in cultural development in infants from different societies and groups.

Activity — *Cultural development*

Below are three descriptions of infants. Can you identify contrasting aspects of cultural development from these accounts?

James, aged 9 months, was born into a moderately wealthy Scottish family in a northern Scottish town. His parents are articulate and introduce him at an early age to the groups to which they belong. He goes to the church crèche when his parents attend their local church, and he was baptised at the church. His parents are his main carers, although he is also cared for by his grandmother while his mother works part-time. He sleeps in a cot in a separate room from his parents. Great emphasis is placed on the importance of developing intellectual and cognitive skills to the extent that, even as a baby, James is surrounded by books and encouraged to look at them. He is told stories at bedtime, his mother reads poems to him and these sources form part of his cultural environment.

Ellie is 18 months old. Her parents are both drug users. Their friends are predominantly drug users and there is no contact with grandparents or other extended family members. They expect Ellie to spend long periods of time entertaining herself. She cannot rely on them for regular meals. They do not introduce her to many influences outside the immediate nuclear family circle and there are few indications of any wider societal culture, except that surrounding drugs and their acquisition, and the television, which is continuously switched on. Ellie often shares her parents' bed at night.

The following is a quote from Hewlett in Rogoff (2003, p. 34) in relation to **Aka children** in Central Africa:

> *Training for autonomy begins in infancy. Infants are allowed to crawl or walk to wherever they want in camp and allowed to use knives, machetes, digging sticks, and clay pots around camp. Only if an infant begins to crawl into a fire or hits another child do parents or others interfere . . . It was not unusual, for instance, to see an eight month old with a six-inch knife chopping the branch frame of its family's house.*

In their camps, Aka infants are held most of the time for the first four months and, although their primary carer is their mother, they are transferred to other caregivers about seven times an hour and have seven different caregivers on an average day. Fathers also play a major role in care giving, spending about 20% of every day holding their infants.

Activity *Cultural development* continued

In each of the above examples, what can be identified as cultural development? Consider:

- expectations about autonomy and responsibility, e.g. sleeping alone or with parents
- who the people are in the child's life and what they do, e.g. the part played by parents, grandparents
- the importance given to different activities, e.g. reading, work
- the nature of the family, e.g. extended or nuclear
- religious and ethnic practices, e.g. importance of baptism, the use of sharp knives
- the emergence of a sense of self within a cultural context
- experience of physical contact – one person or many.

All of these aspects are part of cultural development. The child begins to move towards a greater understanding of what is required and expected by the wider society, and this is culturally specific. Building an identity is part of many aspects of development, but without cultural development this identity is incomplete.

Spiritual development

Building an identity is also part of spiritual development. As with cultural development, there may not be much outward evidence for this aspect of development in such young children, but the foundations are already being laid. Through love and early attachments the infant can begin to feel secure so that a positive, happy sense of self can begin to emerge. Infants can begin to feel at ease with themselves which is the beginning of spiritual development. There will probably be cultural dimensions to this aspect of development, influenced by family beliefs and/or religious practices. The nature of the environment also plays a part. Opportunities for peace, quiet times, imaginative use of colour, music, lighting can all contribute to balance and a sense that all is well with the world.

Table 3.2 Summary of general pattern of development: infancy

Social	Physical	Emotional	Cognitive	Cultural	Spiritual
Interacting/getting on with others	How the body changes	Beginning to gain a sense of identity	How sense is made of the world	Beginning to acquire behaviours associated with culture	Beginning to develop sense of wholeness
• Bonding and attachment - importance of early close relationship(s) • Increasing interest in other children • Parallel play • Communication with others • Move from total dependence to more autonomy	• Increasing control over body • All senses developing from birth • Sitting, crawling, walking, running • Co-ordination, finer hand movements • Brain growing in complexity – sensitive to environmental influences	• Need for warmth, love and closeness • Secure or insecure base • Distinguishing self from others • Emotional responses to others; smiling, crying • Erikson: Trust vs mistrust (0–1yr) Autonomy vs shame and doubt (1–3 yrs)	• Recognition of meaningful people • Development of memory • Developing concept of objects, numbers and problem-solving • Communication and language • Exploration	• Affected by how the family behaves and is structured • Begins to take part in cultural practices • Learning the language reflects in culture • Cultural influences permeate development • Beginning of cultural participation and identity	• Importance of love and attachment • Influenced by all other aspects of development • Emerging sense of self and self-awareness • Cultural influences e.g. religion • Need for periods of quietness and peace

Early childhood: two to five years

Social development

At this stage not only is the child moving outwards emotionally but also socially: from parents to siblings to other children and other adults. The child's social world is usually expanding and spreading beyond the family to nursery, playgroup, public places (shopping, swimming, holidays) and is a mixture of child and adult relationships.

Play is an area which combines all facets of development – social, physical, emotional, cognitive, cultural and spiritual. It is useful to examine here not only how play is part of social development at this stage, but also how it acts to integrate the various facets of development in the process of the growth of a well-balanced person.

At two a child generally participates in parallel play: children play alongside each other rather than with each other. If you watch children at this age, they can be very absorbed by a toy car, or by the toy car with which another child is playing, which they will then proceed to try to obtain. This is more important than any kind of relationship with the other child. Play here is a learning process; it serves to develop physical and cognitive skills and is preparation for a much more social and emotional experience – but it isn't quite there, yet. This process continues slowly until, by the age of five, children begin to co-operate, to divide roles and to share, though play is by no means always a harmonious experience. What the child does in terms of play activity will to some extent be culturally influenced; toy cars will not be present in every culture. The opportunities for quiet periods of play can set the scene for spiritual development.

Physical development

Parents will often have been preoccupied with 'toilet training' for several months preceding the second birthday. Some time from eighteen months to three years magical things seem to happen: the child becomes increasingly able to control both bladder and bowel and can now communicate so well that he or she can begin to predict the need to use a pot and say what is required. This new-found control is very important, for it further frees the child from dependence on adults for physical care. By age two, most children are fully weaned and can eat and drink independently. Development is very much tied up with growth at this stage. As the body grows stronger it also gains in co-ordination and strength. Walking, running, climbing and balancing are increasingly skilled.

CASE STUDY

Matty

Matty is two and a half. He loves to visit the swings and slides. Tentatively he'll climb the ladder and slide down the slide. After ten minutes he's running from the end of the slide to the ladder, up one step at a time and whizzing down with great glee ... time after time after time. He loves to go to the swimming baths and flap around with arm bands on, but needs to know that there's someone close by to help him. By age five he may be going up the really big slide, co-ordinating climbing steps with alternate legs and be confident enough to go head first as well as feet first. Also, by age five, a lot of children are learning to swim without the support of arm bands.

This period from age two to five is one of consolidating skills, of increasing co-ordination of lots of movements, of running around and climbing. Gradually a child can learn to throw a ball and then to catch it, to pedal a tricycle and then to begin to balance on a bicycle. There is increasing skill gained in holding and manipulating toys so that, by age five, children can usually thread beads, create buildings with building blocks and draw by holding crayons quite skilfully and with increasing control.

Figure 3.4 Physical and cognitive development: it may be grey skies over Lanarkshire in reality, but in this child's eye it could be anywhere in the Universe

Emotional development

Emotional development usually, though not always, goes hand in hand with intellectual development. As a child learns communication skills these facilitate interaction with others and the development of relationships. During the period of age two to five years children become considerably less dependent on their parents and strive towards greater autonomy. They can usually be separated from parents for short periods without becoming too distressed. They begin to enjoy the company of others, especially brothers and sisters (siblings), spending as much time with them as with their parents. Siblings often begin to form strong bonds with one another at this stage, talking, playing, imitating, arguing, experiencing difficulties and attempting to sort them out. Sibling relationships are certainly not all plain sailing and some siblings never gain fulfilling, integrated relationships with one another for reasons of both nature and nurture. But there is the potential in sibling relationships for strong bonds to develop which are different from and additional to those with parents and friends. Parents still play a prominent part at this stage, an emotional retreat when the child needs love, stability and reassurance.

It is at this stage that gender identity emerges, and girls and boys become more fully aware of the differences between them. Even before the age of two there are signs that boys and girls are aware that they are different from one another. Physical differences have emotional implications since these differences become part of identity, and children begin to pay attention to the different roles of boys and girls, men and women. The gaining of gender identity can be seen as progressing in four stages.

- Awareness: the child begins to notice gender differences (12–14 months)
- Labelling: the child correctly identifies gender in self and others (2–3 years)
- Stability: the child understands that gender remains over time, that a boy becomes a man and a girl becomes a woman (3–5 years)
- Constancy: the child understands that gender doesn't change when outward appearance changes (5 years).

Cognitive development

Language is one of the main avenues through which cognitive/intellectual development can be gauged at this age. Not only is vocabulary increasing but children are very creative with their language. They do not completely mimic adults but often, once they have learned a few rules of language, they come up with entirely original constructions. Here are some sentences of children in this age range:

> I was tired. My eyes did lie down a little while.
> I not naughty. I just a little terror.
> I knowed Andrew at nursery school. I done some drawing.

Here is a conversation between a three-year-old and a six-year-old, quoted in Bee and Mitchell (1984), about the relative dangers of forgetting to feed the goldfish versus overfeeding them:

> Six-year-old: It's worse to forget to feed them.
> Three-year-old: No, it's badder to feed them too much.
> Six-year-old: You don't say badder, you say worser.
> Three-year-old: But it's baddest to give them too much food.
> Six-year-old: No, it's not. It's worsest to forget to feed them.

These examples show really creative use of language which, although perhaps not grammatically correct, is inventive. One of the delights of this age is this remarkable grasp of some basic rules of grammar combined with experimenting with them in original ways. By age three, children are constructing quite long, complex sentences. They have often replaced their own names with 'I' in their conversations as they gain confidence in themselves and their self-concept becomes more fully developed.

Children of this age are also learning about colours and shapes, numbers and time, what things in their environment are like and what they do. They will play shapes games, putting different shapes through appropriately shaped holes in boxes, they will investigate things to see what they do and feel like, and they will be trying to work out things like distances. One favourite word is often 'why'. 'Why' is sometimes asked out of sheer habit but can also indicate a real desire to know why something is the way it is. 'How far' is also a favourite one, especially on a long journey. 'How far is it? Are we nearly there?' comes from a small voice ten minutes into a three-hour journey, and at five-minute intervals thereafter, unless there's distraction and/or fun going on. It's certainly not far to age five now, but there's still a lot of life's journey to pursue.

Cultural development

From ages two to five, the major determinant of cultural development in Western society continues to be the family. However, other institutions are also beginning to impinge upon the child's life: nursery school, possibly a religious or other spiritual or faith institution, other families, friends. Some children live within contrasting cultures that affect the way they develop culturally. For example, children in ethnically mixed families may have two cultures or a very mixed culture, taking some aspects of one culture, some of another. The child is still likely to accept unquestioningly the culture offered by family and the wider social groups with which he is in contact, but is now able to begin to make comparisons between the way things are for him and for others. This is not well developed at this stage, but this is already a stage at which cultural tolerance or intolerance modelled by those in the child's environment can influence early choices about who to spend time with, who is liked or not liked. These choices are likely not only to be culturally influenced but to influence cultural development. Again, short examples may serve to illustrate this better than any amount of theorising:

Rogoff (2003) tells us that Aka children by the age of three or four years can cook themselves a meal on the fire. They participate in family work from a very early age and see their parents working. By contrast, most children in Scotland see their parents and their activities in the home but rarely also see them at work, unless they work at home. As a consequence they do not get any sense of major areas of activity of their parents in terms of the full range of their economic and social activities. The opportunity of Aka children to see their parents working means that they are more likely to participate in work activities at a very early age. Work is part of their culture and their identity, whereas Western children are expected to have activities completely separate from their parents and very often of a play or educational nature. Indeed efforts to protect children from exploitation and to remove them from the world of work mean that cultural emphasis is placed on children being educated and well-rounded socially, but not on children as major economic contributors. The differing values that different cultures place on different experiences thus influence the child's cultural development.

| Activity | *Observing cultural development in early childhood* |

Through observing two children in the age range 2–5 years in social situations with their families, identify five cultural aspects of development that are presented to them and that they adopt. Try to find contrasting children from different cultural backgrounds.

You may have looked at:

- how children relate to adults
- the values of influential adults in relation to education, play and work, and how these are conveyed to children
- the extent to which children are included in the institutions to which their family and/or carers belong
- how the developing sense of self reflects cultural development.

Activity   *Teegie*

Read the passage below from Rogoff (2003, p. 325) and answer the questions that follow.

> *White folks uh hear dey kids say sump'n, dey say it back to 'em, dey aks 'em 'gain 'n 'gain 'bout things, like they 'posed to be born knowin'. You think I kin tell Teegie all he gotta know to get along? He just gotta be keen, keep his eyes open, don't he be sorry. Gotta watch hisself by watchin' other folks. Ain't no use me tellin' 'im: 'Learn dis, learn dat. What's dis? What's dat? He just gotta learn, gotta know; he see one thing one place one time, he know how it go, see sump'n like it again, maybe it be de same, maybe it won't. He hafta try it out. If he don't he be in trouble; he get lef' out. Gotta keep yo' eyes open.*

1   What things in the description above are important for Teegie in learning his culture?

2   Is this how children you have observed learn about their culture and develop culturally?

3   What other aspects of development are illustrated in this account?

Spiritual development

At age two to five, spiritual development is still in its very early stages. Love, attachment and the child's environment continue to set the scene for later development. However, a curiosity is already emerging about some of the mysteries of life, a need for explanations about how things are as they are. The young child may participate in some spiritual activities that ask and seek to answer ultimate questions such as 'why was I born', for example through religion or other belief systems. Opportunities for contemplation or creative activities away from excessive noise in a secure happy environment can contribute to developing the child's sense of self and whether or not this self is happy.

Table 3.3 Summary of general pattern of development: early childhood

Social	Physical	Emotional	Cognitive	Cultural	Spiritual
Building upon relationships	How the body changes	Developing sense of identity	How sense is made of the world	Behaviour, thoughts and beliefs culturally influenced	Developing sense of wholeness and balance
• Moving outwards; expanding social world • Play: parallel play to playing with other children • Taking on roles in play, including gender roles • Importance of relationships with siblings and other family members	• Steady growth: bigger, stronger but more slender body: increasing skills in walking, running, balancing • Control of bladder and bowel • Eating and drinking independently • Increasing physical independence • Increasing skill in co-ordination	• Less dependence on parents • Greater autonomy if emotionally stable • Emergence of gender identity • Begins to verbalise emotional responses • Developing relationships • Erikson: initiative vs guilt	• Talking and using words and symbols creatively • Learning about everything: colours, shapes, numbers • Curiosity: often asks 'why' • Language as a route to relationships and culture • From self centred to appreciating other's perspective	• Culturally learned from family • Influence of other social institutions reinforces culture • Contrasting cultures in ethnically mixed families • Child can begin to make comparisons • Emergence of cultural identity	• Curiosity about mysteries of life • Participating in spiritual aspects of some cultural practices • Increasing sense of self • Development of beliefs • Potential to be at ease with self

Childhood: age five years to twelve or thirteen years

Childhood has a different time span for different children and for different cultures. In the UK it generally spans the ages of five until about twelve or thirteen, when puberty and adolescence occur. It is the time of starting school, making friends and moving further out from the confines of the family and home to the wider society.

Social development

'Friends' would be an apt title for a TV series about childhood. The peer group, children of the same or similar age, gains in importance as children move increasingly away from social dependence upon adults. Competitive and co-operative play develop alongside one another. Children compete in sports activities, in classroom situations and in their attempts to gain the attention of adults and other children. They also learn co-operation, enhanced in play situations where they act out such co-operative and competing roles as mothers, fathers, doctors, nurses, older brothers and sisters, shop assistants, school teachers and pupils.

Play enables children to learn roles and to empathise with those who perform other roles in their lives. The self-concept, seen as part of emotional development, is developed to some extent through the social situations which the child experiences and through the increasing ability of the child to put him or herself in other roles, to stand outside and to look in. Ideas about self-concept are further developed in Chapter 4.

Group participation, whether through the family, school group, interest group or friendship group, provides avenues not only for co-operation with others, but also for the expression of opinions and the development of relationships. Children of this age have an enormous need for acceptance, which leads to what many adults see as an annoying conformity; children have to dress in similar ways to their peers, develop language patterns which are similar, hair must be just so and things not 'in' are viewed as very 'uncool'. Conformity sometimes looks cripplingly stifling of creativity and achievement, but for many children acceptance by the peer group is of much greater importance. The peer group itself, though, can be a source of creativity, interaction and the opportunity for co-operation and leadership. By age eight or nine, boys and girls are beginning to drift apart into same-sex groups, only to come together again in adolescence.

Adult relationships continue to retain a great deal of relevance, the family is still an important social focal point but other adult attachments often develop. Hero worship of teachers, sports coaches, instructors, guide and scout leaders, youth club leaders, even social workers, can develop. These are usually healthy attachments if the role models are positive and the power that could be associated with these roles is not abused.

For most children this is a happy time socially, with some friendships formed at this stage lasting well into adult life. There are fallings in and out, but gradually as the child develops confidence in him/herself, so confidence develops in relationships. Social development rests firmly in its emotional partner.

Physical development

Of course, children get bigger and bigger, though at different rates. How else do they change and develop before they reach that notorious adolescence? Skills and sex are the two clues to physical development from age five to twelve or thirteen. Skills involve more meticulous dexterity in manipulating their hands and bodies. At age six, children can usually tie laces and cut meat at the table. At age seven, lo and behold, a small person can balance on a plank, leap down several stairs at a time, dress – and undress. By age eight the child is roller-skating or roller-blading on Saturday evening at the sports centre, skipping in the playground and riding a bike at full speed downhill. Sexually, children are inexorably moving towards puberty, girls usually at a faster rate than boys. Girls begin to develop pubic hair and breasts, and some begin menstruation, before they are twelve. Boys do not usually reach puberty at this stage or undergo any major growth spurts. Both sexes make steady progress in their ability to perform complex physical tasks, with the effects of puberty dominating not this stage of development but the next.

Emotional development

Most children become more self-assured between the ages of five and twelve, developing a concept of self which is more confident about their abilities and shows more insight into their own identity. Children from age five to twelve start to question family relationships and emotions, and quite frequently push their parents to the limit of their patience. They like to see how far they can go, though if limits are imposed they are usually adhered to – eventually.

Activity   *Seonaid*

Seonaid wrote the following description of herself at age eleven:

My name is Seonaid. I live in Dundee. My home is a flat. I was born in Fort William and when I was six weeks old I moved to Glasgow and stayed there for seven years. My school in Glasgow was . . . and my best friend was called Joanne. I have brown hair cut short and I wear earrings. My best friend in Dundee is Ellie. I have a younger sister in primary 2 and an older sister in third year. My Mum works in a shop and my Dad is a taxi driver. I go dancing after school every Wednesday. I go swimming quite often too. I collect pictures of cats in a scrap book and I also collect stamps. I have a one-year-old cat called Snowy. My ambition is to look after lots of animals that have been abandoned. I am average size. My home has three bedrooms, a living room, a kitchen and a bathroom. I like skateboards and bikes.

What was important to Seonaid? From this account, identify which parts refer to social, physical, emotional, cognitive, cultural and spiritual development.

Cognitive development

Play continues to have a vital role in cognitive development, though formal learning at school plays an increasing role at this time. Thinking changes in a number of ways. The child usually develops numerical/mathematical ability. For example, by age five a child can count sweets if they are placed in a straight line (though not if they are placed in a circle). By age eight, most children can count sweets placed in a circle. By between age ten and twelve, concepts of addition, subtraction, multiplication and division are being grasped. Measuring and recording can be practised in both formal and informal situations through seeing how long and wide things are, now much items weigh when baking a cake, and so on.

Time becomes increasingly meaningful, and during this stage most children learn to tell the time, understand the calendar in some detail (weeks, months, years), know the date and grasp that it is the same date and time everywhere in the UK. Writing ability is often more developed than speech. The use of increasingly complex sentences indicates growing language competence.

Cultural development

At this stage school is not only a major influence on social and cognitive development but also presents the child with new opportunities for cultural development. Schools now include in their curricula the closely linked aspects of spiritual, moral, social and cultural development. In this chapter moral development is considered to have its basis in cultural development and is not considered separately. As Eagleton (2000, p. 131) states:

> Culture is not only what we live by. It is, also, in great measure, what we live for. Affection, relationship, memory, kinship, place, community, emotional fulfilment, intellectual enjoyment, a sense of ultimate meaning.

CASE STUDY

John

A developing sense of identity is closely related to cultural development. John, aged 10, comes from a family living in a Scottish sea port. Like his parents and school friends, he supports the town's football team, speaks with the local accent, has strong beliefs about what is right and wrong, especially in relation to being true to his friends. John likes to dress similarly to his school friends so that he is not identified as different from them. Which of these factors can be distinguished as part of John's cultural development? The answer is that all of them can. Culture presents ways of belonging and of excluding those who do not belong, though it can also be part of a culture to accept and not judge those who are culturally different.

Spiritual development

The links between spiritual development and cultural development can be seen clearly in the above quotation from Eagleton (2000) where he talks about 'a sense of ultimate meaning'. In some senses this is contrary to culture because it seems to cross cultural difference to indicate a sense of developing common humanity. In other senses, the ways in which this is done are greatly influenced by culture. However, the spiritual dimension of development can begin to ask questions for which culture may not have the answers. These questions begin in childhood but become much more important in adolescence. At this age (5–12) most children are concerned with fairness ('It's not fair' being a rather common expression) which may not seem very spiritual but does begin the establishment of a moral basis for behaviour. An appreciation of different viewpoints emerges. Time and space to be quiet and peaceful, to read, daydream or take part in creative, religious and/or other spiritual activities, and the importance of loving, and more especially being loved, continue to underpin this aspect of development.

Table 3.4 Summary of general pattern of development: childhood

Social	Physical	Emotional	Cognitive	Cultural	Spiritual
Moving outwards from the family	How the body changes	Developing sense of identity	How sense is made of the world	Behaviour thoughts and beliefs of culture	Developing sense of wholeness and balance
• Importance of peers and peer pressure • Competitive and co-operative play • Learning roles and social competence • Group participation • Family still a focal point but child gaining more control over choices	• Increased body strength and co-ordination; rate of growth slows down • Developing skills and co-ordination • Beginnings of sexual development • Progress in doing complex tasks e.g. games and sports • Body proportions more like adult	• Developing self image, self esteem, pride • Questioning about emotions • Increasing independence • Play and its role in identity • Growing sensitivity • Erikson: Industry vs inferiority	• Importance of play: learning by doing • Numerical, language and memory skills increase – importance of education • Grasp of the concept of time • Less self-centred • Some children show particular cognitive needs and/or strengths	• School reinforcing culture • Awareness of other cultures • Education introduces literature, art, etc. • Development of cultural identity • Practising values of culture	• Concern with fairness • Begin to appreciate different viewpoints • Need time and space to be alone • Importance of loving and being loved

Adolescence

Indeed, all the terms that we use for the age group have an awkward feel. There is no neutral way of describing it: 'youth' has an air of causing trouble and needing clubs, 'juveniles' are obviously delinquent, 'adolescents' are most likely to have problems and 'teenagers' to have spots.

(Open University U205 Course Team, 'Birth to Old Age', 1985)

Think about being a teenager. You may still be one, you may have just passed that stage or you may be well past it, not that **adolescence** is ever entirely left behind. What do you think are its most significant aspects? Is it a time of calm, natural transition from childhood to adulthood or a rather stormy passage or a mixture of the two? A lot has been written about this period, which in Western society is often associated with problems, storm and stress; but is adolescence necessarily problematical? Is turbulence in adolescence a biological necessity or are social and cultural factors of paramount importance? Writers and theorists vary enormously in their views. The sections below, combined with your experience and thinking, should enable you to come to a few of your own conclusions.

Social development

Social development is greatly influenced by all other aspects of development in adolescence and bears many resemblances to emotional development. Sexual maturity leads the individual towards sexual relationships. In Western society the search for self and emotional independence from parents establishes a new and different kind of relationship with them and with the peer group. The end of formal school education leads to a transition into the worlds of work or further or higher education or other experiences such as gap years of travel. For some there is the frustrating world of unemployment, uncertainty and lack of money. Whatever avenue is taken by the adolescent, new and often meaningful and long-lasting relationships develop, usually with members of both the same and the opposite sex.

Parents, including step-parents, are a source of support, annoyance and aggravation at this age. One observer (Montemayor, 1983) noted that adolescents and their parents are in conflict in all families some of the time and in some families all of the time. Sometimes serious conflicts can lead to serious problems, which can include running away, drug abuse, under-age pregnancy, attempted and actual suicide and illness, including eating disorders such as anorexia nervosa. Not all conflicts have serious repercussions and not all serious problems are caused by conflict with parents or others. Rayner (1986) also points out that a young person's adolescence brings the opportunity for his parents to be rejuvenated in mind – if not in body.

The peer group or friendship group is of prime importance in adolescence. 'Do I look OK?' doesn't mean 'do I look beautiful?' but 'do I conform to the norms of the peer group?' 'Is my skirt short enough, are the heels high enough, is the hair spiky enough, is the nose-ring in the right place, do the eight ear-rings in one ear conform to the peer group norms but still mark me out as "different"?' Many sets of relationships are being balanced at this stage; those with parents/guardians, those with teachers and/or employers, those with peers and those with whom the individual has a sexual, or potentially sexual, relationship. A fifth relationship, the relationship with oneself, is also vying for attention. The ways in which these relationships develop depend on all of the influences and other aspects of development considered earlier. The person who emerges, the young adult, is the subject of subsequent sections of this chapter.

Physical development

Adolescence is a time of rapid physical growth and development, more so than at any other period except infancy. Probably more so than infants, however, adolescents are very aware of the changes taking place.

The physical changes that an adolescent undergoes are not just ones of growth but ones of transformation associated with the eventual ability to reproduce and to work as an adult. They have many emotional implications. This period of adolescence usually begins with puberty, which occurs at different ages for different individuals and is generally earlier for girls than for boys. The physical development of adolescents can be viewed as falling into three types:

1 **General changes in body shape,** including changes in the way fat and muscle are distributed. In girls, fat is laid down around the hips and breasts, while boys generally lose fat and develop greater muscle mass than girls. The strength and stamina of both sexes greatly increases and they become more greatly differentiated as adolescence progresses.

2 **A growth spurt** occurs in adolescence between the ages of eleven and sixteen. There is usually a rapid increase in height.

3 **There is continuing development of the reproductive system**, with changes in the level of sex hormones in the bloodstream, giving rise to internal and external changes. For boys these changes include a deepening of the voice, enlargement of the penis and the growth of pubic and body hair. For girls the changes include enlargement of the breasts, growth of pubic hair and the onset of menstruation (periods). Menstruation can begin at any age from about ten to sixteen but is usually at around thirteen in the UK. This period of sexual development is known as puberty.

Emotional development

A lot of people would say that the word 'emotional' is quite an apt one to apply to adolescence but would question the relevance of the word 'development'. Is all that storm and tempest really development? Well, yes, it is all part of life's rich, wondrous and varied passage. For many people it is not a period of great trauma and upheaval, although it is certainly a period of change and transition. Children enter and adults emerge (although usually continuing to be adolescent in some aspects of their lives), and a lot of emotional development goes on in between. What is the nature of this development?

The continuing development of a sense of self is one of the main issues of this stage. The adolescent is quite intensely focused on this self, and behaviour is often rather egocentric. The main question is 'who am I?', a question which people often continue to ask themselves throughout their lives. If you look at Seonaid's description of herself, aged eleven, on page 120, she is not really asking questions about who she is but is content to describe herself in terms of where she lives, her interests, her parents, her average size. By sixteen she's writing some quite powerful poetry:

> I feel rejection
> And search for my world
> In a mild way which does not make
> It obvious to them
> Who I really am.
> Maybe one day
> I will be happy
> Not in the way that they believe they are
> But in a way purer than the water I drink
> Where I'm doing what I want
> And don't care what they think
> Because then I'll be at ease with me
> And maybe then they'll see
> That it's not important to be smart and rich
> Because satisfaction is what matters to me
> I could be in the gutter
> And have people mutter
> 'What a waste of a life'
> As they wander by
> But I'd smile to myself
> And think secret thoughts
> At least I am happy and true to my heart
> I don't pretend to be something I'm not.

Activity Seonaid's poem

What aspects of adolescent emotional development are evident in the above poem?

In answering the activity question you may have mentioned the focus on feelings (in this case feelings of rejection), searching for something, a separation from 'them', who are presumably adults, a focus on 'I' (where I'm doing what I want), a rejection of what she considers to be adult ways and an attitude of 'I don't care what they think'. There's an emphasis on being honest to yourself and on not pretending to be something you're not. Not every adolescent has all of these feelings or feels them so intensely but most adolescents have some of them. There is a lot of questioning, which is working towards resolution of what many theorists see as the identity crisis of adolescence.

Connected with the developing sense of self are issues related to sexuality. Part of the 'who am I' questioning is also about being heterosexual, homosexual or of other sexual orientation. Some people find themselves intensely dissatisfied with the conventional options open to them. Many adolescents and young adults experiment with aspects of sexuality until they resolve the conflicts within them. Some adult problems are associated with a lack of resolution of the question of sexuality because it comes into conflict with other aspects of themselves or with the society in which they live.

Separation, both physical and emotional, is one of the aspects of growth and also an issue of anxiety for many adolescents. They desperately want to be independent but many, especially if they continue into further or higher education, are financially dependent on their parents. The nuclear family is less and less important, as partnerships, friendships and sexual relationships increase in importance, yet the family is still a source of financial support, and emotional support in times of crisis. The back and forth, away from and towards the family, away from and sometimes back to (and sometimes away from again) long-established relationships, the contradictions and a move towards their resolution, are all part of adolescence.

There are particular issues in relation to emotional development and establishing an identity in adolescence for those who belong to various ethnic and/or cultural groups, for children who are 'looked after' in children's homes or by foster parents, and for children who are adopted. Can you think of others for whom adolescence may present particular problems?

You may have thought of adolescents with a disability, those who are or have parents who are gay, lesbian or transvestite, those who come from abusive or unstable environments. Although a whole book could be devoted to the issues surrounding all of these groups there just isn't the time or the space here to do the subject justice. Instead two short case studies are presented below for you to consider and discuss.

CASE STUDY

Cathy

Cathy is fifteen. She is looked after in a small, homely children's home. She has had a very difficult emotional life. Her mother was a lone parent and a drug addict who died when Cathy was four years old. Even at the age of four, Cathy was showing signs of disruptive behaviour and an inability to make friends. At the age of six, she was adopted by a loving couple who had one daughter of their own, five years older than Cathy. The adoption was a disaster, with Cathy and her adoptive mother in constant conflict. Cathy had temper tantrums for no apparent reason, used abusive language and didn't seem able to respond to any kind of love or affection shown to her. The adoption completely broke down a year ago and Cathy came to the children's home at that time.

CASE STUDY

Nadia

Nadia Ahmed appears in the case study in Chapter 7. She is eighteen, her parents were born in Pakistan but she was born in Edinburgh. She is part of an extended Muslim family. She is expected to help out at home and with the family shop, and to speak Urdu with her grandmother. Her family hopes that when she marries she will marry within her own faith and community. Nadia attends Edinburgh University where there are many Asian students. She is doing well there, wants to feel part of the social life of the university but is expected to come home at the end of the working day to help with domestic tasks.

Activity — *Cathy and Nadia*

Copy and complete the table below in the light of adolescent emotional development, stating in the first column the main factors which affect adolescents in general, and in the second and third columns the factors which may be additional or different for the two case study adolescents, Cathy and Nadia. The exercise can be repeated in terms of social, cognitive and other strands of development.

Most adolescents	Cathy	Nadia

Cognitive development

As adolescence progresses, each individual is usually moving towards more abstract thought. Thought is not confined to things which can be seen and recognised, but can be applied to unseen things. Ideas and reasoning about one problem can be transferred to similar problems, experiments in thinking can be performed not only with concrete objects but with ideas. The individual is capable of envisaging many possible consequences and not just one or two.

Linda

Sixteen-year-old Linda decides to get a part-time job. She thinks around the problem and initially says something like 'I'd like to work in Tesda'; she makes a phone call to Tesda; she is told that she has to get an application form from the job centre; she is told by the job centre that no application forms are available since Tesda doesn't have any vacancies at present. Linda doesn't stop there but now starts to think more widely around the problem. She realises that she has to use a lot of different strategies and has to keep persisting until she gets a job. She has to telephone, visit, answer advertisements, ask her friends and, if she still wants to work in Tesda eventually, has to keep contacting the job centre until they have application forms. This strategy works. She hears through a friend that people are needed to serve in a café. She takes on that job and works there until she eventually gains employment at Tesda. A pre-adolescent child would have been capable of thinking it would be good to get a job at Tesda but it is unlikely that he or she would have had the ability to see alternative avenues, conduct the experiments needed to find out about how to arrive at an alternative solution or have the persistence to get to Tesda in the end.

Some other aspects of cognitive development in adolescence are the ability to understand the impact of the past on the present and of the present on the future, to begin questioning the views of adults which have previously been accepted (arguments with parents, 'debates' with teachers), to look behind the obvious in books and paintings to appreciate that there is often more than is explicitly stated about life or the world. Adolescents do not confine themselves to progression in logical thought but also progress in creative thought. Some adolescents develop immense creative ability through making imaginative leaps. One famous example is Einstein who, at sixteen, imagined himself as a particle of light travelling away from a planet. This sparked off his thoughts towards what eventually became known as the theory of relativity. Many young people begin to see the world with new eyes at this age and to make creative and imaginative leaps in the production of masterpieces. If you look at work produced for Standard Grade and Higher Art, the combination of analytical thought and creative leaps of imagination is often quite staggering.

Not all adolescents progress at the same rate or in the same way in their cognitive development. Some have reached a stage of analytical thought well before adolescence, some never really reach it, some don't reach it until well into adult life, and some are slow starters but suddenly have an intellectual growth spurt somewhere between age fifteen and twenty-two. This is one of the reasons why some people who do only moderately well in Standard Grades end up gaining first-class honours degrees at university.

Cultural development

> *adolescence begins in biology and ends in culture . . .*
>
> (Herbert, 2002, p. 355)

Whatever the turbulence and search for identity in adolescence, the family, the school and other social institutions continue to be of critical importance in the cultural development of young people:

> *It is exceptional for teenagers to feel torn between the two 'worlds' of parents and peers, certainly on the more important issues of life. There are most likely to be differences of opinion on minor issues such as hairstlyle, fashion, social habits and privileges, where parental views are likely to be rejected in favour of the standards of friends. Where major issues are concerned, it seems that only a minority of adolescents radically depart from their parents' views.*
>
> (Herbert, 2002, p. 357)

There is another viewpoint that many more than a minority of adolescents depart quite radically from their parents' views and culture, and where this happens it can cause difficulties in many areas of development. Sometimes this is associated with failure to do well at school. If a young person sees school and education negatively, this deprives them of a major influence on cultural development. For vulnerable young people who lack stable family backgrounds, such failure may constitute a double deprivation and they may be led into 'cultures' that affect quite detrimentally other areas of development. This is dealt with in more detail in Chapter 5.

Spiritual development

In adolescence young people often think about ultimate questions: the meaning of life, whether or not God exists, who they are and want to be; they are concerned with being true to themselves while still trying to find out who that self is; they are challenging parental and cultural beliefs and testing rules. All this is part of spiritual development.

Activity   *Spiritual development*

Look again at the poem written by Seonaid. What aspects of spiritual development can you identify?

Creative activities can provide opportunities for spiritual development. Poetry provides a medium for expressing feelings and thoughts; similarly art, drama, dance and other forms of expression can be used. Building on the giftedness of everyone, finding the things that interest them, that they enjoy doing, who they are, can also have a spiritual dimension through recognising these things as part of the essential self and necessary for self-esteem.

Table 3.5 Summary of general pattern of development: adolescence

Social	Physical	Emotional	Cognitive	Cultural	Spiritual
Moving further away from the family	How the body changes	Developing sense of self	How sense is made of the world	Questioning cultural assumptions	Developing own beliefs; spiritual searching for self
• Influences of emotional factors • Sexual attraction • Changing relationship with parents • Importance of peer group • Changing roles	• Rapid development/ growth spurt; profound physical changes • Development of reproductive system/puberty – influence of hormones • Changes in body shape • Growth towards adult body shape • Health risks can arise from behavioural issues e.g. anorexia, drug use etc.	• Change and trans-ition • Focus upon self/identity/ feelings/who am I? • Issues related to difference e.g. ethnicity, sexuality • Separation • Extreme emotions; often feel misunderstood • Erikson: Identity vs role confusion	• More abstract and creative thought; understanding impact of past on present, present on future • Presenting arguments • Questioning views of adults • Thinking beyond conventional limits; use of reasoning • Importance of education	• Increasing awareness of other cultures • Questioning and making choices • Increasing influence of friends • Culture reflected in behaviour, dress and activities • Dealing with conflicting cultures	• Understanding other perspectives • Challenging parental beliefs • Testing rules • Need for personal space • Search for identity

Adulthood

Read the case studies of the MacDonald and Ahmed families in Chapter 7, where several adults make an appearance: Linda and Joe MacDonald, Aisha Bibi and Tanveer Ahmed, among others. Below are another two short case studies.

CASE STUDY

Fiona and Alistair

Fiona and Alistair are in their early thirties. They are married. Alistair works as an engineer, and at the moment Fiona, who was a teacher and hopes to be a teacher again, is at home looking after their new baby son, Christopher, and his brother, three-year-old Sam.

CASE STUDY

Alex

Alex is a journalist in his mid-forties. He lives alone and has never married but plays an active role as uncle to his four nieces and nephews. His career is very, very important to him and he loves his work, the unpredictability of it and the fact that he is frequently sent on assignments abroad. He is writing a book about motorbikes in his spare time. He has a boyfriend who is a doctor with whom he has a long-standing sexual relationship. They have considered living together but decided to maintain independent households, especially as they lead such different lives. They do, however, spend holidays together every year.

All of these people are adults but their differing experiences reflect the enormous range of factors to be considered in this section. The period of adulthood examined here is from about 21 to 65, though some people much younger than 21 are functioning as adults, some people of 26 still appear to be experiencing adolescence and some people over 65 are not really older adults but are performing as adults in their middle years. Rayner (1986) emphasises that features of adolescence recur throughout adulthood:

> However, if 'adolescing', with its regression, romance and madness, is not kept alive throughout our lives then we neither have the means to change ourselves nor can we provide the environment for others to change. We become either very dull, shrunken people unable to face crisis, or arthritic martinets, self-satisfied with power and unable to be either humble or flexible.

Social development

The major factors involved in emotional development are also those which influence social development. Forming and maintaining intimate relationships, including friendships, the changing roles brought about by parenthood, work and partnership, and the social networks which individuals form as a result of these roles and relationships, are all part of the pattern of social as well as emotional development. Rather than repeat most of the above section in social terms, the subject of *work* is discussed as a link among all aspects of development.

> *It is a great matter for a man to find his own line, and keep to it. You get along faster on your own rail . . .*

(Janet Aitken in the Glasgow School of Art's magazine, 1893 – 'man' here is an all-encompassing term for 'person'; quoted in Jones, 1990)

The case study below demonstrates some of the links among various aspects of development.

CASE STUDY

Stuart and Eileen

Stuart and Eileen are both senior care workers in a residence for people with sensory and learning disability. They both enjoy their work and, in their desire to further their knowledge and career prospects, they signed up for an evening class in social sciences. They didn't know that they had both signed up for the same course until they met at the first class. They got into the habit of going for a drink after the class and often discussed homework if they were on the same shift. Before long they were seeing each other for social events at the weekend, discovered that they shared similar ways of looking at life and the world and eventually decided that they would like to live together.

This case study shows how work can link social, physical, emotional, cognitive, cultural and spiritual development. The work is care work, which is both a practical and a cognitive process; through mutual interests, empathetic relationships developed which were physical, cognitive, social, emotional, cultural and spiritual in nature.

Work is one of the key sources of self-esteem for the individual and one way in which individuals identify themselves. If someone is asked to describe him/herself, the kind of work done is usually one of the ways in which the individual wishes to be known. In the short case studies at the beginning of this chapter and the longer ones at the end of the book you will see that Alex's role as a journalist is very important to him, Alistair is an engineer, Fiona was a teacher, Senga is a care assistant, Tanveer is an accountant and Aisha works for a voluntary organisation. All of these work roles are bound up with other aspects of the individual's emotional life to promote self-esteem and develop identity. Self-esteem and identity are part of emotional development. Work, though, is also a social role and can be a source of friendship and partnership. In this sense it is also part of social development. Since work has the potential to contribute so much to development it is understandable that the loss of it may cause more problems than just the lack of a wage. It can have an impact on emotional and social life, as well as other aspects of development.

Work is usually a term used to refer to paid employment, but many people do work for which they receive neither pay nor recognition. Unlike unemployment, this can provide a clear role and a strong sense of purpose and worth. Anne Redpath, a Scottish artist born in Galashiels, makes the point that for many years she devoted herself to her family and her home, rather than to painting, and that this was just as relevant to her as any other kind of work. She says:

> *I put everything I had into house and furniture and dresses and good food and people. All that's the same as painting really, and the experience went back into art when I began painting again.*

(Long, 1996)

This passage shows that there can be links between paid work and the work of being at home, and that the one has great relevance for the other. The experience of running a household and bringing up children does go back into and enrich later work experience, yet it is so often undervalued by employers and often people themselves.

Parenthood illustrates the links among all aspects of development. In terms of social development it provides the social roles of mother and father, it creates social as well as emotional bonds between parents and their children. Parenthood also provides networks with other parents through meeting at such places as playgroups, health centres and schools. It is often a source of change in social relationships and roles. As you read the following sections examine parenthood in terms of each aspect of development.

Physical development

Until adulthood, physical development has been a prime force influencing social and cognitive development. In adults cognitive, emotional and social forces influence physical change, development and health to a much greater degree than in earlier life. There are some physical changes, however, which are characteristic of adult life, some associated with younger adult life and others associated with middle adult life. By adulthood physical development, including sexual development, is virtually complete, though sexual identity in terms of heterosexuality, homosexuality or other sexual orientation may not be. Young adulthood is usually the healthiest period of life, when people are at peak fitness. Footballers, for example, usually play at their best in their twenties; athletes are then also at their peak. Serious illness in young adulthood is quite unusual, with the greatest threat to health being accidents, especially road traffic accidents among men in their late teens and early twenties.

> *Young male drivers are the most likely to be involved in road accidents –*
> *In 2005, the number of car drivers involved in accidents represented 4.0 per thousand of the population aged 17 and over, but 9.4 per thousand of the total population of men aged 17–22.*

(Scottish Executive, 2006b)

> *. . . the need for speed, perhaps it's a male testosterone thing – I'm not sure – but I need speed . . . , I need the feeling, the buzz, the adrenaline . . .*

(www.bbc.co.uk, accessed12.08.05)

Activity   *Age of peak fitness*

Find out the ages of ten key players in the Scottish premier football league or another very active sport of your choice. Calculate the average age by adding all the ages together and dividing by ten. This should give you some indication of the age of peak fitness.

Pregnancy and childbirth are among the major physical events for young women. These have enormous implications for their emotional and social lives. The age at which women have their first child is on average much later than it was 20 years ago, though the number of teenage pregnancies has also risen. There are now possibilities for women who would previously have been unable to have children to receive fertility treatment. Pregnancy and childbirth are still risky events in terms of health, though both maternal and infant mortality are at their lowest levels ever. In 2005 only 4 deaths were recorded in Scotland as a result of complications of pregnancy and childbirth. There were 123 child deaths in the peri-natal period, down from 230 in 1987 (NHS Scotland, 2005).

As adulthood progresses, the individual's way of life determines to some extent the physical changes that take place. Many people from their thirties, forties or fifties onwards gain weight and lose physical fitness, but these gains and losses are neither universal nor inevitable. Lifestyle is a major influence, and a combination of diet, exercise and low stress levels can combine to promote good physical health throughout the adult years. Low alcohol consumption and no smoking also contribute to the maintenance of good health. There is some inevitable loss of speed of reaction and of muscularity as adulthood proceeds. This is why winners of the Tour de France, for example, are not usually over 30 years of age. On the other hand, stamina often increases with age and compensates for some of the physical losses. Mountaineers such as Chris Bonnington continued to conquer high peaks well into their fifties, and Beryl Burton, a woman cyclist, continued to compete in 100-mile races into her forties.

One major physical life event affecting women in middle adulthood is the menopause. This is caused by a decrease in levels of the hormone oestrogen, which leads to a cessation of menstruation and the ability to produce children. It does not lead to a cessation of sexual activity, though levels do usually decrease considerably for both men and women as young adulthood gives way to middle age. Like adolescence, menopause can be a time of great emotional upheaval, and a time when women reassess their lives, their relationships and their sense of self and purpose, particularly if they no longer have dependent children to care for.

Emotional development

The self continues to emerge throughout the adult years and is presented with many life experiences and events which contribute to this process. Work, partnership (marriage and other sexual relationships), friendships, parenthood, sexuality, transitions, crises, achievements and interests all play a part. The emerging self is constantly faced with choices and questions which influence the course of this development and the resulting adult identity. Women in their thirties, for example, may be asking themselves 'should I have a baby?' or 'should I have another baby?' or 'should I go back to work, change my career, change my partner, am I happy with him or her?' Some periods of adulthood can be very emotionally stressful. Even quite positive events such as marriage and holidays can create tension. A sufficient number of tense or stressful events, or one extremely stressful one, can lead to a crisis. Usually in a crisis the individual's normal coping mechanisms do not work very well, and support from others may be of vital importance. It is quite interesting for you to look at your own level of stress. One indicator of this is the scale devised by Holmes and Rahe (1967) and adapted by Powell (1997). Do not become too concerned if you score very highly (i.e. in excess of 300). You may just thrive on change and/or be very well supported. You are not necessarily in crisis.

Activity Stress and life events

Look at the list of the major life events listed below. Read through them and circle the major life events which you have experienced in the last twelve months. Once you have done this, add up your score, which will give you an approximate measure of how many life changes you have experienced in the past year and how vulnerable you may be to stress-related problems.

1	Death of your spouse or life partner	100
2	Divorce or separation	75
3	Major illness or injury	70
4	Loss of a job	70
5	Problems with the law/imprisonment	70
6	Death of someone close	60
7	Marital reconciliation	60
8	Retirement	60
9	Illness in your immediate family	50
10	Marriage or moving in with partner	50
11	Moving house or major renovation	50
12	Gaining new family member through birth or adoption	50
13	Pregnancy	45
14	Increase in the number of arguments or disagreements with partner	45
15	Large mortgage, loan or debt	45
16	Changing jobs or a new job	45
17	Unexpected accident or trauma	45
18	Changes at work/increased demands	35
19	Outstanding personal achievement or promotion	35
20	Caring for an elderly or sick relative or friend	35
21	Problems with relatives, family, friends or neighbours	35

Activity   *Stress and life events* continued

22	Financial worries	35
23	Examinations, extra study or having to speak in public	30
24	Changes in social activities	30
25	Changes in recreational activities	30
26	Children going or 'growing' away	30
27	Premenstrual syndrome or menopause	30
28	Starting a new relationship	30
29	Going on holiday	20
30	Family gatherings, e.g. Christmas	20

How to interpret your score

Over 280 (high vulnerability): You have experienced an unusually high number of stressful events in the last year. Illness is not inevitable, however, as a result of such events. Your personality and ability to cope will determine how well you react.

130–280 (moderate vulnerability): You have experienced a number of stressful events in the last year which could increase your risk of stress-related illnesses. The more you know about such events and the likely effects on you, the better prepared you will be for similar events in the future.

Below 130 (low vulnerability): You have experienced few stressful events in the last year and your life seems fairly settled. However, if you are aware of how affected you may be by major events you will be better prepared for future changes.

Most of the events on this scale are either **transitions** or losses. See Chapter 4 for a much fuller discussion of these; only brief consideration is given to them here. Two factors which are important in coping with transition and loss are the degree of support which is available to the individual and the individual's coping mechanisms. Part of emotional development is to find *positive* ways to deal with the many transitions and losses which adult life presents. If this is not achieved, either because the individual has not found ways to cope or because of lack of support or because the level of stress or crisis is just too great, or a combination of all these things, the consequences for psychological and physical health can be severe. Table 3.6 shows a comparison of two possible routes to adjustment in adulthood.

Table 3.6 Adjustment to transition and loss

Positive adjustment	Negative adjustment
Excited about life	Anxious
Keen to seize opportunities	Dissatisfied
At home with self	Feelings of inadequacy
Happy about the future	Feelings of guilt
Well supported by friends and family	Doesn't feel well supported
Able to take transition in stride	Very stressed by transition
Works through loss by facing it and grieving	Experiences prolonged depression as a result of loss

Activity   *Emotional adjustment*

The emotional adjustment of adults to different events in their lives depends on many factors. From the above account and your own experience, list at least six of these factors.

You may have thought of: past history, heredity, level of support, personality and attitude, state of physical health, stage of life.

Support has been mentioned several times as important in adult emotional development. Where does this support come from? One important source is through relationships of intimacy with partners, spouses, friends and relatives. These relationships of intimacy are, at their best, reciprocal, satisfying and a source of stability from which the individual can face the outside world and its challenges. They also contribute to the individual's identity. The roles of partner, husband, wife, friend, daughter, son, etc. all become ways in which the individual identifies him/herself in the outside world. Identity is also enhanced through the creative roles which the individual plays through parenthood, work and/or creative pursuits.

Parenthood is one major life transition which brings change in relationships, lifestyle, roles and responsibilities. Ideally for most people this experience is shared with someone they love and to whom they have made a meaningful, lasting and intimate commitment. This is not always the case, however.

Sexuality influences many aspects of development in adulthood, including emotional development. We have seen statements from Seonaid as a twelve year old and during adolescence. Here she is again, aged 28 and embarking on a degree course, describing the impact of her sexuality.

Seonaid

... as a teenager I realised I was gay, which added to the confusion of who I was and where I belonged ... I had a large group of friends at school but always felt different, never understanding the reasoning for this. Eventually I realised the root cause and kept it secret through fear of being discriminated against ... Lack of awareness of homosexuality increased my discomfort with my own identity, and confused my expectations of those around me. Gradually I became more comfortable and began to tell people, which increased my confidence and self-acceptance. However, it was a long process which was easier around strangers than people I knew. Whenever I began to feel settled in a place, I moved and re-invented myself somewhere new. This constant re-establishment provided insights into various other areas of life, which broadened my understanding of what makes different people act and react in certain ways. From these experiences my eyes were also opened to hardship and suffering, not only my own, but of those around me ... Being part of a minority group provides greater empathy and understanding of those in a similar position. The feelings of uncertainty and unsettlement which disadvantaged people experience, as well as knowledge of the damage discrimination can do, become a part of the personal value base. It also provides a genuine belief that everyone is equal and deserves the same chance in life. I was fortunate enough to meet a partner who encouraged me to recognise the lessons I had learned and put them to use ... I applied for several jobs in the care sector and was employed to work with disadvantaged adults ... Although the job was physically demanding and mentally draining, five minutes of positivity from a service user could overshadow an otherwise disastrous shift. Empowering a person to undertake tasks they were previously incapable of, and seeing the joy this could bring them, made it all worthwhile. It also allowed me to develop an understanding of people with severe learning disabilities, and realise that they are people the same as anyone else, with likes and dislikes, and opinions and ambitions ...

Cognitive development

In adulthood cognitive/intellectual development is associated with knowledge and skills gained through further and higher education, work, hobbies and interests. The application and development of knowledge in relation to everyday life, especially through parenthood, and the passing on of knowledge and skills to other people, are also of importance. Individuals make choices about cognitive development and also differ in the opportunities open to them. Some people see leaving school as the end of their need to develop intellectually, though many feel the frustration and stagnation of this in later years and return to some form of education and/or training. Others lack the opportunities to develop to their maximum potential. Cognitive development is, as a consequence, impaired or delayed. For some adults the intellectual demands of partnership and/or parenthood provide an additional or alternative route to cognitive development and they direct their thinking and learning towards making a success of home and/or family life.

Assuming that one or more of the above avenues of cognitive development is available, most adults show a fairly steady or improving level of ability throughout their young and middle adult years. For example, in a long-term study by Schaie (1994), mathematical ability and verbal comprehension only began to decline after the age of 67. Many adults show improving ability on tests of vocabulary, comprehension and general knowledge, especially if their everyday lives present opportunities for learning or they purposefully pursue intellectually stimulating interests, read a lot and/or travel.

If you look back at the case studies elsewhere in this chapter you will see that the people discussed there have developed cognitively in many different ways in adulthood. For example Fiona and Alistair have undergone training for their respective careers. They have also embarked on parenthood through which they can pass on their own learning and develop the skills of child care. Sconaid's cognitive development has been influenced by her sexuality, and she has used her experience of dislocation and discomfort to think about the needs of others and eventually to embark on a degree course.

> ### Activity *Cognitive development*
>
> Choose two of the adults mentioned at the beginning of this section (pp. 131,132). State how you think they may have developed cognitively during their adult lives, and consider the factors which have contributed to this.

Cultural development

By the time people reach adulthood they will have acquired many aspects of a cultural identity. They will speak in a language, and often a dialect, of others who share the way they do things; they will have customs that they follow, e.g. in relation to marriage or partnership, childbirth, celebrations such as Ramadan, Diwali and Chinese New Year; they may or may not be established geographically in a particular place with an associated cultural identity; they may have tastes in music, art and literature that reflect their cultural heritage and their cultural preferences; there will be agreed norms and behaviours that they will expect of themselves and of others with whom they interact.

> ### Activity *Cultural development*
>
> Identify five aspects of your own life and identity that reflect your cultural development. Contrast these with those of someone with a very different cultural identity.

Spiritual development

> *Spiritual wellbeing, feeling at ease with the essential self, happens when people are fulfilling their potential as individuals and as human beings. They are at ease with themselves at a deep level . . .*
>
> (Bradford Interfaith Centre, 2002)

Adults who have had the opportunity to develop spiritually, to think and make decisions about what is important to them and what they believe in, to be fulfilled and to integrate this into the way they lead their lives, are likely to have a sense of spiritual well-being. It is unlikely that their lives are free from difficulty, but if they have established firm spiritual foundations they are more likely to have an optimistic outlook and ability to cope in times of stress. People continue to need personal space to think and reflect. Questioning is likely to continue throughout life but during adulthood beliefs are likely to become more firmly established and to be reinforced by the choice of friendships, partner and groups to which the individual belongs. Creative activities and an appreciation of the creations of others, also provide opportunities for fulfilment and reflection and can play a part in spiritual development. All of this contributes to enabling people to become themselves, the person they want to be. This is of course a very optimistic view, but something which spiritual development at least gives us the opportunity to strive for.

Figure 3.5 Raft race: some activities meet social, physical, emotional, cognitive, cultural and spiritual needs in one go!

Table 3.7 Summary of general pattern of development: adulthood

Social	Physical	Emotional	Cognitive	Cultural	Spiritual
Relationships	How the body changes	Developing sense of identity	How sense is made of the world	Increasing confidence in cultural identity	Sense of self, wholeness and balance
• Intimate relationships / partnerships • Roles and changes in role • Social networks – may experience stressful periods e.g. mid-life transition • Effects of poverty and discrimination • Parenthood and responsibility	• Importance of cognitive, emotional and social factors • Peak fitness in young adulthood; stamina increases • Pregnancy, childbirth and menopause • Relationship between lifestyle and health • Often loss of speed / increase in bulk	• Influences of work, partnership, friends, parenthood • Transitions, crises and achievements • Importance of support • Roles and identity • Erikson: Intimacy vs isolation (20s) Generativity vs stagnation (late 20s to 50s)	• Different choices and opportunities • Often improving level of ability and creativity • Applying knowledge to work, parenthood and other life situations • Cognitive skills and ability to make moral judgements increase in complexity	• Language and ethnicity as part of cultural identity • Passing culture to next generation • May accept other cultures • Belong to institutions that reflect cultural beliefs • Environment reflects culture	• For well-being need to feel fulfilled and integrated • Gives direction and value • Beliefs more firmly established • Need for personal space to think • Sense of self

Older adulthood

The young photographer said he hoped that he would see his subject the following year. 'I don't see why not – you look in pretty good health to me,' replied Jeanne Calment on the occasion of her 120th birthday.

(Anon, 2007)

In this section a conscious effort is made to get away from the 'all doom and gloom' view of old age. Many older people, even those with illnesses and disabilities, do lead rich and fruitful lives. A class of care students was asked whom they thought were good examples of famous older adults. Here are their suggestions: Sean Connery, the Queen, Jimmy Saville, Dot Cotton, Nelson Mandela, Omar Sharif, Richard Wilson and Clint Eastwood. Their teachers added Paul Newman, Shirley Bassey, Michael Parkinson, Jane Fonda, and Jeanne Calment quoted above, who rode a bike until she was 100. You can probably think of other examples of older people who are active and content in old age. More opportunities are available than ever for older people to learn, to participate in exercise, to live in better health. Relative poverty is, unfortunately, still a problem for many, and efforts need to be made to maximise benefit uptake, for example, and to ensure that those who are young adults now make adequate financial provision for when they are old.

Social development

The influences and events of earlier life are important in the social development of older adults, but are not necessarily determining factors. For some this is a time of rejuvenation, increased social contacts, more friends and time to pursue social activities. Friendship plays a major part in the lives of many older adults. Ishii-Kuntz (1990) found that

> *older people's satisfaction with life has little relationship with the quantity or quality of their contact with the younger members of their own family, but shows a strong correlation to the quantity and quality of their interaction with friends.*

The functions of friendship in later life can be summed up through the three As: aid, affect and affirmation. Friends give and receive help, provide love and affirm people's self concepts. This demonstrates a link between emotional and social well-being.

The initial average increase in social contacts tends to diminish in older adulthood as contact with friends can be lost through death and ill-health. Unless an older adult or others such as care workers and family members make a conscious effort to maintain outside links, isolation can result, which for many is a very depressing experience. Some isolation is aggravated by the restrictions placed on elderly people by low income, though facilitating claims for appropriate benefit entitlements can go some way towards alleviating this. Empowerment can sometimes only be gained through access to cash.

Here is an example from Slater (1995), which relates to the social lives of some older adults:

> *Police had to be called to Highwood Court old people's social club . . . after neighbours complained about the noise coming from a Karaoke session.*
>
> *Mrs Harman now prefers the company of people her own age who can talk about the same things . . .*

Other older adults may enjoy attendance at the community centre, going line dancing, step and tone classes, going to university or college, working in an allotment or going to the library. Heim's (1990) research indicated that, although physical confidence decreases with age, social confidence increases.

Bee and Mitchell (1984) sum up social development as follows. From ages 65 to 75 there is:

> *Usually a maintenance of social contacts, particularly with family. Friends are important here especially for maintaining life satisfaction. Little evidence of any withdrawal or disengagement. Retirement, which occurs during this time for most adults, appears to cause relatively little trauma for most.*

From age 75 on:

> *There appears to be some social disengagement, at least for some older adults, during this period, although most elderly adults continue to see their children and other family members with some regularity and spend time with friends.*

Physical development

> *The really cool thing is that even nonagenarians who have lost muscle strength can get it back . . . we're reaching old age in better and better shape . . .*
>
> (Anon, 2007)

When you first look at old age the evidence does seem somewhat negative: hearing, vision and balance tend to deteriorate, speed of movement decreases, skin loses elasticity and is more likely to wrinkle, there is usually some hair loss and hair pigment loss so that most 'old people' have grey or white hair. The major organs of the body deteriorate, but much more slowly than you probably think. This is all balanced to some extent by fewer physical demands. The physical effects of aging can be ameliorated by exercise, attitude and nutrition as well as inherited genetic characteristics and other environmental influences. When you actually look at older adults the variation is enormous. One person of 80 may be confined to a wheelchair or able only to walk very short distances with a zimmer; she may have a multitude of minor ailments; another will be cycling to play cards with her friends and ploughing up and down the lanes at the swimming pool three times a week. He or she may have several minor ailments but when asked about his or her health will say I'm fine . . . and mean it. There are those who still have an active sex life into their seventies and eighties.

On the positive side, then, gains in health, nutrition and hygiene in recent years mean that fewer people are dying prematurely and that those who do survive into their eighties are generally healthier than they would have been ten years ago. People are living longer in general, with an increase of 14% in the number of people over the age of 75 since the mid 1990s. In 2005 19% of the residents of Scotland were over 65 (General Register Office for Scotland, 2005). A large majority of these people are able to live rich, full lives with health which is at least moderately good. The negative view of old age results not from the effects of primary aging, which is slow and gradual, but from the results of secondary aging resulting from disease, lack of exercise and such pursuits as excessive drinking and smoking. People who continue to be fit and active can usually expect to reap the benefits in a healthier old age.

Emotional development

There is an emotional roller-coaster in older age: down for bereavement and loss, up for becoming a grandparent; down for retirement for some, up for retirement for others; down when a child gets divorced, up for a sense of contentment; down when ill-health occurs, up if health is maintained; down when a family member or friend moves away, up when new friends and activities are gained; down for dependence, up for independence. Some of the losses of old age can have profound effects of either a short- or long-term nature. Loss and bereavement are fully considered in Chapter 4 and are therefore not discussed here. One major transition of old age which has both emotional and social consequences is that of retirement. For many people a part of self-image and identity is their paid or unpaid work. Paid work usually ceases at around 60 to 65 and this, for some people, results in a loss of both status and self-esteem. This is to some extent a reflection of negative attitudes of society to retired people, but there can be compensations. Some people see retirement not as a loss but as an opportunity.

CASE STUDY

Alan

Alan has been employed all of his working life in a brewery but what he had always really wanted to do was to have a beautiful garden. He had always kept his fairly large garden neat and tidy but had never been able to devote much time to it. When he retired he was able to pursue his lifelong passion for plants. He bought a greenhouse, grew some unusual varieties of plant from seed and entered horticultural competitions. He was so successful that within a year of retirement he exhibited some begonia plants in a competition, gaining first prize.

A less positive reaction to retirement is quoted in Rayner (1986):

> *Mrs F went on working in a pub until she was over 70, when she slipped and bruised herself one day. She lost her job through being off sick. She recovered quite quickly but never went back to work . . . she slowly became quiet and apathetic . . . She usually shuffled about the house in boots and several layers of clothing.*

> ### Activity   *Attitudes to retirement*
>
> Research the reactions to retirement of four older people whom you know or are able to talk to. Write a short account of their response in terms of consequences for their emotional lives, including self-esteem and self-concept. If you do not know anyone to talk to, look at relevant websites such as Age Concern.

In care settings it is most important that the way in which care is provided maintains or enhances self-esteem as far as possible. This means promoting empowerment and independence and minimising possible effects of institutionalisation, which can lead to what Goffman (1968) called 'mortification of self' and a state of learned helplessness. Learned helplessness is a decline in the desire and ability to do things beyond what may be expected in relation to a person's state of health. It usually occurs among people who 'give up' because other people won't let them do things or exercise any control over their own lives.

The emotional situation of older people from ethnic minorities deserves some special attention. Most people of Asian and Caribbean ancestry place a very high value on the care of their older people. If they have few or no supports, however, this can result in shame, loss and depression. Fenton (1987) illustrated this in relation to research in Bristol. Emotional problems may be compounded by isolation, poverty, racism and discrimination. Building positive self-esteem among this population can be a vital part of the care task.

There are many positive aspects to growing older. For many older adults, grandchildren can be a source of great joy and emotional satisfaction. Grandchildren come without many of the financial and emotional stresses of parenthood. Grandparents can enjoy their company and care in time-limited amounts, though they still need to work to create positive and fulfilling relationships. Slater (1995) writes about Mrs Patel, who loves the noise and laughter her grandchildren bring. Old age presents a sense of freedom for some older adults. Marjorie Dickens appears to have a great deal of emotional satisfaction in her present state:

> *I like it that I can do as I please, go where I want, and if I can afford it, buy what I want to, and eat what I want.*

(Slater, 1995)

Cognitive development

Slowing down is generally regarded as one of the features of the cognitive state of older adults. This is different from deterioration, for which there is scant evidence except in people experiencing specific illnesses such as Alzheimer's disease.

Here's an example quoted by Slater (1995):

> *I am a 73 year-old 'wrinkly' who, determined not to become a cabbage after retirement, took up the piano at the age of 70. So far I have obtained Grades 1 and 2 . . . Three days a week I work for an international trading company.*

My shorthand is still 120 plus and touch typing is second nature to me. I would like to take up other things but time is too demanding at present . . .

Longitudinal studies (which study the same people over a period of time) show little, if any, drop in mental ability with age (Schaie, 1994). Although there is some slowing down in the rate at which people process information and some decline in tasks which need speed, 'there is no sizable decline in memory, knowledge or the ability to learn'. It is interesting that on a test of 'obscure knowledge' older adults actually did better than younger ones. Do you know what 'deliticulate' means, or for what the Greek writer Antigorus was noted? Older people (over 65) scored higher on such items than younger persons (Slater, 1995).

Evidence from studies of older adults on adult learning courses (e.g. those run by the Open University or the University of the Third Age, which in 2006 has 164,000 students in the UK) illustrate that, although older people may be slower, they have more time to grasp things, persevere more than younger learners and bring wisdom and experience of life which compensates for a lack of speed (Slater, 1995). Birren and Fisher (1992) indicated a link between physical health, exercise and cognitive ability, concluding that exercise may help to ameliorate some of the slowing down in responses related to age. *Mastermind*, the long-lived test of knowledge on televison, was the subject of a study by Maylor (1994), who found that aging didn't seem to affect performance at all on the 'specialised subject' round and that older 'masterminds' did better on general knowledge.

While there are many adults who do show a decline in cognitive functioning in later life, as with physical aging there are enormous variations often related to such secondary causes as disease, lack of exercise and high alcohol consumption. In general, although there is a decline in the speed at which intellectual tasks can be performed, there is stability in solving the problems of everyday life and in knowledge and verbal comprehension.

Cultural development

Cultural development continues into old age and is usually a continuation of the developments experienced in earlier adulthood. As with all aspects of older adulthood, there are both losses and gains. The world and culture of work usually, though not always, become less important in old age, and other aspects of culture may become more important. Some older adults become grandparents and take on new roles which themselves vary from culture to culture. Different cultures have different attitudes and practices in relation to old age. Erikson (see Chapter 4) saw old age as a conflict between integrity and despair. Cultural attitudes of negativity to older adults in many Western countries can lead to despair for some people who can only see their aging process in terms of loss; for others, new roles and opportunities for cultural development lead them towards integrity.

Spiritual development

The positive integration of all aspects of development can lead to the positive spiritual outcomes of feeling respected, valued and worthwhile. There continues to be development in this aspect of life with older adults helped or hindered by their resolution of moral and spiritual dilemmas. They may be helped by their established beliefs towards a feeling of wholeness and balance. If they feel that they have achieved what they wanted to achieve they are likely to feel spiritual well-being, although cultural attitudes towards old age can affect aspects of spiritual development. Whatever the older adult's circumstances, there continues to be a need for opportunities to gain or maintain spiritual well-being through shared and individual activities and periods of peacefulness, respect for their beliefs and opportunities to practise them, and the provision of resources for creative and imaginative activities. A poetry group was one of the highlights of a day centre for older adults in which I once worked. Almost everyone participated either as a writer or as a listener and/or critic. For some people it was a major avenue for expressing feelings, the way they felt about life; they could say things in a poem that it was almost impossible to say through any other medium. Their spiritual development was enhanced in this way.

Figure 3.6 Phoenix and dragon ceiling panels. Kagyu Samye Ling Monastery and Tibetan Centre, Eskdalemuir was established in 1967 and is the first and largest centre of Buddhist wisdom and learning in the West.

Table 3.8 Summary of general pattern of development: older adulthood

Social	Physical	Emotional	Cognitive	Cultural	Spiritual
Relationships	How the body changes	Sense of self	How sense is made of the world	Behaviour, thoughts and beliefs of culture	Sense of self, wholeness and balance
• Friends, family and social networks or isolation • Changing roles e.g. due to retirement • Social confidence • Sometimes improvements in social life and networks – more time for these • Relationships across generations e.g. grandparenting	• Usually healthy; slow but gradual loss of abilities • Importance of exercise/diet • Enormous variation • Dealing with health crises • Greatly influenced by other aspects of development	• Identity issues often related to changing roles • Transition and loss e.g. bereavement • Influence of isolation, discrimination, poverty and their opposites • Changing sense of self • Erikson: Integrity vs despair	• Wisdom and experience • May be slower to grasp new things but usually able to compensate • Continuing ability to learn • Linked with health • Most people mentally alert but may be short-term memory loss	• Attitudes to old age culturally influenced • Maintenance of cultural identity • Culture of work replaced with other activities • Grandparent roles culturally varied • Cultural interests may be developed e.g. art, music	• Search for meaning in life is of great significance • Continuing need for wholeness and balance • Need opportunities for peace and reflection • Need to feel respected, valued and worthwhile • Belief may help process of ageing

SUMMARY

This chapter has encouraged you to look at development as a process which continues throughout life. You should now understand the meaning of behaviour and development along the strands of social, physical, emotional, cognitive, cultural and spiritual. The influences on development and behaviour have been considered, and throughout this chapter you have been encouraged to apply your learning to case study situations. The following areas have been covered in this chapter:

- the meaning of development and behaviour
- the strands of development and behaviour (social, physical, emotional, cognitive, cultural and spiritual)
- influences, including socialisation
- the nature/nurture debate
- development at different stages and ages, from 0–2 to older adulthood
- case studies which encourage you to apply your thinking.

The following activities, in common with all activities in this chapter, underpin the content of the Intermediate 1 and 2, and Higher Care syllabus.

Activity — *The MacDonalds and the Ahmeds*

Read the accounts below and then answer the questions which follow them. The people referred to are described in the case study in Chapter 7 (the MacDonalds and the Ahmeds).

Callum MacDonald, aged 2, is being taken round the supermarket by his Dad Joe. He seems to be quite enjoying himself looking at the objects on display and trying to tell his Dad what they all are. His Dad is ignoring him, intent on getting the shopping done as quickly as possible. At the checkout Callum starts to cry. His Dad is tired and tells him to shut up. The crying just gets louder and louder.

Nabeil Ahmed, aged 19, is very determined to lead an independent life, in spite of his disability. Today he has been to an art show with his fellow students. They are now all going out for a drink and he joins the group, especially pleased of the opportunity since he is very keen on one of the female students in the group. He chats to her over a drink and tells her of his plans to create a large collage of a forest. She tells him of her own plans to create a portfolio of paintings of people travelling on public transport. They arrange to meet again after college the next day.

Activity   *The MacDonalds and the Ahmeds* continued

Joey MacDonald, aged 13, has arranged to go to an evening football match with Fred, his befriender. This is usually an event they both look forward to. They arrange to meet at Joey's house at 5 p.m. But where is Joey? It is now 6 p.m., and kick-off isn't far off. At 6.15 Joey slouches into the house. Without saying anything he goes to his room and slams the door. When Fred asks what's the matter he's told by Joey to go away, that he hates Fred and hates football and wants to be left alone.

Faisal Ahmed, aged 23, has recently completed his studies as an accountant and works in the firm established by his now deceased uncle, Hassan Ahmed. He still lives at home and has just told his mother that he won't be home until late tonight. He is going out to dinner with his Scottish girlfriend whom he met at university. His parents object to this relationship, but his Aunt Aisha encourages it and tells them all not to make such a fuss. Faisal's mother Sira had envisaged that Faisal would marry within the Asian community and that he and his wife would live in the extended family household. Faisal has no such plans.

Fariha Ahmed, aged 80, is not feeling very happy this week and is making everyone feel miserable. She is going to Queen's View for respite care next week while the rest of the family go off to Cornwall for a holiday. She doesn't want to go to Cornwall and wouldn't want to travel such a long distance, but she feels rejected. What if the family don't want her back? Fariha still plays a useful role in the household, often cooking a meal, but she is rather domineering and has been used to having her own way all her life.

Choose two of the above situations and answer the following questions in relation to each one:

1   Copy and complete the table below for each person. Give two features of 'normal' development for a person of this age, for each strand, and below give features of development for each service user (they may be the same, or different from, the norm).

Strand:	Social	Physical	Emotional	Cognitive	Cultural	Spiritual
'Normal'						
development						
Person A						
Person B						

Activity   *The MacDonalds and the Ahmeds continued*

2   Identify four influences on the development and behaviour of each person, and state how you think each of these influences may affect two strands of development.

Suggested reading

Crawford, K. and Walker, J. (2003) *Social Work and Human Development*. Exeter: Learning Matters.
Demonstrates how knowledge of human development helps in establishing effective partnerships with people who use social work services.

Meggitt, C. (2006) *Child Development – An Illustrated Guide*. Oxford: Heinemann. Covers the development of children up to 16 years in a no-nonsense, descriptive and straight-forward way, with lots of summaries and pictures.

Papalia, D., Wendokos, S. and Feldman, R.D. (2001) *Human Development*, 8th edition. New York: McGraw Hill.
A comprehensive guidebook to human development, full of interesting international examples, which has relevance both to this chapter and Chapter 4.

Rogoff, B. (2003) *The Cultural Nature of Human Development*. Oxford: Oxford University Press.
This book focuses on how culture matters in human development and provides interesting examples from many diverse cultures.

Slater, R. (1995). *The Psychology of Growing Old*. Buckingham: Open University Press.
A very positive book about the challenge of later life.

Psychology for Care

Susan Gibb

> *Life can only be understood backwards; but it must be lived forwards.*
>
> (Kirkegaard, quoted in Peter, 1982)

This chapter will look at explanations of how people develop and change over time. You already have some understanding of the many factors which influence human development and behaviour from the previous chapter. It will now be useful to look at a range of explanations offered by three psychological approaches. By so doing you will come to understand more fully the process of human development and behaviour. This understanding will allow you to work with service users more effectively.

The chapter covers Psychology for Care, Intermediate 2 and Higher.

By the end of this chapter you should be able to:

★ define psychology and explain how it helps to understand human behaviour

★ describe three psychological approaches

★ describe key concepts from six psychological theorists

★ explain why people form attachments to others

★ explain how transition and loss affects individuals.

Introduction

Psychology is the scientific study of individuals. It is concerned with their behaviour and how their minds work. Human beings are very complex, and psychologists have developed a number of different approaches to explain and understand human development and behaviour. As you have learned in the previous chapter, people develop throughout life as a result of an interaction of factors – the genes they inherit and the environment in which they are brought up. This is known as the nature/nurture debate. Psychology is concerned with the examination of this interaction of factors.

One of the issues that should be kept in mind throughout this chapter is whether the psychological approaches that have been developed to understand behaviour in the Western world are universally applicable to other cultures and countries. Do people develop differently, in psychological terms, depending on the culture they are brought up in? The field of cross-cultural psychology investigates this question in order to test the generality of existing psychological theories, and it explores other cultures in order to find psychological variations.

Cross cultural psychology is the study of similarities and differences in individual psychological functioning in various cultural and ethnic groups, of the relationship between psychological variables and socio-cultural, ecological and biological variables, and of ongoing changes in these variables.

(Berry et al., 2002, p. 3)

If we look at biology, we can see that every human needs to eat, sleep and drink, but the way these needs are met vary enormously in different cultures: for example, in Spain it is usual to have a siesta after lunch. What about psychological factors such as perception, grieving, conformity, the development of a personality? Do these manifest themselves in different ways, depending on what culture you are raised in? An awareness of this issue is important to the discussion in this chapter, since Scotland is a racially and ethnically diverse country. If the psychological theories that care workers use are 'blind' to the experience of people from some countries or cultures, then there is a likelihood of people being misunderstood and negatively labelled.

How can you use psychology to help explain human development and behaviour in a care context? It may be useful to consider psychological ways of explaining human development and behaviour as 'tools' in a tool box. You will not use all the tools every time you want to understand or assess a client. Rather, you will choose one, or perhaps several, of the tools to help you understand your service users – their past experiences, their feelings or maybe their behaviour. The previous chapter looked at the variety of changes which take place throughout our lives. Psychology seeks to understand this process and explain why people develop and behave in the way they do. After examining the different psychological approaches in this chapter, you will be able to apply this knowledge to help you more fully understand the people with whom you work. During the assessment process, the psychological approaches may help you to understand some of the reasons why service users have developed in the way they have. The different approaches will help to explain the behaviour of service users, staff and carers. This informed approach to assessment should encourage more effective planning, and evaluation of the care process. It will also help you to be clearer about the best ways of working with service users.

Psychological approaches

Three psychological approaches will be considered, each of which takes a different view of human development (see Table 4.1). Each approach has been developed over many years, and has been used by many people involved in the care sector such as nurses, addiction workers, social workers, occupational therapists, psychiatrists, care workers and counsellors. There is not one particular approach which is always the best for every situation: each approach has strengths and weaknesses. In each situation, depending on

Table 4.1 Psychological approaches

Approach	Originated	Main ideas
Psychodynamic	1890s	- people are born with drives and instincts - early childhood experiences influence us throughout our lives - people's behaviour is influenced by unconscious forces
Cognitive/behavioural	1910s	- people are born a 'blank slate' - all behaviour is learned - thoughts are processed and can be changed
Humanistic	1950s	- people are born with a drive for growth - people are motivated to fulfil their potential - the whole person has to be understood, not just one aspect

the needs of the service user, the resources of the care organisation and the training and ability of the worker, a different approach will be more relevant and appropriate. In most cases, a combination of approaches will be used by the worker, depending on the situation.

This chapter does not provide a full discussion of each of these approaches – for that you will need to consult a psychology textbook or look at some of the weblinks provided in this book. Instead, we will look at the aspects of each approach which are most relevant and useful for care settings.

Psychodynamic approach

This is based on the work of Sigmund Freud (1856–1939). Put simply, psychodynamic means 'energy' or 'forces' of the mind. The underlying assumption of this perspective is that the way a person thinks and behaves is determined by the experiences they have had in their early years. Emotional disturbance at any age is caused by unresolved conflicts stemming from childhood. The psychodynamic approach states that these experiences may be buried in our unconscious mind, and so it is difficult to acknowledge the importance they still play in our current life. Behaviour, therefore, is largely seen as being determined by past experiences, of which we often have no conscious memory. In order to understand why people act the way do they do in a care setting, it may be necessary to help them explore their past for possible causes and help them find ways of changing the negative patterns of relating to people and reacting to events which they have developed. This may or may not be part of your particular role, depending on the level of skill and knowledge you acquire.

Freud believed that there were three parts to our personality: Id, Ego and Superego (see Table 4.2). These three aspects develop and interact as we grow up, and will manifest themselves differently in each person, depending on childhood experiences. As adults, we have a combination of all three parts in our personality. For some people their Id is

Table 4.2 Parts of the personality

Id	The 'childlike' part of your personality; the part which demands things *now*, wanting instant gratification; the 'Pleasure Principle'
Ego	The 'adult' part of your personality; the part which knows it may have to wait for your needs to be met; the 'Reality Principle'
Superego	The 'parent' part of your personality; the part which tells you what is right and wrong; your conscience; the 'Morality Principle'

the most powerful force, which means they may be impulsive and spontaneous, whilst for others the dominant force is their Superego, and they may be controlling of self and others, and quite critical. A psychologically healthy person has a strong Ego and is able to balance the demands of both Id and Superego.

All of us encounter situations which make us anxious, and none of us like being in that situation. Freud suggests that we have unconsciously developed ways to protect ourselves from feeling that anxiety. These are called defence mechanisms. They are coping strategies which help us deflect the pain and distress which we experience due to anxiety. These defence mechanisms include: repression – ignoring feelings of fear or hurt; regression – displaying childlike behaviours such as having a tantrum; or sublimation – venting your anger and frustration on an object or an activity, rather than the person who caused it. When we don't want to face up to reality, because it is too painful to admit how we feel, we put up these barriers to protect ourselves from the bad feelings, until the feelings subside enough for us and we can face up to them. Of course, in some circumstances, people are never able to face up to some of their feelings, and this is when it becomes psychologically unhealthy. People develop these defence mechanisms as routine ways of coping with the pressures and hassles they experience, but there often comes a time (because of bereavement, divorce, illness, etc.) when they are unable to keep the defence 'shield' up any more and they have to face up to a lot of unresolved issues at the one time.

The psychodynamic approach can be criticised for the fact that it is all based on ideas that no-one can prove, or dis-prove. No-one can measure the size of your subconscious and, although it is likely that early experiences do influence us in later life, it is impossible to say exactly what degree of importance they have: we have had so many different influences on us throughout our lives, who knows what has been most significant? A lot of Freud's ideas and his methodology have been heavily criticised, but when most people read about this approach in general, they see that a lot of their behaviour can be explained by the key concepts.

Cognitive/behavioural approach

This approach combines two strands: behavioural and cognitive. The behavioural approach explains human development in terms of what a person has learned. Behaviourists believed that the psychodynamic approach was unscientific because it was not based on facts or evidence – and they wanted to research only the part of experience which was observable: behaviour. The initial ideas were developed by researchers, such as Pavlov and Skinner, working in laboratories with animals. They developed the idea that a certain stimulus will trigger certain responses, because an association is made between the two. So, for instance, a researcher walking into a laboratory with a plate of food will trigger the salivary glands in a dog, before it even sees the food, because over time it has developed an association between the door opening and 'mealtime'! Another important part of this process is the consequences of what happens when a person responds in a certain way. The behaviour is more likely to be repeated if it is <u>reinforced</u>, or rewarded. The association between the door opening and salivation would weaken after a while if the food stopped appearing.

Human beings, however, differ from animals in that we don't just act: we are capable of thinking before we act. We think about our feelings, we interpret the situation and we consider what has happened in the past. We don't just react, we respond. The ideas of the behaviourists were developed to make them more appropriate and relevant to human beings by including cognition – or thinking processes. Cognitive/behavioural approaches look at the influence of our perception on behaviour: how we act depends on how we see the situation. If we can change our view of the situation, we will act differently. A lot of work in care settings is based on this cognitive/behavioural model as the work is focused on producing change that is very clear to see, and the work can be carried out in a relatively short period of time.

People criticise the cognitive/behavioural approach by saying that it only deals with the symptoms of a person's problem, not the causes. The approach provides a lot of useful tools to examine and understand *aspects* of behaviour, but it does not look at the whole person, in the context of their whole life. If you were a doctor, for instance, and someone came to you with a bad cough, you would want to know if they had TB, lung cancer or just a bad cold before you decided on the most appropriate treatment. So, if someone in a care setting is getting angry, it can be 'treated' by attending anger management sessions. However, if they never find out the cause of their anger, then it may always be there, ready to cause problems in the future. This medical analogy doesn't quite explain the whole picture, because the situation is often more complex when talking about psychology rather than biology. One key difference is that a doctor could do a test to find out fairly conclusively if someone has cancer or TB, but in psychology there is no simple 'test' to determine what the cause of a person's problem is. Sometimes, it is easier, quicker and more effective just to treat the symptoms.

Humanistic approach

The humanistic approach is based on a positive view of human development and is associated with the work of Carl Rogers (1902–1987). Rogers' work has already been considered in Chapter 2 in relation to communication. Rogers had trained as a psychodynamic therapist, but felt that the people he saw didn't seem to gain the benefits from analysis that he had expected. People could talk in therapy for months and not see any difference in their day-to-day lives. Rogers concluded that this was because the approach concentrated on the past and not the whole picture of the person's life: their feelings, beliefs and spirituality. He also believed that cognitive/behaviourists took a rather narrow view of humans, only looking at what they did and what they could say about their thought processes. After counselling many clients, Rogers came to see that he wasn't the expert in the person's life: they were. There was no sense in him analysing the person or motivating his clients to change: it had to come from the clients themselves. The humanistic approach regards both past and present as having equal importance. It assumes that all human beings are unique, rational and self-determining, that they have free will and that they continuously strive to grow and develop. It sees human beings as having an inherent need to develop their potential to the full. Emotional disturbance happens because individuals are not allowed to 'be themselves'. In an attempt to be accepted by others, individuals suppress their own true nature and make choices, not to please themselves but to please others.

CASE STUDY

Josh

Josh is a 34-year-old man with learning disabilities who attends a day centre near his home in Motherwell. At 10.30 a.m. the tea bar is opened for the morning break. The centre is a very busy place and the queue is very long. Every morning as he stands in the queue Josh becomes very agitated. He begins to shout and swear and becomes abusive to anyone who is standing beside him. His care workers are concerned that he will hurt someone so they take him to the front of the queue. Having chosen his cake and drink, Josh sits quietly at his table with his friends until it is time to return to the activity room. His care workers have tried to stand beside Josh in the queue but have decided that he does not like queues and it is easier to get him served first.

Using information from the three approaches above, what do you think his care workers should have done?

Should they ignore Josh's behaviour? What about restraining or punishing Josh? The care workers could make him stay in the activity room until all the people in the queue had been served. Or they could tell him that if he 'misbehaves' again he will not be allowed to go on the trip to the bowling alley. Do you think this will help? Behaviourists are clear about this and state that, while unpleasant experiences might stop a particular behaviour at the time, it does not mean that future behaviour will be affected. Josh might experiment with different behaviour – screaming, kicking, lying down on the floor – the list is endless! So what is the answer? The answer, according to behaviourists, lies in understanding how reinforcement is working in the present situation, to examine that reinforcement and look for alternatives.

Using the psychodynamic approach might help you to understand that Josh may be experiencing some anxiety in the queue, and is demonstrating this by regressing to 'childlike' behaviour. If staff can use the humanistic approach to try to see the world from Josh's point of view, they might be able to understand more clearly why he is feeling such anxiety. Is he worried he won't get back to his group in time if he doesn't get served first? Has he not had anything to eat before he left home in the morning?

Perhaps Josh's carers could start by placing him near the very front of the queue, spend time with him, talk to him and use a humanistic approach to help understand how he sees the changing situation. Gradually, they could encourage him to stand further back in the queue. They could tell him how good his behaviour is, praise him for his patience while standing in the queue and make him feel good about achieving this new behaviour. Josh will have learned a new piece of behaviour which has been reinforced and this behaviour will be repeated in the future.

Psychological theories

As we have seen, each psychological approach was originally based on the ideas and work of certain theorists, but there are many writers who have developed the ideas of the original theorists. They have the benefit of having listened to discussions about the ideas, and seeing how the approach works in practice. The original theorists sometimes emphasise an aspect of their theory that later turns out to be weak, and only time tells which are the most enduring and useful aspects of the theory. Within each approach, one writer who has developed the original ideas will be considered at Intermediate 2 level, and one writer at Higher level. Aspects of their theory which are most relevant for care settings will be highlighted. Table 4.3 summarises the writers that will discussed.

Table 4.3 Psychological approaches and theorists

Approach	Writer	Theory	Key concepts
Psychodynamic			
Intermediate 2	Eric Berne	Transactional analysis	Ego states
Higher	Erik Erikson	Lifespan theory	8 stages; ego conflicts
Cognitive/behavioural			
Intermediate 2	Albert Bandura	Social learning theory	Observational learning; modelling
Higher	Albert Ellis	Rational emotive behaviour therapy	ABCDE; irrational beliefs
Humanistic			
Intermediate 2	Abraham Maslow	Hierarchy of needs	5 stages; Self-actualisation
Higher	Carl Rogers	Person-centred theory	Self-concept; conditions of worth

Psychodynamic: Eric Berne – transactional analysis

Writing in America more than 50 years after Freud, Berne (1910–1970) would have known all about the ideas of the behaviourist school, and was developing his ideas roughly at the same time as the cognitive and humanist writers. He suggested that people were actors in their own life and 'played games' according to certain 'scripts'. He didn't mean by this that people were false. What he meant, like Freud, was that people were not always consciously aware of why they acted in the way they did but they had developed certain patterns of behaviour, or 'scripts', which they were likely to repeat unless they became aware of the games they were playing.

Berne was interested in the transactions (his word for interactions) between people, and came up with some ideas which are useful in care settings, whether looking at staff or service users. He was the person who coined the phrase 'I'm OK, you're OK'. By this he meant that, in the most successful interactions, both people would be content and feel that they had achieved what they wanted. On the other hand, you can get interactions where the dynamic is 'I'm OK, you're not OK'. This would be when one person thinks they are superior to the other and, perhaps, bullies or undermines them. Equally, some people play the 'I'm not OK, you're OK' game. This situation might occur in a care setting where the service user looks at the worker as the expert, the one who can 'make them better'. This is not a healthy professional working relationship, because it is an unequal relationship, based on a power imbalance. The worker would want to encourage the service user to become more actively involved in decision-making. The final transaction is 'I'm not OK, you're not OK'. This is where both people interact on the basis of their perceived victim status. They both feel worthless, or are people who define themselves by their problems. If an interaction gets stuck in this script, it can stop both people moving on. However, remember that we are talking about a psychodynamic approach, which suggests there may be unconscious reasons why people want to stay in a relationship which from the outside appears negative. For instance, there may be a sense of safety, or familiarity, in their position, no matter how painful it is.

Berne suggests that when we interact with others, we do so from one of three 'ego states': Child, Adult or Parent. These three states link to Feud's three parts of the personality: Id, Ego and Superego. A person's ego is just their sense of self: their picture of who they are when they say 'I'. Berne believes that every person has a mixture of these three Ego states in their personality and that, depending on the situation and the person we are interacting with, we will play out one of these roles.

- The Child ego state is one where we are spontaneous and playful, but also prone to moods and tantrums.
- The Adult ego state is the one where we are balanced, can see our own and other people's strengths and weaknesses and can accept these.
- The Parent ego state is either controlling and punitive or nurturing and caring.

When one person acts in a situation based on an ego state, the other person has a choice about which ego state they respond with. However, since these transactions are happening unconsciously, we often find ourselves reacting to the role. So if someone is in the Parent ego state and criticises you, you may find yourself reacting in Child mode, perhaps by stomping off in a mood, getting angry with them, or bursting into tears. Berne would say that a psychologically healthy person would see what was going on and choose to respond in their Adult ego state. By doing this, it might change the 'game' into an 'I'm OK, you're OK' situation where the person responds in Adult mode, apologises for their tone, and manages to discuss their point without hostility.

(Level Higher) ## Psychodynamic: Erik Erikson – lifespan theory

Erikson (1902–1994) suggested that psychological development is a lifelong process and is not fixed by the time you reach adolescence, as Freud had believed. He also differed from Freud because he believed that the conflicts people encounter are linked to their relationships with other people rather than with their psycho-sexual development. This is why his theory is known as a psycho-social theory of development. Socio-cultural factors such as the person's social class and the political regime in which they live, as well as the cultural expectations of their society will affect the way people develop. Erikson thought that an individual would develop a healthy personality if they were able to resolve the basic psychological conflicts which they meet at different stages of their lives. If they did resolve the conflicts, they would develop a particular ego strength, and this would help them to face up to challenges later in life. He identified eight stages of psychological development: four in childhood, one in adolescence and three in adulthood. Table 4.4 outlines the main stages and the conflict which has to be resolved at each stage.

Table 4.4 Erikson: Eight stages of development

Early infancy	Conflict to be resolved
Trust versus Mistrust	To gain a balance between trusting people and risking being let down, or being suspicious and mistrustful and therefore being unable to relate to others fully. Successful resolution of this stage leads to the ego strength of *hope*.
Later infancy	
Antonomy versus Shame and Doubt	To develop a sense of personal agency and control over behaviour and actions, or to mistrust one's personal abilities and anticipate failures. Successful resolution of this stage leads to the ego strength of *will*.
Early childhood	
Initiative versus Guilt	To develop an increasing sense of personal responsibility and initiative, or to develop increased feelings of guilt and doubt. Successful resolution of this stage leads to the ego strength of *purpose*.

Middle childhood	
Industry versus Inferiority	To learn to overcome challenges through systematic effort or to accept failure and avoid challenges, leading to an increasing sense of inferiority. Successful resolution of this stage leads to the ego strength of *competence*.
Puberty and adolescence	
Identity versus Role Confusion	To develop a consistent sense of personal identity faced with the changes in social role and expectations of adolescence, or simply to become overwhelmed by choices and expectations and to fail to develop a sense of consistent inner self. Successful resolution of this stage leads to the ego strength of *fidelity*.
Young adulthood	
Intimacy versus Isolation	To develop intimate and trusting relationships with others, or to avoid relationships as threatening and painful. Successful resolution of this stage leads to the ego strength of *love*.
Adulthood	
Generativity versus Stagnation	To develop a productive and positive life incorporating recognition of personal achievements, or to stagnate and fail to grow psychologically. Successful resolution of this stage leads to the ego strength of *care*.
Maturity	
Integrity versus Despair	To become able to look back on one's life in a positive fashion and to evaluate one's achievement, or to feel that life has been meaningless and futile. Successful resolution of this stage leads to the ego strength of *wisdom*.

Source: Adapted from Erikson (1968) in Hayes (1994)

In order to resolve the conflicts and develop the ego strengths, we need to have the right people around us at the relevant time. Our parents' care and attention are crucial in our childhood, whereas our friends become more important in our teenage years. If these social conditions and relationships are not positive, then we may fail to resolve the conflict, and this will weaken us psychologically. Equally, positive early experiences of, for example, trust can still be shattered later by negative experiences, but at least we have spent our formative years seeing ourselves and the world from a psychologically healthy perspective. Erikson believed that it was possible to make up for unsatisfactory experiences at a later stage, although it was harder to do so. This is why this model is useful for care workers. If a service user had problems during adolescence, for example, they may never have developed a strong sense of identity. This might explain why as an adult they find it difficult to find a place for themselves in society: they just don't know where they fit in. As a care worker, you can't help them rewind to their adolescence and change things, but you could work with the service user to create tasks which give them a sense of identity now. Erikson's theory helps to remind you that the service users with whom you work are people who, although they have been through a process of development, are still continuing to develop, no matter what age they are.

Does Erikson's model apply to everyone? There are at least two arguments which question the universality of his model: one on the basis of gender-blindness and one on the basis of its cultural limitations. Bingham and Stryker (1995) suggest that development of identity, intimacy and generativity may receive different emphases throughout adulthood for men and women. In Erikson's model, the crisis at this life stage is between intimacy versus isolation. In society in general, men are expected to become self-sufficient, so the male crisis at this stage is one of establishing intimacy. Women, on the other hand, are expected to establish intimate relationships; the female crisis is to develop autonomy, in terms of taking care of themselves emotionally and financially (www.rlc.dcccd.edu/MATHSCI/anth/P101/DVLMENTL/ERIKSON.HTM). Another longstanding debate in psychology is about whether adolescence is a biologically or socially determined life stage.

> *The anthropological evidence from all over the world clearly shows that, while adolescence is everywhere a time for learning new social roles, with attendant psychological tensions, it is not the period of storm and stress claimed by Western psychologists . . . In some cases, such as rural India where children have to fulfil adult tasks from a very early age, not as much time and attention can be spent on adolescence as the western world, and more affluent urban Indians, define it.*

(Berry et al., 2002, p. 39)

Conclusion: psychodynamic approaches

Thus, the psychodynamic approach is not just about a bearded psychiatrist interpreting dreams while the client lies on a couch! It is about looking at the unconscious influences on the development of our ego throughout our life, and trying to understand the way that affects the way we interact with other people. It is often difficult to pinpoint exact reasons from our past that influence the way we act, but we can recognise patterns of behaviour and aspects of our current behaviour which are causing problems with our relationships, at work or at home. Knowing about defence mechanisms, psychological conflicts, ego states, life scripts and ego strengths may help you to understand where changes might be made.

Level Int 2 **Behaviourist: Bandura – social learning theory**

Bandura agreed with the original behaviourist writers that the role of reinforcement was important in determining behaviour, but his research indicated that the process of learning was much more complex than they had detailed. He believed that thought processes allow the individual to interpret the consequences of their behaviour. The interpretation of these consequences exerts its influence on future behaviour by giving the individual information about what effects can be expected if they behave that way in a similar situation.

In particular, Bandura and other social learning theorists believe that a person's development and behaviour are the result of social interaction with others. Social interaction starts when a baby is born and continues throughout a person's life. It involves the process of socialisation, which is discussed in Chapter 3. It is the process whereby a person learns to conform to the norms of society and to act in ways that are considered acceptable. It is therefore a helpful tool in understanding the different social expectations and practices of different cultures and the effects these can have on the development and behaviour of individuals. Social learning theory in general highlights three main ways in which socialisation occurs: imitation and identification; punishments and rewards; and social expectations.

Imitation and identification

From children's earliest stages they will observe the behaviour of others and copy or imitate it. This allows children to learn a range of physical skills very quickly and efficiently, and they will often incorporate this learning into their play activities. Small children love to 'play' at being a grown up. They will play at being mummies and daddies, doctors and teachers, soldiers and fire-fighters. Imitation can be a powerful influence on behaviour. In the experiments he carried out with school-age children, Bandura found that they did not imitate all adult models equally – they were much more likely to imitate models who were similar to themselves, such as those of the same sex. His findings seemed to show that there can be a difference in what children learn and what immediately shows in their behaviour.

Identification is the second part of the process. Not only do children imitate behaviour but, as time goes by, they begin to model themselves on another person, the learning becomes internalised and they come to identify with that person or that role. Role models act as a blueprint of behaviour, attitudes and values which the child may adopt in later adult life. It is believed that identification is responsible for individuals learning social roles such as gender roles.

Punishments and rewards

Another important way in which a child learns to behave is through direct reaction from adults. Behaviour may be rewarded or punished, and through these means the child learns to act in ways which are appropriate and acceptable. There have been several studies carried out to investigate the effects of punishment and rewards. Rewards teach the child the types of behaviour which are likely to bring about a pleasant outcome. Rewards will vary from culture to culture. They may take the form of paying attention to the child, playing with them or giving them sweets, treats or hugs and praise. These rewards do act as reinforcers of appropriate behaviour. However, studies have shown that they are only effective if there is a strong affectionate bond between the child and the adult.

Punishment can take many forms – smacking, hitting, beating, withdrawal of privileges, stopping pocket money or grounding (not letting the child go out of the house). Many social learning theorists believe that punishment often produces hostility and resentment as well as fear and avoidance of the punisher. The child also quickly learns to suppress the punishable behaviour in the presence of the punisher but tends to be more likely to carry out this behaviour out of sight of the adult who has punished them. Punishment only teaches the child what they should not do, not what they should or might do. It may also teach children that behaviour can be controlled by another person by virtue of their age, gender, strength or status. The child may learn to follow this model and could in later years use punishing strategies to control the behaviour of others (their own children, their partner, their friends, their work colleagues or members of the opposite sex).

Why are there sometimes inconsistencies in a person's aggressive behaviour: they are aggressive in some situations but not in others? It may be because their behaviour is reinforced differently in each situation. They have learned to behave differently in the two situations because aggressiveness brings 'rewards' (feeling of power, dominance) in one situation, but not in the other.

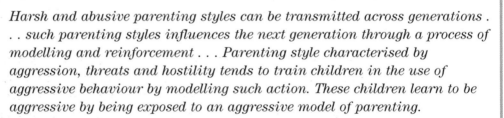

Activity   *Social learning theory and parenting styles*

Read the quotation below, then answer the following question:

Using Bandura's theory, what role do you think that other adults whom these children come into contact with could play in order to break the cycle of violence?

> *Harsh and abusive parenting styles can be transmitted across generations . . . such parenting styles influences the next generation through a process of modelling and reinforcement . . . Parenting style characterised by aggression, threats and hostility tends to train children in the use of aggressive behaviour by modelling such action. These children learn to be aggressive by being exposed to an aggressive model of parenting.*
>
> *The parents' control of the child's behaviour is also often inappropriate in that their responses to deviant (including aggressive) behaviour in the child is not only likely to involve physical punishment (which will be imitated), but also to be inconsistent and ineffective.*
>
> (Messer and Jones, 1999, p. 307)

Social expectations

Social expectations (the type of behaviour which is regarded as appropriate in particular situations) can vary dramatically from one culture to another. The way in which a society's culture is constructed can play a large part in determining the kinds of expected behaviour; this is discussed fully in Chapters 3 and 5.

Cognitive/behaviourist: Albert Ellis – rational emotive behaviour therapy

Albert Ellis (1913–) is one of the many psychological theorists, like Carl Rogers, who started his professional life as a therapist working within the psychodynamic model, but came to believe that it was too limited. He believed that it wasn't what had happened to people that influenced their psychological development, but rather their *perceptions* of what had happened to them, the story they told themselves about their past. By 1961 he had developed the basis of rational emotive therapy, and in 1993 he renamed it rational emotive behaviour therapy (REBT), to show that, although cognition and emotions were crucial, behaviour was also central to his theory. In 2007 (aged 93) Ellis, a colourful and iconoclastic character, was still writing books and developing his ideas. As with all the theorists included in the syllabus, we will focus on particular aspects of his theory which are relevant in a care context.

The main ideas of REBT are that our cognition, the way we think about things, is the key element in determining how we respond to an event and that there is an interaction between our cognition, emotion and behaviour. They are not separate systems that can be examined and 'treated' independently. If we learn to accept ourselves, and do not impose unrealistic conditions on ourselves and others, then we are more likely to achieve a healthy psychological balance in our lives.

Ellis's theory follows an 'ABC' model: An Activating event (the stimulus) results in a Belief (rational or irrational) about the event, which has a Consequence for how the person feels, thinks and behaves. Ellis adds two other steps, D and E, to this basic cognitive model. If the irrational belief is Disputed or debated (either by the person, or by someone else), then there will be a different Effect for the person: they will feel different, because they will develop more effective rational beliefs, their emotional response will be more appropriate and their behaviour will be more in line with their goals. Ellis has developed his theory over the decades and it has been presented in number of different ways. Beware of this if you carry out any background research!

Ellis considers that the beliefs, or thoughts, we have about an event can be rational or irrational. Rational thoughts are logical and flexible – they see the world as it is and not through a distorted lens.

> *[In REBT] humans are seen as having two basic goals: to stay alive and to be happy. While there are shared methods of pursuing the former goal (e.g. seeking adequate shelter from the elements, maintaining a proper diet) there are myriad different ways of pursuing the latter. Humans are remarkably idiosyncratic in what they find personally meaningful or fulfilling. Given the above considerations, the term 'rational' means that* which helps people to achieve their basic goals and purposes.

(Dryden et. al., 1999, p. 6, original emphasis)

Irrational beliefs, on the other hand, are illogical, rigid, stated in 'absolute' terms, are often self-defeating because they impede us from attaining our goals and they are disruptive to our relationships. We develop these irrational beliefs throughout our lives and they become part of a patterned way of thinking and behaving through repetition.

Irrational beliefs fall into four categories:

1   Rigid demands: 'I must be approved of'
2   Awfulising beliefs: 'If I'm disapproved of, it's the end of the world'
3   Low frustration tolerance beliefs: 'I can't tolerate being disapproved of'
4   Depreciation beliefs:

   a) self depreciation: 'I am worthless if I am disapproved of'

   b) other depreciation: 'You are horrible if you disapprove of me'

   c) life depreciation: 'Life is all bad because this tragedy happened'

(Dryden, 2006, p. 276)

A rational belief, such as 'I would like to do well in this Higher Care exam' can so easily transform into an irrational one when a person adds conditions, such as 'must', 'should', 'ought' or 'have to', to the statement. Ellis memorably calls these terms 'musterbations' because they are such clear indicators of the inflexible, absolutist stance that underlies an irrational belief. The statement 'I must do well in this Higher Care exam' tends to have a second part in which the person either explicitly or implicitly states 'or I'll never get into university and move onto the career I want'. The thought processes associated with irrational beliefs are often 'catastrophising', imagining the worst-case scenario. If people can learn to identify and dispute their irrational beliefs, they can reframe their thoughts into more logical perceptions of reality. So the irrational belief would be reformulated into 'I'd like to pass the Higher Care exam', perhaps with a mediating statement at the end such as *'but my future doesn't depend on it'*. This enables the person to give themselves permission to be less than perfect, i.e. human and fallible.

Reframing thoughts like this encourages the person to move away from repetitive, self-defeating thoughts and to stop procrastinating. How often have you put something off time and again, because you don't think you're quite ready to do it, or circumstances aren't quite right yet? When will they ever be perfect? REBT challenges a person to check their underlying beliefs about themselves and about the world, and to make changes.

This theory is useful in a care setting as it responds to some of the observable aspects of a person's situation. It helps clarify what their perception of a situation is, based on their behaviour and how they talk about it. It is a theory that can be used both to understand one-off situations and to facilitate change in longer-term therapeutic work with a service user. It encourages people to actively engage in self-healing by taking responsibility for their perceptions and behaviours.

However, Ellis can be criticised for his lack of sympathy for people who do not actively work to change their perceptions, and this is an aspect of his approach, and indeed of many cognitive/behavioural theorists, that care workers need to be careful not to reinforce. With the wrong emphasis, this could be turned into a criticism of the person for not doing enough to change their situation. Underpinned by a sound care value base, this model could provide a very useful way of working with service users on some issues. Compare it to Egan's three-stage model which was discussed in Chapter 2. Do you see the similarities? Egan states that challenging is an appropriate skill to use *once a trusting relationship has been developed,* and Ellis's theory would also be relevant to use at this stage in working with a service user. The other main drawback of this approach is that, although it can lead to people examining and changing aspects of their perceptions and behaviour, it doesn't examine *where* the irrational beliefs came from in the first place.

Level Int 2   Humanistic: Maslow – hierarchy of needs

One of the main ways in which psychology can help you in your work with service users is in the process of care planning (see Chapter 6). The assessment of needs with the service user represents one of the key components in the care planning process. All human beings have a range of needs, but are any needs more important than the others? As early as 1954, Abraham Maslow put forward the idea that human beings have a number of complex needs and, coming from a humanistic perspective, Maslow believed that all of us constantly strive towards fulfilling these needs. He formulated the idea that needs are not always equally important: some are more important than others at any given time.

He believed that human beings are motivated by two systems of needs – deficiency needs and growth needs. The basic needs are termed deficiency, because when they are not satisfied individuals engage in behaviours designed to remedy this lack of satisfaction. For example, hunger represents a deficiency that can be satisfied by eating. The growth needs are termed growth needs because activities that relate to them do not fulfil a lack but lead towards to the ultimate end of growth: fulfilling your potential.

According to Maslow, needs are organised as a hierarchy – that is, they can only be satisfied if the one below has already been at least partially achieved. As you can see from Maslow's hierarchy of needs in Figure 4.1, the needs at the base are the needs which are necessary to sustain life itself – food, water, rest, shelter and security. It is towards these needs that a person's energy or motivation will be directed as a means of survival and security. Only when these basic needs are satisfied will a person become focused on the next level of needs – social/emotional. As these needs are met, the person can use their energy and attention to move up the pyramid towards the highest point of self-actualisation.

The concept of self-actualisation refers to the potential within all individuals for personal growth – to be the person you want to be, to make full use of your talents and capabilities. Maslow believed that all human beings are born with an innate tendency to strive towards self-actualisation – that is, they are motivated towards reaching their full potential. The satisfaction associated with self-actualisation comes from within the person rather than from outside. In contrast, satisfaction of lower-order needs, such as self-esteem, is associated with external sources of reinforcement (approval and recognition). In an international study of workplaces, self-actualisation is rated as the most important need to meet, but also the least likely to be achieved (Berry et al., 2002, p. 403).

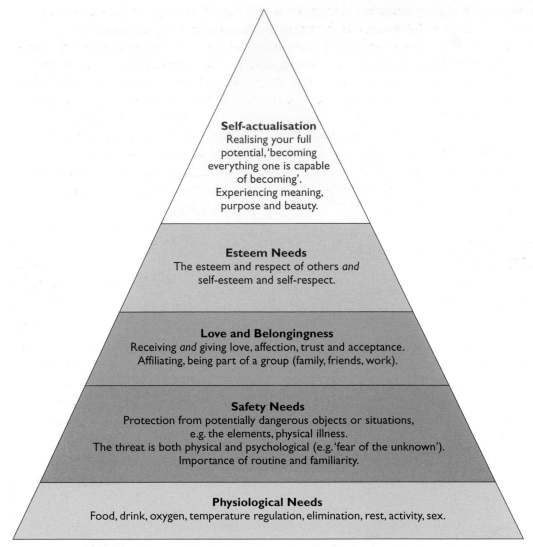

Figure 4.1 Maslow's hierarchy of needs

Those who fail to move towards self-actualisation do so because of circumstances in which they find themselves, e.g. people living in poverty and other circumstances where all available time and energy is spent on meeting the basic needs and coping with struggles at those levels. Other circumstances may cause an individual not to progress towards self-actualisation such as being in the middle of a divorce, losing a job, violence and abuse, or being unable to take part in activities which would be fulfilling. These circumstances and many others will act against the individual being able to move up the hierarchy, towards self-actualisation.

Even people who are highly successful don't stay at the peak of self-actualisation forever. No matter what you have achieved in your life, there is always something else to strive for, and there are always setbacks that you will encounter, as well as all the day-to-day issues of poor health and relationship problems that we all face. It is probably more useful therefore to consider self-actualisation as a process that guides a person towards growth rather than a state that is attained once and for all. It is also important to remember that self-actualisation is relative: we are not all striving for the same thing. Many people have a lifetime ambition to play the piano well, or to get a degree at university, whereas other people have achieved these things and don't particularly value them: they have other things they are striving for. Someone who has had a stroke may view being able to walk unaided as fulfilling their potential, even though they used to jog when they were younger. Someone who has had mental health problems may consider that they have fulfilled their potential by getting out of the house on a regular basis and managing to hold down a job. Someone who has had an addiction in the past may feel a sense of self-actualisation when they are there to see their child winning a race at the first sports day that they have been organised enough and lucid enough to be able to attend. The smile on their child's face is a peak experience which demonstrates to them how far they are into their recovery.

Activity   *Ampin*

How does Maslow's theory help you to understand the needs of Ampin in the case study below?

Ampin is an 84-year-old woman who has been in residential care since her husband died a year ago. Her health is relatively good and she eats and sleeps well. She has her own room, which has many items from her previous house – chair, photographs, clothes, ornaments and a TV. Ampin's only daughter moved away six months ago when her husband's job was relocated to Canada. She writes to her mother once a month and plans to visit her at Christmas time. The staff in the home are very caring towards Ampin. They are concerned, however, that Ampin has not made any friends in the home and tends to sit in her room or on her own in the lounge.

Using Maslow's hierarchy of needs as a guide, it would appear that Ampin's physiological needs are being met. She has food, warmth, shelter and rest. It would also appear that her safety needs are being met. She feels safe, secure and out of danger. Her room contains mementoes and familiar objects from her own home. There are things she knows, things which evoke fond memories and which in themselves make her feel secure.

However, it seems evident that Ampin's need for love and belongingness are not being met. She is obviously missing her daughter and has not made any friends in the home. Since these needs are lacking, Ampin cannot progress towards self-actualisation. It is towards the love and belongingness part of Maslow's hierarchy of needs that Ampin, with the help of the staff, may now want to focus. If Ampin wishes, this will become part of her assessment, and the helping process should work towards meeting these needs and help her progress towards the peak of the pyramid: self-actualisation.

Maslow's hierarchy of needs is a useful 'tool' to develop an understanding of the needs of service users. The humanistic perspective from which it derives encourages a view of service users which demands that they are seen as individuals who are all striving to meet their basic and growth needs. Effective assessment and care planning should be designed to help them to achieve these. Care services are often good at meeting the basic physical and safety needs of service users, by providing warm and comfortable surroundings. But, bearing in mind the positive care environment approach in Chapter 6, they sometimes struggle to provide meaningful and challenging activities for service users. There may be all kinds of reasons for this: lack of staff, poor resources, inadequate training. But it is a real missed opportunity for the workers and organisation to help people make a real difference to their life.

Can you identify any weaknesses in Maslow's theory? Probably the major flaw in the theory is the idea that lower needs have to be at least partially satisfied first before higher needs become important. Some people, for example workaholics, will often neglect their personal needs such as food and sleep in their pursuit to complete a work or college project. Students often hand a piece of work in with the words 'I was up till 3 this morning doing this'. The motivation to complete the work was stronger than their increasingly desperate need for sleep!

(Level **Higher**) Humanistic: Carl Rogers – person-centred theory

One of the major differences between human beings and animals is the ability of human beings to be aware of themselves. This is called self-consciousness or self-awareness. Animals may have consciousness and feel hunger or pain, but only human beings have self-consciousness. This does not mean that people feel shy or embarrassed. Rather, it means that when you think about yourself you are the person doing the thinking but you are also the person being thought about. Cooley (1902) described this as the 'looking glass self'. What he meant by this was that human beings are aware of what kind of person they are, what they think about themselves and what kind of personality they have. They are able to do this because they have self-consciousness: they have an awareness about what others think about them and it is how they develop an impression of what they are like. Robert Burns, the national poet of Scotland, obviously understood this idea. In his poem 'To a Louse' he notes:

> *O wad some Power the giftie gie us*

> *To see oursels as ithers see us!*

Rogers was interested in the ability of people to fulfil their potential and, through his work as a therapist, developed the idea of a self-concept which was made up of three aspects: self-image, ideal self and self-esteem. These three aspects interacted with each other in order to create the person's identity.

Self-image

Activity   Self-image

Try this activity either on your own or with a group of friends or family. Ask each person to write down a list of words or phrases which describe themselves. Ask them to list about 20 things. Remember they can write down some negative aspects about themselves, as well as positive.

Self-image is how individuals describe themselves. An individual's list will probably include three main categories that make up the person's self-image: social roles, personality traits and body image.

- **Social roles:** the person has probably described themselves in terms of their social role: student, sister, father, friend, son. These roles can be verified by others.

- **Personality traits:** the person might also have described themselves in terms of personality traits. These traits or characteristics will be formed from their own opinion about themselves: friendly, under-confident, generous, nervous, bad-tempered. These may be traits they consider themselves to have but other people may not hold the same view.

- **Body image:** The last group on their list might be descriptions of how the person looks, their body image. They might have included descriptions such as tall, fat, thin, blue eyes, attractive, brunette, etc. One of the important features of body image is biological identity, whether someone is male or female. The other important feature of body image is that, as individuals grow and develop, so too do their bodies and appearance. Changes in appearance may be something simple like getting a haircut or having their nose pierced or something more significant such as the change in their body during puberty or their skin becoming wrinkled and their hair turning white when they get older. Some of these descriptions are factual, but others (e.g. attractive) are judgements or opinions, and other people may not agree with them. This is especially the case if the person suffers from an eating disorder such as anorexia. The crucial point is not what the external reality is but what the person believes to be true.

Ideal self

Your ideal self is the kind of person you would like to be. Perhaps you would just like to be a little thinner, a bit wiser, more outgoing or better at sports. Or perhaps you would like to be a better friend, a more caring person or a better mother. At a more extreme level, you may even want to be like someone else! At times this can be a motivation to improve yourself and make positive changes in your life, but at other times it means losing your individuality and becoming a weaker copy of someone else. Socialisation, particularly popular culture in magazines, films, TV, the Internet, etc., plays a major part in defining what looks, lifestyle, house, car are desirable.

Self-esteem

Self-esteem is what an individual thinks about themselves, how they value themselves as a person, how much they like themselves. To a large extent this is influenced by the relationship between their self-image and their ideal self. If they are very unhappy with their self-image and want to be like someone else (ideal self) then most likely their self-esteem will be low. However if they are happy with the person they are, then their self-esteem is more likely to be high. The wider the gap between self-image and ideal self, the lower a person's self-esteem is likely to be.

The type of culture in which people live has a large influence on how individuals view themselves. British culture today holds certain physical attributes in high regard. Women are deemed to be attractive if they are young, tall, slim, have beautiful faces, good skin and long shapely legs. Men are seen as attractive if they are young, tall and slim with a 'six pack', have good skin and look as if they 'work out'. In contrast, other cultures regard fuller-bodied people as attractive. Other aspects of culture, status and orientation will also affect how people see themselves, and how they feel about themselves: race, gender, age, social background, education, marital status or sexual orientation.

Carl Rogers believes our self-concept has been influenced by many things, including the conditions of worth that people have placed on us throughout our lives. These are the sometimes spoken, but often unspoken, expectations about how we should behave and what opinions we should have if we are to be loved by those around us. We encounter these conditions 'You are worthy of my love/approval, but only if you . . .' from all kinds of people throughout our lives: parents, friends, teachers, lovers, children. And remember, you are part of the process too: you will have imposed some conditions on other people throughout your life. People often think they are being caring and 'looking after the best interests' of the person when they make these conditions, but they are seeing the world from their own point of view, and not the point of view of the other person. As a father or

Figure 4.2 Animals do not have self-consciousness (© Andrew Parry and Robin Maclean)

as a wife, you have a certain vested interest in the relationship and it is difficult for you to be completely neutral in your opinions. That is only to be expected. However, it becomes a problem when it starts to constrain and limit the other person. This can lead to the point where they have an external locus of evaluation: they are unable to make up their own mind about things without reference to someone else's opinions. This is often the case in people who have been in care settings for a while, where people have valued them for being quiet and compliant. The staff like them because they are not 'trouble-makers'. However, the person, in the process of fitting into these expectations, loses the last sense of self that they had, and becomes dependent on staff to do things for them that they might be capable of doing for themselves.

Emma

Emma is 23 years old and is of mixed race. She is a lone parent with two children under the age of five and lives in a high-rise block of flats in one of the large housing schemes in Glasgow. She left school at sixteen with no qualifications. She used drugs for several years and her children were in foster care for quite a long time. With help from the local drug rehabilitation team and her social worker, Emma has stopped using drugs and her children have been returned to live with her.

Emma's self-esteem is very low and when her social worker suggested that she attend a college course for adult returners, Emma felt that she was not 'good enough' to go to college with 'a lot of brainy people' from the 'posh area'. After a year off drugs, however, Emma did attend a basic computer course at her local community centre and showed a real aptitude for this subject. The out-reach tutor from the college who taught the course eventually persuaded her to attend a full-time computer course at the college the following year. Emma is now studying for an HNC in computer studies and sees herself as 'as good as anybody else'. Her self-esteem continues to grow.

Independent or interdependent identity?

It is argued that self-concept is one of the psychological concepts which has a cultural dimension, and that this has consequences for how people experience themselves, and how they relate to others.

Read the quote below and write down three consequences this might have for a care organisation working with people from a range of cultures.

> *Generally the western conception of self is of an individual who is separate, autonomous, and atomised (made up of a set of discrete traits, abilities, values and motives) seeking separateness and independence from others. In contrast, in Eastern cultures relatedness, connectedness, and interdependence are sought, rooted in a concept of the self not as a discrete entity, but as inherently linked to others. The person is only made 'whole' when situated in his or her place in a social unit. The independent construal of the self further implies that persons see themselves as unique, promote their own goals, and seek self expression. Persons with an interdependent construal of the self seek to belong and fit in, to promote others' goals, and to occupy their proper place.*
>
> (Berry et al., 2002, p. 101)

Level Int 2 Attachment and separation

> *The term attachment is used to describe a special kind of relationship between two people. Attachments are a special kind of affectional bond. According to Mary Ainsworth (1989) an affectional bond is a relatively long-enduring tie in which the partner is important as a unique individual . . . [and where there] is a desire to maintain closeness to the partner.*
>
> (Cardwell et al., 2004, p. 43)

While attachments can occur at any point in a person's life, psychologists are particularly interested in the first relationships which are formed, as they are regarded as crucial for healthy development. This is because these first relationships are thought to act as a model or example for all an individual's later relationships. Psychologists are concerned with how these relationships are formed and what happens if these relationships are disrupted or disturbed. The bonds of affection that are developed, or not, in infancy and early childhood are seen to be the template for a person's ability to bond with others in adolescence and adulthood, and how well they deal with separation, loss and bereavement. What psychological approach does this remind you of? You will recognise that this topic is based on the psychodynamic approach, with its emphasis on the importance of the experience in our early childhood in determining our adult mental health.

One of the most well-known theorists to first examine this area was John Bowlby. He was asked by the World Health Organisation to investigate the effects on children's development of being brought up in orphanages. In his report, published in 1951, Bowlby argued that babies form a special attachment with one particular person, their mother. They do so by displaying certain behaviours which help to keep them close to their mother, such as crying, smiling, crawling. He also found in his research that there was a critical or sensitive period in which attachment has to take place. For most children, Bowlby thought that this has to take place within the first six months of life. He brought attention to the fact that children who are separated from those they know and love in infancy and early childhood are caused great distress, both on a short-term and long-term basis.

Activity   *Types of separation*

Separation can be short term or long term, but it is implied in the term that it is a temporary situation. When it is a permanent separation, it becomes a loss.

1 Can you think of three examples of short-term or long-term separation which might be experienced at the following ages: 6 months old; 6 years old; 16 years old; 36 years old; 66 years old?

2 At what age do you think each of the following situations would cause most distress, and for whom?

- Mother going out to work in the morning
- Mislaying a favourite toy
- Loved one going into hospital
- Child moving into children's home
- Father going away to work on the oil rigs every two weeks
- Best friend going away on holiday for two weeks
- One parent leaving the family home after a separation or divorce.

Schaffer and Emerson (1964) published the result of a longitudinal study which found that infants, rather than establishing a relationship solely with the mother, were in fact able to develop multiple attachments, i.e. equally important relationships with more than one person. Most importantly the infants formed relationships with people who interacted with them in the most sensitive way. This study found that infants formed attachments with people based on the quality of the relationship.

The role of fathers was also examined in this and other studies. The studies found that infants may seek mothers and fathers for different reasons – the mother as a source of comfort when distressed, the father for particular types of stimulating and fun play. However, the father is not seen as a poor substitute for a mother; rather he offers a unique contribution to the development of the infant. The child is able to form equal attachments to its mother and father, as more than one type of satisfaction can be derived from an attachment figure. Lone parents, whether male or female, can offer a range of behaviour, some like a mother and some like a father. The main factor which determines attachment is based on the quality of the relationship rather than specific behaviour (e.g. rough-and-tumble play, singing songs, cuddling and comforting are all equally important).

One of the most serious criticisms of Bowlby's theory was his belief that failure to form strong attachments during infancy is related to later adjustment problems and to difficulties in establishing loving relationships in adulthood. Studies published by Rutter (1979) questioned Bowlby's notion that maternal deprivation was the cause of children's failure to establish relationships in later years and become delinquent. Rutter found that other factors were much more likely to have caused these problems. In particular he found that the effects of physical and emotional neglect, stress within the family home and the lack of any positive relationships were factors which were more influential than maternal deprivation in affecting children's ability to form relationships. He was also interested in children who had spent time in institutional care, as he believed the impact of this could have a detrimental effect on the ability of children to form positive relationships.

Other psychologists also thought that Bowlby had failed to address the question of whether early deprivation was reversible. That is, would children who had experienced early deprivation be able to form positive relationships at a later date? Studies were carried out by Tizard and Hodges (1978) on children who had experienced early deprivation and had been looked after in children's homes. The study came to the conclusion that children who are deprived of positive attachments within their early years of life are able to make firm attachments later in their life, but this is not automatic. Positive attachments depend not solely on the child being placed within a family but on how parents work at nurturing these relationships. These later studies seemed to produce evidence that, although early experience can certainly cause emotional damage, there is little evidence to suggest that maternal deprivation alone is the major cause of the failure of children to form attachments. More important are factors such as neglect, abuse and stress within the family.

Although Bowlby is best known for his work with children, he developed his ideas throughout his working life in his three-volume work *Attachment and Loss*. The first book looks at *Attachment*, the second at *Separation* and the third at *Loss, Sadness and Depression*. Other people have used the ideas from attachment theory to gain a clearer understanding of adult attachments, looking particularly at how it impacts on the ability to maintain romantic relationships, the propensity to commit violence in a relationship and its role in abnormal personality development. Research is on-going into how children develop 'attachment strategies', or behaviours, in reaction to their early experiences of fear and anxiety associated with perceived danger, and whether these are re-activated when the person experiences stress as an adult.

Activity   *Attachment behaviour*

*Attachment behaviour is any form of behaviour that results in a
person attaining or maintaining proximity to some other clearly
identified individual who is conceived as better able to cope with
the world. It is most obvious whenever the person is frightened,
fatigued or sick, and is assuaged by comforting and caregiving.
At other times, the behaviour is less in evidence. [...] for a person
to know that an attachment figure is available [...] him a
strong and pervasive feeling of security, and [...]
and continue the relationship. Whilst attach[...]
obvious in early childhood, it can be obser[...]
especially in emergencies.*

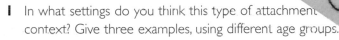

[...]9)

1 In what settings do you think this type of attachment[...]
   context? Give three examples, using different age groups.

2 What is the likely benefit of this type of behaviour for the servi[...]

3 What are the possible problems of this type of behaviour for the ser[...]er?

In care settings, attachment theory is useful when considering how people form,
maintain and end relationships. Attachment theory talks about 'providing a secure base
from which a child or adolescent can make sorties into the outside world and to which he
can return knowing for sure that he will be welcomed when he gets there, nourished
physically and emotionally, comforted if distressed, reassured if frightened. In essence,
this role is one of being available, ready to respond when called upon to encourage and
perhaps assist, but to intervene actively only when necessary . . . Much of the time the
role is a waiting one but it is none the less vital for that' (Bowlby, 1988, p.12). Can you
see the similarities (and differences) with care work in this definition? In care settings, a
major goal is to promote independence, and encourage acceptable risk, so that people
have the opportunity to develop to their full potential. In many cases, people are fearful
of trying new activities, or behaving in new ways, because they are outside their 'comfort
zone'. Care workers can use a knowledge of attachment theory to create a relationship
where the service user feels safe and supported enough (they trust that they won't be
abandoned, or neglected or abused) to try something new.

When the term 'secure' is used, which theorist whom we have already mentioned do you
think about? Maslow's hierarchy of needs puts 'safety and security' as one of the
fundamental needs which has to be met before people are able to meet their esteem and
social needs: before they are able to securely and confidently go out into the world and
achieve their potential. Attachment theory tends to confirm this. A psychologically
healthy individual can cope with routine and non-routine stresses and is able to develop
secure attachments with others such as partners, their children, friends, colleagues. They
are resilient and can recover from setbacks and they will be accepting of themselves and
others. As Bowlby notes, 'Throughout adult life the availability of a responsive
attachment figure remains the source of a person's feeling secure. All of us, from cradle

to grave, are happiest when life is organised as a series of excursions, long or short, from the secure base provided by our attachment figure(s)' (1988, p. 69).

Both staff and service users have to find the least disruptive ways of beginning and ending relationships in a care setting in order to develop secure attachments. Women and children escaping from domestic violence, someone attending hospital for regular chemotherapy treatment: they each have different attachment issues they are bringing to the care setting, and at the same time have to negotiate new relationships with the workers they encounter. Some service users can feel very unsettled and insecure when their favourite worker finishes a shift, let alone goes on holiday for a fortnight or moves to another project. Workers have to acknowledge the impact that these separations may have and work with service users to minimise their impact. Short- and long-term separations can have various impacts on a person, including numbness and withdrawal, searching and yearning for the person (or object), anger (at self, others, or the person who has left) and depression. If the situation is responded to effectively and the service user is supported, then they may come to an acceptance of the separation and they are able to reconnect actively with life once again on a secure footing. For many people who have lost contact with their family, or who have little or no family or friendship network, the care workers they come into contact with are the only source of attachment figures in their life, and this responsibility has to be faced with sensitivity.

Activity   *Attachment*

Read the following article and answer the questions which follow.

Across Scotland there are currently about 1000 young people between the ages of eight and sixteen living in residential schools. Most commonly, they are there because of 'emotional and behavioural needs'. Families vary from the fractured to the chaotic, and they have often missed out on large chunks of their education.

It is hard to appreciate the complexities of working with young people and their families who come from such difficult backgrounds. One boy had not taken his hood down since arriving at the school. He wears it everywhere, even when he goes to bed. One staff member speculates that this must act as some kind of security blanket. There are other mani-festations of the damage that has been done to the young people. Mostly, it comes out in anger and aggression, often in the form of bad language and the trashing of rooms.

But there is another side. Occasionally, in the middle of the night, a young person wakes up after having a nightmare and says that he wants his mum. Indeed, almost all of them constantly refer to missing their mothers and wanting to go home. The staff try to provide a kind of surrogate family for children who have been removed from their families. This creates a bond which will inevitably be broken when the children go home to their own families. 'These children's lives' says the headteacher of one school 'have often been very chaotic, and we try to give them a route back into childhood so that they can get those building blocks which are important for the development of all individuals'.

(Barber-Fleming, 2007, p. 16)

1 How does a knowledge of attachment theory help to explain the behaviour of the young people in the article?

2 What other psychological theory would help understand the behaviour of the young people?

Level Higher Transition and loss

As individuals go through life they experience many changes. These changes affect an individual's development and behaviour and are known as transitions. Adams et al. (1977) have described a transition as 'a discontinuity in a person's life space'. Some transitions are expected (we will all go through puberty; we will all age, if we live long enough), others are routine (starting school, starting a job, getting married) and others are non-routine (car accident, redundancy). A fuller list of life events was discussed in Chapter 3. In this chapter, we consider in more detail the responses that people have to these events.

Adams et al. created a general model which tries to explain the impact of transitions (see Figure 4.3). The seven-stage model tries to show how the experience of transition affects an individual's self-esteem. An understanding of the model can help to understand that people experience a range of feelings when they go through a transitional experience. The feelings are 'normal' and in time they will pass. There is also the idea that the person can have some control over what happens to them.

The stages represent a cycle of experiencing a change. At first the individual may feel in a state of shock, they may 'play down' what has happened, they may feel depressed. As they move through the transition, they may begin to acknowledge the reality of the change, test out new ideas or behaviour, understand themselves and use the experience of the change to modify their behaviour. The level of the person's self-esteem varies across the stages and follows a predictable path. For a transition to be effectively managed, all seven stages would have to be worked through. Individuals seldom move smoothly through all seven stages. Some may never move beyond the earlier stages, others may become 'stuck' in a state of depression. As life unfolds, an individual who has successfully reached the end of the stages after one transition may experience another major problem and be catapulted back to the beginning of the cycle.

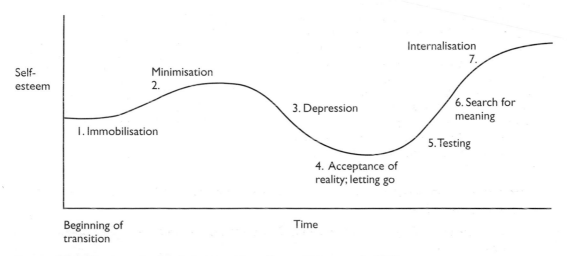

Figure 4.3 Self-esteem changes during transitions (Source: Adams et al., 1977)

Ifrah

Ifrah is 35 years old and has multiple sclerosis. Two years ago she was a senior partner in a large firm of architects in Glasgow. The changes in Ifrah's life had a profound effect on her and she became quite depressed. She no longer went out as she was embarrassed to be seen in her wheelchair, and her mother had to move into her house as Ifrah had lost interest in looking after her husband and children.

After three years the doctors told Ifrah that her condition seemed to be in remission and that they were confident that her condition, rather than deteriorating any further, would be stable at least for a number of years. This news had another profound effect on Ifrah and she seemed to come to terms with her condition. She began to go out again and even did some work for her old firm from the house. Her mother moved back to her own house and, with some assistance from private cleaners, Ifrah was able to manage the upkeep of her house. She began to take an interest in her husband and children again and she felt that her life was beginning again. Five years after her condition was first diagnosed, Ifrah's husband left her, unable to cope with the stress caused by the changes in his life. Her transitional cycle was beginning all over again.

One of the changes which happens in everybody's life is the experience of loss. It is part of everyone's life. Some losses may seem trifling, such as the loss of a book on the bus, but even this could have an effect on a person if the book was a gift from a loved one, or held some other special value for the person. Other losses can have a significant and long-term impact. For example, if your house is burgled and you lose a ring that your mother had given to you, or you lose all your family photographs in a house fire. Loss can have a devastating effect on those who directly experience the loss and it may also have a powerful effect on friends, family and carers.

Activity   *Types of loss*

Can you think of other types of loss which may occur in people's lives and which may have a significant effect on them?

Some that might be on your list are:

- Loss of a job – redundancy or dismissal
- Loss of freedom – imprisonment
- Loss of a pet
- Loss of a limb – accident or illness
- Loss of hearing/sight – accident or illness
- Loss of a partner through divorce or death

Death is the ultimate loss, and some would argue that in Britain the process of dying is being removed from everyday experience. Katz and Siddell (1994) describe this process as the 'unfamiliarity of death' and go on to say that Britain is a 'death denying society'. In many cases, the whole process of death and dying has been removed from the family into the hands of the medical profession. The ever-increasing progress of public health and medical science has meant that people now live longer than they have ever done in the past. No longer do epidemics kill thousands of people, children do not die of childhood diseases such as diphtheria and smallpox, and mothers and babies rarely die in the process of birth. While this progress has no doubt had a positive effect on the health and welfare of the population, it has had a profound effect on how death is viewed. Nowadays death is often seen as a failure of the medical profession to keep someone alive. It is not seen as an integral part of everyday life. Even the language that is used offers some insight into how death is viewed.

Activity — Phrases used to describe death

Make a list of some of the phrases you have heard which either try to be humorous about death, or which use a euphemism to try to 'soften' the idea of death.

Some you might have heard of are:

- she's left us
- he is pushing up the daisies
- he's kicked the bucket
- she's snuffed it;
- he's popped his clogs
- she's gone to her last resting place.

Why do people need to talk about death in this way? Do you think it is healthy or unhealthy to talk about death in this way?

The death of a loved one represents a profound change in people's lives. If there is some agreement that society today has more and more come to ignore the reality and inevitability of death and to a large extent sanitises the whole subject, what implications does this have for individuals who face their own death or experience the death of others? Much work has been carried out to research the process of death and dying, and it is widely acknowledged that grieving or mourning is an essential part of coming to terms with the loss. Grief involves emotional feelings (of sadness, anger, perhaps guilt) but also includes physical aspects (upset stomach, difficulty breathing), cognitive elements (lack of concentration, forgetfulness) and behaviours (poor sleep patterns). It is not a kind of mental illness, but sometimes people feel they are 'ill' because it has disrupted their normal functioning in a number of ways. It is an essential adaptive process, involving a number of phases which people will experience after a loss.

Mourning is another word for how people express their grief. In all cultures mourning has two main parts:

- how people show the feelings associated with grief
- the behaviour which is expected or accepted within a particular culture or society, such as wearing black or reciting prayers.

Different religions have their own rituals. Hindus have a period of 13 days of mourning, when friends will visit and offer condolence. Muslims have an official mourning period of three days (longer for a remaining spouse), and this may include a special meal to remember the deceased. In the Jewish religion, the close family remain at home for a week and pray three times a day. Mourning ends after 30 days, except for children of the deceased who mourn for a year. To find out more about religious and cultural differences in mourning look at the very informative and practical 'If I Should Die' website: www.ifishoulddie.co.uk

When a loss occurs it is inevitable that transitions or changes will occur in a person's life. Transition can be very challenging because people gain a feeling of security from the present pattern of their life. Colin Murray Parkes (1996) describes this as a person's 'assumptive world', or the ideas about their world which are based on how it has always been. It is assumed that this is how it will always be. To think otherwise would cause feelings of insecurity. When loss happens, ideas have to be changed about what is normally taken for granted in order to cope with the world which has changed. The individual has to understand the feelings they are experiencing and face the practical aspects of life after loss. Murray Parkes uses the language of attachment theory, and indeed he worked alongside Bowlby at one time.

Colin Murray Parkes

Murray Parkes's model consists of four phases that people responding to a loss are likely to go through. Some models of loss are sequential, which means that it is expected that the person is likely to go through them in a certain order. Human experience is generally more complex than this, and Murray Parkes believed instead that people had phases that they needed to pass through in order to resolve their grief. These phases will often overlap and a person will work through them in different ways depending on their particular circumstances. The four phases he outlines are:

1 Numbness

- Feelings of detachment and numbness
- These feelings form a psychological barrier to block the pain of loss
- Allows a person to apparently carry on with normal living
- It is a way of staying 'beyond' the pain of grief, temporarily

2 Searching and pining

- Concentration levels fall
- The individual adopts searching behaviours to try to locate that which has been lost
- The individual pines for the lost person and develops 'pangs of grief'

3 Depression

- Realisation that the lost person/object will not return
- Searching becomes pointless
- Anger abates to be replaced by feelings of apathy and despair

4 Recovery

- Former attachments are put behind the individual
- The individual releases themselves from the lost attachment
- The person can now adopt new thinking, relationships and attachments and normal living

Murray Parkes suggests there are a number of factors, *determinants of grief*, which affect the extent and depth to which an individual may experience the grieving process.

> *Those who are concerned with the effects of bereavement have to take into consideration many possible factors when trying to explain the differences between individuals in their response to this event. It is not enough to say that the loss of a love object causes grief, and leave it at that. Grief may be strong or weak, brief or prolonged, immediate or delayed; particular aspects of it may be distorted and symptoms that usually cause little trouble may become major sources of distress.*

(Murray Parkes, 1996, p. 117)

Some of the factors which Murray Parkes suggests may affect a person's grief response include:

- the way in which the person died: was it unexpected, violent, a suicide, an accident, part of a public incident such as a train crash?
- the relationship to the individual: was it their unborn baby, a grandchild, a sibling; their lifelong partner; a relationship that had been kept secret?
- what had happened before the death: what was the relationship like – was it loving or argumentative; were there other stresses in their life anyway?
- previous experiences of when a death has occurred: how did they cope with it then?
- differences in personality: is the person likely to repress their feelings and try to avoid grief, or do they have a tendency towards anxiety?
- different social variables, values and attitudes: does their family/culture allow them to express grief, or expect them to 'keep a stiff upper lip'?

Another factor which has a significant effect on the grieving process is the age and cognitive ability of the bereaved person. Younger people, or people who have limited cognitive or communication abilities, can find it difficult to understand what is happening to them and have difficulty in expressing their emotions. It is vital that care workers find ways of enabling people of all ages and abilities to understand and express their grief, perhaps through use of pictures, objects and physical expression.

Activity   *Applying Murray Parkes's model*

What particular aspects of the situation in the following case study might make it more difficult for Ken to recover from his grief, according to Murray Parkes?

Ken

Ken is 35 years old with a successful career in the computer industry near Edinburgh. Two years ago his wife Angela died of breast cancer. Ken was devastated by his wife's death. Everyone was very supportive of Ken and offered both emotional and practical help for quite a long time after Angela's death.

After two years this support began to scale down as both friends and family felt his period of mourning had 'elapsed' and he should now 'get on with his life'. His married friends began to invite him to parties and barbecues. Ken was initially quite happy to go as it got him out of the house, but he soon realised that there always seemed to be 'an available woman' at these events and it was expected that they would get together. Similarly, his male friends wanted him to 'get back on the scene' again and come out to pubs and clubs. When Ken refused, his friends accused him (behind his back) of wallowing in his grief. Their attitude was that he had no children to look after, he was still young and had enough money to enjoy himself. So he should put Angela's death behind him and start to enjoy life again.

But grief and mourning do not adhere to rigid time scales and Ken was not yet ready to adjust to life without his wife. It may be that Ken needs some help to come to terms with his wife's death in order that he can come through the grieving process.

William Worden

Worden (2003) looks at the process of grieving in a different way from Murray Parkes. He looks not at what happens *to* you, but more at what a person *has to do* in order to cope with the loss. Therefore his is a slightly more active model of loss, which is useful in care work as it suggests things the person, or those around them, might be involved in doing to enable them to work through their process of grief. People use the mourning process to say 'goodbye' to their loved one, and they all do this in a different way. They have different thoughts and behaviours which they develop and then perhaps need to change again if they are to move on. Worden talks about 'tasks' that a person needs to complete before they are likely to move on, rather than stages. This implies a more active engagement with the grieving process than the phase model.

Before we look at his model in more detail, he raises a point which relates to the question that was asked at the very beginning of this chapter: are psychological processes universal?

There is evidence that all humans grieve a loss to one degree or other. Anthropologists who have studied other societies, their cultures and their reactions to the loss of loved ones report that whatever the society studied, in whatever part of the world, there is an almost universal attempt to regain the lost loved object, and/or there is the belief in an after life where one can rejoin the loved one. In preliterate societies, however, bereavement pathology seems to be less common.

(Worden, 2003, p. 9)

Worden identifies four 'tasks of mourning'. He was keen to point out that, although there is some ordering suggested in his definitions, these are not 'stages' which a person *has* to follow in a particular order. It is possible for someone to accomplish some of the tasks and not others. This would mean they would have an incomplete adaptation to the loss, which is similar to having incomplete healing from a physical injury. However, Worden believes that 'Uncompleted grief tasks can impair further growth and development' (2003, p. 27).

Task 1: To accept the reality of the loss

The first task of grieving is to come to terms with the reality that the person is dead, that they are gone and that they are not going to return. Even if the person has been very ill for some time and the family may have known that they were dying, it may still be difficult to accept that the loved one is actually dead.

Some people refuse to believe that the loss is real and get stuck in grieving at this first task. It is very normal after a death to hope for a reunion or to assume that the deceased is not gone. However, for most people, this illusion is short lived and it allows them to move on to Task 2. Sometimes they will engage in 'mummification', where they retain the possessions of the deceased person, or keep their bedroom exactly as it was when they died. This is not unusual in the short term but becomes denial if it goes on for a longer time.

Task 2: To experience the pain of grief

It is necessary to acknowledge and work through this pain or it will manifest itself through some symptom or other form of unusual behaviour. Suppressing pain may prolong the process of grieving. Not everyone experiences the same intensity of pain or feels it in the same way, but it is impossible to lose someone you have been deeply attached to without experiencing some level of pain. Society may be uncomfortable with the mourner's feelings and this might make it difficult to express them honestly. People can deny that they feel pain, by having 'thought-stopping' procedures or keeping very busy so there is no time to think.

Task 3: To adjust to an environment in which the deceased is missing

Now the bereaved person needs to adjust to the environment (home, relationship, family, friends, pastimes) from which the dead person is missing. Bereaved people must restore their self-confidence if they are to overcome their grief. This means different things, depending on what the relationship was and the various roles the deceased played. For many widows in traditional marriages, it takes a considerable amount of time to take on all the roles such as managing the finance, making repairs around the home, etc. Many survivors resent having to develop new skills that their partner used to perform.

Many people, however, struggle to achieve Task 3 by promoting their own helplessness and by not developing the skills they need to cope, or by withdrawing from the world and not facing up to their new situation.

Task 4: To withdraw emotional energy and reinvest it in another relationship

In this last task the mourner should take 'emotional energy' from the relationship with the dead person and reinvest it into different aspects of their lives, such as relationship(s), work, hobbies, activities, etc. This is difficult for some people because they see it as somehow dishonouring the memory of the deceased. In some cases, they might also be frightened by the prospect of reinvesting their emotions in another relationship in case it too ends with loss. Other family members might also disapprove if they start a new relationship. Some people find loss so painful that they make a pact with themselves never to love again. In some way, their life has stopped when the loss occurred.

Managing to achieve these four tasks, in Worden's view, ensures that the person will be able to grieve and mourn for the person they have lost in a way that allows them to move on from the pain of the loss towards a positive readjustment of their own lives. Worden's tasks do offer some help in understanding the grieving process, but care must be taken in applying this model to everyone. All experiences of death are individual and not everyone will 'achieve' Worden's four tasks. There is no time limit to mourning or the feelings of grief. Each person will determine this process for themselves. The model indicates *dimensions* or *aspects* of the grieving process, and this enables you to understand why the person might be experiencing a range of sometimes apparently contradictory feelings.

CASE STUDY

Jin-ming

Jin-ming was a 78-year-old woman who lived in Glasgow on her own in the house she had lived in for over 50 years. Nine years ago when she was 69 her husband Han-chen died suddenly of a stroke. Jin-ming was completely broken-hearted. They had recently celebrated their golden wedding anniversary (50 years) and had a good and happy marriage.

As the breadwinner of the house Han-chen had always been the one to deal with all the money matters in the home. He had paid the mortgage, council tax and all the household bills. He had dealt with all the details of his pension and insurance policies. Han-chen had also taken responsibility for all the DIY tasks in the home. Jin-ming, meanwhile, did all the cooking, cleaning and shopping. Theirs was a traditional type of relationship.

When Han-chen died, Jin-ming found she could not cope with either the emotional or practical aspects of life without him. She stopped going to her church groups and instead never ventured out of the house. She became quite depressed, and her family became worried about her. At first, she refused to go and live with any of them and would not accept a place in supported

CASE STUDY
continued

accommodation in the street next to her eldest daughter. Her daughter realised that her mother might take a while to accept that change was needed, so she didn't insist. Every time her mother came for a visit, she would take her a walk past the supported accommodation and admire the garden. One day they stopped and spoke to some people who were sitting outside and they were invited to stay for a cup of tea. Although Jin-ming never got over the death of her husband, and continued to think about him every day, she decided she wanted to live in the accommodation near her daughter. She was now able to enjoy the new direction her life was taking.

SUMMARY

In this chapter, which covers material at Intermediate 2 and Higher levels, you have been encouraged to look at ways in which psychology can help you to understand the ways in which people develop and behave.

A variety of 'tools' have been used in the form of approaches, theories and models which help to explain aspects of the people with whom you work. These 'tools' offer general guidelines and explanations. They cannot be used as precise answers or explanations because all people are individuals with unique life experiences, but they do at least go some way to give you a body of knowledge which can help you be a more self-aware, and knowledgeable, worker.

The chapter has included discussion of both the strengths and the weaknesses of three different psychological approaches and six psychological theorists, aspects of whose work can be applied in care services. It has considered the effects of attachment, transition and loss on human development and behaviour.

Activity

Applying psychological concepts to the MacDonald and Khan families

1 Using Erikson's 'Eight Stages of Development', outline the stages of development of four members of the MacDonald and Ahmed families (see 'Case study – A tale of two families' in Chapter 7).

2 Choose one person from each of the families in the case study and, using a psychological theory from either Intermediate 2 or Higher level, describe how far their needs are being met.

3 Describe the transitions and losses experienced by one adult in the MacDonald and Ahmed families and the effects they might have on their development and behaviour.

4 What is self-concept? Describe the self-esteem of one member in the MacDonald and Ahmed families.

Suggested reading

Hayes, N. and Orrell, S. (1998). *Psychology: an Introduction*, 3rd edition. London: Longman
This book provides a good basic textbook for this level of study. It has a helpful range of exercises and self-assessment questions. It also attempts to show examples of how psychology can be applied to everyday contexts, or in social or political life.

Berry, J.W., Poortinga, Y., Segall, M. and Dasen, P. (2002) *Cross-Cultural Psychology: Research and Applications,* 2nd edition. Cambridge: Cambridge University Press
This book provides a detailed discussion about the rapidly growing field of cross-cultural psychology. It covers topics such as personality, communication, language and emotions.

Cardwell, M., Clark, L. and Meldrum, C. (2004) *Psychology,* 3rd edition. London: Collins
A comprehensive look at psychology, sometimes at a more detailed level than required for this book. It provides a good introduction to a number of the topics covered in this chapter such as psychological approaches, attachment theory, and cultural bias in psychology.

Messner, D. and Jones, F. (eds) (1999) *Psychology and Social Care*. London: Jessica Kingsley
A detailed look at some aspects of psychology as they relate to care settings. There are chapters on risk assessment, prejudice and discrimination, attachment and separation and dying and bereavement.

CHAPTER 5
Sociology for Care

Susan Gibb

> *Sociology may make us see in a new light the very world in which we have lived all our lives.*
>
> (Meighan, 1981)

This chapter aims to provide a clear and interesting introduction to sociology. The meaning of sociology is examined, together with a consideration of four different sociological theories: functionalist, conflict, symbolic interactionist and feminist.

The material covered in this chapter is relevant to Sociology and Psychology for Care, Intermediate 1 Outcome 1; Sociology for Care, Intermediate 2 Outcome 1; and Sociology for Care, Higher, all outcomes.

By the end of this chapter you should be able to:

★ define sociology and understand key sociological concepts

★ identify and explain four different sociological theories

★ examine aspects of the family and deviance using these sociological theories

★ examine social inequality and its impact on life chances

★ apply your knowledge of sociology to the care context.

Sociology – definitions and concepts

Sociology is a fascinating subject. It provides useful and sometimes unexpected insights into the way society works. It enables us to look at familiar things with different eyes. In common with psychology, it is an alternative to 'common-sense' explanations of human behaviour, and it often turns 'common sense' on its head. It provides concepts – or ideas – to help us understand things, rather than just describe them. There is no one single definition of sociology, and the more you study it the more you will realise that the definition depends to some extent on the viewpoint or perspective that you are taking. Before reading further, imagine that you have said to a friend that you're going to study sociology and your friend says 'What's sociology?' What ideas do you have in your mind about sociology and what it is that you will be studying?

To get you started in your thinking about sociology some brief statements are given below, but do not take these as the whole story. At the end of the chapter you will be asked again to try to define sociology, and hopefully you will be able to give a fuller answer then.

Some statements about sociology:

> *[Sociology is] the study of society. [It] . . . includes the social structure of society, its social institutions and how people live . . . [and] culture . . . [which] deals with the ways in which . . . individual behaviour, values and attitudes are culturally conditioned; and how different people handle the great life experiences of courtship, marriage, birth, growing up, work, old age, death.*

(Younghusband, 1964)

> *Sociology: the science of the development and nature and laws of human (esp. civilised) society; study of social problems.*

(Oxford Dictionary)

> *Sociology is left-wing rubbish.*

(Edwina Currie, formerly Conservative Minister of Health, quoted in Dominelli, 1997)

> *Sociology is a vast discipline characterised by a variety of theoretical approaches and perspectives.*

(Dominelli, 1997)

Sociology and care practice

The aim of this chapter is not to make you a sociologist, but to offer you some sociological insights and ways of looking at the issues you will face in care settings. You will understand more clearly the influence that working and living within systems – the family, a care organisation, society itself – has on people, and you will know more fully how to work within, and at times against, these systems. In fact, some people have seen the study of sociology as potentially damaging to care workers – they fear that too much insight and too much analysis may make workers unduly critical of the structures and ways in which they work, of the bureaucracies in which they are enmeshed and of the institutions which provide social care to thousands of vulnerable people.

Others, however, see sociology as empowering for care workers, as it provides some insights into society, culture and institutions which can enable them to contribute to improvements in the quality of life of those with whom they work. It is this latter view which is promoted in this chapter. Psychology helps us look at individual differences in behaviour, but it is only when people are also seen as part of the group and society within which they live that a more complete picture is possible. Something that is a personal problem affects just the individual and those closest to them. However, when a problem affects a number of people, it becomes a concern for society, and sociology looks at how these problems arise, how they get defined, and how society responds to them. A single chapter devoted to sociology cannot hope to give you more than an introduction to such a wide-ranging subject. You are encouraged to read some of the recommended texts if you wish to take your thinking further.

Sociological concepts

Comte, or, to give him his full name, Auguste Francois Marie Xavier Comte (1789–1857) was the first person to use the term 'sociology' in the late 1830s. Comte saw sociology as the scientific study of society. He stated his belief in these words: '*Savoir pour prevoir et prevoir pour pouvoir*'. This can be translated as: 'To know in order to predict and to predict in order to empower'. For Comte, sociology could be seen as the scientific study of society, seeking to provide an understanding of it. Although the scientific status of sociology continues to be an area of debate and dispute, Comte's aim to understand society, and through this understanding to be able to promote change, continues to be relevant to this day.

In sociology there are some fundamental concepts (ideas) which it is as well to consider at the very beginning of your study so that in later discussion they can be used without further explanation. From the many sociological concepts, brief consideration will be given here to society; culture, norms and values; role and status; social inequality and life chances. Socialisation is also a sociological concept of prime importance but, since it was examined fully in Chapter 3, it is only briefly touched on in this chapter. These are not the only concepts which are relevant to your study, and many others, e.g. discrimination, deviance and the family, will receive consideration at appropriate points in this chapter.

Society

Activity — *What is meant by 'society'?*

Sociology leads to the careful and detailed examination of society and the way it works. But what is meant by 'society'? Before going further a useful activity (adapted from Brown, 1979) is to draw a simple picture, or diagram which represents 'society' for you. You can use shapes and pictures but no words, and spend no more than five minutes doing this.

The picture you drew will say something about your view of society, about where you see people fitting into it and about the assumptions you make about the world around you.

Now examine Figure 5.1 and answer the following questions.

1 What do you think each of these illustrations suggests about society?

2 What do you think the boxes in (c) stand for? Make a copy of the diagram and fill in the boxes.

3 Explain your own diagram and discuss what it says about your own interpretation of society.

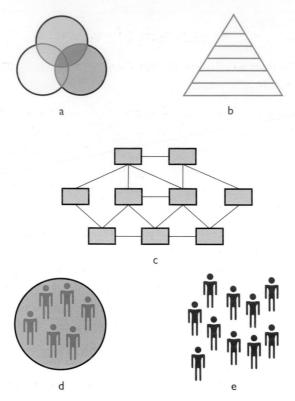

Figure 5.1 Diagrams that illustrate 'society'

Although some theorists argue that we are moving towards a global society, 'society' is still usually regarded as the country or nation-state in which you live. For example, Scotland is increasingly seen as a society which is distinct from other parts of Britain in many ways, though having a great deal in common in other ways. Language often defines a society; laws, education, religion and other aspects of culture distinguish one 'society' from another. Although Scotland shares a language with the rest of Britain, there are distinct Scottish turns of phrase and dialects. Gaelic is still spoken in the Highlands and Islands and is increasingly being taught in other parts of Scotland. Scotland has its own parliament, legal system, education system and religious denominations. Scotland is a multi-cultural society in its own right, but it is still part of Great Britain in many social, economic, political and cultural ways.

Often 'society' is referred to as something distinct and independent, as a thing in itself rather than just the sum total of the members who are part of it. 'Society' is often blamed for things like the inability of people to change their circumstances or the problems that they face. Avril Taylor (1993), for example, in her study of women drug users in Glasgow talks of 'the inability of society either to recognise or to cater for such women's needs'.

Culture, norms and values

As human beings we learn most of our behaviour. We do not just behave instinctively: we use our intelligence, observational skills and learning. We learn how to behave, and we share much of this behaviour with other members of the society to which we belong. This learned, shared behaviour is known as culture. Culture is the way of life of society's members. It includes the values, beliefs, customs, norms and rules which human beings learn as members of a society. Without culture, human society could not exist.

Activity   *Music as an example of culture*

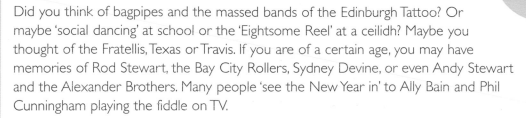

Write down 10 things that come to your mind when you think of the phrase 'Scottish music'.

Did you think of bagpipes and the massed bands of the Edinburgh Tattoo? Or maybe 'social dancing' at school or the 'Eightsome Reel' at a ceilidh? Maybe you thought of the Fratellis, Texas or Travis. If you are of a certain age, you may have memories of Rod Stewart, the Bay City Rollers, Sydney Devine, or even Andy Stewart and the Alexander Brothers. Many people 'see the New Year in' to Ally Bain and Phil Cunningham playing the fiddle on TV.

Most of the above artists are – or were – fairly mainstream Scottish musicians and singers, and they represent a wide enough range. But there are many other musical traditions in Scotland that show even greater diversity even in this one aspect of culture. There is still a very lively tradition of Gaelic singing and the Mod is still held annually in October in a different venue in Scotland. A lot of Scottish bands, such as Salsa Celtica and the Afro-Celt Sound System, have developed fusion music where they mix Scottish instruments and arrangements with musical traditions from other countries. There is Euridyce, a socialist woman's choir who sing contemporary and traditional protest songs, and choirs for asylum seekers that sing songs from all the different countries represented.

Gaelic punk, Scottish-Asian, the list of musical combinations is endless, and that's the point: there is not just one type of 'Scottish music'. You may never pay money to hear the new opera by James MacMillan or Judith Weir, or you might happily avoid going within 10 miles of the Loopallu or Wickerman festivals, but many people in Scotland would make one or the other their priority. That is the diversity of culture: it is never 'one size fits all'!.

Culture is something which can and does change. Sometimes it changes because attitudes change: things which have previously been accepted as 'right' or inevitable come to be seen as unnecessary, oppressive or disempowering. For instance, 100 years ago, women weren't able to vote and people with disabilities were placed in institutions, far away from their local community. Advances in technology have led to other cultural changes such as the use of txt language and the ability of parents to know whether their unborn child has a disability. The impact of the media is much larger now, because people have much greater access to a wide range of images through the Internet and numerous TV channels, and it influences greatly how we understand the world and our place it. Changes in demography – the way the population is structured – have led to other cultural changes, like the increase in the number of older adults who have greater spending power ('the grey pound') but who will also need more care services as their health deteriorates.

Norms are unwritten rules that are generally agreed to be the right way to do things in any situation. You don't often know what they are until you have broken one – especially in a new situation. If you go to hear a Mozart symphony in a concert hall for the first

Figure 5.2 Taiko drummer. The Taiko tradition originates from the west coast of Japan. Each spring, Japanese Matsuri for Glasgow holds a festival in the Botanic Gardens. The aim is to advance education in Japanese culture and heritage, and to promote wide community involvement in the awareness of diverse cultures

time, you may wonder why people don't clap at the end of each section of music. It is the norm (generally so you don't interrupt the focus of the musicians) to wait until the very end to applaud. It doesn't say this on the ticket, or in the programme – you are just expected to know it. You will certainly pick it up very quickly, if you are the only one clapping and other people turn round and glare! Can you remember back to the first few days of your college course, or the start of a new job? People tend to hold back and wait to see how things are (what the norms are) – before they feel they have the true picture of what's going on. For instance, all tutors say that you have 15 minutes for your break, but only some of them make a big deal about it if you are late. For a service user or worker visiting a care setting for the first time, the norms are often more important, and more difficult to work out, than the officially stated rules and policies.

Values are your beliefs about what it is vital to uphold above all else. People have differing viewpoints about what is important or not in life, and this often leads to conflict. Many parents value education as the way for their children to do better in life than they did, but their children may see things differently. They often cannot see the benefit of sticking in at school or college and maybe not even getting a job at the end, or of having to give up the things that they value at the moment: social contact, having a girlfriend/boyfriend, experimenting with drink, etc. In fact a lot of the issues in the 'generation gap' come from this difference in values and priorities. Within care settings, someone in a care home may value peace and quiet while the person in the next room likes to chat and have the TV on, and this can cause conflict. Neither person is right, but it is difficult for both people to meet their needs at the same time.

Activity — Religious attendance and age

Another example of how culture and values vary across age groups is religion. In the Scottish census in 2001, 67% of people reported that they had a religion (42% Church of Scotland, 16% Roman Catholic, 7% other Christian, and the following religions, all with less than 1%: Muslim, Buddhist, Sikh, Jewish and Hindu).

However, of the 28% who reported that they didn't have a religion (5% didn't answer the question at all), there is a big difference when you look at the figures by age group in Figure 5.3.

Using what you know about culture, norms and values can you explain why there is this difference across the age groups?

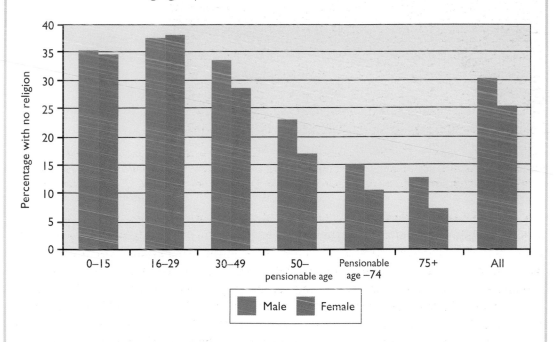

Figure 5.3 Proportion of people with no current religion by sex and age, as a percentage of all people (Source: Scottish Executive, 2005)

Role and status

> All the world's a stage,
>
> And all the men and women merely players:
>
> They have their exits and their entrances;
>
> And one man in his time plays many parts, . . .
>
> (William Shakespeare, As You Like It, 1599)
>
> In a sense, society provides individuals with scripts which enable them, like actors in a theatre, to play their roles.
>
> (Heraud, 1970)

The above quotations refer to people's social roles. Role and status are two further fundamental sociological concepts. A fairly straightforward definition of role is that it is the part an individual appears to play in a group, and the behaviour which is expected from a person in that position. The predictability of behaviour associated with a role (mums are expected to . . ., teachers are generally . . .) enables us to interact more easily with each other. A role has three constituents: part, behaviour and social expectation. A role such as son or daughter is ascribed (given), but other roles are achieved, or chosen, such as teacher or student. Most people have multiple roles. For example, the roles of wife, mother, teacher, daughter can all be held by the same person at the same time, sometimes in harmony, sometimes in conflict with one another. The roles which a person has will, to a large extent, determine the **status** which that person has in society. Status refers to the position a person has in society and the degree of respect which this position commands. As with role, some statuses are achieved and some are ascribed. One status which is largely ascribed is that of social class, though change in social class can be achieved (either up or down) through social mobility. Thus a bank manager has a fairly high status and can be defined as being a member of the middle class. But if she loses her job, can't pay the mortgage, and ends up in a hostel for homeless people, then there is a clear difference in her role and status. Some of the people we work with in care settings have experienced a change in their role or status and are in the process of adapting to this difference.

Social Inequality and life chances

Sociologists believe that social inequality, the fact that there is an unequal distribution of the opportunities and rewards in society, exists not because some people are less motivated, or don't try as hard as others to succeed, but because society is organised in such a way that it is more difficult for people from certain groups to achieve success in society. This has an effect on their life chances: they are more likely to die at a younger age, experience health problems, live in poverty, be unemployed and be less likely to have access to good education. Certain groups are more likely to experience social inequality because of the discrimination they face, for example on the basis of their race or ethnic origin, gender, disability, health status, class, sexual orientation or age.

Socialisation

In Chapter 3 socialisation was defined as the process by which people learn the culture of their society. At this point you are advised to go back to Chapter 3 to read the account of socialisation again, and to remind yourself of the relevant terms: **primary** and **secondary socialisation**; **agents of socialisation**.

Table 5.1 Sociological concepts

Society	Country or nation state; often distinguished from other societies by language, laws, education, religion, etc.
Culture	Learned, shared behaviour; the way of life of society's members
Role	The part which an individual plays in a group and the behaviour which is expected of a person in that position
Status	Position in society and the degree of respect which this position commands
Norms	Unwritten rules which are generally accepted as the way to act in certain situations
Values	Beliefs about what is right and wrong, and what is important or not
Social inequality	An unequal distribution of the opportunities and rewards in society, because of the way in which society is structured
Life chances	The differing possibilities of having access to opportunities in society, e.g. differences in health, employment, housing, education, access to a safe environment
Socialisation	The process by which people acquire and learn the culture of their society

Level Higher Sociological theories

So far you have been introduced to a number of concepts which will be woven through this chapter and the rest of the book. They present the fundamental ideas and building blocks upon which thinking about the behaviour of people in society can be built. In order to gain a fuller understanding of sociology and the way in which it sets out to explain the social world it is also necessary to look at the different approaches, or theories, that sociologists take. Just as you can have a point of view about many things which differs from that of other people (the way you view education, for example, might differ from that of a friend, or someone you meet on holiday) so sociologists differ among themselves about the way they look at people and society. These different viewpoints are called theories, and four different theories are discussed. These are not the only sociological theories but provide an introduction to the main approaches, which can be enlarged through further study.

They are:

- functionalist theory
- conflict theory
- symbolic interactionist theory
- feminist theory.

Try not to be put off by long words here, for what these theories set out to do is to clarify ways of looking at society. The ideas presented in these theories are usually quite straightforward once you have grasped the main terms. They can be split into two different types of theory: macro-sociological and micro-sociological.

Macro-sociological approaches see individual behaviour as being influenced by the demands and constraints of the social system in which the person lives. This includes the functionalist and conflict theories.

Micro-sociological approaches see the individual as capable of exerting influence on society, and not just conforming to the requirements of the systems in which they live. This includes the symbolic interactionist theory.

Feminism is a very wide-ranging theory: some strands come under the micro approach, and others come under the macro approach.

One way of seeing this macro/micro difference in explanation is that individuals are seen as constantly creating their reality in the micro-sociological approach, but in the macro-sociological approach as always being subject to the external forces of the systems in which they live. A 'system', in the way that we are going to use the term here, is any group of people bound by rules and norms. So a family is a system, as is a care organisation, and of course society itself.

Functionalist theory

Functionalism is one of the earliest sociological theories and still remains useful in its emphasis on looking at society as something more than the sum total of individuals who go to make it up. Its early emphasis on scientific method also retains some relevance in sociological thought, as long as this is balanced with other theories.

Emile Durkheim (1858–1917), a professor at the University of Bordeaux and then the Sorbonne in Paris, was a great thinker and writer who developed ideas about society using the term functionalism for the first time. In its earlier stages the essential ideas of functionalism were that social groups and institutions perform functions which are useful to society as a whole. Society is seen as being made up of inter-related parts which form a system, the social system. Understanding of each individual part can only be gained by looking at the functions it has in relation to the whole. Society was compared to the human body, to illustrate the fact that they were both systems which relied on the proper functioning of each constituent part in order to survive. In a human being, the heart has specific functions in relation to pumping blood around the body, but its function can only be understood in relation to other organs which transport oxygen to the blood and take waste products away from it. Similarly, functionalist theory emphasises the importance of looking at parts of society, such as the family, in terms of their function in, and maintenance of, the social system as a whole.

> *The function of any recurrent activity, such as the punishment of a crime, or a funeral ceremony, is the part it plays in the social life as a whole and therefore the contribution it makes to the maintenance of the structural continuity.*

(Radcliffe-Brown, 1935)

There have been many great civilisations in the past, such as Roman, Greek, Inca and Aztec, but they all disappeared because some aspect of their structure began to falter and it eventually led to the downfall of the whole system. Functionalists are interested in this question: why do certain aspects of society exist, and what role, or function, does each aspect play in maintaining that society? In terms of care issues, this is important, because if some parts of society aren't functioning well, the government needs to intervene to address the problems. If the government can be clear about what role that part plays, it can make policies and procedures which aim to bring society back into balance again. For instance, with the change in the structure of the family since the mid 1970s, the role of looking after babies and young children is now not only limited to mothers. Society has adapted to the change of working mothers, and the function of rearing children is now shared with fathers, and with care providers such as nursery schools, partly because governments have provided money to fund the growth of this level of educational provision.

This is the important aspect for Durkheim: it is important not just to have a clear knowledge about a problem, but to know also how we can change things to create social order, or harmony, in society again:

> *Consequently, to explain a social fact it is not enough to show the cause on which it depends; we must also, at least in most cases, show its function in the establishment of social order.*

(Durkheim, 1938)

Consensus about the norms and values was seen to be the ideal situation for a society, and all the inter-connected, inter-dependent parts should work together to maintain the cohesion that would maintain an orderly, well-functioning society. This consensus model can be used to look at all levels and types of 'system' such as a college class, a care organisation or a family. They all have different functions that they need to perform to survive, and some of the people in them will be taking a functionalist view, aiming to keep everything in harmony. Others may no longer be adhering to the values and norms of the system and may be seen as disruptive, like the student who is always late, or the teenager who stays out late without telling his parents where he is. The way the 'system' responds to this is varied, but it might involve re-educating them (sitting down with the student and working out strategies to improve punctuality), or removing them altogether if they are unable to conform.

Criticisms of functionalism

One of the main criticisms levelled against functionalists is that they fail to take adequate account of conflict in society. However, although functionalists do not see conflict as inherent in society, they do not ignore it altogether. Rather, they attempt to explain it in terms of the contribution that conflict can make to the maintenance of social order. Situations of conflict, such as a war with another country, or outrage at the sexual abuse of children, enable society to reconfirm what is important to it. In this sense, dysfunction is useful for society because it helps to clarify what is valued, for example freedom from abuse, and therefore dysfunction is something which society should try to correct.

A further criticism is that functionalists, in concentrating upon social functions and the social system, failed to take account sufficiently of the individual in society. This is a general criticism of all macro-sociological approaches. Feminists have seen much of functionalist theory as being gender-blind and conservative, promoting traditional views of institutions such as the family and in so doing perpetuating patriarchy, the role of women as housewives and mothers, and contributing to their continuing inequality and disempowerment. Finally, through seeing society in terms of functions and harmony, functionalists have failed to emphasise change and the need for progress.

Conflict theory

> *Society is like a more or less confused battle ground. If we watch from on high, we can see a variety of groups fighting each other, constantly forming and reforming, making and breaking alliances.*
>
> (Craib, 1984)

Unlike the functionalist theory, which emphasises equilibrium, balance and shared values, conflict theories rest on the view that conflict is fundamental between various groups in society, because they have inherently different interests from one another. The interests of some groups are better served by the way in which society is organised than the interests of others: some groups of people in society get a better deal from 'society' than other groups. This is not because some people work harder: it results from the way in which society is structured. In any group of people, whether a society or an organisation, there are limited resources and there is competition for these scarce resources. In society, for instance, there may not be enough decent jobs or houses for everyone, and there can sometimes be conflict in communities about who should get the chance to get the resources which do come up. Therefore, competition, not consensus, is the main aspect of human relationships and, according to conflict theory, it is those who already hold power who will be more likely to succeed in this competition. Recognising this structured imbalance of power is the key to understanding the oppression by the dominant group.

In this section two major theorists who have put forward conflict theories will be considered. These are Karl Marx and Ralph Dahrendorf. Karl Marx (1818–1883) was born in Germany, lived for a time in Paris, where he met Friedrich Engels, with whom he formed a lifelong friendship, moved to Brussels and finally settled in London in 1949. He is best known for his views about the importance of economic structures in determining the way a society operates. The Marxist approach put forward a view of society which believed that in capitalist society there is a fundamental conflict of interest between two groups: the ruling class (bourgeoisie) which owns and controls the means of production, e.g. factories, and the subject class (proletariat) which produces labour but which is exploited and oppressed by the ruling class. In Marx's view only when the means of production are communally owned (i.e. equally owned and shared by everyone) will classes and conflict disappear. For Marx economic class and ownership of the means of production were the most fundamental divisions in society and the source of conflicts of interest. Economic relations were the central facts which determined how the rest of the relations in society were structured.

The second conflict theorist to be considered is Ralph Dahrendorf (born 1929). By coincidence he too was born in Germany and subsequently moved to London. He became Professor of Sociology at the London School of Economics. Dahrendorf took Marx's theories as a staring point but argued that in the twentieth century changes took place in society which necessitated a re-evaluation of Marx.

Dahrendorf sees functionalist theories as being utopian or idealistic in their analysis of society and proposes that at least one other way of looking at society is required. For Dahrendorf this is conflict theory. This theory emphasises change as continuous and normal in society. Dahrendorf believed that social conflict is the great creative force that carries along change. He goes on to state that 'wherever there is social life there's conflict, and the surprising thing in society would not be the presence of conflict but the absence of conflict'. He is not here just talking about major conflicts like wars and revolutions but also what happens in your family's house, the local care home or the most recent reality TV show! Thus so far two main concepts in the conflict model are change and conflict. For Dahrendorf a third important concept is constraint.

Unlike the functionalists, who suggest that agreement holds societies and organisations together, Dahrendorf argues that these are held together 'not by consensus but by constraint, not by universal agreement but by coercion of some by others'. Thus for Dahrendorf some groups in society coerce and others are coerced; some groups constrain, others are constrained. This has some similarities to Marx, who argued that the owners of the means of production constrain and coerce workers. Dahrendorf differs from Marx in seeing the situation as much more complicated than this, in seeing other sources of conflict than economic ones and the possibility that in some situations a person may be the source of constraint and in other situations may be constrained. For example, a teacher might constrain students in the classroom but might herself be constrained by the education authority in what she can teach. The essential point to grasp is that conflict, change and constraint, and not consensus, are points of departure in any analysis of social situations.

Criticisms of conflict theory

Dahrendorf again differs from functionalists in stating that the conflict theory is not the only way of looking at society, in a way building in his own criticism of his own theory. Functionalists usually claim that theirs is a comprehensive model and can be used to explain all social phenomena. But Dahrendorf (1964) states:

> As far as I can see, we need . . . both the equilibrium and the conflict models of society; and it may well be that . . . society has two faces of equal reality: one of stability, harmony and consensus and one of change, conflict and constraint.

There is clear evidence that the divisions in society are much more complicated than they were in Marx's day: there was not the large, professional middle class that there is today, and it is sometimes very difficult to identify who actually 'owns' the global multinationals that exist. Feminists and other campaigning groups have demonstrated that the way society is stratified, or structured, has to be seen as multi-dimensional: class alone no longer explains someone's position in society. Depending on the situation, society can also be seen to be divided along lines such as gender, race or age.

The divisions in society are also not static and fixed. Historically, the suffragettes campaigned strongly against the government to achieve votes for women, but withheld their campaign during the First World War, when British society was united against Germany. After the war, they reinstated their campaign vigorously. There are many instances of this type of changing situation when it comes to alliances and divisions in society.

Symbolic interactionist theory

In contrast to the macro approach presented by functionalism and conflict theory, symbolic interactionist theory focuses attention on the meanings which individuals give to social actions. Here interactions among individuals are seen as the starting point, rather than the way society is structured. The importance of society is not denied but social structures are seen as changeable through individual actions and open to varying interpretations. The main emphasis here is on George Herbert Mead's work on symbolic interactionism. Howard Becker's labelling theory, also within the interactionist theory, is discussed later in this chapter in the section on deviance.

In symbolic interactionism symbols are seen as the foundation on which interactions are built. A *symbol* can be defined as:

> *Any gesture, artifact, sign or concept which stands for or expresses something else . . .*

(Abercrombie et al., 1994)

A word can be a symbol. For example, the word 'table' has a symbolic meaning – it stands for a particular set of ideas about a thing called a table, which is immediately understood by those using the symbol and includes some meanings and excludes others. What does the symbol 'table' mean to you? At home it might symbolise the place you sit down to eat and chat, but also the place you have to do your college homework. If this later symbol takes on negative connotations (the work is piling up and never seems to get finished), it may stop having the positive associations it used to have for you. In some situations it has positive connotations and in others it has negative, but it is still the same word. Other words can take on particular meanings because they become associated in popular consciousness with a particular event. Examples of this are Piper Alpha, Dunblane, Lockerbie and 9/11.

A gesture such as a handshake is also a symbol which signifies a particular meaning, and in many societies is used as a welcome. This meaning is, however, culturally determined. The handshake on its own, without its symbolic meaning, would be meaningless to some people. If you try to shake the hand of a child, they often have no idea what to do and why they should do it. If you met someone from Japan, they might bow to you as a greeting. British people sometimes find it awkward to return the bow, perhaps because it symbolises subjection to them, or because it has a religious connotation, or because they are just not familiar with the action.

Clothes are very potent symbols. As a teenager, in particular, they say a lot about what group – or subculture – you identify with (punk, goth, ned, etc.). For all age groups, they convey all kinds of messages about factors such as what you feel about yourself, how much you like to conform, or what your income is. You can 'dress up' or 'dress down' depending on what message you want to convey. And, as anyone living in a house with a teenager knows, piles of washed and unwashed clothes on the floor can symbolise freedom or disrespect, depending on which point of view you are taking! In care settings, many organisations have moved away from requiring staff to wear uniforms as it conveys messages about power and control that they don't want to project to service users.

Symbolic interactionism originated in the USA. Among the founders was George Herbert Mead. Mead (1863–1931) was an American philosopher whose ideas had a great influence upon sociology. One of Mead's central ideas was that individuals develop their interactions and their ideas through their ability to put themselves in the position of others. The process of imagining responses is called role-taking. If I see you crying, for example, my response will be largely determined by me imagining myself in your position. It is likely that my response will be appropriate because I have internalised how to respond to crying and can, in my imagination, take the role of someone crying and respond to it. This process of role-taking is also central to the development of a concept of self.

According to Mead, without symbols there would be no human interaction and no human society. It is the use of symbols which distinguishes human interaction from the interactions of other species. It is only through symbols that the responses of others can be imagined. The individual imagines the effect of symbolic communication (verbal and non-verbal communication, words, gestures etc.) on others and so can anticipate their response. This is done through internal 'conversations' which individuals have with themselves, based on the imagined responses from other people – the generalised other.

Mead, in developing his thoughts about self, distinguishes between the 'me' and the 'I':

> The 'I' is the response of the organism to the attitudes of the others; the 'me' is the organised set of attitudes of others which one himself assumes. The attitude of the others constitute the organised 'me', and then one reacts towards that as an 'I'.

(Mead, quoted in Coser and Rosenberg, 1976)

This distinction between 'me' and 'I' is an important, though rather difficult, one to grasp. 'I' is the self-concept, 'me' is the definition of yourself in specific roles. 'I' has been built up from your reactions to others, their reactions to you and the way in which those reactions have been interpreted. This combination of social interaction and a person's definition of the situation gives rise to people making choices about which roles they take on board and how those roles are performed.

Criticisms of symbolic interactionism

As with the macro-sociological approaches, there are a number of criticisms which can be levelled against this micro-sociological approach, one of which is that there is insufficient consideration given to – guess what? – macro features such as the importance of historical aspects of society and the influences of institutions, power and class. Symbolic interactionists also fail to explain the source or origin of the symbols upon which communication and interaction depend. Why do people shake hands when they meet? Does it matter? Is it important to look at why a type of behaviour started, or is it interesting just to have an accurate record of what people are doing, and understand what it means to them? If symbolic interactionists are more interested at times in describing the variety of social life, rather than analysing the background and context to that behaviour, is it a problem? Part of your response to that might be: it depends on what we want to do with the information.

For care workers, we can use the aspects of any theory which we feel help us understand our behaviour, the behaviour of the people we work with, and the systems within which we operate. Any theory can only hope to explain some aspect of the full picture. Your job as a reflective practitioner is to use *all* your underpinning knowledge to decide which bits are most relevant in the particular situations you find yourself in. Looking back to the chapter on psychology, you can see the similarity: each psychological approach emphasises particular points, and it is only when you compare and contrast all the approaches in any situation that you can identify which are the most appropriate to use at that time.

Feminist theory

So macro approaches are criticised because they don't take account of an individual's power to influence society, and micro approaches are criticised because they don't take enough account of the importance of the way society is structured. The feminist theory adds another dimension to both of these critiques, because it maintains that all theories in the past have undervalued, or completely ignored, the importance of women's role in society. In this sense, it also stands as a useful reminder that the experience of many groups has been neglected by the mainly white, middle-class, heterosexual male academics who developed early sociological theories.

Feminism as a theory sets out to bring to centre stage and explain the position of women in society and to focus attention on how women have been subordinated and oppressed. There are a number of differing strands of feminist thought, some of which take a micro-sociological approach, and others take a macro-sociological approach. The theory as a whole is closely linked to feminism as a social movement, which advocates equality of opportunity for women and men, and the eradication of the economic, social, political and sexual inequalities that exist between them. As a sociological theory, feminism has only relatively recently made its way into general sociological literature. For example, a book published in 1971 entitled *Sociological Perspectives: Selected Readings*, edited by Thompson and Tunstall, had no mention of feminism, and out of 44 readings not a single one was by a woman or addressed issues specifically related to women. By 1991, *Sociology: Themes and Perspectives*, by Haralambos and Holburn, was giving considerable attention to feminist thought.

In spite of the relatively recent emergence of feminist theories in sociology, feminist ideas have been around for a long time. Mary Wollstonecraft expressed an equal rights doctrine as early as 1792 in her 'Vindication of the Rights of Women'; the Suffragettes fought for votes for women at the beginning of the twentieth century; feminist writers such as Simone de Beauvoir in France and Germaine Greer in Britain gained prominence in the 1950s and 1970s. More recent feminist thinkers have emphasised the diversity of feminist thought. Several strands of feminist thought can be identified, such as liberal feminism, radical feminism, Marxist feminism and black feminism.

All of the above developments can be referred to as the three waves of feminism:

Wave 1 – the beginnings of feminism, fighting for women's civil rights, especially equal rights to vote and to property;

Wave 2 – a more radical focus seeking reform of society in order to promote an equality of power in society and to eradicate male domination of women from all spheres of life;

Wave 3 – postmodern feminism, emphasising the diverse needs of different groups of women, e.g. black women, working-class women, while retaining the main focus of eradicating all inequalities.

To understand more fully the ideas behind feminist theory, we have to look at the ideas associated with gender and patriarchy. Many people have argued that differences in biology between men and women justify the domination of women by men and that they should occupy different roles in society. For example, one argument runs: because women can become pregnant and bear children they should stay at home to look after the children they produce; this is their 'natural' role. Since it is their 'natural' role to bear and look after children and be at home with them, it is also 'natural' that they should do the housework while they are there. Women, it is argued, make unreliable workers anyway, always taking time off to have children or to look after them when they are ill.

Feminist theory seeks to give insight into why there is absolutely nothing 'natural' about this situation. Feminists claim that there is nothing in female biology which determines that women should perform childcare or housework or should be any less reliable than men, given the same opportunities and rights. In the 1970s, Ann Oakley gave research status for the first time to the subject of housework, based on the feminist principle that the 'personal is political'. (You can see that this approach reflects a micro-sociological approach: individuals *can* influence society.) Before this, such a subject would not have been considered worthy of sociological research. Oakley and others argue that, although male and female are biological terms, gender roles in society are culturally, not biologically, determined. Most feminist thinkers support this view and feel that confusion between sex (male and female) and gender (masculine and feminine) has been used as an excuse to promote the subordination of women, through placing them in roles which are given inferior status in society.

Figure 5.4 Tug of war. Women have many more opportunities in all areas of life: here the women of Knoydart take on the men in a tug of war.

This social construction of gender is an essential aspect of patriarchy, the systematic structuring of male dominance in society. This strand of feminist thought takes a macro approach, looking at the impact that society has on the lives of women. For instance, in the Health and Social Work sector in Scotland, although 82% of the workforce is female, women make up only 19% of the Chief Executives in the Health Service (Fitzgerald and McKay, 2006) And this is despite the fact that there has been sex discrimination and equal pay legislation for more than 30 years! In terms of decision-making in society, only 20% of MPs in the House of Commons are female. The Scottish Parliament fares a lot better, with women making up 39% of MSPs, although this is still far from equal representation in positions of power. Some feminists would argue that if there is better representation of women in the policy-making process, then the laws that get made are more likely to reflect the interests and values of women. For instance, the Scottish Parliament has had a lot of initiatives on improving community care, reducing sexual violence against women and zero tolerance of domestic abuse.

Criticisms of feminist theory

There are criticisms of feminist theory both from within the ranks of feminism and outside them. Many people have criticised the second wave of the feminist movement for being 'colour-blind' and not paying enough attention to the particular issues of black women and the racism they experience. Any person who is a member of more than one oppressed group should have all aspects of their life acknowledged in a full exploration of the multiple discriminations they face. There is still an on-going debate about whether you can talk about 'feminism', even at the most general level, as a single theory because there are more differences between women – for instance on the basis of race, class or sexuality – than there are similarities. However, the one thing that all feminist writers agree on is that there are gender divisions in society, that these are historically based and are still perpetuated today.

Feminists have also been criticised in the past for their emphasis only on the gendered oppression of women, and for neglecting the problems encountered by men by the social construction of masculinity. For instance, although more men are choosing to work in care settings, the workplace is still a very gender-divided area: only 2% of childcare workers and 10% of nurses are male, but they still make up 89% of the workforce in construction (DTI, 2006). But how does this square with the fact that men still dominate the key positions in most of the large organisations in society? It points to the fact that you can't understand a social problem from one point of view only. Looking at gender alone is too narrow: it has to be matched by an analysis of the other dimensions of the problem such as class, education and employment opportunities.

It is with this need to take an overview that we will now move on to look at the next two sections. The sociological concepts and theories are used to help us understand the family and deviance as aspects of society, and to look at social inequality, concentrating on the example of people with disabilities.

Activity — *Table of main sociological theories*

Draw up a table which illustrates the main sociological theories, summarising the most important points of each one, the advantages, disadvantages and main theorists. You will then have this to refer to as you read the following sections. This will be a useful exercise to help you learn the key features of each theory, which you are often asked for in exam questions.

Level Higher — Aspects of society

So far this chapter has tried to give you different ways of looking at society, different viewpoints from which to look at what is familiar to you. In doing this you are developing what the American sociologist C. Wright Mills called 'the sociological imagination'. With these concepts and theories, and the resulting sociological imagination, some aspects of society are now considered which are of particular relevance to care practice: the family and deviance.

The family

We used to be able to talk about the family; now we've got to talk about families because there are lots of different forms of the family.

(Frude, 1997)

The family – that dear Octopus from whose tentacles we never quite escape.

(Smith, 1938)

The family as an institution is not a static entity, stereotyped in its forms, or unchanging in its functions. It is a dynamic system, susceptible to change; it's influenced in the short term by the personality, development and relationships of its members, and in the longer term by the pressures of economic events and historical processes.

(Herbert, 1986)

The first thing to recognise when talking about 'the family' is that there is not only one 'family type'. Today, there are many differing manifestations of the family. Families are part of the social structure and as such are affected by, and affect, the culture in which they exist. This culture is in turn influenced by many social, economic and historical forces such as social class, ethnicity and regional differences. Scotland today is characterised by a great variation in family patterns and this has repercussions on how 'normal' families are defined.

Activity   Is there such a thing as a 'normal' family?

What do you see as a 'normal' family? Is there such a thing? What percentage of the 20 people you know best in your age group live in what you have defined as a 'normal' family?

A definition of the family, such as George Peter Murdock's (1949) quoted below, can no longer be seen as universally relevant. Murdock took a sample of 250 societies ranging from small hunting and gathering bands to large-scale industrial societies and developed the following definition:

A family is a social group characterised by common residence, economic co-operation and reproduction. It includes adults of both sexes, at least two of whom maintain a socially approved sexual relationship and one or more children, own or adopted, of the sexually co-habiting adults.

Although this might have been the norm in 1949, even then it hardly encompassed all possible family types. Married or co-habiting couples in the absence of children, for example, can be regarded as a family in the support that they provide one another. A definition more applicable to the realities of twentieth-century Britain is taken from *Social Trends* (Office for National Statistics). This is a definition of a nuclear family, explained below.

A family is defined as a married or co-habiting couple, with or without their never married children who have no children of their own, or a lone parent with such children. People living alone are not considered to form a family.

(*Social Trends,* 1998)

The variety of household types in Scotland in 2003–2004 are represented in the following table. How many of these categories would be included in the definition of 'nuclear family' given above?

Table 5.2 Household types in Scotland 2003–2004 (Source: Scottish Executive, 2004)

	Frequency	Percentage	Cumulative percentage
Single adult	5000	16.2	16.2
Small adult	5161	16.7	33.0
Single parent	1779	5.8	38.7
Small family	4249	13.8	52.5
Large family	2003	6.5	59.0
Large adult	2937	9.5	68.5
Older smaller	4641	15.1	83.6
Single pensioner	5053	16.4	100.0
Total	30822	100.0	

Sociological concepts which relate to the family

Before going on to discuss the family in terms of different sociological theories there are some sociological concepts which contribute to an understanding of the family and the changes which are taking place within it. The first distinction to be made is that between the extended and the nuclear family. An extended family consists of all family members related by blood or marriage, beyond the nuclear family, and this has both vertical (grandparents, grandchildren) and horizontal (aunts and uncles, in-laws) dimensions. The nuclear family accords with the definition from *Social Trends* above and usually takes one of three forms: a couple in a socially recognised union and child or children; a single parent and child or children; or a couple without children, all sharing the same household. 'Socially recognised union' includes married and co-habiting couples, step-families, adoptive and foster families. In 1976–1980, the proportion of babies born in Scotland to unmarried parents was 10%, which was more or less unchanged from when records first started in 1855. However, by 2001–2005, this figure had leapt to 45.3% of all live births (General Register Office for Scotland, 2006). Since civil partnerships became legal in 2005, there has been a wider social recognition of gay partnerships. Although the numbers are small, 343 were recorded in the first six months of the Act (General Register Office for Scotland, 2006); this has enormous symbolic importance as same-sex unions are now officially recognised by the state. Another symbolic change was brought about by the Adoption and Children (Scotland) Act 2007, which enables both partners to legally adopt as a couple. Although it had never actually been illegal in Scotland for a gay person to adopt a child, the Act caused considerable debate in the Scottish Parliament, as will be seen later in the chapter.

To clarify further the present nature of the family in Britain an excellent article by Peter Willmott, reproduced in O'Donnell (1993), is summarised below. In 1957 Peter Willmott and Michael Young published a now famous study of family life in Bethnal Green, London. At that time this was a fairly stable working-class community where most residents had lived for a long time and over 90% of residents had some relatives living in the district. Kinship was a very important element in people's lives and kinship contact from and to the extended family, in the form of face-to-face support, was a common part of life, with a high proportion of married women with children seeing their own mothers on a daily, or at least weekly, basis. Willmott makes the point that, by the 1980s, although enormous changes had taken place in what were old established areas and in the way society functions, the role of kinship and the role of the extended family were (and still are) very important in the lives of a high proportion of the population. In a study of a London suburb (Willmott, 1986, reprinted in O'Donnell, 1993) the proportion of couples seeing relatives at least weekly was precisely two thirds. O'Brien and Jones updated Willmott's study in 1996 and discovered that 'kin contact and association do not appear to have changed significantly since Willmott's study in the 1950's' (quoted in Haralambos and Holborn, 2004, p. 489).

Two important changes have served to influence contact with relatives: greater mobility, especially by car, and the telephone. To quote Willmott:

> *Greater mobility has helped give kinship a new face: proximity no longer matters as much as it did . . . Today the wider family could equally well be called the 'telephone family'.*

Willmott goes on to suggest that there are now three broad kinship arrangements in Britain:

- The *local extended family* with relatives living near each other providing mutual aid on a continuing basis. This kind of arrangement applies to approximately one in eight of the adult population of Britain and is more common in Scotland, the Midlands and the north of England than in southern England.

- The *dispersed extended family* where members of the extended family still maintain contact and, although they are not all living in one locality, support is still provided both in an emergency and on a regular basis. Research evidence from many sources suggests that this operates for about half the adult population.

- The *attenuated extended family* is a term used to describe people who still have an extended family but only maintain limited contact with it either from choice or because distance or finance prevents this, or for a mixture of other reasons. For example many students break away for a time from their family of origin (though they often return in the vacations) and for them friends matter more and family less than at other stages in their lives.

Families today have to be looked at in their widest sense, as 'extending' as well as 'extended'. Many people live with people who are not blood relatives, but who are part of a 'step', 'half' or foster family. Indeed many people are part-time members of two different family groups: generally one which includes their biological/adoptive mother and another which includes their biological/adoptive father.

Activity   *Drawing your own 'extended family'*

Look at your own family and draw a diagram to illustrates it. Does it include just the people you share a house with? How many of the people are actually related to you by blood? Do you feel this makes a difference to the relationships within the family?

The evidence points to the family, in all its different forms, as an important institution in its continuing relevance to people's lives. But what about the family and sociological theories? How can different theories enhance our understanding of this major aspect of society? The four theories outlined earlier in the chapter are now returned to and assessed in terms of their contribution to the understanding of the family in Britain today.

The family and functionalist theory

Functionalist sociologists concentrate on looking at the family in terms of its functions both for society and for the individuals in that society. Some functionalists have made the leap from trying to demonstrate that the family is universal to saying that if the family is universal then it must also be necessary. For example Murdock (1949), in his study of 250 societies, suggested that the family is found in every society and has four main functions which he called sexual, reproductive, economic (providing food and shelter) and educational (socialisation).

Activity **The MacDonalds and the Ahmeds**

Read the case study of the MacDonald and Ahmed families in Chapter 7 and say how you think these families achieve the four main family functions suggested by Murdock.

In a similar way to Murdock, Talcott Parsons argued that there are two 'basic and irreducible' functions of the family: primary socialisation (i.e. early childhood socialisation which serves to internalise culture and develop personality) and the stabilisation of adult personalities through emotional security and the performance of appropriate social roles. However, there is an impact for both the individual and for society when a family is disrupted, through divorce or death. In their paper on 'Divorce in Scotland', The Centre for Research on Families and Relationships (2002) notes:

> *The form of family disruption may be significant, as outcomes vary depending whether the loss of a parent is through separation or death. For example, the proportion of young people who used drugs was 20% for those living with both parents, higher (37%) among those losing a parent through separation – but higher still (47%) for those losing a parent through death. Early pregnancy too was more common among those whose parents were separated (14%) than among those living with both parents (6%) – but higher again among those losing a parent through death (40%). This study also found that young people reporting more conflict with parents were more likely to have health problems and lower self-esteem.*

Although living in an intact family is a functional arrangement for society, a 'good' divorce, where there is not too much conflict between the parents, may be less harmful for the children than a bad marriage where there is conflict over a period of time. Remember that, from the earlier discussion of socialisation, the family is only one of the influences on young people. Especially among teenagers, behaviour and attitudes are also greatly influenced by peers and the media.

Both Murdock and Parsons have been criticised for presenting a rather idealised picture of family life, especially since their theories implied that families are harmonious and integrated. There was little consideration of the problems that beset many families, such as divorce and single parenthood, or of diverse family patterns and cultures in a multi-cultural society, or of the ways different families allocate and perform social roles.

Some of these criticisms have been partly met by later functionalist sociologists who appreciate the problems which families may experience and the changes which have taken place in family structures, but maintain that families in some form or another still perform useful functions today. Sociologists such as Ronald Fletcher (1988) and Young and Willmott maintain that family functions may have changed but they have not diminished. Young and Willmott, using their research in London, claim that the family:

> . . . can provide some sense of wholeness and permanence to set against the more restricted and transitory roles imposed by the specialised institutions which have flourished outside the home.

(Willmott and Young, in O'Donnell, 1993)

Fletcher maintains that the functions of the family have increased in detail and importance. The family's role in socialisation is as important as ever, the family has a responsibility for the health and welfare of its members, and the family is a major consumer of goods and services.

The family and conflict theory

By contrast with the functionalist view, which emphasises the family as a positive force, conflict writers present a theory which views the family as serving the needs of some sections of society more than, and often at the expense of, others. For example, from a Marxist viewpoint the family favours the interests of the owners of the means of production. Marx's friend and colleague Friedrich Engels was a major proponent of this view. He saw the monogamous nuclear family developing alongside and supporting capitalism. For Engels, a nuclear family structure provides the owners of the means of production with a way of passing wealth from one generation to another through the male line. At the same time workers are stabilised within families, which inadvertently perpetuates the capitalist system because they are dependent on their waged labour to support themselves and their families. Later Marxists have emphasised that in modern society the family consumes the products of the capitalist system and that people must continue in paid employment in order to maintain their families. They depend upon the products produced through their labour and perpetuate the need for them, which gives the owners of the means of production (capitalists) the power to continue to make a profit.

The somewhat different emphasis of Dahrendorf's conflict theory provides a more complex and complicated analysis of the family in conflict terms. If you look back at the account of Dahrendorf's theory you will be reminded that the three central concepts were change, conflict and constraint. Change in Dahrendorf's view is a natural social phenomenon. Society and its parts are in a perpetual state of change, a phenomenon which is not adequately accounted for if society is viewed using functionalist theory. Change in the family is illustrated in many ways: increases in the divorce rate, increases in the number of step-families, the presence of single-parent families as an accepted part of the social structure, the emergence of gay and lesbian families, multi-cultural families. All illustrate changes in the family which are not inherently good or bad, or necessarily functional or dysfunctional. They are just part of the inevitable movement which is always taking place in society.

Constraint upon the family by external factors is illustrated through laws and social policy, and the promotion of norms and values. For example, parents have legal responsibilities to their children as outlined in the Children (Scotland) Act 1995, and most religions continue to promote heterosexual marriage and the procreation of children within marriage as the only acceptable way of leading family life, while being highly critical of gay marriages. Conflict theorists believe these laws, norms and values constrain individuals, and, by doing so, prevent individual creativity, diversity and achievement.

When Edmund Leach (1971) made the following statement he was expressing a conflict theory analysis of the family:

> *Far from being the basis of the good society, the family, with its narrow privacy and tawdry [grubby] secrets, is the source of all our discontents.*

He goes on to say that within the family 'parents fight, the children rebel' and his solution was not that dissimilar to that of Engels when he says that:

> *. . . children need to grow up in larger, more relaxed domestic groups centred on the community rather than on mother's kitchen . . .*

Dobash and Dobash (1980), in a Scottish study of domestic violence, said:

> *For most people, and especially for women and children, the family is the most violent group to which they are likely to belong. Despite fears to the contrary, it is not a stranger but a so-called loved one who is most likely to assault, rape or murder us.*

Over two decades later, this is still the case. Scottish Women's Aid reports that of the 36,010 incidents of domestic abuse reported to police in Scotland in 2002, 90.5% involved a female victim and a male perpetrator; 8.5% involved a male victim and a female perpetrator, 0.6% involved a male victim and perpetrator, and 0.4% involved a female as victim and perpetrator. These figures still don't represent the full picture: domestic abuse is still the least likely violent crime to be reported to the police. Only one out of three crimes resulting in injury is reported. In 40–60% of cases of domestic abuse child abuse is also occurring, and an NCH study found 75% of mothers said their children had witnessed domestic abuse, 33% had seen their mothers beaten up and 10% had witnessed sexual violence. Each year, 45% of female homicide victims are killed by present or former male partners compared with 8% of male victims. This means that, on average, two women per week are killed in the UK by their partners/ex-partners (www.scottishwomensaid.co.uk).

Conflict theory, however, does not account for the fact that many people continue to live harmoniously within nuclear families and see their families as a major source of comfort and emotional support. These theorists do not acknowledge that the family can provide the emotional stability from which individual creativity and achievement can emerge. It fails to explain that, whatever its faults, only a small proportion of the population has no contact with any other family member.

The family and symbolic interactionist theory

One of the most relevant features of a symbolic interactionist theory in relation to the family is its part in the development of a self-concept. If you look back at the account of this theory, you will see that the starting point is the way the individual interacts with society. The individual's experience of family is one of the foundations upon which the self is constructed. For most people the family contributes to the framework that helps us define 'the self': Mead's idea of the 'generalised other'. Individuals learn the symbolic meaning of family and family roles initially through play. They gradually acquire knowledge of the expectations and attitudes of others about family roles. Their experience of roles, including gender and family roles, enables people to be members of 'a community' or of society. There are, however, still choices which the individual 'I' can make about which roles are taken on board and how these roles are performed.

The interactionist view, in seeing individuals as both shaped by their social environment and actively influencing this environment, explains the diverse ways in which family roles are performed, or even chosen at all. The symbolic interactionist view of the family differs fundamentally from the functionalist view of the family because it emphasises the part the individual plays in creating his or her own social world, while at the same time recognising that this world is also being influenced through the performance of social roles.

The symbolic importance of language is also relevant when considering the family. Many women retain their maiden name after marriage, and couples make a variety of arrangements about what surname their children should have. These decisions just weren't available to most people 50 years ago. Another example is that the terminology used in the Children's (Scotland) Act 1995 has changed the way post-divorce arrangements for children are spoken about. It talks in terms of the child having 'residence' (with the main parent/guardian) and 'contact' with other relevant people. Previously, people spoke in terms of one parent having 'custody' of the child and other people having 'access'. That was the language of prisons, and implies more of a conflictual 'us and them' situation, rather than the partnership approach that is being encouraged today, which puts the child's needs, rights and opinions at the centre of the discussion. The language reflects, and helps to create, these new social arrangements.

Activity

Family roles in the MacDonald and Ahmed households

Now look at the case study of the MacDonald and Ahmed families in Chapter 7 using the symbolic interactionist theory, paying particular attention to Andy and Tanveer.

How have Andy and Tanveer acquired knowledge of family roles? What other influences, as well as their families, do you think have affected Andy and Tanveer in the creation of their self-concepts?

The family and feminist theory

Feminist theorists have had a field day with the family, backed up by some very substantial evidence that, even in the twenty-first century, women still perform most of the housework, most of the childcare, still experience most of the violence which occurs in the home and are far from equal in their status as family members or as members of the workforce. Patriarchy and oppression are alive and well, and feminist theory of the family focuses on the relationship between women, the family and society. As discussed previously, it is closely related to the political stance of pursuing equality and empowerment within the family and elsewhere.

Gender is the starting point for examining what happens in the family from a feminist point of view. Ann Oakley (1985) was one of the first researchers to identify the power imbalance between men and women when it comes to participation in housework and childcare. She found that few marriages could be defined as egalitarian. Although there was greater equality among middle-class than working-class families, in only 15% of the families she studied did men have a high level of participation in housework, and in only 25% did men participate in a high level of childcare. In 2005, the picture had changed little. The Living in Britain survey found that 74% of men in Britain didn't do any of the four main household tasks (grocery shopping, cooking, cleaning/hovering and washing/ironing), and this figure rose to 82% if just men in Scotland were counted, and 93% if those men were aged between 16 and 29 years old. Feminists would argue that it is this subjugation of women into carrying out time-consuming and tiring tasks that makes it more difficult for them to have the time and energy to be active participants in other areas of community and work life.

When Oakley showed that women still do most of the housework and the childcare she also demonstrated that these tasks are associated with culture. Women are socialised to perform these roles and it continues to be in the interests of men to keep women in these subordinate roles. The role of mother/wife, even in an age of enlightenment, is still passed from one generation to the next:

> *. . . the female is chronically disadvantaged from the start by the socially constructed framework of values and norms which constrain her options.*

> (Allan, 1985)

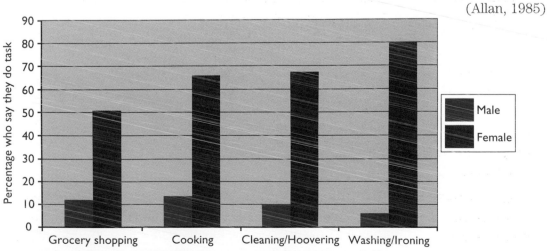

Figure 5.5 Housework: who does what (Source: Institute for Social and Economic Research)

Lena Dominelli (1997) discussed housework in terms of black women:

> Black women have, therefore, carried the burden of doing the housework for the world. This included working as domestic servants for white middle class women ... Consequently black women's oppression is not the same as white women's even if they share the same gender and class.

However, there have been other social changes related to the division of labour within families. With one in five women being the major breadwinner in their household, many couples have decided that the best childcare arrangement is for the man to stay at home. In 1996, 5,000 men in Scotland were 'stay-at-home' dads, but by 2003 there were more than 20,000 (Wilson, 2003). The government has recognised this change in attitude about the more active role men want to play with their children and has responded by legislating for improved paternity leave. Statutory Paternity Pay and Leave was introduced in Britain in 2003 and was extended in the Work and Families Act 2006 to enable fathers to take Additional Paternity Leave and Pay. Evidence shows that involvement of the father in childcare during the first 18 months of their child's life can have strong beneficial effects on the child's cognitive development, if the mother is working (DTI, 2006).

Conclusion: using sociological theories to understand the family

This discussion of the family demonstrates the complex situation that sociologists face: there are all kinds of changes within the dynamics of the family, and it is very difficult to state exactly what the current picture is. In the last 20 years, more men are staying at home to look after children, but there doesn't seem to be any change in the number of household tasks that men in general do. The home is still the place where most women are likely to be assaulted, but it is also a place of safety and comfort for many others. There is an enormous range of family shapes, and many more people are choosing to divorce, or remain single.

What sense can we make of these differences? For a care worker, the question always has to be: how can this help me work with the service users better? How can it help me understand my situation and their experience? Knowing how other families lead their lives can give clues about how to organise your own and help other people manage their situations. A lot of family life happens behind closed doors, and people often feel that they are the only person or family which experiences a particular problem. Abusers often use this as one of their strongest weapons in maintaining the silence of their victim. The shame of admitting to problems in public, and the threat 'You don't want the family to split up, do you?' are often enough to keep people in abusive relationships for years, as their confidence to make decisions dwindles with each passing event.

As a care worker, you know that there are all kinds of 'family' possibilities for people, and that you are actively engaged in helping people build personal, family and community lives for themselves in which they can thrive. Some people using care services are not part of traditional families – they may live in a care home and their children live abroad, their parents may be drug addicts and they live in residential care with their siblings, they may have had mental health problems and cut themselves off from their family years ago, and the care setting provides some of the functions of the family. It might help care for their physical and mental health, it provides encouragement and support to meet their goals, it helps them gain and maintain a job, and it provides a sense of purpose and belonging. What the care worker needs to ensure is that the time and energy they give to the workplace doesn't dilute the time and energy they have left for their own life and their own family. Don't forget yourself: knowing about division of labour and work/life balance applies as much to the worker as to the service user!

Activity   *Gay adoption*

Outcry at new laws allowing gay adoption

Linda Gray

Gay couples in Scotland will be able to adopt children for the first time under controversial new laws passed by the Scottish Parliament yesterday. The Adoption Bill, which will also allow unmarried couples to adopt, sparked furious debate in the Scottish Parliament and protests from religious organisations. Roseanna Cunningham, MSP for Perth, tabled the amendment against gay couples adopting. 'We have a pattern of family life which we have had for generation upon generation,' she said. 'All the research shows it is the best way to raise children and I do not think we should depart from that. We cannot bemoan the consequences of family breakdown and at the same time do things that undermine the traditional family.'

Murdo Fraser, deputy leader of the Tories, also raised concerns: 'Many people believe that children need a strong male and female role model and are concerned that adoption by same-sex couples excludes that possibility and is not in the best interests of children,' he said. 'People who express these [views] are not homophobes, or extremists or religious nutters, as some would suggest. They have genuine concerns and their concerns should not be dismissed.'

Cardinal Keith O'Brien, the leader of Scotland's Catholics, also said children should be brought up by a man and woman. He said: 'Of course it is better for a child to be in a loving home. But a loving home means a mum and dad.'

However Patrick Harvie, Green MSP, who is gay, argued that Ms Cunningham's amendment made homosexual couples and their children into 'second-class citizens'. He said: 'It is an absurd argument. Over millions of years of evolution, diversity is clearly the norm. There have always been gay couples and same-sex parents with children. What we are doing is making sure those children have the same rights as any other child in Scotland.'

Around 400 children a year are adopted, compared with 1,000 two decades ago, and there are 6,500 youngsters in the care of local authorities. Barbara Hudson, director of the British Association of Adoption and Fostering, said any adoptive parent was robustly assessed, not only for the stability of their relationship, but their ability to deal with discrimination. She said: 'There are already gay parents bringing up children with strategies to deal with that. We would regret if other people's prejudice stopped children from having a loving family.'   (Gray, 2006)

Activity   *Gay adoption* continued

1   How does an understanding of norms, values and culture help you understand these differing views about adoption?

2   What sociological theories of the family could help you understand the different sides of this debate?

Deviance

Deviance is a crowd puller. It generates curiosity and interest. Perhaps this has something to do with the fact that deviance, as Durkheim reminds us, is exciting and innovative.

(Stephens et al., 1998)

There's something fascinating about **deviance**. Perhaps people are sometimes attracted by, as well as sometimes repulsed by, things that go considerably beyond the bounds of what is considered to be 'normal' behaviour. As with most other sociological concepts, there is a great deal of controversy about what deviance is and how it should be defined, and no single definition can be completely satisfactory. Definition to a large extent depends on the theory being used. Here are two definitions that you might want to bear in mind as you read through the chapter. Which theory do you think they belong to: feminist, conflict, functionalist or interactionist?

Deviance refers to those acts which do not conform to the norms and values of a particular society.

(Haralambos, 1996)

The deviant is one to whom that label has successfully been applied; deviant behaviour is behaviour that people so label.

(Becker, 1963)

You would be correct if you said the first definition describes a functionalist viewpoint and the second takes an interactionist perspective.

Deviance has generated much discussion within all branches of sociology, and to look at it with only one or two theories is almost as limiting as it is illuminating. A combination of theories is needed and, although theories are examined separately, a grasp of several is necessary to examine all of the ways in which deviance occurs, and to seek explanations for it. As with all the topics looked at in this chapter, explanations cannot be complete without also taking into account the range of psychological explanations of behaviour. These were examined in Chapter 4.

Crime is one of the ways in which people deviate from the norms of society. Although a lot of research into deviance has involved investigation of criminal behaviour, sociologists, unlike criminologists, consider a much broader range of issues within their definition of deviance including sexual deviance, drug and alcohol abuse, and behaviour within subcultures. Two small points are emphasised here, which may seem obvious but which need to be made:

- all crime is deviance but not all deviance is criminal
- deviance is not only negative; it can be positive in a number of ways, and may lead to social change.

Sociological studies of deviance, however, usually focus on those forms of deviance which are regarded negatively, especially since positive deviance in the form of non-criminal innovation is really only partial deviance since it is often carried out within the framework of socially approved norms and values. For instance, Elvis Presley, the Beatles and the punk movement were all seen as breaking major taboos when they first played their music, and there was moral outrage from some sections of society. But they were all also part of a tradition of young people channelling their energies into ideas, in this case via music, which challenged the preceding generation. In each case, within a relatively short period of time, their music became an accepted part of youth culture.

Activity   *What is deviant?*

1 None of the following actions is illegal, but which would you see as deviant? Do you feel they break the rules or norms of society? Does it depend not only on the action, but where it takes place? Does it depend on whether there are any witnesses to it? Does it depend only on whether someone objects to it, or if there is some other negative consequence?

- Skipping the queue in a fast-food restaurant
- Self-harming
- Calling your parents by their real name (e.g. Joanne, Paul) rather than mum or dad
- Over-eating to the point of obesity
- Wearing bright colours to a funeral
- Passing wind in public
- A man wearing mascara
- Getting so drunk you don't remember what you did the night before

2 List five other things which you consider to be deviant, and describe why you consider them to be deviant.

As you read though the chapter, try to relate the reasons you have given to the different explanations of deviance given below.

A functionalist theory of deviance

Our old friend Durkheim was among the first sociologists to study deviance, and his theories still receive serious consideration in sociological literature. He saw the potential for deviance to be functional in society, as long as its levels were not too high or too low, arguing that social change might begin with some form of deviance. This is because the deviant behaviour challenges the socially accepted norms and values and makes people reconsider whether these values and norms are still relevant, or not.

Activity   *Positive change resulting from 'deviance'*

Here are some positive social changes which began with deviance:

- Nelson Mandela became the president of South Africa. He spent more than 25 years of his life in prison for committing 'terrorist acts' in his fight against apartheid.

- Former gangland killer Jimmy Boyle, who served 15 years for murder, became, in 1998, a member of a Scottish task force to tackle social exclusion. He is also an author and sculptor.

- Oscar Wilde, the author of many famous plays including *The Importance of Being Earnest*, was arrested in 1895 for being a homosexual; he has come to be seen as a pioneer in the fight for equal rights for homosexuals. A statue of him was unveiled in London in November 1998. The Culture Secretary, Chris Smith, said of him: 'It's due to Oscar Wilde in many ways that we today can celebrate a society that generally appreciates diversity and the richness of diversity in our community.'

Can you think of two other examples of deviance which have led to positive social change?

Durkheim developed the concept of anomie in relation to deviance. He saw this as a condition of normlessness. This occurs when people do not feel connected to the norms of society. It may be because they don't value the prevailing norms, or it may be because they feel they can't achieve them. Having a secure job, owning a house, or being part of a family unit doesn't feel like a possibility for them, so they don't strive to achieve the rewards of society. If these people are prevented by social structural factors from achieving what are the 'accepted' values and norms of society, they can become alienated and feel they don't fit into society. It is a problem for the individual if they feel dislocated in this way, but it is also a problem for society, because they are a potential threat to the stability of society.

Since Durkheim's day, many different terms have been used to describe this group, such as the 'underclass'. Today for instance, there is growing concern about NEET's, young people who are Not in Education, Employment or Training. These are three key factors which help us build up our adult identity, give us a purpose in life, a reason to get up in the morning, and a reason to keep on the right side of the law, as we have so much to lose if we don't. If there are too many 'outsiders', who are detached from society and its values, then there is a greater possibility of disharmony.

Durkheim studied suicide, a form of deviance, in one of the first great sociological studies to use statistical evidence, and concluded that increases in suicide rates occurred when anomie increased. In Scotland today young men are the most likely group to commit suicide and it is often because they have a sense of hopelessness, a sense that things are bad and will never get better. Their situation (perhaps unemployed, perhaps living in an environment where there is drug and alcohol misuse and violence, perhaps having been abused in the past or being brought up in care) feels inescapable, and they may feel that taking their own life is the only way to get out if it. Merton (1968) developed Durkheim's theory of anomie in his studies of North American society in the 1930s to the 1970s and saw the USA as a particularly anomic society. The goal of success through the attainment of wealth and material possessions is stressed, without providing the means for large sections of the population to attain them. Jeremy Seabrook's account of property crime in the UK in the 1990s echoes what Durkheim and Merton said about anomie:

> *The upsurge in crime is the only logical response by certain sections of the poor to the exacerbation of their condition . . . They are not only relatively poorer, but they also see the good life, which requires ever more money, receding from them at an accelerating pace.*

(Seabrook, 1990)

Other studies of deviance have examined subcultures such as bikers, or people who get a lot of tattoos and piercings, which provide a 'solution' to the 'failure' of members within conventional society. Subcultures may be seen as functional for society because they allow people who reject, or are disengaged from, mainstream norms to succeed within the norms and values of their subgroup. They are connected to the others in their group, and develop their identity and a sense of purpose from having a role within the group.

A conflict theory of deviance

One of the main criticisms of functionalist theory is that it fails to take sufficient account of the power structures within society. This has been addressed by Marxists and other conflict theorists who have examined deviance, particularly criminal deviance, not only in terms of who commits crime but in terms of who makes the law, which crimes are acted upon by police and the different treatment received by 'criminals' of different social classes. Marx saw the law as one means by which the dominant class kept everyone else in check and maintained their position of power in society. For example, criminal legislation has historically given prominence to the protection of property.

Many non-functionalist sociologists have thought that Marxism is an inadequate theory for looking at deviance, feeling that it goes too far in its emphasis on relative power and in underestimating the importance of working-class crime. A group of sociologists, known as left realists, developed a theory which seeks to redress the balance by taking all kinds of crime seriously, including domestic violence, sexual harassment, blue collar and white collar crime. Left realists such as Matthews and Young (1992) have carried out a number of victimisation studies (studies of the victims of crime rather than criminals) demonstrating that crime is often unreported and is a very real problem to ordinary members of the population. Rather than the straightforward power/non-power explanations of Marxists they put forward an explanation for crime based on relative deprivation, subculture and marginalisation.

These explanations, although often referred to as neo-Marxist, do not fall neatly into any one theory but combine aspects of conflict and interactionist explanations of deviance and of Durkheim's theory of anomie. Relative deprivation occurs when people see themselves as deprived relative to others in the population. As mentioned previously, forming a subculture is one possible response to feelings of deprivation whereby members have their own values and norms which are distinct from, though related to, the dominant culture. Marginal groups are those which lack legitimate social organisations to represent their interests: for example, they do not work or study. Terms like social exclusion are used to describe marginalised people in society. Tackling deviance, especially criminal deviance, involves tackling all three of these areas, through reducing poverty, increasing prospects of employment and through community involvement.

An analysis of the prison population is a clear example of how poverty and deprivation are key factors in crime. Andrew McLellan, HM Chief Inspector of Prisons for Scotland, notes in his 2005–2006 annual report:

> *Any prison inspector, or indeed any casual visitor to a prison, cannot help recognising who our prisoners are. Before I took up this office I wrote* You do not need a degree in social science to observe that we lock up a disproportionate amount of Scotland's poor people. The reasons for that are complex; but what you do about it is not lock up more poor people, but rather change for good the crippling, destructive effects of poverty on so much of our society.

> *Since then some real social science has offered some remarkable statistics. Roger Houchin carried out a survey which received some press attention in 2005. There are 1440 local authority wards in Scotland. One quarter of all of our prisoners come from 55 of these wards, and these wards are the very poorest in the country. One half of all of our prisoners come from 120 of these wards, and these wards are the poorest in the country. In one part of Glasgow one 23 year-old man in every nine is in prison. Only when we transform life for our poorest young men will overcrowding in our prisons disappear.*

> *When Lord Scarman investigated riots in London twenty years ago he famously concluded* There can be no criminal justice without social justice. *How often in the last four years have I said* We will only have better prisons when we have a better Scotland.

(Scottish Executive, 2006d)

A symbolic interactionist theory of deviance

Symbolic interactionist explanations of deviance differ from functionalist, Marxist and left realist theories in focusing not upon the breaking of society's rules but upon the interaction between the individual 'deviant' and those who define him or her as deviant. Howard Becker was one of the first and major exponents of this theory, emphasising that it is only once someone has been labelled as deviant that the consequences of 'being a deviant' come into operation. Becker (1963) states that

> *. . . social groups create deviance by making the rules whose infraction constitutes deviance, and by applying those rules to particular people and labelling them as outsiders. From this point of view, deviance is not a quality of the act the person commits, but rather a consequence of the application by others of rules and sanctions to an 'offender'. The deviant is one to whom that label has been applied; deviant behaviour is behaviour that people so label.*

The above passage gives the essence of the interactionist approach, which emphasises the deviant label and its consequences. In saying that deviant behaviour is behaviour that people label as such, Becker is implying that there are behaviours which could be labelled as deviant but they aren't. He gives the example of a brawl involving young people. In a low-income area it might be defined by the police as delinquency, a deviant label. In a wealthy area it might be defined as youthful high spirits and no deviant label given or gained. Becker also makes the point that there are behaviours which aren't necessarily criminal or offensive but which by being labelled as deviant become deviant.

Becker went on to describe a deviant career, which often follows once a deviant label has been applied. Firstly the label, e.g. delinquent, nutter, pervert, is applied to the individual. This leads to a public reaction and quite often rejection by family, friends and neighbours. This may encourage further deviance because other more legitimate avenues of behaviour are blocked. The 'deviant' may also join a deviant group which develops a subculture with its own deviant norms and values, and the deviant career is now well and truly established. The deviant identity becomes incorporated into the individual's self-concept. Tim in *A Glasgow Gang Observed* (Patrick, 1973) illustrates this point very well. His identity and status became increasingly linked to his gang membership and the delinquent activities of the group. He felt that school had rejected him and he in turn had rejected school. Gang membership gave him some sense of belonging. He committed crimes of theft and violence as a member of the gang, was labelled as delinquent by the police, sent to what was then an approved school and gained status in the gang from this. Once this pattern of behaviour was established his deviant career was well and truly launched.

Labelling occurs not just in relation to the criminal, but also in relation to the *type* of sentences that are handed out. The following extract from HM Chief inspector of Prisons Annual Report 2005–2006 outlines the process that leads to negative views of non-custodial sentencing:

> *It is difficult to visit prisons regularly and not be regularly struck with the thought that there are people in prison who should not be there. For some the underlying mental health difficulties, addiction problems, family crises are not likely to be made better by imprisonment. Scotland has more forms of sentencing available to the courts than many countries, and yet the numbers going to prison continue to increase. There is a circle of confidence here: the public will have little confidence in punishments in the community as long as judges have little confidence; and judges will have little confidence in them as long as these community disposals are under-resourced; and they will be under-resourced as long as the public have little confidence in them. At the same time the press does little to help the public form a clear view about the relative value of punishment in the community and punishment in prison for crimes which are less serious. So Scotland continues to be a highly "imprisoning" country. In the spring of this year I visited Sweden and Norway. Figures provided by the International Centre for Prison Studies show that the Scottish rate of imprisonment is 141 per 100,000, in Sweden it is 78 and in Norway it is 68.*

> (Scottish Executive, 2006d)

Since non-custodial sentences are judged as 'soft options' by the media and public, even though they could alleviate the overcrowding in prison and may help the perpetrator make amends for their crime in the community, judges feel they have to give custodial sentences. You might want to consider why Scotland as a nation has such a high rate of imprisonment, compared with other countries.

Interactionism, therefore, emphasises that defining deviance is by no means straightforward and directs attention to the social reaction to the act, as well as to the deviant act itself. For instance, committing suicide is not illegal, but it does contravene some religious codes and it still has an element of social stigma: if a member of your family has committed suicide, people often want to cover it up, and explain the death away in other terms. However, assisting someone who is ill to commit suicide *is* illegal and has led to people being imprisoned, but many people feel that it is a moral and ethical thing to do. Assisting someone to have a death which is free from fear and pain is symbolised as a noble and moral act. Euthanasia is legal in some European countries, and there has been an on-going debate about making it legal in Britain, but politicians and public opinion have not moved sufficiently to recognise it officially. There are still some circumstances in which it is legal to kill someone: in war for instance, or maybe in self-defence, but not yet as a planned end to someone who has been diagnosed with a terminal illness.

A feminist theory of deviance

Looking at studies of deviance before 1970, you are immediately struck by the almost total absence of reference to, or studies about, women in the context of deviance. Does this mean that there weren't any women who were deviant? Does it mean that the deviance of women was unimportant sociologically? These are the kinds of question which a feminist asks. Other theories have ignored women as significant or failed to consider that a separate consideration of women in relation to deviance is important.

Feminist sociologists and criminologists see the study of deviance before the 1970s as having been written by men, about men, and with a male readership in mind. Fortunately there has been some redressing of the balance since then. Apart from gender blindness (women literally were just 'not in the picture' when deviance was being studied), one reason for fewer studies of female deviance, especially female crime, may be that statistically fewer women than men are convicted of crimes. Although there has been a sharp rise in the number of women being sent to prison in Scotland, only 4.9% of the daily average of 6,779 prisoners in Scotland in 2006 were female (Scottish Parliament, 2006).

In 1985 Frances Heidensohn tried to explain why women commit fewer serious crimes and argued that male patriarchy with its elements of power and control make it more difficult for women to deviate from 'society's' norms, with control operating at home (women are expected to look after children and to do more housework than men), in public (women are often afraid to go out in public at night, for example) and at work (through predominantly male hierarchies).

Is this still the situation today? Although these factors would still appear to be true for many women, there have been significant changes in the intervening years. One social trend that is likely to make more of an impact in the next decade or so is the increasing number of young women coming to the attention of the Children's Hearing system. In 2003–2004, 40% of the 45,793 children referred to the Reporter were female (SCRA, 2004). The following article from the *Scotsman* newspaper demonstrates that crime among adult women has also increased, and gives some possible explanations.

Violent crime by women up 50 per cent in past 4 years

VIOLENT crime committed by women in Scotland has soared, with more than 327 women committing non-sexual violent crimes, such as serious assaults and attempted murder, in 2004–5: up almost 50% in four years. Criminologists yesterday blamed the increasing use of drugs, binge drinking and wider changes in society for women's increasing criminality. The figures, released by the Scottish Executive, showed that more than 21,000 women were found guilty of a crime in 2004–5, up from almost 16,000 four years earlier. But violent crime was rising even faster, with the number of women convicted for serious assault and attempted murder rising from 80 to 118 over the same period and the number convicted of robbery increased from 44 to 79.

Statistics also revealed the number of women found guilty of drugs offences stood at 640 in 2000–1, increasing to 746 the following year and 1,018 in 2004–5 – a 59% rise in four years. Crimes of indecency rose from 159 to 229 – 44% up – while convictions for dishonesty offences, such as housebreaking and shoplifting, also rose. Non-sexual violent crime convictions rose from 221 six years ago to 375 in 2003–4, dropping back to 327 in 2004–5.

Susan Batchelor, a criminologist at Glasgow University who works with female prisoners, said: 'The primary problem is an increase in drug use. Most of these crimes are a direct result of a drug problem. Women may be stealing or working as prostitutes or they may assault someone they are stealing from, but the underlying cause is almost always drugs.' The figures have been released on the heels of a report into Stirling's Cornton Vale Prison, Scotland's only all-female jail, which found the number of women prisoners has doubled in the past decade.

(Harrell and Howie, 2006)

Activity *Deviance*

How could you use the different sociological theories to explain the issues raised in the following report?

Young offenders and victims of crime are often the same people

The Edinburgh Study of Youth Transitions and Crime, led by Professor David Smith and Dr Lesley McAra, School of Law, University of Edinburgh, shows that boys offend only slightly more often than girls at the ages of 13–15, if every kind of offending is included. Girls are more likely to smoke and drink than boys are by the age of 15. Yet the study reveals considerably higher levels of serious offending in boys compared with girls.

Professor Smith said: 'These findings suggest there is something about males, or a risk factor to which males are prone, that is implicated in serious offending but is not identified by our current research.'

Being a victim of crime at the age of 12 is one of the most powerful indicators that a child will offend at 15. Likewise, offending at age 12 brings a strong possibility of victimisation at 15. One explanation of this link is that young offenders tend to group together and commit offences on each other. Another is that young people who get into risky situations together – such as late-night clubs or amusement arcades – end up both committing offences and being victims of crime. A third point is that personality traits such as being impulsive and taking risks lead both to offending and victimisation.

Finally, people may bounce backwards and forwards between offending and victimisation, as when they have their possessions stolen or trashed when in prison. Victims may be traumatised, leading to later offending or simple retaliation.

Dr McAra said: 'Few youngsters are specialists in violent offending, instead certain lifestyles provide opportunities for getting involved in various kinds of trouble. The study shows that violent boys are very similar as people to those who are not, suggesting that the phenomenon is a normal expression of masculinity for teenaged youths.

'By contrast, violent girls are very different from both other females and aggressive boys. They are much more likely to be drug users, gang members, truants, and from a lower class background.'

A fifth of 15-year-olds were members of gangs, although only five per cent belonged to a gang with a name and a saying or sign. Offending was higher among gang members than others. Members of organised gangs were typically male, from broken families, and lower-class backgrounds. Gangs provided moral support, encouraging and excusing violence and criminal activities.

(ESRC, 2003)

Social inequality and life chances

Inequality exists when there is a difference between two groups. Social inequality exists because there is a gap between, for example, people who are affluent and people who are deprived. Sociologists argue that it is not just a coincidence, or a matter of individual psychology, that certain people are more likely to experience inequality. The way a society is organised, through its educational system, legal system, benefits system, public services and employment practices, has an influence on the life chances a person has. Inequalities are structured into the system. The family and community in which you are brought up influence the opportunities you have and the decisions you make, and these will affect your mental and physical health throughout your life. Living in poor housing affects your physical health negatively; living in a community where there is violence and vandalism affects your mental health; and living in an area of high unemployment affects your ability to live a life free from financial stress.

There can be no clearer indication of inequality than the fact that people who live in certain communities are likely to die younger than people brought up in more prosperous communities. Women living in deprived areas have a life expectancy 6% lower than women in affluent areas, which corresponds to 4.5 years, and men living in deprived areas will live, on average, eight years less than men in affluent areas (Scottish Executive, 2003). When you consider particular illnesses such as cancer and coronary heart disease (CHD), which are linked to poverty and deprivation, then the statistics are quite stark, as the graphs below demonstrate.

Although you can see that there has been a decline in coronary heart disease for both groups over the 10 years, which indicates an improvement in health in the overall population, the gap *between* the two groups has actually widened, which indicates a greater inequality in health. This is because a lot of the factors which relate to these diseases, such as poor diet and smoking, still affect more people from lower-income families.

But health isn't the only indicator of inequality. Inequality is demonstrated by the fact that certain people and groups are more likely to experience deprivation than others. The Scottish Indices of Multiple Deprivation (SIMD) were established in 2003 to examine different aspects of deprivation at a very detailed local level in Scotland. These will form the basis of a long-term Scottish Executive strategy to measure deprivation and monitor the extent to which the Executive's policies are reducing deprivation. Again, it clearly demonstrates that people living in certain geographical areas experience poorer life chances, in a number of different ways, compared with other geographical areas.

The SIMD indices measure deprivation in seven different 'domains', or categories: Income; Employment; Crime; Education, Skills and Training; Health; Geographical Access to Services. Each of these has a number of specific items against which different geographical areas can be compared. For instance, of the 37 indicators, one indicator of whether an area is likely to be deprived on the Income category is the number of people on Income Support. An indicator of likely deprivation in the Education, Skills and Training category is the number of absences from secondary school. An indicator of possible deprivation in the Health domain is the number of babies born with a low birth

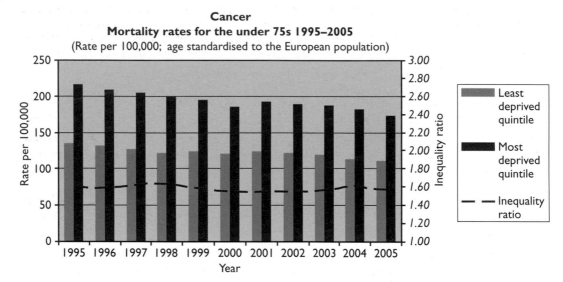

Figure 5.6 Mortality rates for cancer and coronary heart disease (Source: Scottish Executive, 2003a)

weight. As you can see, there is a wide variety of factors which, when combined, are likely to indicate whether an area experiences deprivation. The full list can be accessed at www.scotland.gov.uk/Resource/Doc/151578/0040731.pdf

Education has always been seen as one possible route out of the cycles of deprivation that exist in certain communities, but educational attainment varies widely between schools in different areas. Although overall more than a third of Scottish school children cannot write properly by the time that they leave primary school, there are wide differences in attainment between schools in different areas. For instance, in 2005 in Edinburgh, 92% of pupils in Cramond School achieved the expected reading level before going onto secondary school, but only 15% of pupils in Royston School achieved this level (School League Table, *Scotsman*, 21 May 2007).

Figure 5.7 Getting into shape: some young people from Drumchapel practise ball skills at the Donald Dewar Leisure Centre, which opened in the Glasgow housing scheme in March 2003. The centre is named after Donald Dewar, who was MP for Garscadden and also MSP for Anniesland, and who died in October 2000. The politician refused to accept that Drumchapel residents or people of any community should have diminished dreams or lesser lives simply because of where they were born.

Thus, some people find it difficult, from an early age, to get their foot onto even the first rung of the ladder of educational success. If you can't read by the time you leave school, it limits not only your job opportunities in later life, but also your health (unable to read health promotion literature or prescription advice) and social opportunities (unable to read a newspaper or websites).

At the other end of the age spectrum, inequality is happening not on the basis of where you live, but because of your age: older adults do not receive the same level of health care as younger people. The basic right to quality health care is not guaranteed to these citizens because of prejudice and stereotypes about older adults and their 'worthiness' for treatment. In the 'Adding Life to Years' report, it is noted by NHSScotland that:

> *Ageism has been defined as 'systematic and negative age discrimination', and can exist at individual and institutional levels. But there are many other ways in which negative attitudes to older people can be demonstrated, or displayed to older people, or perceived by them. Areas of concern and recent discussion about ageism in NHSScotland include: decisions about resuscitation; access by older people to various treatments and interventions; the quality of care experienced by older people; attitudes of NHS staff; and the quality of the environment in which care is provided.*

(Scottish Executive Health Department, 2002)

The failure of NHSScotland to adapt to the changing needs of a changing population could also be seen as 'structural ageism'. In other words, a traditional service designed around isolated episodes of care within well-defined specialties and agencies cannot fully meet the needs of increasing numbers of older patients, especially those with chronic, multiple and recurrent medical problems.

The above statistics are clear indications that inequality exists in Scotland – in educational attainment at primary school, in health provision for older people, in the life expectancy of people from different areas and in the likelihood of experiencing deprivation.

However, the problem with statistics is that they quickly go out of date. In the field of inequality and deprivation, the government and many other organisations are working hard to reduce the disadvantages that certain people and groups experience, as we shall see below. Whether for better or for worse, the statistics quoted above will change.

Carry out an Internet search, using the above topics and websites as a start, and see if there has been a change in any of the issues mentioned.

Why do inequalities exist?

As we can see from the above information, there is clear evidence to indicate not only that inequality still exists, but that in many cases it is getting worse. Is it not just inevitable and natural that inequality exists? There will always be a range of outcomes for people in any society: not everyone is going to get an A in their Higher English, be Prime Minister, or score the winning goal in the Scottish Cup final. *Functionalists* point out that for a system to work, all functions must be met in some way, not just the aspects people like doing: someone has to do the boring, dirty or meaningless jobs at work or in the house. Someone has to work in a garage or clean the toilet! *Symbolic interactionists* point out that different people have different perceptions, and so not everyone will see the same situation in the same way. Working in a garage may be great for someone because there's not much responsibility, it gives you time to play the guitar and hang out with your friends, or it's helping to pay your way through university. But *conflict theorists* would say that we need to look at those oppressive structures: did people have the same chance to start off with? Did they start off on a level playing field? Was it more or less destined from birth that some people were more likely to succeed and that others were being prepared for low-paid menial jobs, or unemployment (being a reserve of labour, when capitalism needs it), from an early age?

The concepts examined earlier will help explain why this is the case. People brought up within a family or community where there is not a *culture* of having a job, may find it more difficult to adjust to the demands of the workplace, such as turning up on time. They will not have had *role* models from whom to copy the habits of regularity and consistency, and they may have missed crucial *socialisation* because they have had poor attendance at school. In terms of the Scottish Indices of Multiple Deprivation looked at earlier, the reason that things like eating fruit and vegetables regularly are included are that they are *symbolic* of having enough money to buy fruit and vegetables (that is why communities in deprived areas establish food co-opertives, so that people can have access to healthy but cheap produce locally) and the motivation to think about a healthy diet. If people are living with violence or mental health problems or caring for relatives on benefit, a healthy diet is often the least of their priorities. And factors such as poor dental health might be symbolic of the fact that children a) have had a poor diet; b) their parents haven't checked they have brushed their teeth every night and morning; and c) they have haven't taken them to the dentist for regular check-ups. It's not the *norm* in their family or community. Other people aren't doing it, therefore it doesn't become part of their routine either.

In terms of society's response to inequality, there are mixed views from the different theories. *Functionalists* would see that it was good for society that the state is taking on a lot of the functions of the family by providing an economic safety net for people through the benefit system, and for the physical nurturing of children through the provision of free fruit at school, free school meals, dental checks at school, etc. Many families can no longer provide these services to their family, so it is adaptive that other institutions do. Day nurseries look after the rearing of children, paid carers look after family members who are unable to care for themselves. *Conflict theorists* though would argue that all these measures only serve to maintain the existing inequality gap. If people didn't have the safety net of the Welfare State, they might really wake up to the inequalities in the system and challenge it. An alternative view points to the fact that the voice of those who are deprived is not going to be heard because these are the people who are *marginalised*. Because they are struggling to cope with poor health, and poverty, and violence, and unemployment, and addiction, they don't always have the power to stand up and state their case. *Symbolic interactionists* might point to the many initiatives that people make in their local communities to improve their life chances by setting up and getting involved in various groups.

Disability and social inequality

People who have a disability are further disadvantaged because of the way in which society views, and responds to, their disability. The definition of disability has been extended since it was developed in the 1995 Disability Discrimination Act (DDA). The original definition covers people with physical, sensory and mental impairments, and includes people with a range of health conditions such as diabetes, epilepsy and long-term depression. Since December 2005, it has included people with cancer, HIV and multiple sclerosis from the point of diagnosis. In 2006, there were 10 million people in Britain who had rights under the Act (Disability Rights Commission, 2006).

However, despite the creation of the Disability Discrimination Act in 1995, there are still many examples of inequality in the life chances of people with disabilities. For instance:

- Disabled people die younger than non-disabled people.
- A quarter of all disabled people have experienced hate crime or harassment rising to 47% of mental health service users and 9 out of 10 people with learning disabilities.
- 73% of people with mobility or sensory impairments experience difficulties in accessing services, yet disabled people's spending power is £80 billion per annum.
- At 31 March 2003, only 696 out of 22,464 appointments to non-departmental public bodies (NDPBs) were held by disabled people, representing just 3.1% of total posts.

(Disability Rights Commission, 2005)

Two other factors which affect a person's life chances are housing and health care provision. Without the provision of good housing that provides them with a safe and stable base, people are often unable to fulfil their other needs. And when a person experiences mental and physical health problems, they need to know that there will be accessible, appropriate care which is offered in a non-discriminatory way. However, people with disabilities often face obstacles when trying to access both these services, as the following excerpts demonstrate.

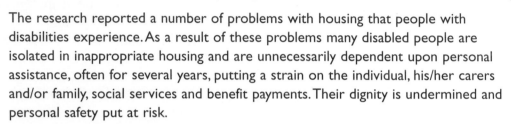

Activity *Disability and housing*

Housing: A contemporary view of disabled peoples' experience, provision and policy directions

The research reported a number of problems with housing that people with disabilities experience. As a result of these problems many disabled people are isolated in inappropriate housing and are unnecessarily dependent upon personal assistance, often for several years, putting a strain on the individual, his/her carers and/or family, social services and benefit payments. Their dignity is undermined and personal safety put at risk.

For those that become literally roofless, hostels for homeless people and accommodation provided for women escaping domestic violence are often inaccessible. The only alternative is unsuitable B&B or other temporary accommodation where they may be isolated and lacking essential support services for protracted periods.

Some specific problems identified in the report include:

Information

– Houses, show homes, estate agents and letting agents offices are often inaccessible.

Supply

– There is a lack of supported housing options, particularly for adults with learning difficulties. MENCAP reported that 60% of adults with learning difficulties live with their parents or are inappropriately housed in hospitals for lack of an alternative.

– In Scotland much of the existing housing in the cities is tenement style and many rural locations are very isolated and therefore unsuitable for the majority of disabled people. It is estimated that 20,000 more wheelchair accessible units are required and 124,000 suitable for people with ambulant disabilities.

Activity   *Disability and housing* continued

Costs

- House prices and rents are inflated in urban centres where, as a general rule, there are more support services, amenities and accessible facilities, and for ground floor, larger and therefore more flexible accommodation.

Attitudes

- Neighbourhood harassment, including individual or collective reaction to proposals to provide a shared/supported housing unit, is commonplace.

- Assumptions are often made about people with learning difficulties' abilities to make appropriate choices.

(Adapted from Brothers, 2003)

Health inequalities experienced by people with schizophrenia and manic depression

The report examined aspects of the health and primary care provided by GPs to people with serious mental health problems and explored whether their needs and experiences are in any way different from those of other people.

The analysis found some worrying differences in ill health and some differences in the services provided. Rates of obesity and smoking were higher for those with serious mental health problems than in the rest of the population, and ischaemic heart disease, stroke, hypertension, epilepsy and diabetes were all more common too. Some tests were carried out less frequently, even for people with known physical health problems, and women were less likely to have had cervical or breast screening.

(Adapted from Disability Rights Commission, 2006)

1 Name four problems people with disabilities may experience, in relation to housing or health care provision.

2 Discuss what effect this might have on their life chances, that is, their ability to lead a life where they fulfil their potential.

How does taking a sociologiocal approach help address problems of social inequality?

As a care worker, you are likely to be interested not only in trying to understand the problem but, because of your desire to help people fulfil their potential, and your belief in equality and social justice for everyone, you will want to know how to use your understanding to combat these inequalities. We have looked at anti-discrimination strategies in Chapter 2, at personal, organisational and structural levels. What is examined here is the role that sociology plays in underpinning the value and purpose of those strategies.

Sociology highlights the fact that are likely to be a range of structural reasons why problems exist in a society and, therefore, that there could equally be a range of ways in which these problems could be tackled. Just as there is not only one cause of any problem, there will always be a number of possible solutions. Here are a number of ways in which adopting a sociological approach can help you to understand and tackle social inequality.

Carry out research to define the problem clearly

As mentioned at the beginning of the chapter, sociology attempts to turn 'common sense' on its head. Quite often what people believe, and what is actually the case, are two different things. It is crucial that policy makers accurately understand what the problem is, so their attempts at creating solutions are targeted effectively. From a functionalist point of view, research helps establish what the current norms are in a society, and how they, and the values they represent, have changed.

The following information from the Scottish Executive, for example, will help determine how best to allocate money for mental health services. It will also help determine, over time, whether initiatives such as 'Breathing Space', which targets people at risk from committing suicide, are having an impact.

- *People living with chronic disease, especially those with mental health problems, is an increasing challenge for society. Depression and anxiety were the 3rd and 4th most common conditions reported in GP consultations in 2003/04.*

- *There has been a continuous increase in the number of prescriptions for antidepressants – from 1.16 million in 1992/93 to 3.48 million in 2004/05, with a commensurate increase in cost. Estimated daily use of antidepressant drugs by the population aged 15 to 90 increased from 1.9% in 1992/93 to 8.3% in 2004/05.*

- *In Scotland in 2004 there were 835 suicides (including events of undetermined intent), the same level as in 1994 and 1995. Numbers of suicides showed an upward trend from 1995 up until 2002. They dropped from 899 in 2002 to 794 in 2003. Around three quarters of suicides each year are by males.*

(www.scottishexecutive.gov.uk/Topics/Statistics)

Understand where the power lies: create legislation

Conflict theory is about understanding power differentials, and using that knowledge to make relevant changes. There are a number of ways of doing that and one way, working within exisitng systems, is to create legislation. Creating new Acts of Parliament and creating strong organisations to monitor and implement the legislation should help enhance the life chances of those who experience discrimination and deprivation. One of the key ways in which society responds to social problems is through the creation of laws which seek to redress some of the inequalities in society. Although conflict theorists maintain that legislation reflects the values of the ruling political party, it would be fair to say that, in general, to take an interactionist perspective, most political parties are more responsive to public opinion than they have been in the past. The Scottish Parliament, in particular, has been set up to consult widely with a number of representative groups before deciding on any new legislation. You can see what issues they are currently consulting on at www.scottish.parliament.uk/vli/consultations/index.htm

Most pieces of legislation go through quite a long process before they are finalised in an Act of Parliament. Special groups may have met and prepared reports which outline the need for change and detail proposals for parliament to consider, such as the Millan Commission, which set out the points that were developed into the Mental Health (Care and Treatment) (Scotland) Act 2003, or the Griffiths Report, which led to the NHS and Community Care Act 1990.

For people with disabilities, there were years of protest and challenge before the Disability Discrimination Act was introduced in 1995, two decades after the Sex Discrimination Act and Race Relations Act. One of the main reasons for this was the potential cost of implementing any changes. Introducing gender and racial equality required organisations to change their policies and procedures, but introducing equality for people with disabilities would also involve changing the physical structure of buildings and transport, and this would cost much more money. The powerful lobbying group of the business community was against any compulsory measures, but effective and highly public campaigning from people with disabilities (e.g. by chaining themselves to the Houses of Parliament), lots of media coverage and a change in public perception meant that the government had to respond to pressure. Demographic changes such as the number of people with disabilities living longer due to changes in improved medication and health care provision, and social changes such as the closing of long-stay institutions resulting in a move to increased care in the community, also played a part in making people with disabilities more visible in society, and more vocal about demanding their rights.

Like all pieces of legislation, although Acts have been through a long process of consultation, it is only after an Act has been tested by people taking cases to court or employment tribunals, that we can see how it really works. In many cases, Amendments to Acts are published to deal with significant changes. For instance, three other pieces of legislation have been created to compensate for limitations in the original Disability Discrimination Act 1995 (DDA):

1   Originally, the body created to monitor the Act was called the National Disability Council, but it did not have the powers to take test cases to court or to organise investigations into poor practice so, after a lot of campaigning, the Disability Rights

Commission was created by a separate piece of legislation, the Disability Rights Commission Act 1999.

2 Equally, educational establishments were exempt from the provisions of the DDA when first published, but given that education is such a crucial foundation for the achievement of other life chances, this was rectified with the creation of the Special Educational Needs and Disability Act 2001.

3 The Disability Discrimination Act 2005, as mentioned earlier, has extended the range of illnesses which are covered by the Act and created a duty to promote disability equality for the public sector.

Creating legislation does not in itself solve a problem, but it gives a clear message to society that things need to change. It cannot change people's attitudes, but it can require them to modify their behaviour and this is a necessary step in any process of social change. Legislation can help protect people from harm and abuse, it can promote positive practices and it can prevent certain behaviours from going unpunished.

Use an understanding of all the agents of socialisation to help change attitudes

There are a number of organisations who use the *media* to focus on certain groups in order to challenge stigma and discrimination and promote healthy lifestyle choices. Many agencies now target young people specifically by *advertising* on music and chatroom websites, or by presenting information in formats that young people are likely to pick up. For example, the Scottish Association for Mental Health produced a CD of well-known Scottish bands which it handed out free in colleges and other venues. A CD was much more likely to be picked up by students than a leaflet which had the same information. Zero Tolerance campaigns use stark images on billboards to publicise the message 'Domestic abuse. There is no excuse', and sexual health adverts are shown during the intervals to TV programmes popular with young people.

Schools have an important part to play in the development of children as citizens. For example 99% of schools provide drug education to their pupils. This will include *education* on all of the following areas: safe use of medicine, alcohol, tobacco, solvents and controlled drugs. All drug education has to take account of the age, stage and maturity of the children involved and it is accepted that education on controlled drugs may not be appropriate until later in primary school (**www.scotland.gov.uk/stats**).

In terms of addressing issues of social inequality, the *government* has a crucial part to play. Apart from its role in creating relevant legislation, it is the major financer of *care and health projects* to combat inequality. Or rather, you are, because the government gets its money through taxing your income, petrol, cigarettes, alcohol and the clothes you buy, among many other things. There is not an endless source of money to fund all the projects that would combat inequality, so the government has to set priorities about where the money goes. It goes beyond the scope of this chapter to discuss this in detail, but you are probably aware that, at a local level, your local authority has to publish a Community Care Plan every three years after consultation with all relevant groups, which states what services will be provided to the variety of service user groups. And the Scottish Executive sets targets such as the 'Social Justice Milestones', against which they measure progress. This includes many items which have direct relevance to care, items such as 'All our young people leaving local authority care will have achieved at least

English and Maths Standard Grades and have access to appropriate housing options' and 'Increasing the proportion of older people able to live independently by doubling the proportion of older people receiving respite care at home and increasing home care opportunities' (Scottish Executive, 2003b).

Conclusion

At the end of the chapter it is useful to return to the question posed at the beginning: 'What is sociology?' Hopefully you will be able to write a fuller and clearer definition now. You will have realised by reading through to the end of the chapter that sociology is not about seeing the world from one point of view. It is about keeping your eyes, ears and mind open to a variety of ways of understanding how society works. Human behaviour is constantly changing, and sociologists have to keep generating new research to update the current picture. Beware though: you always have to be careful about where you get your information. There seems to be no end of surveys in magazines and newspapers that claim to tell us the 'truth' about one aspect of our life or another. A sociological approach will take evidence from credible sources and use this to help analyse a situation.

But analysis is not enough. In care practice we want to use that understanding to help us to become better workers and to help the people we work alongside achieve all they can in life. We want to enhance their opportunities and life chances. An understanding of the way society is structured, in addition to a knowledge of psychology, and underpinned by care values, is a solid basis for positive care work. The concluding activity should further your thinking about these questions.

SUMMARY

At the beginning of the chapter attention was given to defining sociology and some key sociological concepts. Four sociological theories were considered: functionalist, conflict, symbolic interactionist and feminist. Functionalist theory emphasises a view of society as a system made up of interrelated parts which perform functions in relation to the whole. 'Society', according to this theory, is seen in terms of consensus and agreement rather than conflict and change. Conflict theory, on the other hand, rests on the view that conflict is fundamental, inevitable and even desirable between the various groups in society which have differing interests from one another. Both the functionalist and conflict theories can be regarded as macro or large-scale approaches which take the influence of society on individuals as their starting point. Symbolic interactionist theory focuses attention upon the meanings that individuals give to social actions, and the active part an individual plays in constructing their own reality. It is an example of a micro-sociological approach. Feminist theory sets out to explain the position of women and to focus attention on such issues as the subordination and oppression of women in society. Feminist sociology may take a macro- or micro-sociological approach, in combination with a central focus on the role of gender in any issue.

All of these theories were used to examine two aspects of society: family and deviance. Social inequality was considered in relation to the experience of people with disabilities, looking particularly at housing and the provision of health care. Throughout the chapter opportunities were provided for you to apply your thinking to care situations.

Activity

Sociological theory, the MacDonalds and the Ahmeds

Assess the relevance of any one sociological theory in understanding either the MacDonald or the Ahmed family, described in the 'Case study – A tale of two families' in Chapter 7. (If you are working in a group situation, you could divide into four groups, with each group considering a different theory.)

Suggested reading

Haralambos, M. and Holborn, M. (2004) *Sociology: Themes and Perspectives*, 6th edition. London: Collins
More academic and thorough discussion of sociological ideas touched on in this chapter.

O'Donnell, M. (1997) *Introduction to Sociology*, 4th edition. London: Nelson.
A well-written and interesting introduction to sociology.

CHAPTER 6
Care in Practice

Janet Miller

> *The person at the centre of the plan is the person whose contributions we've not had enough of yet.*
>
> (Judith Snow in Ritchie et al., 2003, p. 39)

This chapter aims to enable you to understand the care planning and helping process and to place the service user firmly at the centre. You are introduced to models of care and need and also to exchange and person centred approaches to care planning. A positive care environment approach is discussed in relation to implementing care plans. The importance of the value base, communication and relationships discussed in Chapter 2 is emphasised throughout the chapter.

The material in this chapter is relevant to Values and Principles in Care, Intermediate 2 Outcome 3 and Higher Outcome 3.

By the end of the chapter you should be able to:

★ understand a model of care based on assessment, care planning, implementation and evaluation

★ explain needs, wants, wishes and dreams in relation to aspects of development and a PROCCCESS approach

★ explain assessment and tools of assessment

★ distinguish between exchange and person-centred approaches to care planning and explain the care planning process

★ implement care plans according to a positive care environment approach

★ carry out evaluation through monitoring and review.

The foundations of good practice

The foundations of good practice have been laid in Chapter 2, through the development of a sound value base and the ability to build helpful, supportive relationships with people. These are really the most important things, since without them care practice is just a chore without the interests of people at its centre. They are not enough, however, to promote the best possible practice. Good practice needs to give service users as much

239

power in their lives as possible, as much choice and as much say about how they wish to lead their lives. This imposes a duty on care workers to develop their own knowledge and skills about needs and the care planning and helping process, so that they can optimise their role in working with service users to enhance their quality of life. This must be done in ways which empower and include service users by making sure that they are at the centre of the process. This has not always been so and, unfortunately, it is still the case that some people in care situations feel that things are done *to* them rather than *with* them. Here are some quotes from service users which reflect this:

> There are so many reviews, reports and everything else that they put together about your child. They do not talk about the person, their character, their gifts or anything like that . . .

(Ritchie et al., 2003 p. 26)

> Everyone got together, staff, family and did your meeting and got my future sorted out without me.

> When I got my plan typed up the four things I wanted had been left out, but some things staff wanted were there.

(Sanderson et al., 1997)

Would you like it if other people decided how you should live your life?

Care practice

Care practice is part of a process which begins with working with someone to explore needs and wants. Needs refer to those things which it is considered the person's right to have, whereas wants refer to things that a person would like, wishes for, dreams about and/or that would make life easier. The dividing line between needs and wants is rather a blurred one. Person-centred work takes into account not only those things that are considered to be needs, but also the wishes and dreams people have. A good plan will attempt to incorporate both while recognising that for service users, as with anyone else, it is impossible to have everything you wish for. However, a lot of what people do in life is probably about working towards not only meeting their basic needs but about improving their life and achieving at least some of their wants, wishes and dreams.

In care practice the initial exploration of needs and wants is usually called an assessment. As a result of this a plan is made about how those needs and the wants identified for action will be achieved, by whom and in what time scales. This plan has to be implemented, i.e. put into action, and it should be constantly evaluated through processes of monitoring and review. The mode and timescale of evaluation should be built into the plan. If evaluation indicates that the plan is not meeting need and agreed wants, then it should be changed. Flexibility is essential in this process, and frequent opportunities should be presented to the service user to discuss and evaluate the plan of care. Implementation in this chapter is examined in terms of four environments: therapeutic, physical, organisational, community.

Figure 6.1 illustrates the care planning and helping process in the form of a tree. The roots of the tree represent values and principles, communication and other skills, and knowledge, some of which are explained in other parts of this book. The trunk of the tree represents the relationships which are made with service users and other relevant people, emphasising especially the qualities put forward by Carl Rogers (1991) of empathy (understanding), congruence (genuineness) and unconditional positive regard (acceptance) (see page 65, Chapter 2 for a full explanation of Roger's qualities). The crown of the tree is the care planning process, a process which begins with assessment and care planning and progresses to implementing and reviewing, but which goes round and round because care planning should never be regarded as complete. It is a process which continues for as long as the service user needs services, and is adapted to changing needs and wants

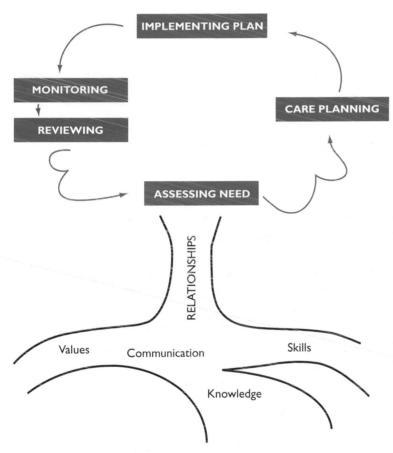

Figure 6.1 The tree of a model of care

Assessment

Assessment is the first step in the care planning process. It involves examining needs, wants and opportunities as a basis for a care plan which aims to ensure that the service user reaches a quality of life which is as good as it possibly can be. Right at the centre of this process, guiding its course as much as possible and making decisions, is the service user. A good assessment will also take into account the needs of other people in the service user's life, especially carers and family members, but the focus of this assessment should always be this service user. Under Community Care, Disability, Carers and Children's legislation other people in the service user's life may be entitled to assessments and plans in their own right in order that their own needs are promoted.

Activity *Assessment and care planning*

Before proceeding to a more detailed examination of the elements of assessment, think about, and if possible discuss, the ten essential points about assessment and care planning identified in Figure 6.2 below. Most of these have been contributed by care students after they have been on placement and worked in a care service for the first time. A fresh pair of eyes often sees things more clearly than people who have worked somewhere for years! Would they be your priorities? Do you have other suggestions?

Assessment and care planning should:

1 – rest upon a firm value base with respect for the dignity of every individual and promotion of choice, rights, empowerment and protection, at the forefront;

2 – have the service user at the centre; be with, and not of, the service user and be available to him or her – the aim is to empower and optimise the participation of the service user in developing an agreed care plan;

3 – have good communication, including listening, at the core of the process;

4 – be part of an on-going process which should never be regarded as complete;

5 – be needs led and not service led; 'needs led' means focusing on a full examination of needs; 'service led' means the way in which, in the past, people were assessed for a particular service for which they had been referred – service came first, needs second;

6 – be based on accurate, up-to-date information. It is important to distinguish clearly what is fact, what is opinion, intuition or something else;

7 – guard against labelling, stigmatising or making a scapegoat of a person – for example, if Joe is described as 'difficult' in an assessment this is a label which can lead to stigma (a negative sign), which can lead to scapegoating (being unjustly blamed for everything which goes wrong);

8 – be specific about who is responsible for what, and outline the responsibilities, as well as the rights, which the service user has in the process;

9 – have a built-in evaluation procedure;

10 – emphasise that there is not just one right care plan; there are no absolutes, and assessment and care planning should be tailored to individual needs.

Figure 6.2 Ten essential points about assessment and care planning

Needs

This section reminds you of some of the things which it is important to consider when examining need. The term need is used here to incorporate many kinds of need, including those identified in Maslow's hierarchy (see Chapter 5) ranging from physiological to self-actualisation, and needs which reflect aspects of development in terms of SPECCS: social, physical, emotional, cognitive, cultural and spiritual development (see Chapter 3). Another model, which includes and expands upon both Maslow and SPECCS, and which is useful in a consideration of needs in a helping context, is the PROCCCESS model (Miller, 2005). This model is examined in further detail below. The categories of need examined in the PROCCCESS model are as follows:

- physical needs
- relationship needs with carers and other professionals
- organisational and operational needs
- communication needs
- cognitive/intellectual needs
- cultural needs
- emotional needs
- social needs
- spiritual needs.

Physical needs

Everyone has *physical needs* associated with keeping the body in good working order and as healthy as possible. For people who need some help it is essential to identify those needs which the individual is unable to meet and to provide enough help to meet these, while at the same time maximising independence, maintaining dignity and promoting empowerment. The quotation below gives an example of providing adequate housing as a way of enabling people, including informal carers, to meet needs, especially physical needs, of children with physical disabilities:

> *The home was often these children's most restrictive environment. Often they simply could not use their equipment such as walking or standing frames around their homes because of the cramped and confined conditions.*
>
> *Parents were worried that their children were not getting the exercise or therapy they believed they need because of space constraints and the two mothers of visually impaired children complained that their children spent a lot of time colliding into furniture and doors.*

(Anon, 1998c)

Compare this with the experience of Debbie after moving to a new, specially built home:

> *Within 24 hours of being in this house it was like – Wow! She was a different child. Her confidence increased overnight. I can't describe to you the difference in Debbie.*

(Anon, 1998c)

Meeting physical needs for housing, however, also has to be balanced with meeting other needs. The example below illustrates the links between meeting physical needs and meeting social and cultural needs. In an article about single people who have been homeless or have mental health problems Gerard Lemos states:

> *Making a flat or a house a home depends almost as much on who or what is nearby as it does on the flat itself. Being near family members and friends, places of worship and interests, groups and activities are what makes an area feel like your community.*

(Lemos, 2006)

Relationship needs with carers and other professionals

One part of the care planning process which is often neglected is the need for service users and care workers to build up relationships with the providers and organisers of care. Informal carers such as parents, partners and friends, professionals such as doctors, social workers and community nurses, and other people with whom the service user interacts such as neighbours and befrienders, are all potentially important components of the planning process. In one school of care planning, person-centred planning, which is explained in greater detail later in the chapter, the service user chooses who is to be part of the planning process. In other situations, especially where statutory requirements must be met in relation to children or people with mental health problems, there are some people who must be part of the planning process and others who can be chosen by the service user.

Organisational and operational needs

A knowledge of organisations which have the potential to provide for need, and of the operations necessary to access their services, is a vital part of the care worker's repertoire. The more a care worker knows about what resources can be utilised or may be available, the greater the choice which can be given to the service user. Sometimes all that is needed is information about how to access various forms of help, for example what benefits are available, where there is a day centre, or which college runs appropriate courses in computing. Armed with this information the service user may then be able to pursue avenues of interest or care independently. Among the agencies which are able to provide a great deal of useful information are the Citizen's Advice Bureaux in many locations around Scotland and the rest of the UK, Department for Work and Pensions (UK benefits), Social Work or combined Departments, Health Centres and LearnDirect Scotland.

Communication needs

Although communication needs could be included in the section on cognitive/intellectual needs they are considered separately here, mainly at the suggestion of service users who feel that this is an often neglected area. Many people experience some form of communication difficulty or disability such as hearing or speech impairment or have a first language which is different from that of the care worker. It is important that their communication needs are met, for example by providing signers for someone who is deaf and communicates by signing, and/or by learning some signing yourself.

Joan

Joan, a social work assistant on a disability team, wanted to gain a qualification. She is deaf and communicates by signing. She visited her local college where she was offered a place on a course. Her employer was prepared to finance a signer, Joan successfully completed her care course and is now keen to further her education by taking an Open University degree. By meeting Joan's communication needs, cognitive needs were also achieved and Joan was enabled to move towards self-actualisation.

Cognitive/intellectual needs

If you look at Chapter 3 you will see that there are different cognitive needs at each stage of development. The young child needs education, usually at school, and stimulation at home, especially through play and communication. The adult also needs opportunities to continue to develop cognitively and these should be explored as part of the planning process. Whenever possible, people should be enabled to access resources which are available to everyone. Many colleges at present provide special courses for people with a learning disability. It is often assumed that these students would be unable to access mainstream courses when in fact additional support rather than special courses may fulfil their needs. Care workers can be advocates for people to access resources in the community which contribute to the fulfilment of cognitive needs. Remember, however, that cognitive needs are not just about gaining qualifications and learning new things. For some people with learning difficulties or dementia their cognitive needs may be about what television programme to watch or what meal to eat. Cognition is about making decisions and formulating opinions, in whatever way is relevant to the person.

Cultural needs

Cultural needs are often seen as part of social needs but are in danger of being neglected if not considered separately. Culture includes values, language and customs. The care worker should try to familiarise him/herself with the different cultural practices of those with whom he or she works and should take these into account in shared planning. Different cultural groups have different practices in relation to diet, physical care and coping with death. For Muslims, for example, Islam governs the way of life and forbids eating pigs in all forms, and other animals which have not been slaughtered ritually. During the month of Ramadan a Muslim fasts from sunrise to sunset, although those who are sick are not expected to fast. A Muslim who is dying may wish to face towards Mecca. In Jewish families there is a tradition of circumcising their new-born sons. An example of the way in which such cultural practices can cause difficulty is provided by Neil Pollack, who is Jewish, and his wife, who isn't. When they announced to Neil's parents that they had decided not to have their son circumcised they were told that he would therefore not be recognised as their grandson. His mother said: 'Your wife is immaterial here. You can't betray 6,000 years of Jewish tradition' (Pollack, 2007). Fulfilling cultural needs is not always straightforward!

Emotional needs

Emotional development depends on the fulfilment of emotional needs. These include the need for love, belongingness, self-esteem and opportunities to develop a positive self-concept. Exploration of emotional needs rests very much upon spending time getting to know the service user, listening actively to verbal and non-verbal communication and, from this, gaining a picture of the individual's emotional life and the extent to which emotional needs are fulfilled. The time and patience required to explore the significance of relationships and how the individual sees and feels about him/herself can have spin-offs in many areas of life.

The account below, provided by a care student, about a man who attended a day resource centre, provides a good example. The service user had no speech and couldn't say how he felt. Other care staff had said this was not a great concern!

> *I thought about making up a chart of faces with different expressions so that the service user could show me how he feels and we could start working together and getting to know each other. By doing this it would promote effective care practice for the service user as he is getting to know how he feels and he can deal with it . . . Within 2 weeks I was getting results and he was showing me and telling me how he was feeling.*

Social needs

Social needs include the need for relationships, and opportunities to build these in a variety of contexts.

When you look at the opportunities which service users have to develop social relationships how far do these meet social needs and is there any support needed to develop these? Have community links been thoroughly explored in order that service users have opportunities which are as far as possible equal to the opportunities open to all citizens? The answers to these questions provide indicators for planning and implementation.

CASE STUDY

Mary and Jean

Here is an example contributed by a student with the permission of the service users.

Mary has a physical disability which restricts her movement, and is a wheelchair user. She also has a mild learning disability. She loves the cinema, going to pubs and enjoys going to chapel on Sundays. She has a good friend Jean who lives in the same supported living house and with whom she enjoys going out. Jean also has a learning disability but is able to walk and is physically quite fit. Because of Mary's mobility problems and her inability to travel independently she has few opportunities to go out socially with her friend. I asked if I could be of any help in enabling Mary and Jean to do something they would enjoy together. They discussed this and said that they would love to go to see the film *Braveheart* . . . I discussed this with the care team and it was agreed that I could arrange this outing with maximum help from Mary and Jean, and that I would accompany them to assist with Mary's wheelchair, but would only sit with them if they wanted me to . . . the outing was a huge success and enhanced their relationship with one another, fulfilling both social and emotional needs.

Spiritual needs

Spiritual needs could perhaps have been encompassed in the discussions of emotional and social needs, but there is a danger that they are given insufficient emphasis. Spiritual needs include the need for contemplation, for the pursuit of religious belief and/or the sharing of ideas about the meaning of life and mortality. Mary, written about in the previous section, fulfilled some of her own spiritual needs through attending chapel, though it wasn't always possible for her to achieve this need, because someone had to organise this and accompany her. In their book *Spiritual Wellbeing of Adults with Down Syndrome*, Margaret Crompton and Robin Jackson (2006) emphasise the importance of assessing and meeting spiritual needs through attention to spiritual wellbeing:

> *Every individual, irrespective of intellectual or physical ability, race, religion or any other attribute, has the right to respect for and nurture of spiritual wellbeing. Failure to ensure this may cause impairment of the whole life development and experience.*

Other considerations in the assessment process

Before proceeding to a consideration of tools of assessment, there are other things that should be taken into account in the assessment process. These include:

- wants, dreams and nightmares
- gifts and giftedness
- opportunities.

Wants, dreams and nightmares

Wants refer to things a person would like but doesn't necessarily need, though it does depend on how you define 'want' and 'need' and where you draw the line between the two. It used to be the case that if you had a roof over your head, enough food and clothing you could be considered to have your needs met. Happily we have progressed beyond this to legislate for needs to be met in many additional areas of life and at a level beyond that of mere subsistence. Dreams can be seen as wants which perhaps don't seem realistic in the immediate future but are things that can be imagined as making life more satisfying and uplifting. They are worth having because they present possibilities for the future which could just be achieved with the will, the 'right' support and enthusiasm from everyone involved in the helping process. Nightmares are those things which an individual definitely does not want to happen. Assessment needs to identify those things that shouldn't happen as well as those things that should.

Vicky

Vicky, aged 33, has learning difficulties, lives with her parents and attends a day centre five days a week. She has various wants, dreams and nightmares identified below.

Table 6.1 Wants, dreams and nightmares

Wants	Dreams	Nightmares
To live in a flat away from her parents	To share a flat with her boyfriend John	To live in a large institution
To have a mobile phone	To have a computer and to learn to use it	To be cut off from her friends and family
To manage her own care budget through direct payments	To earn enough in a job to live on	To be dependent on others for all decisions that relate to her
To have a holiday abroad every year	To go abroad with John to a place they choose	Not to have any holidays

Gifts and giftedness

Assessment in the care planning process considers 'gifts' as part of looking at needs. Gifts in this context, refer not to exceptional talents such as singing well for example, but to the recognition that every individual is unique, has a personality, a presence and characteristics which distinguish him or her from everyone else. These gifts need to be recognised so that they can be used and built upon in care planning. Judith Snow in Sanderson et al. (1997) has written beautifully about how giftedness can be seen as based on presence and difference:

> But . . . everyone has gifts – countless ordinary and extraordinary gifts. A gift is anything that one is or has or does that creates an opportunity for meaningful interaction with at least one other person. Gifts are the fundamental characteristics of our human life and community.

> There are two simple gifts that all people have and that every other gift depends on. The first is presence. Since you are here you are embodying the possibility of meaningful interaction with someone else.

Secondly you are different from everyone else – in countless ways. Difference is required to make meaning possible . . . human interaction arises from presence and difference. You are different from the next person in hundreds, perhaps thousands of ways – in your body, your thinking, your experience, your culture, your interests, tastes and desires, your possessions, your relationships, and more. Therefore you are a bundle of hundreds, perhaps thousands of gifts. So is everyone else.

Opportunities

Opportunities are things which can be used to produce a favourable outcome. They may exist already or they may have to be created. They may be the gifts and qualities of an individual as outlined above or they may exist outside the person in the form of resources; they may be here within this agency or they may be outside in the wider community. They are important in assessment and care planning because they present the means by which the plan can be put into action. A care worker needs to build up a picture of what these opportunities are, what needs to be done to access them or create them or fight for them. Resources refer to anything which can be helpful: money, people, services in the statutory, voluntary and private sectors including day centres, educational opportunities and respite care. The assessment and care planning focus should be needs led but must also be realistic in terms of what may be possible. This doesn't mean abandoning dreams, which should be fought for, but it does mean that a worker has to be honest both with herself and with the service user about what opportunities exist or are likely to exist. The one great resource which a good care worker needs to develop is imagination, since many care plans can be implemented using all available resources imaginatively. Befrienders, volunteers, shared carers, everyday facilities in the community such as coffee shops and pubs, family members, friends, can all be useful resources providing opportunities for fulfilling many needs.

Tools of assessment

Assessment builds up a picture of needs, gifts, dreams and nightmares. There are some tools available to the care worker which can help in building this picture over a period of time, some of which are a necessary requirement of the agency, and some of which can make the process enjoyable rather than a chore. The emphasis is on building relationships as a prerequisite to good assessment and on taking time, rather than attempting to complete an assessment and plan in one short meeting. Below is an account of some of these tools, which are examined in terms of their merits and disadvantages.

Assessment meetings

An assessment meeting can take many forms. In person-centred planning, for example, the service user can invite those people whom he or she chooses to a meeting (or if necessary, meetings) at which needs, dreams and people who are to be part of implementation are discussed with an aim of making a plan which is truly focused on this individual. Another form of meeting is a multi-disciplinary one which is attended by the service user and as many people involved in his or her care as possible. Meetings need to be as non-threatening as possible, to be relaxed so that everyone feels confident enough to make a contribution. Meetings have the advantage of bringing many people together but are only one aspect of the assessment/care planning process. They can be rather formal occasions unless a determined effort is made to avoid this.

At one assessment meeting I attended, the chair of the meeting began by taking this opportunity to discipline the service user. Why do you think this defeated the purpose for which the meeting was called? The service user was immediately put on the defensive, his mother was furious, other people at the meeting felt extremely uncomfortable and were completely taken by surprise by this approach. Although efforts were made to rescue the situation, the participation of the service user and his mother was effectively lost. When you read the section on person-centred planning you will see an emphasis on meetings being facilitated rather than chaired, with a facilitator representing and advocating for the service user where necessary. Some situations may require both some formal structure and a degree of advocacy, for example when assessment and planning are taking place with a child at risk.

Assessment forms

Assessment forms have their uses but should never be the be all and end all of the assessment and care planning process. They are only a tool. Most local authorities and health boards have assessment forms of some description which summarise useful information, usually under such headings as: personal details; family members and contact with these; housing situation; physical and psychological health; dependencies on e.g. drugs or alcohol; informal support received from e.g. family members; formal support/services received; service user's views; carer's views; any disagreements between the two; people contacted as part of the assessment process; a summary of needs; a summary of areas to be carried forward to the care plan.

These forms are often used as a way of arguing for resources and often don't contain the kind of information that a care worker needs to know about everyday life. For this reason many agencies also have their own forms asking for the kind of information they need for work on a day-to-day basis. These forms may include such details as likes and dislikes, medication, how to respond if a particular emergency should arise, contact numbers and a photograph. The form is only the written account of a process which should be personal, built upon thorough knowledge and relationships. Forms have the advantage of providing a written summary but are limited by the questions asked which may not always be the most appropriate ones.

As discussed in Chapter 1, agencies are increasingly using a *single shared or unified assessment process*, with only one process and one set of forms to cover all or many services received. This has been established to overcome problems associated with duplication, and aims to promote an effective response to meeting needs. The Scottish Executive produced guidance on single shared assessment in 2001 to local authorities, NHS Scotland, housing agencies and other relevant organisations in the independent sector (Scottish Executive, 2001). Special forms have also been developed for *looked-after children* to ensure an integrated system of assessment, planning, review and monitoring, with a focus on development across the following areas of life:

- health
- identity
- social presentation
- emotional and behavioural development
- education
- family and social relationships
- self-care skills.

In 2007 education received a particular focus because evidence, published in the *Herald* (16 January 2007) indicated that 50% of children leaving care at 16 do not have any qualifications. This issue is also examined in Chapter 5. Good assessment, planning and implementation can begin to address such issues.

Checklists

Checklists are sometimes used in care practice to establish what a service user can do in relation to a set of tasks, as a way of planning what needs to be achieved to make progress. They may be used, for example, with people with learning disability to establish a baseline from which a plan in relation to defined tasks can be made e.g. handling money, making a meal or planning a journey. These checklists have many of the pitfalls which have already been seen to apply to forms. They are only as good as the questions asked and there is a danger that they can become the main focus of work when they are only one tool in the care planning and helping process.

Observation

Observation doesn't mean that a person's every move and action needs to be watched and recorded but that a care worker's and other's observations of the service user can be of relevance in the assessment process, especially in situations where the service user has difficulty in communication. Observed changes in behaviour, difficulties in relating to some people more than others, observations of likes and dislikes can all be important aspects of assessment. If, for example, you are working with a child with a learning disability whom you observe to become very agitated and to exhibit challenging behaviour when there is a lot of noise, you may build into the care plan opportunities to have quiet times away from other service users.

Asking questions

As with observation, asking questions is a very straightforward way of obtaining information if the service user or those being asked have the communication skills to provide adequate answers. This method is quick and is a very good way of obtaining factual data. Wheal (1994) emphasises that the issues covered on the forms for looked-after children, ranging from health to family and social relationships, can provide a good basis for asking questions. Asking questions can, however, be seen as rather threatening and sometimes people give the answer they think you would like to hear rather than what is really concerning them. There may be issues of power or fear transferred from other situations which can limit the use of questions, or the questions themselves may not be sufficient to elicit information about what is really worrying the service user. Other information is just as well gained through one of the other more informal ways set out below which may, in the end, produce a more accurate picture.

Diaries and scrapbooks

Diaries record day-to-day events of significance. A care worker can suggest to a service user that he or she keeps a diary for perhaps a period of two weeks, writing down (with help, if necessary), all of the things which are important during that time: activities, people, classes, outings and so on. In this way a picture of the service user's everyday life and the network of people who are important to him/her can be built up as a basis for assessing need and looking at things which should and should not happen in the plan of care.

CARE IN PRACTICE

Stephen

A care worker worked on a diary with Stephen, a boy of thirteen resident in a care and education centre. Stephen enjoyed going over his day, and the care worker realised from the diary just how important routine was to Stephen. One of the most vital parts of the day was a morning shower, without which Stephen felt very uncomfortable. Keeping the diary not only enabled the care worker and Stephen to identify needs and activities which should be incorporated in the care plan, but as a spin-off it improved their relationship with one another and gave Stephen the opportunity to improve his literacy skills in an enjoyable way.

A diary may also be a useful tool for the care worker to keep, recording events in relation to a specific service user over a set period of time. In this way it may be possible to identify patterns of behaviour, triggers to challenging behaviour, issues which are of importance, social contacts, likes, dislikes and needs which have not previously been evident. Carers too, for example family members or carers in shared care situations, can facilitate the assessment process through the use of diaries from which needs can be identified. Shared care refers to situations where people offer care in their own home to share the care with family members and provide them with regular, planned breaks.

Where communication, especially written communication, is difficult, a scrapbook of pictures could be built up as a shared exercise enabling the service user to identify needs and people of importance through photographs and magazine pictures.

Shared activities

Sometimes needs can be identified when the focus isn't on assessment at all but on an enjoyable activity which is shared between service user and worker.

Linda

When Linda and her care worker went to the cinema together they had a good chat afterwards about the film and about all sorts of other things too. Linda talked about her family, about how she wished she could see her sister more often, about her great love of the cinema and going bowling and swimming; she mentioned her key worker several times and expressed a dislike of one particular night shift worker. All of this contributed to building up a picture of her needs, which could subsequently help in developing her care plan.

The above are not the only ways in which information for an assessment can be gained. You may be able to think of others which work just as well. They do, however, provide a start and a basis on which a plan of care can be formulated.

Care planning

A care plan is an action plan in working with service users. As plans are written down and shared with users, they emphasise the contractual nature of the service provided.

Planning is a practical activity that:
- *gives a sense of purpose to meeting needs;*
- *takes action in advance of any problems;*
- *ensures that service users do not get overlooked.*

(Social Care Association, An Introduction to Care Planning, 2000b)

Plans can be staged according to which needs are to be met in what time scale. For example, there will be some needs to be met immediately, some in one month, some in three months, some by next year and some which will be worked towards at some point in the future. The essential features of a care plan, from the above definition and the preceding discussion of assessment, are that:

- it is the basis for action (not just a paper exercise)
- it is written down
- it is shared with the service user
- it is a contract – providers and users agree about what is to be done by whom
- it is a practical activity
- all team members should be working to this plan which is the service user's, not theirs
- the plan should state specifically what is to happen, who should be doing what and in what time scale
- monitoring and review of the plan should be built into the planning process

- the plan should clearly identify any statutory/legal requirements, implications or constraints. For example, some care plans for children incorporate a supervision requirement which is legally enforced by the children's hearing or the courts. Any other likely constraints which may affect the care plan should be detailed.

Models used in the care planning process

The above discussion has drawn heavily upon two models of planning: the exchange model and person-centred planning. Both of these emphasise the importance of placing the service user at the centre of the planning process. However, person-centred planning goes much further than this and presents exciting possibilities for the service user to make supported choices ranging from who attends planning meetings to how the future is to be lived.

The exchange model

The exchange model is described in Coulshed and Orme (2006) and emphasises an exchange among service users, carers and workers of their knowledge and skills, including knowledge of methods of helping and of resources and skills in the process of problem-solving. The model recognises that people with needs and those in their network know more about their problems than any worker who comes along to help them, though workers have their own areas of expertise. The process of producing a plan is an exchange among everyone involved and should be multi-disciplinary in nature. A plan emerges which is a balance-sheet of everything which has been presented. One person, usually a key worker or social worker, coordinates the plan and negotiates agreements about who is to do what, for whom, in what time scale. The focus is on the social situation and everyone in the service user's network. Smale et al. (1993) summarise the main tasks of this model:

- facilitate full participation in the process of decision-making
- make a 'holistic' assessment of the social situation, and not just of the referred individual
- help create and maintain the flexible set of human relationships which make up a 'package of care'
- facilitate negotiations within personal networks about conflicts of choices and needs
- create sufficient trust for full participation and open negotiations to actually take place
- change the approach to all these broad tasks as the situation itself changes over time.

Person-centred planning

Most of the text of this section was based on material from Ritchie (2003), and is used with permission.

> *Person-centred planning creates a compelling image of a desirable future and invites people to join with the person to make it happen.*
>
> (O'Brien and Lovett in Sanderson et al., 1997)
>
> *Person-centred planning is a way of helping people who may wish to make some changes in their life. It is an empowering approach to helping people plan their future and organise the supports and services they need. It seeks to mirror the ways in which 'ordinary people' make plans.*
>
> (Sanderson et al., 1997)

Person-centred planning has developed from ideas presented by O'Brien and Lovett (1992), mainly in relation to people with learning disability who are now beginning to find a place 'in the community', often after spending many years in hospital. Some of its central ideas, however, can be transferred to care planning in general and can be useful with any service user who wants and is in a position to make changes in his or her life. It is an exciting advance upon traditional models of care planning, moving away from professionals organising the process, towards placing as much control and decision-making as possible in the hands of the service user. Various forms of care planning are based upon the person-centred approach, including Personal Futures Planning and Essential Lifestyle Planning, and many agencies, among them the Outlook project in East Dunbartonshire and Richmond Fellowship, Scotland, are embracing person-centred planning as central to their work. The potential of this approach for empowering service users is enormous and exciting and for this reason it is given considerable space in this section of the book. Unlike the exchange model, the focus is well and truly on this service user, rather than a social situation and a plan which must account for the needs of many people. The roots of person-centred planning are illustrated in Figure 6.3.

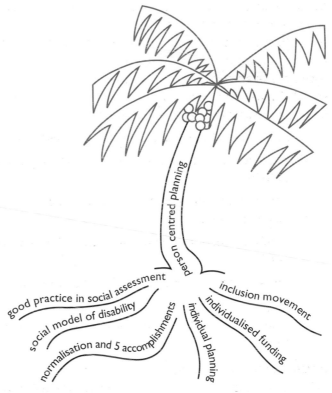

Figure 6.3 The roots of person-centred planning (Source: Ritchie et al., 2003; reproduced with permission of P. Ritchie)

Person-centred planning is often very visual, using diagrams and charts to assist in building a plan. Figures 6.4, 6.5 and 6.6 show some of the ways in which visual material is used in the planning process, illustrating 'building a shared understanding', 'relationship circles' and 'when a meeting is needed'.

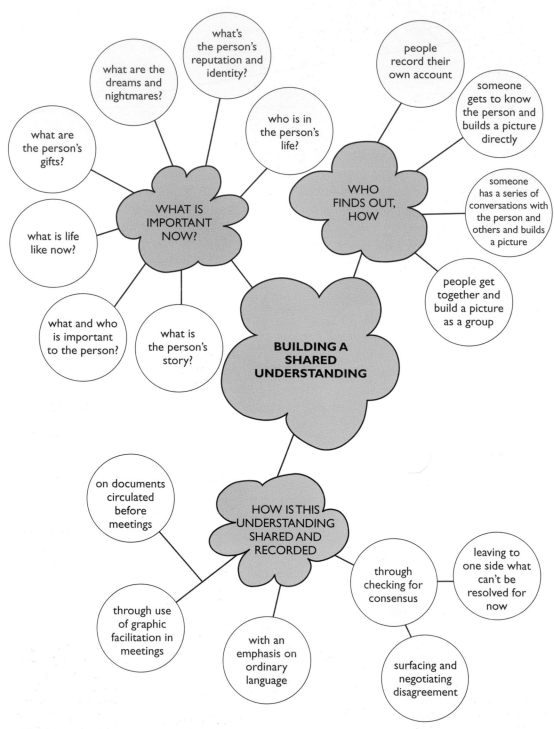

Figure 6.4 Building a shared understanding (Source: Ritchie et al., 2003; reproduced with permission of P. Ritchie)

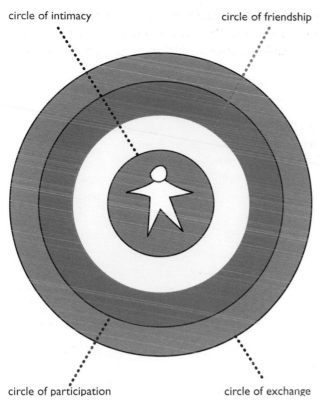

circle of intimacy

circle of friendship

circle of participation

circle of exchange

Figure 6.5 Relationship circles (Source: Ritchie et al., 2003; reproduced with permission of P. Ritchie)

We need to look creatively at these issues with the person and think about how decisions can be made in the most empowering way.

Figure 6.6 When a meeting is needed . . . (Source: Ritchie et al., 2003; reproduced with permission of P. Ritchie)

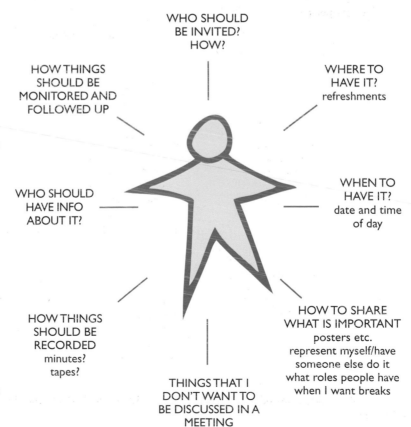

WHO SHOULD BE INVITED? HOW?

HOW THINGS SHOULD BE MONITORED AND FOLLOWED UP

WHERE TO HAVE IT? refreshments

WHO SHOULD HAVE INFO ABOUT IT?

WHEN TO HAVE IT? date and time of day

HOW THINGS SHOULD BE RECORDED minutes? tapes?

THINGS THAT I DON'T WANT TO BE DISCUSSED IN A MEETING

HOW TO SHARE WHAT IS IMPORTANT posters etc. represent myself/have someone else do it what roles people have when I want breaks

Three ways of working which are essential to the person-centred planning process are now considered:

- sharing power
- building a shared picture
- building a capacity for change.

Sharing power is not always easy, especially when service users have experienced many years of powerlessness in institutional settings. For this reason, planning may also have an educational element, showing and informing the person about what is possible. It may also require enormous patience and a very positive belief that the person is capable of growth and participation. The use of visual materials is one of the ways in which people are both empowered and can begin to build a shared picture of their future. Building a capacity for change may involve investigating and utilising community resources in creative and new ways. Here are some ways in which agencies share power and build up a shared picture. Outlook (Kirkintilloch) asks the service user who he or she wishes to invite to a planning meeting, and the meeting is at the user's, and not anyone else's, pace. Ritchie (2003) advocated looking at the best possible day and the worst possible day for the person, going right through a 24-hour period and looking at every detail. The important thing about this is that it focuses attention on the small details of life, such as what this individual likes for breakfast.

Person-centred planning is a comprehensive way of planning for people. There may still be some formalities to be completed in order to access some aspects of the care plan. It will probably still be necessary, for example, to complete a community care assessment form, but the process of getting there in person-centred planning is unique to this service user who is being empowered to make these changes in his or her life.

Table 6.2 is a summary of what person-centred planning is moving from and towards.

Table 6.2 Moving towards person-centred planning

Moving from . . .	Towards . . .
clinical descriptions of people	seeing people as human beings
professionals being in charge	sharing power
professionals inviting people	the person choosing who attends meetings
meetings in offices at times to suit professionals	meetings in a venue chosen by the person, when it suits her/him
meetings being chaired	meetings being facilitated
not asking what the person wants	encouraging the person to dream
assuming inability	looking for gifts in people
filing plans away	giving the plan to the person
writing notes of meetings	graphic facilitation of meetings
professionals putting the plan into action	all team members having some responsibility for implementing the plan

Implementing care plans

The helping process aims to implement the care plan in ways which respect worth and dignity, empower and include the person and promote rights and welfare. A lot of people think of helping as a very active process of doing things for other people. From the value base, skills and qualities already explained, you will have realised, however, that helping is really about empowering and enabling people to do as much as possible for themselves, empowering them to make decisions and have opportunities which are available to most other people. This should always be considered to ensure that helping does not become patronising, discriminating or demeaning. With these factors in mind, a positive care environment approach to implementing care plans is explained below. This sets out some useful skills and methods in the context of different care environments, which aim to improve the service user's quality of life.

Before reading this, it is useful for you to think about the skills which you already have. These are some of the suggestions made by a group of care students on placement when asked what skills and methods they used to implement plans:

- I use empathy when I'm helping people, just imagining what they may want and how they're probably feeling.
- I always demonstrate respect so that people aren't embarrassed when they need help.
- I talk to the young people, get to know them first.
- I try to motivate the older adults I work with by providing some interesting activities and a choice of things to do.
- I play with the young people and try to help with their socialisation and their education plan.
- Communication, communication, communication – verbal and non-verbal; anything that works.
- I assist people to the toilet and with bathing, always being careful to find out how much they can do for themselves first, and I always talk to them and ask how their son or daughter is or whoever is important to them.
- I write up notes in the log at the end of the day and attend the handover meetings so that I know what is being achieved in the care plans and others have an idea about what has happened during my shift.
- I take one lady shopping. It sometimes takes us an hour to get out of the house because she's quite slow at getting ready and the other care staff seem to think this isn't relevant work. I think this is what the job is all about. We go to the post office and collect her pension, then we'll go for a coffee and take our time, then a walk back in time for lunch. Admittedly you can't do that every day, but it's an important part of care work.
- I've been helping a group of children with life story books so that they have a reminder about who has been important to them and important places, holidays and so on.

- I've been doing something similar with some older adults, making a scrap book to represent old times. We have some amazing conversations about some of the pictures. Some people in their 90s remember the first world war.

- I used to be a hairdresser and when we're going on an outing I ask if anyone wants their hair done. Lots of them do. While you're doing their hair or their nails you talk to them and they tell you all sorts of things they never would usually, because they're so relaxed.

What do you notice about the above examples? Most of them illustrate skills which are part of everyday life: talking to people, playing with children, making scrapbooks, going shopping. The importance of the value base and communication are emphasised again and again and are an essential part of all care work. Building upon these foundations, a useful model for implementing care plans is presented below. You will see that this rests firmly upon the foundations of value base and communication discussed above and set out in Chapter 2.

(Level **Higher**) ## The positive care environment approach

Implementation can be considered in many ways but one useful framework that promotes assessment, planning, implementation and review in person-centred ways is 'the positive care environment approach'. This approach ensures that all relevant issues are taken into account in the care process while the focus remains firmly on working with service users to optimise their quality of life. Using the word 'environment' may at first sound rather impersonal, but environment refers to the surroundings and conditions in which a person lives and/or conducts their life or parts of it, whether the physical location is their own home or a residential, day care other setting. Care workers and what they do are not only part of the environment, but their work can make an enormous difference to the many environments affecting the service user. In addition to this, the environments can themselves be used in helpful ways. Beginning with the therapeutic environment ensures that the service user is placed firmly at the centre.

Four strands of the care environment are considered:

- **the therapeutic environment (working with service users)**, that is, how the care environment, including communication, relationships and the place in which care takes place, can be utilised to provide a life for service users which is as fulfilling as possible and as the backdrop to creative therapeutic approaches

- **the organisational environment (staff and how well they work together)** including the way the organisation is led and managed, the quality of staff training, development and supervision, and the supporting organisational policies

- **the physical environment (the building and other material factors),** which includes the building and grounds, their location, the things in them, the way they are maintained and adorned, food, clothing and comforts and luxuries to enhance well-being

- the community environment (external links), which concentrates on links with families and the wider community.

These threads are inextricably intertwined but for the purposes of discussion, of necessity, they are examined separately.

The therapeutic environment – working with service users

> In promoting people's well-being consideration should be given to reducing emotional and physical pain, creating positive care environments, developing networks and circles of support and promoting spiritual well-being.
>
> (Miller, 2005)

'Therapeutic' is interpreted very broadly to mean healing or having a good effect. It doesn't necessarily refer to specific treatments or the use of any particular methods of working, though it can include these if they have a healing or positive benefit. The therapeutic environment should enable service users to have lives that are as fulfilling as possible. Contributing factors include:

- love and relationships
- communication and oomph
- direct care and attention to the importance of daily life
- effective care planning, implementation and evaluation
- critical thinking and reflective practice
- activities and holidays
- availability of specialist therapeutic approaches.

Rather than deal with all of these in detail we will select some of them and incorporate the importance of love, relationships and communication, already discussed in Chapter 2. 'Love' is interpreted to mean caring through warmth, empathy and being genuine, as in the philosophy of Carl Rogers (1991). It is a precondition of helping where children and vulnerable adults have lacked the conditions to form attachments or to feel secure.

Direct care and attention to the importance of daily life

The enormous importance of the direct care role is often undervalued, underestimated and certainly under-rewarded. The everyday life of any establishment is enhanced if attention is paid to how the tasks of everyday life are achieved. In addition, it is often these everyday tasks which provide the greatest opportunities for establishing warm and genuine relationships with service users, sharing activities and using their potential for working with difficult behaviour or developing social skills. One care worker I spoke to said that one of her outstanding memories was of helping a child to tie his shoe laces on his first day at school. It was so important to him that someone cared about how he looked and realised how important this day was to him. The help was as symbolic as it was practical. It set the seal on an on-going and productive helping relationship. The importance of the symbolic relates to the discussion of symbolic interactionism in Chapter 5.

The establishment of a daily routine which incorporates specific tasks that have to be achieved can also be of great importance to some service users. This can provide structure to previously unstructured lives and enhance skills in daily living (such as shopping, washing up and cleaning). Where these skills are lacking they can be modelled by the care worker and practised by the service user. The discussion of Bandura's work on imitation and identification in Chapter 4 is relevant to modelling behaviour. The care setting provides the ideal opportunity for this in an environment that is comfortable for the user and with someone with whom he or she has a close and trusting relationship.

The importance of crucial events and tasks in everyone's lives is also often undervalued in care services. The way in which these events and tasks are tackled can make the difference between people feeling good about their lives and people feeling absolutely dreadful. Staff who see as chores having to assist people at meal times, or to get up in the morning, cannot be cheerful about them. They do not make an effort to converse or make these events pleasant, and this sets the tone for a bad day. It is poor practice.

Activities and holidays

Doing an activity together is a splendid way of getting to know the service user group, for them to get to know you, of adding interest, challenge, development of skill and enjoyment to the lives of those with whom we work. It can also be very therapeutic, in the sense that it helps to relieve stress, raise self-esteem, and it has spin-offs in other areas of life. Similarly holidays can have lots of spin-offs apart from being, in general, thoroughly enjoyable experiences. They can be an occasion for:

- enabling service users to choose where to go and what they want to do
- planning
- gaining new experiences
- sharing
- feeling free from the constraints of everyday life
- staff and service users to get to know one another in a relaxed and friendly way
- sharing memories after the event, which gives a sense of bonding to those who participated.

Availability of specialist therapeutic approaches

Other approaches, such as using counselling skills and group work, lend themselves to being implemented within a care environment both by trained and experienced care workers or by specialists in particular approaches. Social workers, psychologists and any number of other workers may also be involved. If several people are working with a service user, possibly from different disciplines, it is essential that they work together, rather than in separate compartments. It is so easy for care workers to be by-passed unless they can articulate their work to these others in the multi-disciplinary team and demonstrate their skill, understanding and value base. The value of 'the other 23 hours' can be overlooked by professionals who come in for an hour or two (or less) for a therapeutic purpose and then attribute all of the progress to their own input – unless the care workers themselves can demonstrate their value and participate fully in the assessment, planning, implementation and evaluation process.

Care workers have many advantages over others involved in the care of the service user. They are often with him or her for more hours of the day and night than anyone else, they get to know his or her preferences and habits and can implement plans along with the tasks of everyday life. All of this gives care workers a unique advantage for helping in the context of the care environment. This has given rise to theoretical approaches which incorporate aspects of those approaches already discussed into a blend specially adapted to care settings. Such ideas have been developed by Adrian Ward in his discussion of opportunity-led work.

Opportunity-led work

The concept of Opportunity-led Work is a framework that has been designed to enable workers to think through the stages of handling and responding to the many unplanned moments and events in a day's work in order to make their responses more productive and helpful.

(Ward, 2006)

Opportunity-led work is an approach developed by Adrian Ward to build on what happens during the course of every day. Many things that take place in a care service offer opportunities for working productively with people if they are thought about, even just a little and quickly. The skill lies in building up processes and a bank of questions to ask yourself. It involves thought and using your experience to advantage, rather than responding to every issue and event reactively.

For example, a young person, Josie, during the course of an evening discussion in a children's home, suddenly loses her temper and storms out. The key worker instinctively gets up and follows her out shouting 'What do you think you're doing? Come back NOW.'

Is this a good response? Perhaps not. The drawback is that it was not associated with even the quickest of thought processes. It was just a reaction. Such responses lose any advantage that may be gained from what is potentially an opportunity to improve quality of life.

Ward advocates a four-stage process in working with events that happen during the course of everyday work, an approach that can be practised until it can become second nature. The stages are:

- observation and assessment
- decision-making
- action
- closure and evaluation.

The first stage is crucial since it consists of weighing up what is happening, who is involved and what is likely to happen next. Questions associated with the key words what, why, how, when, who, can enable the worker to weigh up quickly the possibilities of the situation and begin to make decisions about what to do. Action will depend on decisions about the answers to the questions posed: for example, what is happening, who is involved, who is affected, etc.; what are the priorities, what is actually possible and what is ethical. The worker needs to examine the desirable result and how to get there given the current and future time scales. Consideration also needs to be given to what shouldn't happen under any circumstances and avoiding this: for example, shouting back when someone shouts at you; giving straight back what is received – hitting back, swearing in response to swearing. Strategies include what is called 'first aid', dealing with the immediate situation, together with a decision about whether or not a longer-term strategy is required.

In the immediate situation, here and now, 'first aid' has to be administered through:

- working on a one-to-one basis, for example through what Redl (1966) has called 'emotional first aid on-the-spot' to help the individual express and leave behind anger, sadness or anxiety
- supporting the individual through the group, for example helping the group to be sensitive to this person's situation or distress and/or supporting group activities 'in order to override the disruptive effects of one member'
- managing the group through focusing on key individuals, for example by drawing the group's attention to how one individual may have been discriminated against without the group being aware that this is what they were doing
- managing the group, for example by establishing ground rules and reminding the group when these are breached.

There are some specific strategies in addition to these which may be used in a conflict or difficult situation:

- offering alternatives – for example, you can go to your room and miss the outing or you can come back and join us and we'll all go on the outing together
- preventing the build-up of tension through defusing the situation, for example being sensitive enough to know that when Josie wrings her hands she will quickly lose her temper unless you change the subject or introduce an activity
- allowing and helping people to climb down with dignity, for example if Josie has often caused offence in the group situation, giving her the opportunity to apologise quietly afterwards to those concerned.

The short-term emotional first aid may be all that is needed but it may also be necessary to use some of the other longer-term strategies associated with more specialised therapeutic intervention.

Activity   *Josie*

In the light of the above guidance, what might have been a more positive response to Josie than 'What do you think you're doing? Come back NOW' when she left the evening discussion, if you know that:

- she usually comes back when she leaves in a temper
- she can react violently to any form of direct criticism
- she usually values the group discussions.

The organisational environment – staff and how well they work together

As important as the therapeutic environment is the way an organisation is run and managed. The following are among the organisational factors which contribute to a positive care environment:

- ethos – the values, mission and vision
- team work, partnerships and collaboration
- leadership and management
- supervision and mentoring
- providing and supporting learning and development.

Ethos

All staff should be given some guidance by those in responsible positions about what their organisation is striving for (its mission and vision), what values and ideas guide the thinking behind the care that is provided and what the end result of all the work and thought should be. This is the ethos which establishes the organisation's culture. Preferably staff and service users should have a say in how this is developed. Some agencies have set out their ethos very clearly for everyone to read; others seem never to have thought about it, except perhaps in terms of aiming to make ends meet or make a profit. Below I reproduce two statements by organisations which encompass their ethos in terms of a mission and vision statement and charter. These should be read critically by readers and adapted to meet the needs of their own agencies. The first statement is from Kibble Education and Care Centre for young people:

Mission
[The Centre] . . . exists to provide a stable, purposeful, safe and happy environment for young people in trouble. It aims to be a place where:- Pupils and staff live and work together in a spirit of trust, mutual respect and co-operation. By investing in people and setting high standards of work and behaviour, individuals and teams develop their full potential in learning, changing and growing.

Vision
[The Centre] . . . aims to be at the forefront of effective and innovative services for young people in trouble.

Values
[The Centre] . . . will conduct its activities with dedication, integrity and honesty. All goals will be reached ethically and morally. It recognises its place in the wider community and obligation to be a good neighbour.

Equal Opportunities
[The Centre] . . . is committed to Equal Opportunities and ensures that all persons receive equal and fair treatment and are not discriminated against or victimised on grounds of sex, marital status, race, sexual orientation, religious beliefs, disability or age.

The second example is set out as a residents' charter in a residential and nursing home for elderly people. This is handed to clients and staff, with a further copy framed and hung in the entrance hall:

Residents . . . have the right to:

- *dignity; to respect by staff of all beliefs and choices of lifestyle and in all circumstances*
- *kindness*
- *privacy*
- *confidentiality in all matters, personal and medical and protection of interests, social and legal*
- *freedom of movement and activity, subject only to safety*
- *freedom of choice, so far as is practicable*
- *a homely and safe environment*
- *feel and be treated as a valued member of the small community of the . . . Home*
- *have visitors whenever and wherever wanted*
- *associate with others and build up relationships, both inside and outside the Home*
- *have spiritual, emotional and physical needs respected and met*
- *a high standard of care, be given details of medical condition on request and to choose their own General Practitioner and Dentist*
- *be consulted on all aspects of living in the Home and nursing care, and have the right to say, 'No'*
- *go to bed at the chosen time and to have a lie-in as they choose*
- *have access to the Head of Home, Chief Executive and Inspectorate; have complaints taken seriously and dealt with promptly and fully.*

(reproduced with permission of the Retail Trust, Glasgow)

Team work, partnerships and collaboration

. . . team work should never be regarded as an optional extra in this sort of work: it is the heart of the matter . . . A worker who initiates and tries to sustain a large amount of individual work without reference to the team is actually undermining the strength of the team . . .

(Ward, 2006)

Team work, partnership and collaboration are all about everyone working together to achieve the best possible results for service users and carers, both within the organisation and across boundaries with other organisations and disciplines. It is only in this way that needs will be adequately met and aims and objectives implemented. Some things that contribute to effective team work, partnership and collaboration are:

- everyone feeling valued
- communication which is transparent, open and inclusive
- flexibility, which includes open-mindedness and a willingness to share and learn from others
- working in partnership to share ideas, work practices and relevant information, whilst also respecting confidentiality and boundaries
- having opportunities to share in decision making and the allocation of work
- feeling that everyone is pulling together to reach the same place
- having opportunities to discuss how things are going and how improvements could be made
- positive meetings that tackle the needs of service users and staff members
- regular meaningful supervision
- a willingness to address and resolve conflicts through discussion and negotiation within a no blame culture
- supportive leadership and management.

Leadership and management

> *Leaders are those who in some way embody, articulate, channel and construct the values …*
>
> (Grint, in Martin, 2003, p. 24)
>
> *Conventionalists and rationalists wear a metaphorical hard hat. Leaders must be different and wear sombreros.*
>
> (Bennis, 2001)

Effective leaders have vision and are supportive. They both help to create, and embody, the ethos of their organisation. In today's world they must lead change and also undertake the tasks of management. Appointed leaders are not the only ones, however, who should exercise leadership. Everyone in an organisation is in a position to exercise qualities of leadership to some extent.

From the literature about leadership and management, and from my own experience, there do seem to be a few things that stand out in relation to what makes an effective manager who is also a leader:

- a commitment to the agency, its ethos and a care value base
- self-awareness and a lack of personal agendas to be achieved
- a commitment to sharing leadership with team members and to optimising everyone's development
- a willingness to get to know staff and build relationships with them
- a thorough grasp of the strategic issues to be tackled

- a willingness to share decision making with staff and service users while at the same time establishing authority to make decisions when necessary
- relevant experience which enhances understanding of the jobs which care workers do
- an ability to stay calm under pressure
- being sufficiently present to know what is going on, to influence it, to lead when necessary and to provide opportunities for everyone to gain experience in leadership in areas of interest or expertise
- and, as Bennis says, 'wearing a sombrero'!

The quality of leadership can usually be judged by the quality of work done when the leader is not there, as well as when they are. A good leader will have established an ethos that is evident whether they are present or not:

> . . . *they will have done this through creating a vision, inspiring others through effective communication of the vision, encouraging others to think creatively and question the way things are done and coaching people to be responsible for their own development and effectiveness.*

> (Taylor Clarke Partnership, 2003)

Good leaders value their most precious asset, the workers. They will give people the confidence to feel that what they are doing is worthwhile, they will include people in the decision-making process, they will empower people to be as autonomous as possible and trust them to take control of work for which they are responsible, they will be open about the decisions that are made and how they were reached and, most importantly, they will value workers both as individuals and as team members.

Supervision and mentoring

Supervision is very often overlooked because managers may make the excuse that there is not enough time for it. It is seen as an optional extra 'if there's time for it'. But time must be made for it. It is a vital element in maintaining quality and is included in the National Care Standards (2002) which specify that:

> *You can be assured that staff and volunteers are properly supervised and appraised and have access to advice and support.*

Even when the care service is understaffed and overworked, supervision is a vital component of care. Indeed, it is probably more important in this situation, since workers will require more support, and may encounter non-routine incidents they need to discuss. Thompson (2002) identifies the tasks of supervision as follows:

- *Monitoring work tasks and workload*
- *Supporting staff through difficulties*
- *Promoting staff development*
- *Acting as a mediator between workers and higher management where necessary*
- *Problem solving*

- *Ensuring legal and organisational requirements and policies are adhered to*
- *Promoting teamwork and collaboration*

While supervision provides opportunities for discussion about work within the organisation, mentoring can provide opportunities for work-related discussion and development with someone outside the care service. This has the advantage of not being connected to line management issues or work relationships that may be hampering progress.

Supporting learning and development

Organisations that support learning and development, both professional and personal, provide ways in which people can improve their practice and learn to meet changing demands. Rogers (2002) refers to learning as follows:

> . . . *learning is an activity in which we take part all the time in the course of everyday living. It is the process by which we face, cope with and use our experience. Throughout our lives we face situations in our work, in our domestic settings and in our wider relationships that were not conceived of when we were at school or college, and they all call for new learning.*
>
> *We need to learn to meet the changing demands of our various occupations, whether heart surgeon, historian or handicraft expert. All the tasks we engage in, whether they comprise paid employment or work in the home call for new knowledge, new skills and new attitudes at various stages.*

(Rogers, 2002, pp. 46–7)

Learning takes place in many ways, for example through formal training, supervision, attendance at conferences, reading and through becoming a reflective practitioner. Developing the habits of reflective practice enables you to think beyond the obvious and to think on your feet, often a requirement of the busy worker. Schon (1983) expressed the view that workers build up a catalogue of experiences and reactions to those experiences like a repertoire they can draw upon: a central feature of reflective thought.

The physical environment – the building and other material factors

> *Children care about shabby, run-down buildings, lack of privacy in bedrooms, showers, toilets and bathrooms. They recognise them as indicators that they are undervalued and that their needs have been overlooked.*
>
> (Kahan, 1994)

Any care environment offers potential for both good and harm. One of the greatest dangers is that of institutionalisation, discussed in detail in Chapter 1. To recap briefly, institutionalisation is a state of being characterised by apathy and an inability to make independent choices. It results from a deprivation of choice, an over-insistence on routine and practices which ignore each person's individuality. Planners and care workers should strive to create an environment which is free from institutionalising forces. In any kind of care environment, even the person's own home, there is inevitably a stress between the needs of individuals for personal choice and individual expression and the needs of the agency to be well organised, hygienic, efficient and cost effective. Care workers are responsible for maximising the former (as well as giving attention to the latter), for looking at the care environment in which they work and ensuring that it is not only predominantly keeping the needs of service users paramount but also creating and using the environment in partnership and collaboration with them. The physical environment plays a part in this.

The National Health Service and Community Care Act 1990, still one of the key influences on the way care is planned and provided, talks about providing *homely settings* in the community for those who are unable to live in their own homes, and maintaining people in their own homes in so far as this is possible. A homely setting is somewhere that 'feels like home'. Among the things which count here are care workers who are concerned about what the place looks like and feels like, and who care about consulting the people who are spending time in this environment.

Figure 6.7 Royal National Institute of the Blind (RNIB) Centre

Figure 6.7 shows how an RNIB employment and learning centre makes the most of technology. The computer is an absolute boon to many people with poor sight as the font size can be increased to a size where they are able to read the text and also see their typed responses. It also gives a wonderful sense of empowerment to those who thought they were condemned to a life of being cut off from visual communication with society at large.

Some other things which can enhance the physical environment include:

- participation of service users in decisions about the environment
- a warm, welcoming, carpeted entrance area (and warm, welcoming staff)
- attractive, well-framed pictures on the walls of corridors and rooms, chosen by service users and perhaps contributed by service users, relatives or local artists
- a colourful, much-used garden with garden seats
- photographs of service users and staff, informal and formal ones

- items of furniture and other belongings brought by service users
- a tea room which service users help to run for the benefit of themselves, their relatives and friends
- pets
- a cupboard full of items which could be used in reminiscence sessions: old photographs, clothes, household items, etc.

And additionally, in a children's centre:

- murals painted by the children and staff in the main lounge/play room
- a play area free from the need to be careful with the furniture, and with enough space for some physical activity
- a cosy, private room where children can have some peace and quiet and can take family members and other visitors
- enough computers, books and play equipment for all children to be able to participate in creative activity
- sturdy, challenging play equipment in the grounds.

Food, clothing, and comforts and luxuries to enhance well-being are also important aspects of the physical environment. Enabling service users to choose the meals they eat and participate whenever possible in their preparation, to have such luxuries as pleasantly smelling toiletries which they have selected, and the opportunity to live in a place that not only looks good but also feels good, all contribute to a positive physical environment.

The community environment – external links

Since they are closely integrated into all of the aspects of the care environment approach, the importance of family/friendship ties and links with the wider community should be emphasised. There will be service users who may need protection from some of the negative aspects of these links or a great deal of support in maintaining them, and there are links with the wider community which could be seen as intrusive and invasive. This whole issue, then, should be approached with care and thought, and it should not be assumed that the promotion of such links is always necessarily a good thing. However, there is a great deal of evidence which suggests that care environments which fail to promote links with family and community networks can become isolated, institutionalised and are more likely to give rise to settings in which service users are neglected or abused. For example, the Waterhouse Report (2000) into the wide-scale abuse that took place in residential homes in Wales reported systematic abuse, a climate of violence and a culture of secrecy that existed for more than two decades. These abuses took place in settings which received few outside visitors and were not integrated or included in local communities.

Care in Practice – community links

As a conclusion I mention emphasis on seeing care settings as part of the community and as community resources. One building, previously only used as an Adult Resource Centre, now also houses a community nursery, a drop-in coffee shop, a crêche, and a welfare benefits adviser. It has developed links with the local community college which students attend and which also uses the centre for some outreach courses, including an

English course for people for whom English is not their first language. Students of the resource centre often gain work placements in the nursery, and boundaries among the various services have become very flexible. The development of such centres seems to be one way forward in breaking down barriers, though such provision must be carefully planned to take account of all service users' needs.

Evaluation: monitoring and review

The final link in the care planning and helping process is to evaluate all of the work which has been done. This involves looking at the process and at the outcomes of the work done. It should be achieved on an on-going monitoring basis, and at regular, scheduled intervals, for example every six months, usually through a review meeting. The aim of evaluation is to determine whether the plan is being implemented properly, how far needs are being met, and whether the plan is still appropriate or requires to be changed in the light of the person's changed needs or circumstances. Evaluation can also be used to improve practice in the future, help others to improve their practice, justify the use of any resources which were used, and to identify any unexpected or unplanned outcomes.

The evaluation should not be the task of one person, since it needs to be as objective as possible and to include the views of those who participated. In care practice, as with all other aspects of the helping process, evaluation should focus on the service user and be done with the service user at the centre of the process. The service user, relevant family members and friends, care staff and professionals across a multi-disciplinary spectrum are among those who can play a part in the review process. Participants should come prepared, with a review of their own work and role, in order that a comprehensive picture of all aspects of the helping process can be achieved.

SUMMARY

This chapter has introduced you to a model of care practice based on assessment, planning, implementation and evaluation. The importance of thorough, clear assessment of need has been emphasised. Need was considered from several perspectives including a return to Maslow's hierarchy and SPECCS (social, physical, emotional, cognitive, cultural and spiritual) and an examination of the PROCCCESS model. Assessment is built on a consideration of need, and plans are built on assessment. Assessment was discussed, together with two models of care planning: the exchange model and the person-centred model. Implementation was discussed in relation to a positive care environment approach. The importance of evaluation and building this into the helping process was emphasised.

Suggested reading

Davis, L. (1992) *Social Care, Rivers of Pain, Bridges of Hope.* London: Whiting and Birch.
An interesting and varied collection of Davis's writing over a number of years, about caring, feelings, management, stress and many other things; the book also provides an international perspective. There are lots of literary quotes, and it is an enjoyable as well as an enlightening read.

Ritchie, P., Sanderson, H., Kilbane, J. and Routledge M. (2003). *People, Plans and Practicalities.* Edinburgh: SHS Ltd.
Explores the practical application of person-centred planning using lots of interesting examples.

Sanderson, H., Kennedy, J., Ritchie, P. and Goodwin, G. (1997). *People, Plans and Possibilities.* Edinburgh: SHS Ltd.
An interesting and well-illustrated exploration of person-centred planning.

Ward, A. (2006) *Working in Group Care,* Birmingham: BASW/Policy Press.
This is an excellent book which looks at work in group care, the service user's stay and the worker's shift.

CHAPTER 7

Integration and Conclusions

Janet Miller and Susan Gibb

> *Education is the most powerful weapon which you can use to change the world.*
>
> Nelson Mandela (1994–)
>
> *The best way to find yourself is to lose yourself in the service of others.*
>
> Mahatma Gandhi (1869–1948)

Introduction

The chapters of the book so far have separated related subjects for individual study. The task of this chapter is to weave the subjects together to enable you to begin to see the ways in which they are connected, and to evaluate some of the material we have covered. This is achieved partly through reference to the case study, 'A tale of two families', and also through revisiting some of the subjects already discussed, relating them to one another. Some concepts, such as socialisation, needs and equality are seen as link words connecting the subjects of the book. Several activities enable you to make your own connections. At the end of the chapter some conclusions are presented, together with guidelines for future study.

Integration

In the Intermediate 2 and Higher external exams in Care, marks are now set aside for a question which enables students to integrate the knowledge they have gained from the three key topics: Values and Principles in Care, Sociology for Care and Psychology for Care. At Intermediate 2 level, 5 marks are allocated to this question and, at Higher level, 25 marks are allocated in question 4, Paper 2. The format of these integrated questions will vary, but all will involve pulling together information from more than one Unit in the answer. The Sample Question 4 for Higher Care in the Specimen Question paper on the Scottish Qualifications Authority (SQA) website is 'Care workers benefit from a knowledge of sociology and psychology when supporting service users. To what extent do you agree with this statement?'. The question is divided into four sub-sections which help the student present their argument clearly: visit the SQA website for full details of the Specimen Question Paper and Marking Instructions, and Past Papers with marking instructions.

The content of these integrated questions in the future can't be predicted, but possible connections between the topics covered in the preceding chapters are discussed below. They are presented in the style of Frequently Asked Questions (FAQs) found on websites: a quick way of getting to the essential knowledge required on a topic. These are the types of questions that care tutors have been asked by students in the past. In the answers, there is also an element of analysis and evaluation, as separate marks are given in both the internal exams (NABS) and the external exam for analysis, evaluation and application. The integration of the Units is also dealt with in the imaginary dialogue between the descendants of some famous theorists, and in the discussion of the case studies of the MacDonald and Ahmed families, which have been referred to throughout the book.

Frequently asked questions

1 *Is it important to know all the details of each psychological and sociological theory to be a good care worker?*

The emphasis on a Care course is not just about gaining a knowledge and understanding of the topics, but in developing the ability to *apply* the knowledge to care settings and to *evaluate* the relevance of the topic for particular care settings. The psychological and sociological theories that have been considered in this book have been developed over a long period of time in academic and practical contexts. They are very detailed, and people can study any one of the theories for many years before they become an expert practitioner.

Care courses at Intermediate and Higher levels only consider limited aspects of each theory, chosen because they have relevance for care settings. The aspects that were examined in Chapters 4 and 5 can be used by non-experts to aid their understanding of human behaviour, and to develop effective ways of working with service users. As care workers, you will work with a lot of professionals who are experts in particular fields and you will see how a particular approach can be used in a very focused and specific way in certain situations. Psychiatrists, counsellors, addiction workers, family therapists, social workers, community nurses and occupational therapists all have areas of expertise that may help the person you work with to make a desired change in their life. An individual care worker can't hope to meet all the needs of any particular service user, so it is essential that there is collaborative work with other people in the person's life, to enhance their ability to meet their goals.

Thus, being a good care worker is not about knowing all the details of one particular theory. It is about picking up the aspects which may be relevant for you in your particular role, and working within a team, using the range of skills and abilities of team members for the benefit of the service user. The broader the base of knowledge you acquire through courses and continuing professional development, the more resources you will have at your command in any situation. And there is an important point to be made about the difference between knowing and understanding. You may have memorised Erikson's eight stages, or Ellis's ABCDE theory, but unless you have the skills, qualities and values of a good care worker discussed in Chapter 2, it is unlikely that you will be able to use your knowledge effectively to develop a positive working relationship with a service user.

> *The only person who is educated is the one who has learned how to learn . . . and change.*

Carl Rogers (1991)

2 Isn't a little bit of knowledge a bad thing?

No, as long as you don't misuse it! Care workers encounter a number of different situations and it is useful to have as wide a range of strategies as possible to use. Care work is often about being creative in your way of working, as illustrated in the example of John and Ben discussed in Chapter 1.

Most work in a care setting is part of a planned process as discussed in Chapter 6. There should have been full discussion and collaboration among the relevant people about which particular ways of working alongside a particular service user will be the most suitable. Care workers should receive regular training and support to ensure that they are capable and competent to fulfil the requirements of their role, and they should have a number of opportunities, such as supervision and team meetings, to reflect upon their work.

> *When planning for a year, plant corn. When planning for a decade, plant trees. When planning for life, train and educate people.*

Chinese proverb: Guanzi (c. 645 BC)

3 Why is there never a definite answer to any question in a sociology or psychology assessment?

Because it is human beings we are talking about, not robots or machines! Humans are complex and there is *always* more than one way of understanding and responding to any situation. There has probably been at least one occasion in the life of every Care tutor, when they have thought, 'Why didn't I choose to study maths? In Maths, there are right and wrong answers. When a student asks a question, I could say "Yes" or "No" instead of 'Maybe . . . But have you thought about . . .?"' Then again, we would miss all the fascinating discussions that such a lack of certainty promotes in a class, and the development of self-awareness that both staff and students experience on the course.

A number of key psychological and sociological concepts were explained in Chapters 3, 4 and 5. These will have to be applied to a range of different situations and case studies in both internal and external assessments. It is the task of the student to interpret the situation presented in the exam and use the most relevant concepts in their answer. There will be a number of ways to present the answer and each student has to decide how best to analyse and evaluate the situation and apply their knowledge. The more practice a student gets at writing assessment answers, the more they will improve their ability to write good answers. Examiners are interested in the way that an individual student pulls together their knowledge and presents it in answer to the *specific question* asked.

4 Do all the psychological and sociological theories apply to everyone?

There has also been a discussion throughout the book about whether the concepts used are universal: do they apply to everyone in every situation? It was noted in Chapter 4 that some psychological concepts (such as grieving) are found across all cultures, yet others (such as independence / interdependence) are more culture specific. The notion of Nigrescence was discussed in Chapter 3, and the gender-blindness of various psychological and sociological approaches was discussed in Chapters 4 and 5. The key point to remember is that everyone is an individual, and has to be seen as such, in relation to their social context.

Ethnocentrism, a term first coined by W.G. Sumner in 1906, is used to describe prejudicial assumptions made in theorising and explaining human behaviour and aspects of society which favour one group over others. The implication is that 'our' attitudes, customs and behaviours are regarded as superior to others. The term is further used in criticising some theorists whose research rests upon 'narrow, parochial assumptions drawn from their own society' (Abercrombie et al., 1994). Although a great effort has been made in the text to avoid ethnocentricism and to give a multi-cultural view, it is nevertheless recognised that much of the book rests upon western, British and Scottish perspectives. The Scottish perspectives have, to a large extent, been intentional and the aim has been not to assume that this perspective applies elsewhere.

Activity   Level Higher   *Cultural diversity*

1   Look at the perspectives presented in Chapters 4 and 5 and discuss one of them in terms of the extent to which it can be seen as ethnocentric (seeing the world from only one point of view: that of the dominant group).

2   Look at Tanveer Ahmed in the 'Case study: A tale of two families' and consider how an understanding of his situation may be enhanced through taking account of ideas about nigrescence.

3   To what extent do you think that Erikson's lifespan perspective is ethnocentric? Give at least two reasons why you think it either can or cannot be applied equally to the MacDonalds and the Ahmeds in the case study.

Nothing is permanent but change.

Heraclitus

5 What is it more important for care workers to know about: sociology or psychology?

Look back at question 3: there is no definite answer to this question! Sociology and psychology look at human development and behaviour from different angles, and at times there is quite a lot of cross-over.

Activity *Similarities between sociology and psychology*

1 What sociological theory is most like a psychological theory?

2 What psychological theory emphasises the importance of a person's social context?

Students can quickly see the relevance of psychology to their own life, and to care work, because it is concerned with looking at an individual's needs, motivations, behaviour, thoughts and emotions. They can see when people in their class go into a Child–Parent transaction, and they can identify when their physical needs for lunch overrides any higher level to learn! Students gain insight into the behaviour of their friends and family, and, if they go on placement, they come back with lots of examples about how relevant psychology is in a care setting.

It sometimes takes students a bit longer to see the relevance of sociology in a care setting, because it looks at situations at a wider, more abstract level. However, the concepts that are covered at the beginning of Chapter 5 (such as socialisation, culture, norms, roles) help care workers to understand, on a day-to-day basis, the social context within which psychological development takes place. And sociology isn't just about abstract structures and systems. Remember that the symbolic interactionist approach is based on the premise that an individual helps to create their own reality, and this makes it as close to some psychological theories as it is to some of the macro-sociological ones. Similarly, some of the psychological theorists, such as Erikson and Bandura, acknowledge that a person's social context *has* to be considered in order to understand the way they develop and behave.

Thus, although it may appear that psychology has more immediate relevance for one-to-one work in a care setting, sociology provides many concepts which are also useful on a day-to-day basis, as well as providing an overview of human behaviour and a context to look at individual and group behaviour.

The difference between a sociological and psychological response to a problem is neatly summed up by the following quote:

> *If you don't like something, change it. If you can't change it, change your attitude.*

Maya Angelou

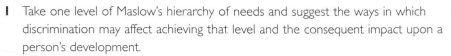

Activity — Level **Int 2** — *Integrating concepts from sociology and psychology*

1 Take one level of Maslow's hierarchy of needs and suggest the ways in which discrimination may affect achieving that level and the consequent impact upon a person's development.

2 Choose a stage of development as identified in Chapter 3. Write a paragraph about how development at any one stage may be affected by discrimination. Try to make at least three separate points.

6 What is the most important thing I should take away from this book?

Look back at question 3: it won't surprise you (again) that there is no definite answer to this question! It all depends on what you knew before you started reading this book. A lot of people sitting Intermediate and Higher courses in Care have been service users or carers in the past. Some are still involved with care services while they complete their course. They have lots of experience of the assessment process and have a clear awareness of what good practice (and poor practice) looks like. They may benefit from the underpinning theory offered by the psychology and sociology chapters (3, 4 and 5), as this might help them place their individual experience in context. Other people may find Chapters 2 and 6, on values and principles, and care planning, essential to give them an insight into how the caring process works.

The main message we have tried to repeat throughout the book, which we think is fundamental to everyone working in care, is always to remember that the service user is at the centre of the process. The therapeutic relationship between care worker and service user is one of the most important transformational tools: it doesn't matter so much *what* you do with someone; the important factor is *how* you do it. This can't be emphasised strongly enough. Chapter 2 looks in detail at the qualities, skills and values that a care worker is likely to have, and the care planning process is considered in Chapter 6. All the other information is provided to help you work with the service user in the most effective way possible.

7 Why do I need to know about legislation? Is that not the employer's responsibility?

One of the things that is emphasised throughout the book, and particularly in Chapter 1, is that *everybody* in a care organisation has responsibilities under law. Managers, staff *and* service users have to abide by legislation which deals with issues such as health and safety and discrimination.

In the past there have been instances of abuse, neglect and poor practice in care settings, and legislation attempts to minimise the possibility of this happening again. However, the example of the problems surrounding the Adult Support and Protection (Scotland) Bill in Chapter 2 demonstrate that it is not always easy to create a piece of legislation that meets the needs of every stakeholder.

Every care organisation has to develop policies and working practices which implement the law, but every individual within the organisation also has particular responsibilities. It can be illegal to be a bystander to an offence (such as abuse, breach of health and safety regulations or smoking in a public place) and do nothing about it: the witness is culpable alongside the perpetrator, if they don't report it.

Legislation changes all the time and, as it is often different in Scotland from the rest of the UK, it is important that care workers know that they are informed of the accurate and most up-to-date information. For instance, Neil MacLeod of the Voluntary Sector Social Services Workforce Unit notes that devolution has ensured that different approaches are taken to the registration of care workers throughout the UK. Scotland has opted to use the term 'social services' instead of 'social care' and so the regulatory body is called the Scottish Social Services Council.

> *The SSSC's registration timetable for social service workers commenced in April 2003 with the registration of social workers – staff within residential child care services and managers of care homes for adults were subsequently asked to register as part of this first phase . . . The register of workers in adult residential care is due to open in 2007 and for housing support workers in 2009. Post Registration Training and Learning Requirements have also been set for staff.*

(Macleod, 2007, p. 13)

8 The National Care Standards are mentioned in almost every chapter. Why is this?

Because they are central to good care work in Scotland. The National Care Standards and the principles contained in them (dignity, privacy, choice, safety, realising potential, and equality and dignity) underpin all work of social service providers in Scotland, whether domiciliary, day care or residential. All care organisations are inspected against these standards, and so it is important that students become very familiar with them.

The reason care workers need to know about psychology and sociology is to enhance their ability to meet the needs of their service users. In order to demonstrate the principle in the National Care Standard of 'equality and diversity', for instance, it is important to know about prejudice and stereotypes, and types of discrimination, as well as how to promote anti-discriminatory practice, as discussed in Chapter 2.

9 Chapters 1 and 5 seemed to be quite political at times. Do I need to be political to be a good care worker?

You do not need to be political in the specific sense of being involved in a political party, but you do in the general sense of 'being aware of power structures in society'. Care workers are motivated by a desire to help the people they work with to achieve as much as they can in their life. In so doing, they often come up against obstacles because of the way society is organised. A care worker may realise that, no matter how positive and fulfilling their relationship with a service user is, some changes will not occur unless action is taken at an organisational or structural level. Many service users, carers and workers have taken a stand against particular examples of injustice and inequality, and many changes have been made as a result of this, as noted in the example about the creation of the Disability Discrimination Act in Chapter 5. However, as can be seen from the evidence in Chapters 1 and 5, there are still many examples of discrimination and inequality in Scotland, and it is important for workers to be aware of the various ways in which they can tackle this, at different levels, and in different ways.

Activity — Level **Int 2** — *Discrimination and Maslow's hierarchy of needs*

Choose one form of discrimination, for example: ageism, racism, sexism, disablism. What effects on belongingness and esteem do you think this discrimination might have?

You may have suggested:

- feeling excluded from groups in education, work or leisure
- feeling uncomfortable in many social situations because of discriminatory attitudes
- standing less chance of belonging to a chosen work group or profession
- self-exclusion from situations in order to avoid the above feelings or because you feel that your safety or sense of security may be threatened.

The process described above need not be inevitable. A more positive outcome may be achieved for emotional development for those who are able to counter the negative impact of discrimination. This is discussed fully in Chapter 2.

Never doubt that a small group of thoughtful committed citizens can change the world. Indeed it's the only thing that ever has.

Margaret Mead

10 There's so much information in the book: how can I remember everything?

Chapters in the book introduce material at three different levels: Intermediate 1, Intermediate 2 and Higher. It is likely that there will be information in each chapter which is not relevant for your course of study. Always check your class notes to ensure that you are studying the correct theorist for your course. The way the information is presented in the chapters enables you to see the links between your level and the next, and hopefully this is helpful rather than confusing. However, if you are short of time, stick to the topics that are directly relevant for your course of study.

The basic information is the same for all three levels (in sociology, socialisation is mentioned at all three levels, but the depth of knowledge you require increases as you study at a Higher level). There are a number of techniques a student can use to retain information, such as using a study map, which is a pictorial representation of the key ideas. See Figure 7.1 for an example of a study map related to Higher Psychology. It uses colour to link groups of ideas, and lines to separate each extra level of detail.

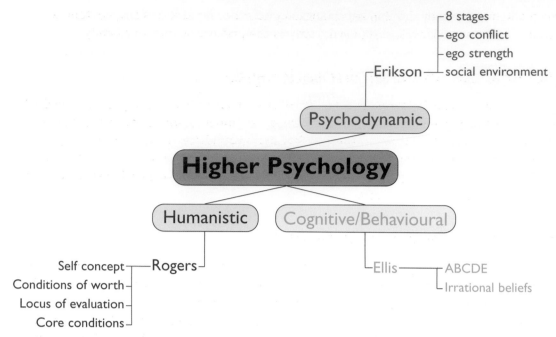

Figure 7.1 Psychology Higher study map

An imaginary dialogue

Socialisation is taken as an example to illustrate the relationships among the various topics that have been discussed in the book. One way to show these relationships is through the invention of a dialogue. Imagine a scenario where several Scottish descendants of some rather famous theorists come together to discuss socialisation.

McMaslow (humanistic psychologist)

If you look at my uncle's hierarchy of needs you'll appreciate that although it doesn't specifically mention socialisation, it plays a big part in reaching self-actualisation. An individual who has not acquired any ideas about how to behave in society, through the socialisation process, will have little sense of belonging to anything and won't know how to behave properly in situations. Their behaviour will end up being seen as strange and they might attract the wrong type of attention and probably won't feel safe. You can't progress up the hierarchy of need towards self-actualisation if you don't feel safe. An individual who hasn't been socialised into some form of family life probably won't be able to form meaningful relationships, to benefit from the school system or reach anything like his or her potential. Socialisation underpins the ability to move up the hierarchy of needs.

McFreud (psychodynamic psychologist)

I think socialisation is important too, though I'd stress that much of it takes place at an unconscious rather than a conscious level. What happens in families in the very early years of a child's life, including the ways in which children are socialised into male and female roles, how they are toilet-trained and how they are loved, is of vital importance to the ways in which they develop psychologically later on. We are, to a large extent, a product of our past socialisation, particularly of the primary agents: our family.

McDurkheim (functionalist sociologist)

Forget the individual for a moment. I want to direct your attention away from individuals to look at society itself. Socialisation performs a vital function for society by ensuring that people absorb the culture of their society and learn about social roles. Society couldn't do without it, culture wouldn't be perpetuated without it, and our institutions would fall to pieces if people didn't acquire an internalised idea of social norms, and the roles which they need to perform.

McErikson (lifespan psychologist)

That's all very well, but you sociologists generalise too much for my liking. If you take a lifespan perspective you can see exactly how socialisation applies to specific individuals. All individuals face conflicts at each stage of development and it is how they deal with these conflicts which determines whether they emerge positively or negatively into the next stage. Socialisation certainly does play a part here in resolving the conflicts which apply to each stage, especially during childhood. I have always given importance to the social context of people's lives, their families, work and relationships. Good socialisation helps children to build up trust by promoting consistent values, it helps to build autonomy and identity through encouragement in taking social roles and it can help to build initiative through encouraging responsibility. It has a most important role to play in the development of the adult towards an eventual resolution of the conflict of integrity versus despair.

McMarx (conflict sociologist)

The conflict of integrity versus despair – that's a good one! What about the conflict between the haves and the have nots; that's the one that seems most important to me. A lot of socialisation is a con as it stands in the present capitalist society. People are socialised to accept a capitalist system in which power rests with the people who control the means of production, and everyone else is socialised into the subordinate and accepting role of being a good industrious worker. A Scottish parliament may be a start . . . but don't forget the revolution.

McEllis (cognitive/behavioural psychologist)

You sociologists put too much emphasis on the power of society. People are not puppets; they can think and act and feel and make decisions for themselves. They don't need to change the world: they only need to change their perception of it. That alone will mean that there will be a change in the person's life. And if they change, then there will be a change in their relationships, and this will have a knock-on effect in the places where they interact with people, such as work and their wider social circle. They will be meeting their own goals to be happy, but it will also help other people take responsibility for meeting their needs as well.

McMead (symbolic interactionist sociologist)

For goodness sake – I don't agree with a single one of you. You're all barking up the wrong tree as far as I'm concerned. My symbolic interactionist theory, which I have developed from the small beginnings made by a venerable ancestor from Chicago, nicely combines the best of sociology with the best of developmental psychology, acknowledges the importance of socialisation in the emergence of the self with, on the one side, 'me', an organised socialised being, and on the other side, 'I', choosing what I'd like to do in relation to 'me'. I'm sure you understand what I'm getting at.

McWollstonecraft (feminist theorist)

I understand that you've left the woman until last, as usual, but at least I have the final word on this subject. Socialisation is all very well. We certainly do need some means whereby we can acquire the best of the culture of our society. But socialisation as it stands gives women a pretty raw deal. Look at my research into socialisation. It shows that most girls in our society play with dolls and learn to be a good mother, play house and learn to do the housework and choose subjects at school they will be able to use in a career which will fit around children and a male partner. Well, like my ancestors before me, I've campaigned for years for women to have equal opportunities in all walks of life, that was my successful slogan when I stood for election to the Scottish Parliament, and that's what socialisation should be doing too.

Annie

Annie is 86 years old and lives in a local authority residential home. One of her care workers lacks an understanding of human development, hasn't reflected on her value base or had any training on equality and diversity. How might this person respond to Annie? Do these short-comings have an impact on her interpersonal skills?

She might fail to understand or empathise with the fact that some older people may be slower to respond to requests, and may have experienced a number of losses throughout their life, resulting perhaps in depression. She might also fail to understand that older people who receive stimulation, interest and respect can lead happier lives. The care worker might have incorrectly concluded that because a person is old and physically frail it isn't worth trying to encourage, stimulate and respond with empathy. She might also have failed to understand that development is possible at any stage of life and that people who are encouraged and stimulated retain their physical and mental abilities much longer than people who are subjected to 'institutional' regimes. The lack of understanding by the care worker is in itself a form of prejudice because it is based on a stereotypical view of 'old age' instead of a realistic understanding of the potential of this stage of development. Lack of a value base or any understanding of equal opportunities might lead the care worker to be extremely insensitive to Annie's needs and to have very poor interpersonal skills.

One day Annie wandered into the staff room at the home. Another care worker was in there alone taking a tea break. 'What do you think you're doing in here? Go straight back to the lounge.' shouted the care worker. An understanding of human development and behaviour would have allowed for Annie's disorientation, while recognising that Annie is an older adult, able to respond and to be addressed as an adult, not as a child. An understanding of equal opportunities and a value base would have enabled the care worker to appreciate that Annie should be given the same opportunities as anyone else to receive respect and to be valued as a human being. An understanding of the effects of institutionalisation would have encouraged the care worker to enhance rather than diminish Annie's self-esteem, and all of these things would have enhanced the care worker's own interpersonal skills.

In this one case study you can draw upon information from every chapter of the book: institutionalisation in Chapter 1, equal opportunities, the value base and interpersonal skills in Chapter 2, human development and behaviour (Chapters 3, 4 and 5) and needs and opportunities (Chapters 3 and 6).

Case study – a tale of two families

The MacDonald and Ahmed families in 2007

For people who read the first edition of this book, here are the MacDonalds and the Ahmeds again, but they are now eight years older. So that you can see what has changed in those eight years, the original accounts are included as Appendix 1.

Senga MacDonald and her children live in the same five-apartment semi-detached house in Edinburgh in which they lived in 1999. The house is no longer rented, however, since Senga took the opportunity to purchase the property from the Council. She now pays quite a hefty mortgage but feels that it's worth making some long-awaited changes. The area has maintained its air of reasonable respectability in spite of one rather noisy pub which attracts a mixture of young loud and older loud people, and a fair number of young people who hang around in the evening. The adjoining tenement area has acquired an even more diverse population with an influx of workers from Eastern Europe. The Ahmed family have stayed in their large, comfortable, owner-occupied second-floor tenement. Joe MacDonald, Senga's former husband, no longer lives with this girlfriend of eight years ago, but has remained living in the same area as the Ahmeds in a rented flat with his new girlfriend and their 2-year-old son, Callum. Schools, shops and local services are shared by people in both areas.

The MacDonald family in 2007

Senga MacDonald, aged 44, works full-time as the depute manager of Queen's View, a privately run home for older adults. She works hard and in the past five years has acquired the first qualifications of her life, gaining her SVQ3 in Care and a Management certificate. She has tried to set a good example to her children, both throughout her studies and through giving up smoking last year. She hasn't yet lost the weight she hoped to lose. She would never consider leaving Edinburgh where she was born and brought up, and has a good circle of friends in the neighbourhood and through her interests in dressmaking and dancing. Since her divorce five years ago she has remained single. This isn't altogether to her liking since she does not feel emotionally fulfilled, but she prefers this to living in a difficult relationship.

Joe MacDonald. It is now 10 years since Joe, now 50, and Senga separated. Joe lives in rented accommodation with his 32-year-old girlfriend Vicky and their 2-year-old son Callum. Joe has tried several times to turn over a new leaf but his lifelong addiction to drink and cigarettes, combined with what he calls his frequent 'knock-backs' in the world of employment, have meant that his good intentions haven't amounted to much. As in 1999, he occasionally has work as a driver for various home-delivery Chinese and Indian restaurants.

Callum MacDonald, aged 2, was born one month prematurely and got off to a rather slow start. He has made up for lost time since then and now walks and runs competently and has a vocabulary of about 100 words or so, making himself understood and learning to imitate animal sounds; moo, neigh, meow. He attends 'The Five Trees', a local authority nursery, five mornings a week and enjoys the company of other children.

Andy MacDonald, 24, was a rebellious teenager. He left school after gaining, to his surprise, two more Standard Grades to add to the four he had already, in addition to modules in art and music. His ambition to be rich and famous hasn't materialised yet but he is working on his guitar playing with a group at the Further Education college he now attends. He's taking courses in painting and decorating with a view to going into business with one of his old school friends. He continues to smoke about 10 cigarettes a day. After leaving school he took several jobs mostly in the building and painting and decorating trades before deciding to go to college at the age of 23 to qualify in his chosen profession. He has a girlfriend, Emma, but has no thoughts of settling down just yet. He continues to live at home with his mum.

Linda MacDonald's development has been greatly affected by cerebral palsy but she has an independent spirit and with her family's support has moved to supported accommodation at Newton Road run by a voluntary organisation. She is now 21 and attends courses in basic skills (numeracy, literacy, crafts and household skills) at the local college and has surprised everyone with how well she is managing her tenancy. She is supported by care workers on a shift basis and her social worker has worked with her to develop a person-centred plan, taking account of her needs, wishes and dreams. Her family are in close touch with her and exchange visits frequently.

Joey MacDonald is now a very lively 13 year old, interested in everything and doing well at school, especially in sport. He has been encouraged in this by his male befriender Fred who has been a stabilising influence since he was 5 years old and has become a good friend of the family. Fred is employed by 'Buddies', the local authority befriending scheme.

Senga's mother Jean is now 72 and going strong. She has a very active retirement, seeing friends, volunteering at the local hospital tea shop and attending the Doward, a centre for older people, twice a week. There is a very full programme of activities ranging from an exercise class to craft afternoons. She says it is definitely not a care centre, but it provides useful support for older people and plays a big part in health promotion. Jean's mother Annie died three years ago just after her 90th birthday. She had spent many years in a local authority residential home, which unfortunately closed when Annie was 89. She was transferred to a privately run home and never really settled there, becoming ill shortly after her move.

Senga's sister, Maureen McKay, has had several admissions to the McTavish Unit, a small supportive unit of the local psychiatric hospital. She has experienced several bouts of depression and has times when she just can't cope with life any more. Her family and GP now recognise her symptoms and she is supported for short stays in hospital, and attendance at the McTavish Day Unit when she is living at home. After a rocky start her son Alistair McKay, now 22, is not finding life as an adult as difficult as he found life as a child in care. He has recently gained employment and started a Modern Apprenticeship in the building trade. He likes to go drinking with his pals on a Friday night but is adamant about not taking drugs. He often stays with his Aunt Senga and cousins.

The Ahmed family in 2007

Hassan Ahmed would have been 53 this year but sadly died of a heart attack two years ago. The accountancy firm which he set up with a fellow student continues to flourish. His nephew Faisal qualified as an accountant last year and is now working in the business.

Aisha Bibi, Hassan's wife, is now 43. The death of her husband was a severe blow to her and initially she needed some help to recover from a prolonged grieving process. She attended counselling at the Westgate Clinic and was helped her to recover from a very difficult time. When she later announced that she had taken a full-time post with Barnardo's, a voluntary sector child care organisation, and intended to take a post-graduate social work degree with the Open University, her family were supportive of her decision.

Tanveer Ahmed, 23, achieved his ambition to take an engineering degree in spite of his visits to McDonalds instead of the library. He left home for Glasgow University at the age of 18 and hopes eventually to go to the USA to work. His mother is very upset about this but at the same time encourages his independence of thought and action.

Nabeil Ahmed, aged 19, has already had 12 operations in his short life. His heart condition, which resulted in a stroke and severe disability, continues to cause concern. His family has always included him in family life. Like many people of 19, he wants his independence. He is supported at 8 Newton Road, a house with four other people with disabilities, next door to and run by the same voluntary organisation that accommodates Linda MacDonald. He attends the local FE college where he is taking courses in art. He would like to go to art school and is working on preparing a portfolio of large collages, which are his speciality.

Hassan's older brother Afzal and his wife Sira Ahmed and their children **Faisal, 23, Asif, 20, and Nadia, 18**, continue to live in their owner-occupied tenement flat in the same area as Aisha, their sister-in-law. They still run their successful general store in which many family members help out. Afzal's mother, Fariha, now 80, continues to be a domineering presence and misses her visits from her nephew Tanveer, who is now only home occasionally. She has mild dementia and severe arthritis which limits her mobility. Twice a year she goes, reluctantly, for a period of respite at Queen's View. She also attends Queen's View day centre two days a week.

In the above study there are several members who require care both on an informal basis by family members and a formal basis in care or support situations. These family members are **Linda MacDonald**, 21, who has cerebral palsy and lives at 6 Newton Road, next door to **Nabeil Ahmed**. **Senga**'s sister **Maureen** has admissions to the **McTavish Unit** and also attends the Day Unit there, **Afzal's mother Fariha** goes to Queen's View for respite care twice a year, Senga's mother **Jean** attends the **Doward**, **Callum MacDonald** attends the **Five Trees Nursery**. **Joey MacDonald** has **Fred**, a befriender from **'Buddies'**, the local authority befriending service.

Two family members work in Social Work Services. Senga MacDonald is the depute manager of Queen's View home for older adults. Aisha Bibi is working for Barnardo's, a large voluntary sector child care organisation, and is training to be a social worker.

Each of the social services which the families use or work in in 2007 is described below.

Queen's View home and day care centre for older adults is a privately run home with 40 residential beds, 10 respite beds and a day centre for 20 people, open five days a week. All residents have a single room with bathroom. A new nursing care wing was added to the home three years ago expanding the total number of beds from 30 to 50 and adding the beautiful new day unit. Meals both in the residential and day units are eaten communally at set times. In the past five years a lot of resources have been put into enabling staff to gain qualifications. Currently 30% of staff members hold a relevant qualification, such as a Nursing diploma or Health and Social Care SVQ; a further 20% of staff are working towards qualifications. All staff take an induction course when they are first employed which introduces them to organisation and to the values and principles of care practice. Following recommendations from the Care Commission, a programme of activities and outings has been established which enhances the quality of life for both residents and day care attendees. There is a cheerful atmosphere in the home and people seem to enjoy living there.

The Five Trees Nursery is a local authority nursery and provides places for children aged 0–5. It opens at 8 a.m. and closes at 6 p.m., enabling parents to bring their children early if they have jobs to go to. Hours are allocated on the basis of child and family need. Nursery staff work closely with parents and other service providers to ensure that nursery provision optimises the child's development in all areas: social, physical, emotional, cognitive, cultural and spiritual. The nursery itself is bright and modern with plenty of space and equipment to enable children to learn and play. Staff are well-trained, with all staff possessing relevant qualifications or working towards them.

6 and 8 Newton Road are two large adjoining houses in a residential area of Edinburgh. They were purchased several years ago by a large voluntary organisation to accommodate eight people with disability in their own tenancies. Each resident has a small flat and each house has a communal lounge and communal cooking and eating facilities. Care staff work on a rota basis to support the tenants according to their individual needs. A lot of emphasis is placed on enabling tenants to have a fulfilling life and to gain the skills for leading as independent a life as possible. All staff either have or are working towards the qualifications relevant for their job.

Buddies is the local authority befriending service for young people. It was set up as a preventative service to help young people where issues could lead potentially to problems in the future. For example, Joey's lack of a father figure combined with his hyper-activity led to a referral and the allocation of Fred to his family. This has enabled Joey to have a male role model and to pursue his interest in football. It has also provided the family with reliable and consistent support over a period of years.

The Doward is a community centre established 25 years ago by a local businessman to meet the needs of anyone over the age of 55 living in the local area. It is a place with a real buzz about it run by a committee mainly made up of people who use the service themselves. It has registered charity status and is a non-profit-making voluntary organisation run for the local community by the local community. There is a full programme of activities available five days a week, ranging from exercise classes, arts and crafts to formal learning for certificates in computing and other subjects. The centre is staffed by a mixture of volunteers and employees, all of whom have a culture of learning to be the best that they can be. The manager of the centre promotes her belief in everyone's abilities and that the centre should not only be fun but should make a contribution to the life of the whole local community.

The McTavish Unit is run as a partnership between the local authority social work department and the health board to meet the needs of people who experience mental health difficulties. There is a day centre and 15 individual rooms with bathrooms for short-stay residents. The aim is to enable people to continue to live their lives in the community while providing on-going support and a haven during periods of crisis. Staff come from a variety of backgrounds with varied skills, ranging from social work and social care to nursing and health care. The centre aims to promote a social model of care with emphasis on the dignity of the individual and meeting needs through focus on the environment. There is a wish to create a safe place for individuals to flourish and deal with the issues that create stress for them.

Barnardo's is a large, national voluntary organisation which provides a variety of services in many locations to children and young people in need of support. Aisha Bibi is working in a support service for children who have been accommodated by the local authority but who are moving on from a care situation, either back to their families, to live with other families or to live in other settings in the community. Often they are also at the stage of leaving school and making decisions about their future. This is demanding work with young people who have often experienced difficult lives and may have complex issues to deal with. Barnardo's is supporting staff to gain the qualifications relevant to the work. Aisha Bibi is receiving support to undertake the Open University post-graduate social work qualification.

The Open University

The Open University is a university which operates through distance learning, with a style of teaching called 'supported open learning'. Aisha Bibi is working towards her social work qualification with the Open University. This route is only open to people who are working in social service agencies and are supported by their employer.

Westgate Clinic

Westgate Clinic specialises in providing counselling support to people who have experienced difficulties in their lives. A person-centred approach is used, based on Egan's three stage model. People are initially encouraged to explore their current situation and difficulties as a way of moving towards new understanding. With new understanding they are supported to identify and take action that will move them towards more satisfying and fulfilling lives.

The MacDonald and Ahmed families have been referred to many times throughout this book. It is useful to look at them in terms of what they can illustrate about the content of the book and to undertake the activities that relate to them in the text.

Conclusion

> *And some kind of help*
> *Is the kind of help*
> *That helping's all about.*
> *And some kind of help*
> *Is the kind of help*
> *We all can do without.*
>
> (Shel Silverstein, 1974)

By now it should be possible to distinguish between good, empowering help and poor, patronising 'help'. The above discussion has also attempted to enable you to discover links among the many threads of this book and the several subjects which you have studied. There has been an emphasis on a holistic approach, seeing both people and societies as wholes made up of interacting parts. Your development as a care worker can be carried further through gaining experience of care practice and through further training. Courses such as the HNC in Social Care or Health Care, the Diploma in Social Work and SVQs are all ways of enhancing your development. The foundations have been laid. It is now up to you to apply your knowledge, skills, understanding and value base to improve the quality of life of those with whom you do or will work.

Suggested reading

At the end of a course you usually feel like a holiday. The suggested reading below should enable you to take your thinking further, while at the same time providing something enjoyable and reasonably undemanding to do on the beach!

Axline, V. M. (1990) *Dibs in Search of Self.* Penguin

Haddon, M. (2004) *The Curious Incident of the Dog in the Night.* Vintage

Walker. A. (1990) *The Colour Purple.* The Women's Press

You might also like to try works by Scottish authors such as Iain Banks, Lewis Grassic Gibbon, Alasdair Gray, Liz Lochead, George Mackay Brown, Ali Smith and Irvine Welsh.

Appendix 1

The MacDonald and Ahmed Families in 1999

The following account of the MacDonald and Ahmed families appeared in the first edition of this book. It is reproduced here for comparative purposes.

The MacDonald family in 1999

Senga MacDonald and her children live in a rented five-apartment council house a few miles from the centre of Edinburgh. The area in which they live is one of a large 1950s housing scheme which has gained an air of reasonable respectability, with a mixture of houses and flats rented from the local authority and properties which have been purchased and are now owner-occupied. The scheme borders on tenement land which stands between it and the city centre. The tenements are a mixture of properties which are privately owned, rented from the council or privately rented, and the population is culturally diverse, with a mixture of religious and ethnic groups. It is here that the Ahmed family lives in a large, owner-occupied second floor tenement. Joe MacDonald, Senga's former husband, also lives in this area. The children of the MacDonald family and the Ahmed family attend the same schools, shop at the same shops and their teenage children sometimes hang about on the same streets.

Senga MacDonald, aged 36, works part-time as a care assistant in a home for older adults. She has to work very hard and regrets that she didn't stay on at school or gain any qualifications. She tries to encourage her children with their school work. She has recently been trying to cut down on her smoking (about 10 cigarettes a day at the moment) and to lose weight. She was born and brought up in Edinburgh in the area in which her ex-husband now lives.

Joe MacDonald, aged 42, left the family home two years ago and lives in a tenement with his girlfriend, aged 29. He is unemployed but has occasional work as a driver for various home-delivery Chinese and Indian restaurants. He says that he can't see the point of getting qualifications. He enjoys a drink and smokes about 20 cigarettes a day. Joe seems to have lost interest in his children since he and his girlfriend got a flat together, though his son, Andy, goes to visit him sometimes, especially if he needs money.

Andy MacDonald, aged 16, lives at home with his Mum, sister and brother. He is still at school taking some modules after gaining four Standard Grades at general level last year. He would rather have left school but couldn't see much chance of getting a job. He plans to go to the local FE College next year. He'd like to be rich and famous but is having such a struggle with his modules that he thinks there must be an easier way. Although he's very fond of his mum and definitely doesn't want to end up like his dad, he also wants to establish his independence from both of them. His friends at school encourage him to go drinking and clubbing at weekends and sometimes evenings in between. His mum despairs about this but Andy doesn't seem to take any notice of anything she says. He smokes about 10 cigarettes a day depending on how much money he has.

Linda MacDonald, 13, has cerebral palsy. She has difficulty with speech, has a mild learning disability and is unable to walk. She attends a special school and goes there on the school bus each morning. She is still very dependent on her mum, who has to attend to all of her needs when she is at home. Linda and her family have a social worker who attends her reviews, supports the family when necessary and has arranged respite care for Linda on a rolling basis every six weeks. This provides her mum with a much-needed break.

Joey MacDonald is 5, a little clown with a great sense of humour and huge quantities of energy. He loves his toy building games and a toy garage. He is in P1 and loves it. He never seems to stop, and Senga finds him quite exhausting, especially if she has had a hard day at work. He has just been allocated a male befriender by the Social Work Department and Senga hopes that this will provide him with a stabilising influence and will give her a break sometimes.

Senga's mother, Jean, aged 64, lives locally and offers support on an occasional basis, but she works in a shop and doesn't have a lot of spare time or energy. Her second husband (not Senga's father) died two years ago and her 86-year-old mother, Annie, is in a local authority residential home not far away. Jean visits Annie a couple of times a week after work and at least once at the weekend. Annie has severe arthritis, which limits her mobility, and mild dementia.

Senga's sister, Maureen McKay, lives on a housing scheme a few miles from the city centre. She has three children and has had a very chequered life with a partner involved in both drink and drugs. Maureen has spent periods in a homeless unit and has now left her partner for good. Her oldest child, Alistair, is looked after by the local authority in a children's unit after committing a series of offences.

The Ahmed family in 1999

Hassan Ahmed, aged 45, is an accountant who qualified when he was in his early 30s. He set up his own practice in partnership with a fellow student. He works very long hours, spends less and less time with his family but is improving the business – he and his partner have almost doubled the number of clients in the past five years. He has some worrying health complaints and thinks he may have an ulcer, but hasn't got time to go to the doctor. He has gained quite a lot of weight recently. He is very determined that his children get a good start in life and stresses the importance of a sound education.

Aisha Bibi, Hassan's wife, is ten years younger than her husband, a very cheerful person most of the time, but recently she has become very concerned about her husband's health. She works part-time for a voluntary organisation, supervising a sheltered housing complex, and loves her work. She tries to encourage other Asian women to assert their independence but is viewed with some suspicion by many of their husbands and families. She also encourages her children to do well at school and helps them with their homework. Her own family viewed education as the key to success and Aisha attended Edinburgh University where she gained a degree in languages (French and Spanish).

Tanveer Ahmed, aged 15, attends the local secondary school. He is doing well there and is expected to achieve several credits in his Standard Grades and to continue at school to achieve Advanced Highers. He wants to be an engineer but for the time being works one or two evenings a week in his uncle's shop. He also is expected to help with his younger brother at the weekend. Tanveer has a great wish to be accepted by the boys in his class at school, who often tease him about his colour and his younger brother who has a disability. Whenever he gets the chance he lingers after school with a group of boys and goes to 'McDonald's' with them for a laugh, a coffee and a cigarette. He tells his mum he goes to the library.

Nabeil Ahmed, aged 11, was born with a severe heart condition which has necessitated several operations. After one major operation he had a stroke which affects his left side. He has delayed development, has great difficulty with speech and is unable to walk. His doctors think that he may eventually catch up intellectually and may gain some power of speech, though it is unlikely that he will ever walk. He faces the prospect of more heart operations in the future. He attends the same school as Linda MacDonald, though is in a different class. He is well-loved and supported by his family, though they took a long time to accept his illness and disability. His mother is especially concerned that he has all the opportunities possible to develop in the same ways as other children. Although the family has been reluctant to request outside help they have approached the Social Work Department to assist with day care for Nabeil during the summer so that Aisha can continue to work.

Hassan's older brother, Afzal, his sister-in-law Sira and their three children, Faisal, Asif and Nadia, live in another apartment in the same area. Hassan and Afzal originally set up in business together to run a shop but Afzal now owns the shop, whilst Hassan runs his accountancy business. The brothers do help one another out and attend the mosque together. Their mother, who speaks very little English, lives with Afzal and his wife. She is very helpful with housework and cooking but is a very domineering woman with rather traditional views. Sira resents her constant presence and her attempts to influence her children's behaviour. Tanveer gets on well with his grandmother whom he visits most days. She is always giving him little treats and telling him how she expects great things of him. Although this sometimes makes him uncomfortable, they have a good rapport which is without the stresses which his parents and aunt and uncle experience in her presence.

In the above study there are several members who require care both on an informal basis by family members and on a formal basis in care situations. These family members are: Linda MacDonald who goes for respite care at Ivy Unit; Alistair McKay who is looked after by the local authority children's unit at 16 Fir Street; Nabeil Ahmed who will attend Heron Day Centre during the summer; Hassan and Afzal's elderly mother who is due to go for a week of respite care at a home for older people, Queen's View.

Two family members work as care workers. Senga MacDonald works as a care assistant in a home for older adults. Aishi Bibi works for a voluntary organisation, supervising a sheltered housing complex.

Each of the units which the families use or will use is described below.

Ivy Unit is a twelve-bed, purpose-built voluntary organisation respite care unit for children with disabilities. Each of the 50 children who attends comes for respite every six weeks (three nights Friday to Monday alternating with four nights Monday to Friday) and also for a one-week summer holiday. There is a good staff ratio and a committed and trained staff team. Staff work well together, have regular meetings to discuss their work and aim to meet the needs of the children who attend through a combination of care and activities.

16 Fir Street is a small children's unit at present accommodating seven children in the age range twelve to sixteen who are looked after by the local authority. Most of the children attend local schools, though two of the children, including Alistair McKay, attend a care and education centre as day pupils. Here they are taught in small classes and their usual disruptive behaviour can be 'managed' by a trained and dedicated care and teaching team. There is a high rate of sickness among staff at Fir Street, so this means that there either aren't enough staff on duty or unfamiliar sessional staff cover for absence. Although the staff want to do a good job, only four out of eight have any kind of qualification at present. The local authority is hoping that all of the others will receive some training in the next couple of years.

Heron Day Centre is run by a voluntary organisation and accommodates ten children with moderate to severe disabilities during the summer months. A mixture of trained staff and untrained temporary staff are employed to work with the children, whose ages range from three to twelve. They assess the needs of each individual child through meetings with them, their families and other workers and devise a programme to meet these needs.

Queen's View home for older adults is a private home with 25 residential beds and five respite beds. Everyone has a single room with bathroom. Meals are eaten communally at set times. Very few of the staff have a formal qualification in care but the unit manager ensures that all staff have an induction training in the values and principles of care practice. There is a cheerful atmosphere in the home and people seem to enjoy living there. Some of the more active residents, however, regret the fact that there are not more opportunities for outings and activities.

Appendix 2

Codes of Practice for Social Service Workers and Employers (reproduced with permission of the Scottish Social Services Council)

Employers of Social Service Workers

Introduction

This document contains agreed codes of practice for social service workers and employers of social service workers describing the standards of conduct and practice within which they should work. This introduction, which is also reproduced in the Code of Practice for Social Service Workers, is intended to help you understand what the codes are for and what they will mean to you as a social service worker, employer, service user or member of the public.

The Scottish Social Services Council began its work on 1 October 2001, at the same time as the General Social Care Council, the Northern Ireland Social Care Council, and the Care Council for Wales. The Councils have a duty to develop codes of practice and have worked together in developing these codes as part of their contribution to raising standards in social services.

The two codes for workers and employers are presented together in this document because they are complementary and mirror the joint responsibilities of employers and workers in ensuring high standards.

What are the codes?

The Code of Practice for Employers of Social Service Workers sets down the responsibilities of employers in the regulation of social service workers. Again, this is the first time that such standards have been set out at national level.

The code requires that employers adhere to the standards set out in their code, support social service workers in meeting their code and take appropriate action when workers do not meet expected standards of conduct.

The Code of Practice for Social Service Workers is a list of statements that describe the standards of professional conduct and practice required of social service workers as they go about their daily work. This is the first time that standards have been set in this way at national level, although many employers have similar standards in place at local level. The intention is to confirm the standards required in social services and ensure that workers know what standards of conduct employers, colleagues, service users, carers and the public expect of them.

The codes are intended to reflect existing good practice and it is anticipated that workers and employers will recognise in the codes the shared standards to which they already aspire. The Councils will promote these standards through making the codes widely available.

How will the codes be used?

The codes are a key step in the introduction of a system of regulation for social services in the four countries of the UK. The Councils are responsible for the registration of those working in social services The register will be a public record that those registered have met the requirements for entry onto the register and have agreed to abide by the standards set out in the Code of Practice for Social Service Workers.

The Councils will take account of the standards set in the Code of Practice for Social Service Workers in considering issues of misconduct and decisions as to whether a registered worker should remain on the register.

What will the codes mean to you?

As a social service worker you will have criteria to guide your practice and be clear about what standards of conduct you are expected to meet. You are encouraged to use the codes to examine your own practice and to look for areas in which you can improve.

As a social service employer you will know what part you are expected to play in the regulation of the workforce and the support of high quality social services. You are encouraged to review your own standards of practice and policies in the light of the standards set in the code.

As a user of services or member of the public the codes will help you understand how a social service worker should behave towards you and how employers should support social service workers to do their jobs well.

Code of Practice for Employers of Social Service Workers

The purpose of this code is to set down the responsibilities of employers in regulating social service workers. The purpose of workforce regulation is to protect and promote the interests of service users and carers. The code is intended to complement rather than replace or duplicate existing employers policies and it forms part of the wider package of legislation, requirements and guidance that relate to the employment of staff. Employers are responsible for making sure that they meet the standards set out in this code, provide high quality services and promote public trust and confidence in social services.

Status

Relevant regulatory bodies in Scotland will take this code into account in their regulation of social services.

To meet their responsibilities in relation to regulating the social service workforce, social service employers must:

- Make sure people are suitable to enter the workforce and understand their roles and responsibilities;
- Have written policies and procedures in place to enable social service workers to meet the Scottish Social Service Council (SSSC) Code of Practice for Social Service Workers;
- Provide training and development opportunities to enable social service workers to strengthen and develop their skills and knowledge;

- Put in place and implement written policies and procedures to deal with dangerous, discriminatory or exploitative behaviour and practice; and

- Promote the SSSC's codes of practice to social service workers, service users and carers and co-operate with the SSSC's proceedings.

1 *As a social service employer, you must make sure people are suitable to enter the social service workforce and understand their roles and responsibilities.*

This includes:

1.1 Using rigorous and thorough recruitment and selection processes focused on making sure that only people who have the appropriate knowledge and skills and who are suitable to provide social services are allowed to enter your workforce;

1.2 Checking criminal records, relevant registers and indexes and assessing whether people are capable of carrying out the duties of the job they have been selected for before confirming appointments;

1.3 Seeking and providing reliable references;

1.4 Giving staff clear information about their roles and responsibilities, relevant legislation and the organisational policies and procedures they must follow in their work; and

1.5 Managing the performance of staff and the organisation to ensure high quality services and care.

2 *As a social service employer, you must have written policies and procedures in place to enable social service workers to meet the SSSC's Code of Practice for Social Service Workers.*

This includes:

2.1 Implementing and monitoring written policies on: confidentiality; equal opportunities; risk assessment; substance abuse; record keeping; and the acceptance of money or personal gifts from service users or carers;

2.2 Effectively managing and supervising staff to support effective practice and good conduct and supporting staff to address deficiencies in their performance;

2.3 Having systems in place to enable social service workers to report inadequate resources or operational difficulties which might impede the delivery of safe care and working with them and relevant authorities to address those issues; and

2.4 Supporting social service workers to meet the SSSC's Code of Practice for Social Service Workers and not requiring them to do anything that would put their compliance with that code at risk.

3   *As a social service employer, you must provide training and development opportunities to enable social service workers to strengthen and develop their skills and knowledge.*

This includes:

3.1 Providing induction, training and development opportunities to help social service workers do their jobs effectively and prepare for new and changing roles and responsibilities;

3.2 Contributing to the provision of social care and social work education and training, including effective workplace assessment and practice learning;

3.3 Supporting staff in posts subject to registration to meet the SSSC's eligibility criteria for registration and its requirements for continuing professional development; and

3.4 Responding appropriately to social service workers who seek assistance because they do not feel able or adequately prepared to carry out any aspects of their work.

4   *As a social service employer, you must put into place and implement written policies and procedures to deal with dangerous, discriminatory or exploitative behaviour and practice.*

This includes:

4.1 Making it clear to social service workers that bullying, harassment or any form of unjustifiable discrimination is not acceptable and taking action to deal with such behaviour;

4.2 Establishing and promoting procedures for social service workers to report dangerous, discriminatory, abusive or exploitative behaviour and practice and dealing with these reports promptly, effectively and openly;

4.3 Making it clear to social service workers, service users and carers that violence, threats or abuse to staff are not acceptable and having clear policies and procedures for minimising the risk of violence and managing violent incidents;

4.4 Supporting social service workers who experience trauma or violence in their work;

4.5 Putting in place and implementing written policies and procedures that promote staff welfare and equal opportunities for workers; and

4.6 While ensuring that the care and safety of service users is your priority, providing appropriate assistance to social service workers whose work is affected by ill health or dependency on drugs and alcohol, and giving clear guidance about any limits on their work while they are receiving treatment.

5   *As a social service employer, you must promote the SSSC's codes of practice to social service workers, service users and carers and co-operate with the SSSC's proceedings.*

This includes:

5.1 Informing social service workers about this code and your responsibility to comply with it;

5.2 Informing social service workers about the SSSC's Code of Practice for Social Service Workers and their personal responsibility to meet that code;

5.3 Making service users and carers aware of this code and the Code of Practice for Social Service Workers and informing them about how to raise issues through your policies and, if necessary, contact the SSSC in relation to the codes;

5.4 Taking account of the SSSC's Code of Practice for Social Service Workers in making any decision that relates to the conduct of workers;

5.5 Informing the SSSC about any misconduct by registered social service workers that might call into question their registration and inform the worker involved that a report has been made to the SSSC; and

5.6 Co-operating with SSSC investigations and hearings and responding appropriately to the findings and decisions of the SSSC.

Social Service Workers

Introduction

This document contains agreed codes of practice for social service workers and employers of social service workers describing the standards of conduct and practice within which they should work. This introduction, which is also reproduced in the Code of Practice for Employers of Social Service Workers, is intended to help you understand what the codes are for and what they will mean to you as a social service worker, employer, service user or member of the public.

The Scottish Social Services Council began its work on 1 October 2001, at the same time as the General Social Care Council, the Northern Ireland Social Care Council, and the Care Council for Wales. The Councils have a duty to develop codes of practice and have worked together in developing these codes as part of their contribution to raising standards in social services.

The two codes for workers and employers are presented together in this document because they are complementary and mirror the joint responsibilities of employers and workers in ensuring high standards.

What are the codes?

The Code of Practice for Social Service Workers is a list of statements that describe the standards of professional conduct and practice required of social service workers as they go about their daily work. This is the first time that standards have been set in this way at national level, although many employers have similar standards in place at local level. The intention is to confirm the standards required in social services and ensure that workers know what standards of conduct employers, colleagues, service users, carers and the public expect of them.

The Code of Practice for Employers of Social Service Workers sets down the responsibilities of employers in the regulation of social service workers. Again, this is the first time that such standards have been set out at national level.

The code requires that employers adhere to the standards set out in their code, support social service workers in meeting their code and take appropriate action when workers do not meet expected standards of conduct.

The codes are intended to reflect existing good practice and it is anticipated that workers and employers will recognise in the codes the shared standards to which they already aspire. The Councils will promote these standards through making the codes widely available.

How will the codes be used?

The codes are a key step in the introduction of a system of regulation for social services in the four countries of the UK. The Councils are responsible for the registration of those working in social services. The register will be a public record that those registered have met the requirements for entry onto the register and have agreed to abide by the standards set out in the Code of Practice for Social Service Workers.

The Councils will take account of the standards set in the Code of Practice for Social Service Workers in considering issues of misconduct and decisions as to whether a registered worker should remain on the register.

What will the codes mean to you?

As a social service worker you will have criteria to guide your practice and be clear about what standards of conduct you are expected to meet. You are encouraged to use the codes to examine your own practice and to look for areas in which you can improve.

As a social service employer you will know what part you are expected to play in the regulation of the workforce and the support of high quality social services. You are encouraged to review your own standards of practice and policies in the light of the standards set in the code.

As a user of services or member of the public the codes will help you understand how a social service worker should behave towards you and how employers should support social service workers to do their jobs well.

Code of Practice for Social Service Workers

The purpose of this code is to set out the conduct that is expected of social service workers and to inform service users and the public about the standards of conduct they can expect from social service workers It forms part of the wider package of legislation, practice standards and employers' policies and procedures that social service workers must meet. Social service workers are responsible for making sure that their conduct does not fall below the standards set out in this code and that no action or omission on their part harms the wellbeing of service users.

Status

The Scottish Social Services Council expects social service workers to meet this code and may take action if registered workers fail to do so. Employers of social service workers are required to take account of this code in making any decisions about the conduct of their staff.

Social service workers must:

- Protect the rights and promote the interests of service users and carers;
- Strive to establish and maintain the trust and confidence of service users and carers;
- Promote the independence of service users while protecting them as far as possible from danger or harm;
- Respect the rights of service users whilst seeking to ensure that their behaviour does not harm themselves or other people;
- Uphold public trust and confidence in social services; and
- Be accountable for the quality of their work and take responsibility for maintaining and improving their knowledge and skills.

1 *As a social service worker, you must protect the rights and promote the interests of service users and carers.*

This includes:

1.1 Treating each person as an individual;

1.2 Respecting and, where appropriate, promoting the individual views and wishes of both service users and carers;

1.3 Supporting service users' rights to control their lives and make informed choices about the services they receive;

1.4 Respecting and maintaining the dignity and privacy of service users;

1.5 Promoting equal opportunities for service users and carers; and

1.6 Respecting diversity and different cultures and values.

2 *As a social service worker, you must strive to establish and maintain the trust and confidence of service users and carers.*

This includes:

2.1 Being honest and trustworthy;

2.2 Communicating in an appropriate, open, accurate and straightforward way;

2.3 Respecting confidential information and clearly explaining agency policies about confidentiality to service users and carers;

2.4 Being reliable and dependable;

2.5 Honouring work commitments, agreements and arrangements and, when it is not possible to do so, explaining why to service users and carers;

2.6 Declaring issues that might create conflicts of interest and making sure that they do not influence your judgement or practice; and

2.7 Adhering to policies and procedures about accepting gifts and money from service users and carers.

3 As a social service worker, you must promote the independence of service users while protecting them as far as possible from danger or harm.

This includes:

3.1 Promoting the independence of service users and assisting them to understand and exercise their rights;

3.2 Using established processes and procedures to challenge and report dangerous, abusive, discriminatory or exploitative behaviour and practice;

3.3 Following practice and procedures designed to keep you and other people safe from violent and abusive behaviour at work;

3.4 Bringing to the attention of your employer or the appropriate authority resource or operational difficulties that might get in the way of the delivery of safe care;

3.5 Informing your employer or an appropriate authority where the practice of colleagues may be unsafe or adversely affecting standards of care;

3.6 Complying with employers' health and safety policies, including those relating to substance abuse;

3.7 Helping service users and carers to make complaints, taking complaints seriously and responding to them or passing them to the appropriate person; and

3.8 Recognising and using responsibly the power that comes from your work with service users and carers.

4 As a social service worker, you must respect the rights of service users while seeking to ensure that their behaviour does not harm themselves or other people.

This includes:

4.1 Recognising that service users have the right to take risks and helping them to identify and manage potential and actual risks to themselves and others;

4.2 Following risk assessment policies and procedures to assess whether the behaviour of service users presents a risk of harm to themselves or others;

4.3 Taking necessary steps to minimise the risks of service users from doing actual or potential harm to themselves or other people; and

4.4 Ensuring that relevant colleagues and agencies are informed about the outcomes and implications of risk assessments.

5   *As a social service worker, you must uphold public trust and confidence in social services.*

In particular you must not:

5.1   Abuse, neglect or harm service users, carers or colleagues;

5.2   Exploit service users, carers or colleagues in any way;

5.3   Abuse the trust of service users and carers or the access you have to personal information about them or to their property, home or workplace;

5.4   Form inappropriate personal relationships with service users;

5.5   Discriminate unlawfully or unjustifiably against service users, carers or colleagues;

5.6   Condone any unlawful or unjustifiable discrimination by service users, carers or colleagues;

5.7   Put yourself or other people at unnecessary risk; or

5.8   Behave in a way, in work or outside work, which would call into question your suitability to work in social services.

6   *As a social service worker, you must be accountable for the quality of your work and take responsibility for maintaining and improving your knowledge and skills.*

This includes:

6.1   Meeting relevant standards of practice and working in a lawful, safe and effective way;

6.2   Maintaining clear and accurate records as required by procedures established for your work;

6.3   Informing your employer or the appropriate authority about any personal difficulties that might affect your ability to do your job competently and safely;

6.4   Seeking assistance from your employer or the appropriate authority if you do not feel able or adequately prepared to carry out any aspect of your work, or you are not sure about how to proceed in a work matter;

6.5   Working openly and co-operatively with colleagues and treating them with respect;

6.6   Recognising that you remain responsible for the work that you have delegated to other workers;

6.7   Recognising and respecting the roles and expertise of workers from other agencies and wor` the learning and development of others.

Scottish Social Services Council
Compass House
Discovery Quay
11 Riverside Drive
Dundee
DD1 4NY
Lo-call 0845 60 30 891
Telephone 01382 207101
Fax 01382 207215
Email enquiries@sssc.uk.com
www.sssc.uk.com

Glossary

Acceptance   Taking people as they are without judging them; an absence of rejection.

Adolescence   The stage of development between childhood and adulthood, usually seen to begin with puberty and to end with responsibility and independence.

Advising   Telling others how they might act, feel or think rather than letting them decide for themselves.

Advocacy   Actively promoting and representing the cause of another; speaking on behalf of someone as if speaking as that person.

Ageism   Discrimination applied to or experienced by people because of their age. This term is applicable both to older and younger people.

Agency   An establishment or organisation providing a service to service users.

Agents of socialisation   The groups from whom we pick up our culture: family, friends, media, religion, etc.

AIDS   Acquired immune deficiency syndrome caused by the human immunodeficiency virus (HIV).

Anti-discriminatory practice   Practice which acknowledges, understands and challenges the many negative effects of discrimination.

Assessment   An exploration of service user needs as part of the process of care or health promotion in order to enable the service user to reach an optimum quality of life; the basis for planning.

Attitude   The way something is viewed in an evaluative manner; an habitual mode of regarding anything. Attitudes affect the way people behave.

Behaviour   How people conduct themselves. The way they do things and act in their relationships with others.

Belief   An opinion or conviction which is held to be true, often without any sort of proof.

Body language   Non-verbal communication expressed through the position, attitude and expression of the body, or parts of the body, e.g. the way you sit, the degree of eye contact.

Care/formal care   Caring for people in society, other than self or family, in an agency whose codes of practice are dictated to and guided by legislation, policy and professional ethics.

Care plan   An agreement arising from an assessment about what needs are to be met, how this will be achieved and how problems are to be dealt with.

Choice   Promoting choice means giving different and realistic options from which the service user can select as independently as possible.

Client   The recipient or user of a service. Although 'service user' is the term used in this book, 'client' is still an accepted term in care practice and counselling.

Communication   Communication occurs whenever people receive and/or give messages which they regard as significant. It can be verbal, non-verbal or symbolic.

Community   A network of people who are linked, usually by sharing a geographical locality; may also refer to those linked by occupation, ethnic background and/or other factors.

Community care Providing the services and support which people need to be able to live as independently as possible in their own homes or in 'homely' settings rather than institutions.

Confidentiality Maintaining the right to privacy of information; not divulging personal information without consent.

Congruence Being genuine; ensuring that your verbal and non-verbal behaviour give the same messages.

Counselling A process which aims to help people help themselves through communication to make better choices and become better decision makers.

Culture The way people live, lifestyles, values; can also be seen as consisting of all the messages received from society about what is good, bad, desirable, undesirable etc.

Development Gradual unfolding; increase in complexity involving change and movement. Human development can be social, physical, emotional, cognitive, cultural and spiritual.

Deviance Behaviour of individuals or groups that is outwith the socially defined normal limits of behaviour.

Disablism Discrimination applied to, or experienced by, people with physical or learning disabilities.

Discrimination The process whereby some groups or individuals in society, as a result of prejudice and stereotypes, treat others less favourably.

Empathy Putting yourself in someone else's shoes and attempting to imagine how they feel.

Empowerment Enabling people to take control of their lives; gaining the power to make decisions and choices.

Equality of opportunity The belief that everyone should get an equal chance to access the opportunities in society.

Ethnic group A group with a long shared history and cultural tradition of its own. Other important characteristics may be common geographic origin, language, literature and religion.

Ethnocentrism Prejudicial assumptions made in theorising and explaining human behaviour and aspects of society, which favour one or some groups over others; may lead to accounts which make false assumptions and which are biased.

Exclusion See 'Social exclusion'.

Feminism Sets out to explain the position of women in society; to focus attention upon how women have been subordinated and oppressed and how this can be changed.

Gender The term used to describe socially constructed differences between men and women. Sex refers to biological differences.

Genetic The influence of genes, which are inherited from parents and determine bodily aspects such as eye colour to some illnesses, e.g. haemophilia.

Holistic care Care which sees the whole person in a social situation and attempts to satisfy physical, intellectual, communicational, emotional, cultural and social needs.

Ideology A set of beliefs and ideas that are held by a group, e.g. the ideology of the Scottish Nationalist Party.

Implementation Putting plans into effect; carrying out what has been agreed upon in the planning process.

Inclusion   See 'Social inclusion'.

Independence   Having as much control as possible over your life and decision-making.

Institution   A part of society which has regular and routine practices, regulated by social norms.

Institutional discrimination   The routine, day-to-day, ingrained discrimination which exists in any of the different institutions in society.

Institutionalisation   Becoming dependent upon the routines and narrow confines of an institution, resulting in such characteristics as apathy, lack of initiative and inability to make personal plans.

Keyworker   A worker who is allocated to work more closely with a service user than other workers and who has a coordinating role with that service user within the agency.

Labelling   Attaching a (usually negative) name to acts or conditions which then becomes a 'master status', e.g. labelling people as deviant, neurotic or difficult.

Learned helplessness   A decline in the desire and ability to do things beyond what may be expected in relation to a person's state of health, usually because too much assistance is being given.

Legislation   The law; Acts of Parliament.

Marginalisation   Literally means to 'place at the edge' and refers to the process whereby some groups are forced to live outside the mainstream of society and are denied opportunities to participate as full citizens.

Modelling   Demonstrating behaviour, feelings or thoughts to others which may, if adopted, improve the quality of life for the service user.

Monitoring   On-going evaluation; keeping a check on what you are doing to ensure that it meets objectives.

Nature/nurture debate   Refers to the discussion about the extent to which nature (inherited characteristics) or nurture (the environment, socioeconomic factors and socialisation) influence behaviour and development.

Normalisation   Affording all citizens the same rights and opportunities to develop and contribute to society in ways which are socially valued; developed predominantly as an attempt to promote the aim of integrating people with a disability fully into society.

Norms   The shared, unwritten rules in a society that define acceptable behaviour.

Oppression   Abuse of power by a group or individual over a less powerful group or individual, with the effect that those less powerful are denied their rights.

Patriarchy   The systematic dominance of men over women in society.

Prejudice   A strongly held negative attitude or set of attitudes based upon irrational beliefs, lack of understanding and/or stereotypes, rather than fact or reason.

Primary socialisation   The first influence on how your culture is acquired, usually through family.

Principles   The practical manifestation of values.

Psychology   The study of mind and behaviour.

Racism   Discrimination applied to, or experienced by, people on the basis of their race, nationality or ethnic origin.

Record   A written account of significant information including decisions, incidents, feelings, actions and monitoring of the implementation of assessments/plans.

Relationship   Being connected in some way with another; a helping relationship is characterised by empathy, genuineness and unconditional positive regard.

Respite care   A temporary period usually spent in a supported, residential environment in order to give carers a break and/or to provide help and a change for those in need of care. It can also be used as an opportunity for assessment or re-assessment.

Scapegoats   Individuals or groups of people who have been inaccurately and unjustly targeted as being responsible for a problem.

Secondary socialisation   Groups apart from the family who influence how we pick up our culture, e.g. friends, school, the media, work, etc.

Self-concept   The view you hold about yourself.

Self-esteem   A sense of your own worth. This can be a positive or negative evaluation of yourself.

Service user   One who avails themselves of help or assistance towards fulfilling need and/or improving their quality of life; sometimes also called a client or resident.

Sexism   Discrimination applied to, or experienced by, people on the basis of their gender.

Siblings   Brothers and sisters.

Social class   People in the same or similar socioeconomic circumstances. Socioeconomic differences result in disparities of wealth, power and life chances.

Social exclusion   The prevention of some people/groups from taking a full and valued part in society, e.g. those who are marginalised because of poverty or disability.

Social inclusion   Taking positive steps to assist and include people who have traditionally been excluded from society; includes treating everyone as a valued member of society and facilitating participation in that society.

Socialisation   The process or way in which people learn the culture of their society.

Society   Usually, but not always, the country or nation-state, defined in terms of language, laws, education and religion.

Sociology   The study of societies and the analysis of the structure of social relationships as constituted by social interaction. No single definition is satisfactory because of the diversity of sociological perspectives.

Status   Position in society or social institution; what a person is; can also mean the prestige associated with that position.

Statutory   Provided by, or connected with, central or local government.

Stereotype   A fixed, general, over-simplified and usually negative image of what a particular individual or group is like because of the possession of certain characteristics, e.g. the false 'stereotypes' that all gay men are promiscuous or all people from Aberdeen are mean.

Stigma   A distinguishing mark or characteristic which is both noticeable and regarded as objectionable by some individuals or groups. Stigmas have the power to affect a person's social and personal identity.

Summarising   Making statements which briefly give the main points of what you or another person has been saying; may include feedback from you.

Support   Giving whatever is needed to another, including encouragement, help, understanding and warmth.

SVQ   Scottish Vocational Qualification; awarded at different levels upon successful completion of a detailed assessment of practice by an approved workplace assessor.

Symbolic communication   Messages, behaviour and actions which represent something else, e.g. an unwelcoming physical environment says 'we don't care about you'.

Team   A group of people who work together to achieve the philosophy and goals of their agency.

Transitions   Changes from one life state to another which people undergo during their lives, e.g. marriage, loss of a partner, retirement.

Transsexual   A person who has made hormonal or surgical changes to their body in order to live as a member of the opposite sex, adopting a name, clothes and lifestyle of that sex.

Transvestite   A person who dresses in the clothes of the opposite gender.

Value   That which is desirable and worthy for its own sake.

Voluntary organisation   A not-for-profit, non-statutory organisation; often a charity.

Bibliography

Abbot, P. and Wallace, C. (1997) *An Introduction to Sociology: Feminist Perspectives*, 2nd edition. London: Routledge.

Abercrombie, N., Hill, S. and Turner, B. (1994) *The Penguin Dictionary of Sociology*, 3rd edition. London: Penguin.

Adams, G., Guillotta, T. and Montemayor, R. (1992) *Adolescent Identity Formation*. Newbury Park: Sage.

Adams, J.D., Hayes, J. and Hopson, B. (1977) *Transition: Understanding and Managing Personal Change*. London: Martin Robertson.

Alexander, M. (1995) *Painters First*. Bordon: Leader Books.

Allan, G. (1985) *Family Life: Domestic Roles and Social Organization*. London: Blackwell.

Allan, J. (1935) Farmer's boy, reprinted in Maclaren, A. (1976) *Social Class in Scotland*. Edinburgh: John Donald.

Amato, P.R. (1993) Children's adjustment to divorce: theories, hypotheses and empirical support, *Journal of Marriage and the Family*, 55, 23–38.

Anderson, C. and Wilkie, P. (1992) *Reflective Helping in HIV and AIDS*. Milton Keynes: Open University Press.

Anon (1998a) Parents hands tied by Euro judgement, *Scotsman*, 24 September.

Anon (1998b) Girl kept in attic, *Guardian Weekly*, 2 July.

Anon (1998c) *Community Care*, 1 October.

Anon (2007) The 100 club wants you, *Guardian Weekly*, 12 January.

ASH (Action on Smoking and Health), BMA (British Medical Association) and HEA (Health Education Authority) (1988) *Two Good Reasons for a Tobacco Pricing Policy* London: ASH/BMA/HEA.

Bamford, C. (1995) *Equal Treatment and the Law: A Guide to European Community Law in Scotland*. Edinburgh: European Commission representation in Scotland.

Bandura, A. (1965) Influence of model's reinforcement contingencies on the acquisition of imitative responses, *Journal of Personality and Social Psychology*, 1, 589–95.

Bandura, A., Ross, D. and Ross, S. (1963) Imitation of film mediated aggressive models, *Journal of Abnormal and Social Psychology*, 66, 3–11

Barber-Fleming, P. (2007) Seven days society. *Sunday Herald*, 18 February 2007

Barnard, A. and Burgess, T. (1996) *Sociology Explained*. Cambridge: Cambridge University Press.

BBC (2005) Meet Tanni Grey Thompson. BBC Sport/Disability Sport. Accessed from: news.bbc.co.uk/sport1/hi/other_sports/disability_sport/4354422.stm

Becker, H. (1963) *Outsiders: Studies in the Sociology of Deviance*. New York: The Free Press.

Bee, H.L. and Mitchell, S.K. (1984) *The Developing Person*. New York: Harper and Row.

Bell, N. and Vogel, E. (1959) *A Modern Introduction to the Family*. London: Collier-Macmillan.

Bennis, W. in van Maurik, J. (2001) *Writers on Leadership.* London: Penguin.

Beresford, P. (2007) Service user wishlist goes back to basics, *Community Care*, 11 January.

Beresford, P. and Branfield, F. (2004) Shape up and listen, *Community Care*, 4 November.

Berry, J.W., Poortinga, Y., Segall, M. and Dasen, P. (2002) *Cross-Cultural Psychology: Research and Applications,* 2nd edition. Cambridge: Cambridge University Press.

Biggart, A. and Furlong, A. (1996) Educating 'discouraged workers': Cultural diversity in the upper secondary school, *British Journal of Sociology of Education*, 17 (3), 253–66.

Bingham, M. and Stryker, S. (1995) *Things Will be Different for my Daughter: A Practical Guide to Building her Self-esteem and Self-reliance*. New York: Penguin.

Bion, W. (1968) *Experiences in Groups*. London: Tavistock.

Birren, J.E. and Fisher, L.M. (1990) Aging and slowing of behaviour, in *Current Theory and Research in Motivation*, 39, pp. 1–37. Lincoln, NB: University of Nebraska Press.

Black, N., Boswell, D., Gray, A. and Murphy, S. (eds.) (1984) *Health and Disease: A Reader*. Milton Keynes: Open University Press.

Blakemore, K. and Drake, R. (1996) *Understanding Equal Opportunities Policies*. London: Prentice Hall/Harvester Wheatsheaf.

Blane, D., Brunner, E. and Wilkinson, R. (eds.) (1996) *Health and Social Organisations: Towards a Health Policy for the 21st Century*. London: Routledge.

Bottomore, T. and Ruben, M. (eds.) (1963) *Karl Marx: Selected Writings in Sociology and Social Philosophy*. Harmondsworth: Penguin.

Bowlby, J. (1951) *Maternal Care and Mental Health*. Geneva: World Health Organisation.

Bowlby, J. (1953) *Child Care and the Growth of Love*. Harmondsworth: Penguin.

Bowlby, J. (1969) *Attachment and Loss,* Vol. 1: *Attachment*. New York: Basic Books/ Hogarth Press.

Bowlby, J. (1973) *Attachment and Loss*, Vol. 2: *Separation: Anxiety and Anger*. New York: Basic Books.

Bowlby, J. (1980) *Attachment and Loss*, Vol. 3: *Loss: Sadness and Depression*. New York: Basic Books.

Bowlby, J. (1988) *A Secure Base: Clinical Applications of Attachment Theory*. London: Routledge.

Bowles, S. and Gintis, H. (1976) *Schooling in Capitalist America*. London: Routledge & Kegan Paul.

Bradford Social Services Department, Community Health NHS Trust and Bradford Interfaith Centre (2002) *Spiritual Wellbeing: Policy and Practice*. Leeds: NIMHE.

Bradshaw, J. (1972) The concept of social need. New Society, 30 March.

Branfield, F. and Beresford, P. (2006) *Making Service User Involvement Work: Supporting Service User Networking and Knowledge*. York: Joseph Rowntree Foundation.

Breitenbach, E. (1995) *Quality through Equality: Good Practice in Equal Opportunities in Scottish Local Authorities*. Glasgow: Equal Opportunities Commission.

Bronfenbrenner, U. (1974) The origins of alienation, *Scientific American*, 231, 53–61.

Brothers, M. (2003) It's not just about ramps and braille: disability and sexual orientation. Disability Rights Commission, 21 October 2003. Accessed from: www.drc.org.uk/library/policy/other_issues.aspx

Brown, C.H. (1979) *Understanding Society*. London: John Murray.

Brown, G.M. (1995a) *Beside the Ocean of Time*. London: Flamingo.

Brown, G.M. (1995b) *Winter Tales*. London: Flamingo.

Brunner, E. (1996) The social and biological basis of cardiovascular disease in office workers. In Blane D. et al. (eds.) *Health and Social Organisations*.

Bryman, A. (1988) *Quality and Quantity in Social Research*. London: Unwin Hyman.

Burnard, P. (1989) *Teaching Interpersonal Skills*. London: Chapman and Hall.

Cardwell, M., Clark, L. and Meldrum, C. (2004) *Psychology for A2 level*, 3rd edition. London: Collins

Carlen, P. (1988) *Women, Crime and Poverty*. Milton Keynes: Open University Press.

Carstairs, V. and Morris, R. (1991) *Deprivation and Health in Scotland*. Aberdeen: Aberdeen University Press.

Centre for Research on Families and Relationships (2002) Research Briefing Number 6 Divorce. Accessed from: www.crfr.ac.uk/Reports/Resbriefing6.pdf

Chambliss, W.J. and Mankoff, M. (1976) *Whose Law? What Order?* New York: John Wiley.

Cheetham, J. (1992) *Evaluating Social Work Effectiveness*. Buckingham: Open University Press.

Chiesa, A. (2007) National champion for children in care. *The Herald*,16 January 2007.

Clough, R. (1987) *Scandals in Residential Centres*. An unpublished report for the Wagner Committee, University of Bristol.

Commission for Racial Equality (1995) *Annual Report*. London: CRE.

Commission for Racial Equality (1997) *Annual Report*. London: CRE.

Community Care Magazine (1998) Deaf people from ethnic minorities feel isolated, *Community Care*, 13–19 August, p. 5.

Community Care Magazine (1998) Scots unclear about Children Act Legislation, *Community Care*, 9–15 July, p. 4.

Community Care Magazine (1998) Study paints picture of isolation, *Community Care*, 28 May–3 June, p. 3.

Comptroller and Auditor General (2004) *Improving Patient Care by Reducing the Risk of Hospital Acquired Infection: A Progress Report*. London: The Stationery Office.

Comte, A. (1986) *The Positive Philosophy*. London: Bell and Sons.

Cooley, C.H. (1902) *Human Nature and Social Order*. New York: Shocken.

Coser, L. and Rosenberg, B. (eds.) (1976) *Sociological Theory: A Book of Readings*. New York: Macmillan.

Coulshed, V. and Orme, J. (2006) *Social Work Practice*, 4th edition. Basingstoke: Palgrave.

Craib, I. (1984) *Modern Social Theory*. Brighton: Wheatsheaf Books.

Crawford, K. and Walker, J. (2003) *Social Work and Human Development*. Exeter: Learning Matters.

Crompton, M. and Jackson, R. (2006) *Spiritual Wellbeing of Adults with Down Syndrome*. Portsmouth: Down Syndrome Educational Trust.

Currie, E. (1989) *Life Lines: Politics and Health 1986–88*. London: Sidgewick and Jackson.

Dahrendorf, R. (1964) Out of Utopia. Reprinted in Coser, L. and Rosenberg, B. (eds.) (1976) *Sociological Theory: A Book of Readings*. New York: Macmillan.

Dalrymple, J. and Burke, B. (1995) *Anti-Oppressive Practice: Social Care and the Law*. Buckingham: Open University Press.

Davies, M. (ed.) (2002) *The Blackwell Companion to Social Work*, 2nd edition. Oxford: Blackwell.

De Beauvoir, S. (1972) *The Second Sex*. Harmondsworth: Penguin.

Department of Health and Social Security (1976) *Prevention and Health: Everybody's Business.* London: HMSO.

Disability Rights Commission (2005) Disability rights, equality and human rights – Queen's speech debates briefing 2005. Accessed from: www.drc.org.uk/docs/10_686_rights_briefing.doc

Disability Rights Commission (2006) Public sector professions fall foul of anti-discrimination laws says DRC, 18 December 2006. Accessed from: www.drc.org.uk/the_law/drc_formal_investigations/equal_treatment_investigation.aspx

Dobash, R. and Dobash, R. (1980) *Violence Against Wives.* New York: The Free Press.

Dominelli, L. (1997) *Sociology for Social Work.* London: Macmillan.

Donohue, E. (1985) *Echoes in the Hills.* Surbiton: SCA Publications.

Douglas, J.W.B. (1964) *The Home and the School.* London: Macgibbon and Kee.

Douglas, J.W.B. (1975) Early hospital admissions and later disturbances of behaviour and learning, *Developmental Medical Child Neurology*, 17, 456–80.

Douglas, T. (1978) *Basic Groupwork.* London: Routledge.

Dryden, W. (2006) in Feltham, C. and Horton, I. (eds.) *The SAGE Handbook of Counselling and Psychotherapy*, 2nd edition. London: Sage.

Dryden, W., Neenan, M., Yankura, J. and Ellis, A. (1999) *Counselling Individuals: A Rational Emotive Behavioural Handbook* 3rd edition, London: Whurr.

DTI (2006) *Work and Families: Choice and Flexibility.* Department of Trade and Industry. Accessed from: www.dti.gov.uk/files/file23932.pdf

Durkheim, E. (1938) *The Rules of Sociological Method.* New York: The Free Press.

Eagleton, T. (2000) *The Idea of Culture* Oxford: Blackwell.

Earle, M. (2003) *Obesity.* Edinburgh: Scottish Parliament.

Eastbank Health Promotion Centre (1997) *First Annual Report.* Glasgow: Greater Glasgow Health Board.

Eaude, T. (2006) *Children's Spiritual, Moral, Social and Cultural Development.* Exeter: Learning Matters.

Edgell, S. (1980) *Middle Class Couples.* London: Allen and Unwin.

Egan, G. (1986) *The Skilled Helper.* Monterey: Brooks/Cole.

Eldridge, J.E.T. (1970) *Max Weber: The Interpretation of Social Reality.* London: Joseph.

Engels, F. (1972) *The Origin of the Family, Private Property and The State.* London: Lawrence and Wishart.

Equal Opportunities Commission (1997) Making equality work: The challenge for Government. EOC Annual Report (Scottish Extract), Manchester: EOC.

Equal Opportunities Commission (2006) Twenty years on from landmark case, sexual harassment remains all too common. Accessed from: www.eoc.org.uk/Default.aspx?page=18860

Erikson, E.H. (1968) *Identity: Youth and Crisis*. New York: Norton.

ESRC (2003) Young offenders and victims of crime are often the same people. ESRC Press release 10 August 2003. Economic and Social Research Council. Accessed from: www.esrcsocietytoday.ac.uk/ESRCInfoCentre/PO/releases/2003/august/young.aspx

Fenton, S. (1987) *Ageing Minorities: Black People As They Grow Old in Britain*. London: Commission for Racial Equality.

Ferguson, A. (2007) Passing of Bill belies problem, *Scotsman*, 23 February. Accessed from: http://news.scotsman.com/opinion.cfm?id=291122007

Field, D. and James, N. (1993) Where and how people die. In Clark, D. (ed.) *The Future of Palliative Care*. Buckingham: Open University Press.

Fitzgerald, R. and McKay, A. (2006) Gender equality and work in Scotland: A review of the Evidence base and the salient issues. Equal Opportunities Commission. Accessed from: www.eoc.org.uk/PDF?gender_equality_and_work_in_Scotland.pdf

Flanagan, C. (1996) *Applying Psychology to Early Child Development*. London: Hodder and Stoughton.

Fletcher, R. (1988) *The Family and Marriage Under Attack*. London: Routledge.

Ford, J. and Sinclair, R. (1987) *Sixty Years On: Women Talk About Old Age*. London: Women's Press.

Frude, N. (1997) *Understanding Family Problems*. London: Wiley.

Furlong, A. and Cartmel, F. (1995) Aspirations and opportunity structures: 13-year-olds in areas with restricted opportunities, *British Journal of Guidance and Counselling*, 23 (3).

General Register Office for Scotland (2005) *Scotland's Population 2005*. Edinburgh: GRO.

General Register Office for Scotland (2006) Table 1.1 Population and vital events, Scotland, 1855 to 2005. Accessed from: www.gro-scotland.gov.uk/files/05t1-1.pdf

Gill, A. (1999) Do you recognise this family? *Scotland on Sunday*, 31 January 1999.

Glasgow City Council (1997) *Language Matters: A Guide to Good Practice*. Glasgow: GCC.

Glasgow University Media Group (1980) *Bad News*. London: Routledge & Kegan Paul.

Goffman, E. (1968) *Asylums.* Harmondsworth: Penguin.

Gough, E. (1959) Is the family universal? The Nayor case. In Bell, N. and Vogel, E. (eds.) *A Modern Introduction to the Family.* London: Collier-Macmillan.

Gould, R.L. (1978) *Transformations: Growth and Change in Adult Life.* New York: Simon and Schuster.

Gray, L. (2006) Outcry at new laws allowing gay adoption. *Scotsman,* 8 December. Accessed from:
http://news.scotsman.com/politics.cfm?id=1822862006

Greer, G. (1970) *The Female Eunuch.* London: MacGibbon and Kee.

Gross, R. (1996) *Psychology: The Science of Mind and Behaviour.* 3rd edition, London: Hodder and Stoughton.

Haralambos, M. (ed.) (1966) *Sociology: A New Approach.* 3rd edition, Ormskirk: Causeway Press.

Haralambos, M. and Holborn, M. (1995) *Sociology: Themes and Perspectives.* London: Collins Educational.

Haralambos, M. and Holborn M. (2004) *Sociology: Themes and Perspectives.* 6th edition, London: Collins.

Harrell, E. and Howie, M. (2006) Violent crime by women up 50 per cent in past 4 years, *Scotsman,* 1 September. Accessed from:
http://thescotsman.scotsman.com/index.cfm?id=1290372006

Hayes, N. (1994) *Foundations of Psychology: An Introductory Text.* New York: Routledge.

Health Education Board for Scotland (1997a) *Scotland's Health at Work.*

Health Education Board for Scotland (1997b) *Strategic Plan 1997 to 2000.*

Heidensohn, F (1985) *Women and Crime.* London: Macmillan.

Heim, A. (1990) *Where Did I Put My Spectacles.* Cambridge: Allborough Press.

Heraud, B.J. (1970) *Sociology and Social Work (Perspectives and Problems).* Oxford: Pergammon Press.

Herbert, M. (1986) *Psychology for Social Workers.* Leicester: British Psychological Society Imprint.

Herbert, M. (2002) The human life cycle: Adolescence. In Davies M. (ed.) *The Blackwell Companion to Social Work,* 2nd edition. Oxford: Blackwell.

HMSO (1968) *Social Work (Scotland) Act.* London: HMSO.

HMSO (1987) *British Crime Survey.* London: HMSO

HMSO (1990) *National Health Service and Community Care Act.* London: HMSO.

HMSO (1992) *Scotland's Health: A Challenge to Us All.* London: HMSO.

HMSO (1995a) *Children (Scotland) Act.* London: HMSO.

HMSO (1995b) *Disability Discrimination Act*. London: HMSO.

HMSO (1998a) *Scottish Statistical Survey*. London: HMSO.

HMSO (1998b) *Social Trends.* London: HMSO.

Holmes, T.H. and Rahe, H. (1967) The social re-adjustment rating scale, *Journal of Psycho-Somatic Research*, 11, 213–18.

Institute for Social and Economic Research (2006) Living in Britain, What the papers say. Accessed from:
http://libsurvey.essex.ac.uk/reports/2002LIB_RR.htm

Ishii-Kuntz, M. (1990) Social interaction and psychological well-being: Comparison across stages of adulthood, *International Journal of Ageing and Human Development*, 30(1), 15–36.

Jones, A. (1990) *Charles Rennie Mackintosh*. London: Studio Editions.

Joseph Rowntree Foundation (2002) Poverty levels remain high in Scotland despite falling unemployment. Pressroom. Accessed from:
www.jrf.org.uk/pressroom/releases/051202.asp

Kahan, B. (1994) *Growing Up in Groups*. London: HMSO.

Katz, J. and Siddell, M. (1994) *Easeful Death: Caring for Dying and Bereaved People*. London: Hodder and Stoughton.

Kidd-Hewitt, D. and Osborne, R. (1995) *Crime and the Media: The Post-Modern Spectacle*. London: Pluto Press.

Kinsey, R. (1993) *Policing in the City: Public, Police and Social work*. Edinburgh: Scottish Office, Central Research Unit.

Labov, W. (1973) The logic of nonstandard English. In Young, T. (ed.) *Tinker, Taylor… The Myth of Cultural Deprivation*. Harmondsworth: Penguin.

Laing, R. and Esterson, A. (1970) *Sanity, Madness and the Family*. Harmondsworth: Penguin.

Lawson, T. (1991) *GCSE Sociology: A Conceptual Approach*. Chester: Checkmate Publications.

Leach, E. (1971) *A Runaway World?* London: BBC Publications.

Lemos, G. (2006) More than a place to stay, *Community Care*, 29 June.

Levin, E. (2004) *Involving service users and carers in social work education*. London: Social Care Institute for Excellence (SCIE).

Lewis, I. and Munn, P. (1987). *So You Want to Do Research*. Edinburgh: The Scottish Council for Research and Education.

Lishman, J. (2005) *The Case for Change*. Aberdeen: The Robert Gordon University, Leading to Deliver Module 2 paper.

Long, P. (1996) *Anne Redpath 1895–1965*. Edinburgh: National Galleries of Scotland.

McCurry, P. (1999) Wired for work, *Community Care*, 14–20 January.

McLaren, A. (1976) *Social Class in Scotland*. Edinburgh: John Donald.

McLellan, D. (1980) *Karl Marx 1818–1883: Selections in English*. London: Macmillan.

Macleod, N. (2007) Registration of the social care workforce: A UK agenda. *Care Appointments*, Issue 21, March 2007.

Macoby, E.E. (1980) *Social Development, Psychological Growth and the Parent Relationship*. New York: Harcourt Brace Jovanovich.

Mallinson, I. (1995) *Keyworking in Social Care*. London: Whiting and Birch.

Mannheim, H. (1960) *Comparative Criminology*. London: Routledge & Kegan Paul.

Martin, V. (2003) *Leading Change in Health and Social Care*. London: Routledge.

Marx, K. and Engels, F. (1915) *Manifesto of the Communist Party: Authorised English Translation*. Chicago: C.H. Kerr.

Matthews, R. and Young, J. (1992) *Issues in Realist Criminology*. London: Sage.

Matthews, Z. (1998) The outsiders, *Nursing Times*, 94(37), 16 September.

Maylor, E.A. (1994) Ageing and the retrieval of specialized and general knowledge: Performance of masterminds, *British Journal of Psychology*, 85(1).

Mead, G.H. (1934) in Morris, C. (ed.) *Mind, Self and Society*. Chicago: University of Chicago Press.

Meggitt, C. (2006) *Child Development: An Illustrated Guide*. Oxford: Heinemann.

Meighan, R. (1981) *A Sociology of Education*. London: Holt Rinehart.

Merton, R.K. (1968) *Social Theory and Social Structure*. Enlarged edition, New York: The Free Press.

Messer, D. and Jones, F. (eds) (1999) *Psychology and Social Care*. London: Jessica Kingsley.

Miller, J. (1996) *Social Care Practice*. London: Hodder and Stoughton.

Miller, J. (ed.) (2005) *Care Practice for S/NVQ 3*. London: Hodder Arnold.

Mills, C.W. (1959) *The Sociological Imagination*. New York: Oxford University Press.

Montemayor, R. (1983) in Adams, G. et al. (1992) *Adolescent Identity Formation*. Newbury Park: Sage.

Moonie, N. (1994) *Health and Social Care*. Oxford: Heinemann.

Moonie, N. (ed.) (1996) *Advanced Health and Social Care*, 2nd edition. Oxford: Heinemann.

Morison, M. (1986) *Methods in Sociology*. London: Longman.

Murdock, G.P. (1949) *Social Structure*. New York: Macmillan.

Murray Parkes, C. (1996) *Bereavement: Studies of Grief in Adult Life*, 3rd edition. London: Penguin.

Naysmith, S. (1994) Out in the cold. *The Big Issue* (in Scotland), 6(94), 22–3.

Nelson-Jones, R. (1988) *Practical Counselling and Helping Skills*, 3rd edition. London: Cassell.

NHS Scotland (2005) *Scottish Health Statistics*. Edinburgh: ISD (NHS Information Services Division).

Nobbs, J., Fielding, R., Hine, B. and Flemming, M. (1989) *Sociology*, 3rd edition. London: Macmillan Education.

Oakley, A. (1974) *Sociology of Housework*. Oxford: Martin Robertson.

Oakley, A. (1982) Conventional families. In Rapoport, R. (ed.) *Families in Britain*. London: Routledge & Kegan Paul.

Oakley, A. (1985) *Sex, Gender and Society*. London: Gower/Maurice Temple Smith.

Oakley, A. (1993) *Essays on Women, Medicine and Health*. Edinburgh: Edinburgh University Press.

Oakley, A. (1997) *Man and Wife: Richard and Kay Titmuss – My Parents' Early Years*. London: HarperCollins.

Oates, S. (1982) *Let the Trumpet Sound*. London: Search Press.

O'Brien, J. and Lovett, H. (1992) *Finding a Way Toward Everyday Lives: The Contribution of Person-centred Planning*. Harrisburg: Pennsylvania Office of Mental Retardation.

O'Donnell, M. (1993) *New Introductory Reader in Sociology*. Walton-on-Thames: Nelson.

O'Donnell, M. (1997) *Introduction to Sociology*, 4th edition. Walton-on-Thames: Nelson.

Office for National Statistics (2004) *Family Resources Survey*. London: Office for National Statistics.

Oldman, C. and Beresford, B. (1998) A space of our own, *Community Care*, 1–7 October.

Open University U205 Course Team (1985) *Birth to Old Age*. Milton Keynes: Open University Press.

Papalia, D., Wendokos, S. and Feldman, R.D. (2001) *Human Development*, 8th edition. New York: McGraw Hill.

Parsons, T. (1937) *The Structure of Social Action*. New York: McGraw Hill.

Partridge, C. and Barnitt, R. (1987) *Research Guidelines: A Handbook for Therapists*. London: Heinemann.

Patrick, J. (1973) *A Glasgow Gang Observed*. London: Eyre Methuen.

Payne, G. and Abbott, P. (eds.) (1990) *The Social Mobility of Women: Beyond Male Mobility Models*. London: Falmer Press.

Payne, M. (1991) *Modern Social Work Theory*. London: Macmillan.

Peter, L. (1982) *Quotations for our Time*. London: Methuen.

Pilsbury, B. (1984) Doing the month. In Black, N. et al. (eds.) *Health and Disease: A Reader*. Milton Keynes: Open University Press.

Pollack, N. (2007) *Like father, like son?* The Guardian, Manchester, 3 February.

Powell, T. (1997) *Free Yourself from Harmful Stress*. London: DK Publishing.

Radcliffe Brown, A. (1935) Structure and function in primitive society, *American Anthropologist*, 37.

Rapoport, R.N., Fogarty, M.P. and Rapoport, R. (eds.) (1982) *Families in Britain*. London: Routledge & Kegan Paul.

Rayner, E. (1986) *Human Development*, 3rd edition. London: Unwin Hyman.

Redl, F. (1966) *When We Deal with Children*. New York: Free Press.

Richardson, A. (1995) *Preparation to Care*. London: Balliere Tindall.

Ritchie, P., Sanderson, H., Kilbane, J. and Routledge, M. (2003) *People, Plans and Practicalities*. Edinburgh: SHS Ltd.

Robinson, L. (2002) The human life cycle: Nigrescence. In Davies, M. (ed.) *The Blackwell Companion to Social Work*, 2nd edition. Oxford: Blackwell.

Rogers, A. (2002) *Teaching Adults*. Berkshire: Open University Press.

Rogers, C. (1991) *Client-centred Therapy*. London: Constable.

Rogers, J. (1990) *Caring for People: Help at the Frontline*. Milton Keynes: Open University Press

Rogoff, B. (2003) *The Cultural Nature of Human Development*. Oxford: Oxford University Press.

Rosser, R. and Harris, C. (1965) *The Family and Social Change*. London: Routledge & Kegan Paul.

Rowlands, O. (1998) *Informal Carers: An Independent Study*. Office for National Statistics, Social Survey Division. The Stationery Office.

Rutter, M. (1979a) Maternal deprivation (1972–78): New findings, new concepts, new approaches, *Child Development*, 50, 283–305.

Rutter, M. (1979b) *Maternal Deprivation Re-Assessed*, 2nd edition. Harmondsworth: Penguin.

Sanderson, H., Kennedy, J., Ritchie, P. and Goodwin, G. (1997) *People, Plans and Possibilities*. Edinburgh: SHS Ltd.

Schaefer, N. (1978) *Does She Know She's There*. London: Harper and Row.

Schaffer, H.R. and Emerson, P.E. (1964) The development of social attachments in infancy, *Monographs of the Society for Research in Child Development*, 29.

Schaie, K.W. (ed.) (1988) *Methodological Issues in Aging Research*. New York: Springer.

Schaie, K.W. (1994) The Course of Adult Intellectual Development, *Developmental Psychology*, 19, 531–543.

Schaie, K.W. and Labouvie-Vief, G. (1974) Generational versus ontogenetic components of change in adult cognitive behaviour: A fourteen year cross-sequential study, *Developmental Psychology*, 10, 305–20.

Schon, D. (1983) *The Reflective Practitioner: How Professionals Think in Action*. London: Temple Smith.

Scotland on Sunday (1999) Letter from student (Claire Gordon, Aberdeen), 7 February.

Scottish Executive (2000) *The Same as You?* Edinburgh: The Stationery Office.

Scottish Executive (2001a) *Joint Future Agenda in Community Care and Health Bill 2001*. Edinburgh: Scottish Executive.

Scottish Executive (2001b) *Single Shared Assessment Guidance*. Edinburgh: Scottish Executive.

Scottish Executive (2002) *National Care Standards: Care Homes for Children and Young People*. Edinburgh: Scottish Executive.

Scottish Executive (2003a) *Inequalities in Health: Report of the Measuring Inequalities in Health Working Group*. Edinburgh: Scottish Executive. Accessed from: www.scotland.gov.uk/Resource/Doc/47171/0013513.pdf

Scottish Executive (2003b) Social Justice: A Scotland where everyone matters. Indicators of progress. Accessed from: www.scotland.gov.uk/Publications/2003/12/18693/31047

Scottish Executive (2004) Scottish Household Survey 2003–04. Accessed from: www.scotland.gov.uk/Topics/Statistics/16002/shs-search

Scottish Executive (2005a) *Smoking, Health and Social Care (Scotland) Act 2005*. Edinburgh: Scottish Executive.

Scottish Executive (2005b) Analysis of Religion in the 2001 Census: Summary Report. Accessed from: www.scotland.gov.uk/Publications/2005/02/20757/53570

Scottish Executive (2006a) *Changing Lives: Report of the 21st Century Social Work Review*. Edinburgh: Scottish Executive.

Scottish Executive (2006b) *Key 2005 Road Accident Statistics*. Edinburgh: Scottish Executive.

Scottish Executive (2006c) *Scotland's Social Services Labour Market Report*. Edinburgh: Scottish Executive.

Scottish Executive (2006d) HM Chief Inspector of Prisons for Scotland: Annual Report 2005–2006. Accessed from:
www.scottishexecutive.gov.uk/Publications/2006/10/26121221/3

Scottish Executive Health Department (2002) 'Adding Life to Years: Report of the Expert Group on Healthcare of Older People, Chapter 5 'Ageism in NHSScotland'. Accessed from:
www.sehd.scot.nhs.uk/publications/alty/alty-05.htm

Scottish Office (1991) *The Patient's Charter*. London: HMSO.

Scottish Office (1997) *Scotland's Parliament*. London: HMSO.

Scottish Office (1998a) *Working Together for a Healthier Scotland: A Consultation Paper*. London: HMSO.

Scottish Office (1998b) Social Work Research Findings No. 11. The range and availability of domiciliary care services in Scotland. Accessed from:
www.scotland.gov.uk/cru/documents/sw-find11.htm

Scottish Parliament (1999) *Poverty in Scotland: Research Note 04.06.99*. Edinburgh: The Information Centre.

Scottish Parliament (2006) Justice 2 Report, Volume 2 Evidence. Accessed from:
www.scottish.parliament.uk/business/committees/justice2/reports-06/j2r06-16-Vol02-00.htm

SCRA (2004) Annual Report 2003–04. Scottish Children's Reporter Administration. Accessed from: www.scra.gov.uk/

Seabrook, J. (1990) Law and disorder, *New Statesman and Society*, 5 October, p. 18.

Sharp, D. (ed.) (2006) *Annual Abstract of Statistics 2006*. London: Office for National Statistics.

Sharrock, D. (1993) Anthony Quinn's lust for life results in 11th child at age 78, *Guardian*, 20 August.

Sheridan, M. (1997) *From Birth to Five Years*. London: Routledge.

Skidmore, W. (1975) *Theoretical Thinking in Sociology*. Cambridge: Cambridge University Press.

Slater, R. (1995) *The Psychology of Growing Old*. Buckingham: Open University Press.

Smale, G., Tuson, G., Biehal, N. and Marsh, P. (1993) *Empowerment, Assessment, Care Management and the Skilled Worker*. London: HMSO.

Social Care Association (1993) *The Social Care Task*. Surbiton: SCA.

Social Care Association (2000a) *SCA Handbook*. Surbiton: SCA.

Social Care Association (2000b) *An Introduction to Care Planning*. Surbiton: SCA.

Social Care Association (2002) *SCA Handbook.* Surbiton: SCA

Spender, D. (1983) *Invisible Women: Schooling Scandal.* London: Women's Press.

Spitz, R.A. (1965) *The First Year of Life.* New York: International University Press.

Spitz, R.A. and Wolf, K.M. (1946) Anaclitic depression, *Psychoanalytic Study of the Child,* 2, 313–42.

SRC (1993) *Training Package in Residential Care.* Glasgow: SRC.

SSSC (2002) Codes of Practice for Social Service Workers and Employers. Dundee: Scottish Social Services Council.

SSSC (2005) New body boosts sector skills. *SSSC News* No. 14, Autumn 2005. Dundee: Scottish Social Services Council. Accessed from: www.sssc.uk.com/nr/rdonlyres/2f3c13f3-02f8-475e-b8a2-c5087cf6d2d3/0/autumn05.pdf

Stapleton, K. (1998) Signs of improvement, *Community Care,* 30 April–6 May, 26–7.

Stephens, P., Leach, A., Taggart, L. and Jones, H. (1998) *Think Sociology.* Cheltenham: Stanley Thornes.

Strathclyde Regional Council (1991) *Strathclyde Social Trends, 1988–1995.* Glasgow: Business Information Centre.

Taylor, A. (1993) *Women Drug Users.* Oxford: Clarendon Press.

Taylor Clarke Partnership (2003, 2005) *Leading to Deliver.* Course Pack for Module 1, Changing to Lead.

Taylor, S. and Field, D. (eds.) (1993) *Sociology of Health and Healthcare.* Oxford: Blackwell.

Thompson, K. and Tunstall, J. (1971) *Sociological Perspectives.* Middlesex: Penguin in association with the Open University Press.

Thompson, N. (2006) *Anti-Discriminatory Practice,* 4th edition. Hampshire: Palgrave Macmillan

Thompson, N. (2002) *People Skills,* 2nd edition. London: Palgrave Macmillan.

Thomson, H. and Manuel, J. (1997) *Further Studies for Health.* London: Hodder and Stoughton.

Thomson, H., Holden, C., Hutt, G. and Meggit, C. (1995) *Health and Social Care for Advanced GNVQ,* 2nd edition. London: Hodder and Stoughton.

Thorne, B. (1992) *Carl Rogers.* Thousand Oaks, CA: Sage.

Thorpe, N. (1998) Scottish women: Second class citizens, *Scotsman,* 20 November.

Tizard, B. and Hodges, J. (1978) The effect of early institutional rearing on the development of eight year old children, *Journal of Child Psychology and Psychiatry,* 19, 99–118.

Tossell, D. and Webb, R. (1994) *Inside the Caring Services*, 2nd edition. London: Edward Arnold.

Townsend, P., Davidson, N. and Whitehead, M. (eds.) (1992) *Inequalities in Health: The Black Report and The Health Divide*. Harmondsworth: Penguin.

Vernon, G. (video) *Stand up the Real Glynn Vernon*.

Wagner, G. (1988) *Residential Care: A Positive Choice*. London: HMSO.

Ward, A. (2006) *Working in Group Care*. Birmingham: BASW/Policy Press.

Ward, B. and Houghton, J. (1967) *Good Grief: Exploring Feelings of Loss and Death with Over 11s and Adults*. London: Cruse.

Waterhouse, Sir R. (200) *Lost in Care*. London: Department of Health.

Wheal, A. in collaboration with Buchanan, A. (1994) *Answers: A Handbook for Residential and Foster Carers of Young People aged 11–18 years*. Brighton: Pavilion.

Wilkinson, R. (2005) *The Impact of Inequality*. London: Routledge.

Williams, L. (1994) *Finding Out About Society*. London: Bell and Hyman.

Willis, P. (1977) *Learning to Labour*. Farnborough: Saxon House.

Wilson, G (2003) Stay at home fathers hit a record high, *Scotsman*, 26 October.

Worden, W. (2003) *Grief Counselling and Grief Therapy: A Handbook for the Mental Health Practitioner*, 3rd edition. East Sussex: Brunner-Routledge.

Young, T. (ed.) (1973) *Tinker, Taylor ... The Myth of Cultural Deprivation*. Harmondsworth: Penguin.

Young, M. and Wilmott, P. (1957) *Family and Kinship in East London*. London: Routledge & Kegan Paul.

Younghusband, E. (1964) *Social Work and Social Change* London: Allen and Unwin.

Zeldin, T. (1995) *An Intimate History of Humanity*. London: Minerva.

Index

Activities, case studies and figures are not indexed